ENVIRONMENTAL NGOs AND ACCESS TO JUSTICE BEFORE THE CJEU

This book tells a fascinating legal mobilisation story. Analysing EU environmental litigation over the last 30 years, it illustrates how the European environmental movement has patiently attempted to expand access to justice – and succeeded – before the EU Courts.

This is despite the longstanding reluctance of the EU Court of Justice to soften its standing requirements for private applicants bringing cases directly to Luxembourg. This research draws on both doctrinal analysis and qualitative methods of socio-legal inquiry. At its heart are interviews with key stakeholders: environmental lawyers, plaintiffs, and activists, which give an invaluable and innovative perspective on strategic litigation before the EU judiciary.

With the growing emergency posed by the climate crisis and resultant increased litigation, this book makes a significant scholarly contribution to the study of environmental movements, to our conceptualisation of legal mobilisation, and to our understanding of the impact of litigation in European environmental law.

Volume 136 in the Series Modern Studies in European Law

Modern Studies in European Law

Recent titles in this series:

EU Trade and Investment Treaty-Making Post-Lisbon: Moving Beyond Mixity
Gesa Kübek

The Normative Foundations for EU Criminal Justice: Powers, Limits and Justifications
Jacob Öberg

EU Neighbourhood Law: Wider Europe and the Extended EU's Legal Space
Alessandro Petti

The Dynamics of Powers in the European Union
Edited by Christina Eckes, Päivi Leino-Sandberg and Anna W Ghavanin

The European Convention on Human Rights and Private Law: Comparative Perspectives from South-Eastern Europe
Edited by Mateja Durovic and Cristina Poncibò

Judging Composite Decision-Making: The Transformation of European Administrative Law
Filipe Brito Bastos

EU Diplomacy in Multilateral Fora
Edited by Christine Kaddous and Frank Hoffmeister

The Market Citizenship Illusion: Free Movement Rights for Atypical Workers
Alice Welsh

Actors and Roles in EU Disability Law
Edited by Delia Ferri and Eva S Krolla

The Impact of War (in Ukraine) on the EU
Edited by Inge Govaere, Sacha Garben and Eleanor Spaventa

The European Judiciary: A Community of Law and a Community of Judges
Edited by Alejandro Saiz Arnaiz and Joan Solanes Mullor

Dissensus over Liberal Democracy: Insights from European Judges
Edited by Ramona Coman, Viktor Kazai, Leonardo Puleo and Andrew Bradley

Structural Principles of EU Law
Marcus Klamert

Environmental NGOs and Access to Justice before the CJEU
Mario Pagano

For the complete list of titles in this series see www.bloomsbury.com/uk/series/modern-studies-in-european-law/

Environmental NGOs and Access to Justice before the CJEU

Mario Pagano

•HART•
OXFORD • LONDON • NEW YORK • NEW DELHI • SYDNEY

HART PUBLISHING

Bloomsbury Publishing Plc

Kemp House, Chawley Park, Cumnor Hill, Oxford, OX2 9PH, UK

1385 Broadway, New York, NY 10018, USA

Bloomsbury Publishing Ireland Limited, 29 Earlsfort Terrace, Dublin 2, D02 AY28, Ireland

HART PUBLISHING, the Hart/Stag logo, BLOOMSBURY and the Diana logo are trademarks of Bloomsbury Publishing Plc

First published in Great Britain 2025

A catalogue record for this book is available from the British Library.

A catalogue record for this book is available from the Library of Congress.

ISBN: HB: 978-1-50998-000-0
ePDF: 978-1-50998-002-4
ePub: 978-1-50998-001-7

Typeset by Compuscript Ltd, Shannon

To my parents

ACKNOWLEDGEMENTS

I am particularly grateful to my PhD supervisor, Professor Joanne Scott, who guided me in my years in Florence at the EUI, where this research was born and raised. I am also grateful to Professors Áine Ryall, Claire Kilpatrick and Scott Cummings for their encouragement, as well as for their valuable comments and insights. I want to thank the EUI administration, the staff of the library – where I spent so much time – and of the Law department, which have always been extremely generous and dedicated. Thank you to my friend and colleague Virginia Passalacqua, who initiated me to the study of legal mobilisation and deeply supported me in the writing of this book. I also want to thank Marta Morvillo, Pola Cebulak and Stefan Salomon, who organised two wonderful workshops in Amsterdam in 2023 and 2024 on 'Strategic Litigation in the EU'. Such workshops were truly inspiring and helped frame my research better. Thank you also to the people who kindly accepted to be interviewed in the frame of this research. Your contribution was essential and completely changed the way I look at EU law and legal mobilisation in environmental matters.

Finally, I want to thank my family. My parents, Gianpiero and Natalizia, as well as my sister Giulia, for bringing stability and joy to my life, despite the distance. Thank you also to my partner Soraya, who supports me every day.

Mario Pagano

Brussels, 25 March 2025

CONTENTS

Acknowledgements ... *vii*
Acronyms ... *xiii*

Introduction ... 1
I. Legal Mobilisation as a Theoretical Framework ... 1
II. My Research ... 7
III. Methodology ... 11
A. Case Selection ... 11
i. Actions for Annulment ... 12
ii. Actions for Annulment Brought under the Aarhus Regulation ... 12
B. Direct Observation and Semi-Structured Interviews ... 13
i. In-House Lawyers/Members of ENGOs ... 15
ii. Other Sources ... 16
IV. Structure ... 17

1. The *Plaumann* Test ... 22
I. Introduction ... 22
II. The *Plaumann* Test ... 23
III. Stein's and Vining's Contribution ... 24
IV. Rasmussen's Contribution ... 25
V. van Wolferen's Contribution ... 27
VI. The *Greenpeace* Case ... 29
VII. Mobilising against *Plaumann* in the pre-Aarhus Period ... 31
A. Treating the Environment Differently ... 31
i. Treating ENGOs Differently ... 33
B. Effective Judicial Protection ... 34
C. EU Law Consistency ... 35
i. Consistency with EU Secondary Law ... 36
ii. Consistency with the Case Law of the CJEU ... 37
VIII. AG Jacobs and *Plaumann* ... 40
IX. Conclusions ... 41

2. Circumventing *Plaumann* via National Courts ... 44
I. Introduction ... 44
II. 'Complete', Yet not Perfect ... 45

III. Using AG Jacobs' Opinion 47
IV. Opening Legal Opportunities at National Level 52
V. Training National Judges and Practitioners....55
VI. ENGOs and the PRP on Validity....60
A. The *Associazione Italia Nostra* Case 62
B. The *Xylella* Case 63
C. The *Blaise* Case....65
D. The *Vereniging Hoekschewaards Landschap* Case....68
E. Preliminary Conclusions on ENGOs and the PRP on Validity 69
VII. Conclusions....73

3. Shaping the Aarhus Convention 77
I. Introduction....77
II. The Aarhus Convention 77
III. ENGOs and the Aarhus Negotiation 81
IV. The Introduction of the 'Justice' Pillar....84
V. The EU Adhesion to the Aarhus Convention....86
A. The Aarhus Regulation....87
VI. Mobilising against *Plaumann* in the 'Post-Aarhus (I)' Period 89
VII. The Arguments of the Applicants in *Stichting Natuur*....90
A. An Act of 'Individual Scope'....90
B. Compliance with International Environmental Law 92
VIII. Conclusions....94

4. Using the Aarhus Convention against *Plaumann*....97
I. Introduction....97
II. The Role of the ACCC 98
A. Composition and Functions....98
B. The Scrutiny of the Compliance Committee 99
III. ClientEarth as a 'Legal ENGO' 101
IV. ACCC/C/2008/32....102
V. Mobilising against *Plaumann* in the 'Post-Aarhus (II)' Period....105
A. The Non-Binding Character of the ACCC's Findings 107
B. The Impact of the ACCC Findings....109
VI. The Impact of the ACCC's Findings on EU Decision-Making....110
A. The Commission's Study and Report 113
VII. The *ClientEarth v EIB* Case....117
A. Comment on the *ClientEarth v EIB* Case....120
VIII. Conclusions....121

5. The New Aarhus Regulation 124
I. Introduction 124
II. Shaping the New Aarhus Regulation 124
III. The New Definition of 'Administrative Act' 128
A. Other Main Amendments 130
IV. Contesting EU Regulatory Acts: Where Do We Go? 131
A. The *ClientEarth v Commission* Case 136
V. Conclusions 138

6. *Plaumann* and Climate Change before Non-EU Courts 141
I. Introduction 141
II. The Global Climate Litigation Trend 143
III. Understanding Strategic Litigation at GPI 147
IV. Framing 'Judicial Comfort' 150
V. Building Blocks and 'Incrementalism' 153
A. The *People v Arctic Oil* Case 154
VI. Preliminary Conclusions on GPI: An 'Obsolete' Court 156
VII. Understanding Strategic Litigation at GLAN 158
A. The *Duarte Agostinho* Case 159
B. The Court's Judgment in *Duarte Agostinho* 162
C. Comment on the *Duarte Agostinho* Case 165
D. The *Müllner v Austria* Case 167
E. EU Climate Change Law and the *Bosphorus* Presumption 168
F. The Political Impact on the EU of CCL in Strasbourg 175
VIII. Conclusions 178

7. *Plaumann* and Climate Change before the Court of Justice of the European Union 181
I. Introduction 181
II. Using Article 263(4) TFEU in CCL 182
III. Constructing the *Carvalho* Case 183
A. Lawyers Seeking Plaintiffs 185
B. Litigation and Communication 190
IV. The *Carvalho* Case before the EU Judiciary 192
A. Establishing Causation in *Carvalho* 197
V. The Aftermath of *Carvalho* 200
VI. Contesting EU Policy on Biomass Energy 204
A. Constructing the *Sabo* Case 205
VII. The *Sabo* Case before the EU Judiciary 207
A. Which Fundamental Rights? 208
B. Establishing Causation in *Sabo* 209
C. Standing and Aarhus 211
D. Is Aarhus Enough? 212

VIII. The Aftermath of *Sabo* ... 214
IX. Conclusions ... 215

Conclusions ... 220
I. Who? ... 220
II. Why? ... 223
III. How? ... 225
A. Turning Defeats into Opportunities ... 225
B. Combining Legal and Non-Legal Mobilisation Strategies ... 227
IV. What? ... 229
V. Grounds for Future Research ... 233

Bibliography ... *235*
Index ... *251*

ACRONYMS

ACCC	Aarhus Convention Compliance Committee
AG	Advocate General
AR	Aarhus Regulation
CAN Europe	Climate Action Network Europe
CCL	climate change litigation
CFI	Court of First Instance
CJEU	Court of Justice of the European Union
CSOs	civil society organisations
ECHA	European Chemicals Agency
ECHR	European Convention on Human Rights
ECtHR	European Court of Human Rights
EEB	European Environmental Bureau
EFSA	European Food Safety Authority
EIA	environmental impact assessment
EIB	European Investment Bank
ENGO	environmental non-governmental organisation
EPAW	European Platform Against Windfarms
ETS	emissions trading scheme
EU	European Union
EUCFR	EU Charter of Fundamental Rights
FRs	fundamental rights
GC	General Court of the European Union
GLAN	Global Legal Action Network
GP	Greenpeace

GPEU	Greenpeace European Union
GPI	Greenpeace International
HRs	human rights
ICEL	International Council for Environmental Law
IUCN	International Union for the Conservation of Nature
LOS	legal opportunity structure
MS	Member State
MOP	Meeting of the Parties
NECPs	national energy and climate plans
NGO	non-governmental organisation
PIL	public interest litigation
PPP Regulation	Plant Protection Products Regulation
PRP	preliminary reference procedure
REC	Regional Environmental Centre for Central and Eastern Europe
TEU	Treaty on European Union
TFEU	Treaty on the Functioning of the European Union
TIJC	Transnational incremental judicial comfort
UNECE	United Nations Economic Commission for Europe
WWF	World Wild Fund for Nature

Introduction

In spring 2017, I was a bluebook trainee at DG ENV of the European Commission, in the unit dealing with environmental implementation. Thanks to that experience, I had the privilege to follow, at least until the end of my traineeship (in July 2017), the development of the 'Aarhus saga' – concerning the tensions between access to justice before the CJEU and the Aarhus Convention – from the inside of the European Commission. In September of the same year, I was to come back home to Italy to start a PhD at the EUI and I was super excited about the new adventure.

The bluebook experience gave me the chance to grasp the European Commission's perspective on the direct access of environmental NGOs to the Court of Justice of the EU (CJEU). I was also aware of the CJEU's perspective on direct access, which could be inferred from the Court's judgments and the vast legal scholarship produced on the subject. But I wanted to know what NGOs had to say about direct access before the EU Courts. This is how I became interested in the topic addressed in the present book and why I decided to devote my research to exploring the NGOs' perspective on *Plaumann* and access to justice in environmental matters.

In this regard, I hope that this book will provide useful insights not only to legal scholars working on legal mobilisation or to any reader interested in the subject (of course), but also to NGOs and practitioners who intend to use courts to achieve change.

In this first section, I will now outline the theoretical framework adopted in the present book, that is the one of legal mobilisation. Then, in the following sections, I will set out the main research question embedded in my research and justify how my research is situated within the existing literature and how it contributes to advance the state of the art. The final sections of this introduction will then set out the methodology deployed to carry out the present research and provide a general overview to the structure of the whole contribution.

I. Legal Mobilisation as a Theoretical Framework

The literature on legal mobilisation is situated at the intersection between different social sciences, such as law, political science, and sociology. For decades, social movements have incorporated legal strategies into their mobilisation campaigns, in order to achieve their specific objectives.[1] The typical example that is often

[1] Emilio Lehoucq and Whitney K Taylor, 'Conceptualizing Legal Mobilization: How Should We Understand the Deployment of Legal Strategies?' (2020) 45 (1) *Law & Social Inquiry* 166.

referred to in order to show how courts have been used by civil rights movements is the advancement of minority rights in *Brown v Board of Education* in the US. This judgment prohibited states from segregating public school students on the basis of race.[2] In clearer terms, the term 'legal mobilisation' usually refers to the strategic use of law and legal institutions to achieve political or societal change.[3] Although there is no consensus in socio-legal scholarship as to what kind of activities and litigants specifically constitute 'legal mobilisation',[4] in the present research I identify 'legal mobilisation' in very broad terms, along the lines of Lisa Vanhala's definition, namely as 'any type of process by which individual or collective actors invoke legal norms, discourse, or symbols to influence policy, culture, or behaviour'.[5] In the frame of the present research, 'strategic litigation' – that can be defined as the strategic deployment of legal disputes before a judicial or quasi-judicial body intended to achieve broader socio-political purposes – should thus be understood as one of the possible forms of legal mobilisation (although probably the main one).

Through the lenses of legal mobilisation, courts have come to be considered as 'reactive institutions', which normally 'do not acquire cases on their own motion, but only upon the initiative of one of the disputants'.[6] On this point, Galanter emphasised the 'radiating effect' of courts: these can be seen not only in their traditional dress as dispute-settlement agencies, but also as bargaining forums, where judges contribute deeply to the 'dissemination of messages rather than the pronouncement of authoritative decisions and application of sanctions'.[7]

Legal scholars have written extensively on the 'impact' that courts' 'messages' are able to produce. The most famous contribution in this regard is probably *The Hollow Hope*, written by Gerald Rosenberg and published in 1991.[8] In his book, Rosenberg theorised about the US Supreme Court's limited capacity to produce compelling societal reform. He identified several constraints on achieving social change via court rulings. These include the limited nature of constitutional rights, courts' traditional unwillingness to 'take the heat' generated by politically sensitive decisions and courts' lack of implementing powers (necessary to execute their own decisions).[9]

[2] *Brown v Board of Education of Topeka*, 347 US 483 (1954).

[3] See Frances Khan Zemans, 'Legal Mobilization: The Neglected Role of the Law in the Political System' (1983) 77 (3) *The American Political Science Review* 690–703; Mark Kessler, 'Legal Mobilization for Social Reform: Power and the Politics of Agenda Setting' (1990) 24 (1) *Law & Society Review* 127.

[4] Lehoucq and Taylor, n 1, 174.

[5] Lisa Vanhala, definition of 'legal mobilisation', (2021) Oxford Bibliographies. Available at: www.oxfordbibliographies.com/display/document/obo-9780199756223/obo-9780199756223-0031.xml.

[6] Marc Galanter, 'The Radiating Effects of Courts', in Keith O Boyum and Lynn Mather (eds), *Empirical Theories About Courts* (New York, Longman Inc, 1983) 135.

[7] ibid.

[8] Gerald N Rosenberg, *The Hollow Hope: Can Courts Bring about Social Change?* (Chicago, University of Chicago Press, 1991).

[9] ibid.

However, other leading scholars like Michael McCann disagreed with Rosenberg, stressing that – despite constraints – courts can still produce significant 'indirect effects', such as mobilisation of societal groups and increased leverage in workplace negotiations, even when judges' decisions themselves fail to directly produce significant societal change.[10] More recent contributions have followed McCann in his line of reasoning, claiming that legal scholars should go 'beyond a focus on winning or losing in the courts' and understand that strategic litigants can also use litigation loss to 'articulate rights-based demands, provide a public narrative and forge a group-based identity'.[11] The present research supports this claim. Indeed, the 'indirect effects' of litigation also include ways in which case law may influence 'social actors' perceptions of their rights, their discourse about their rights and their pursuit of those rights, whether through political or legal means'.[12]

Besides the scholarship focusing on the 'impact' of strategic litigation, other major contributions have theorised about the 'factors' hindering or facilitating legal mobilisation. In particular, Chris Hilson in 2002 started a strand of research on so-called 'legal opportunity structures' (LOS).[13] The 'legal opportunities' present in a given 'structure' refer to those dimensions of the legal system that increase or decrease actors' likelihood of using litigation and being successful in doing so.[14] In fact, there is still no consensus on the definition of LOS and, in some contributions, legal opportunities seem to indicate 'anything that affects opportunities for mobilization'.[15] However, for reasons of clarity, in the present research I rely on De Fazio's conceptualisation of LOS, considering only the factors *external* to collective actors as part of LOS, namely (i) the possibility of having access to courts; (ii) the availability of justiciable rights; (iii) the degree of judicial receptivity.[16]

Besides the existing legal opportunities present in a given legal system, some scholars have also shown that there is no such thing as 'objective' opportunities and that even the 'perception' that strategic litigants have of the available opportunities deeply affects their willingness to trigger legal mobilisation.[17] For instance, 'courts'

[10] Michael W McCann, *Rights at Work: Pay Equity Reform and the Politics of Legal Mobilization* (Chicago, University of Chicago Press, 1994). See also Gerald N Rosenberg, 'Hollow Hopes and Other Aspirations: A Reply to Feeley and McCann' (1992) 17 (4) *Law & Social Inquiry* 761–78.

[11] Ceren Ozgul, 'Beyond Legal Victory or Reform: The Legal Mobilisation of Religious Groups in the European Court of Human Rights' (2017) 45 (3–4) *Religion, State & Society* 319.

[12] ibid; see also Lisa Vanhala, 'The Diffusion of Disability Rights in Europe' (2015) 37 *Human Rights Quarterly* 831–53.

[13] See, *inter alia*, Chris Hilson, 'New Social Movements: The Role of Legal Opportunity' (2002) 9 (2) *Journal of European Public Policy* 238–55; Ellen Ann Andersen, *Out of the Closets and into the Courts: Legal Opportunity Structure and Gay Rights Litigation* (Ann Arbor, University of Michigan Press, 2009); Gianluca De Fazio, 'Legal Opportunity Structure and Social Movement Strategy in Northern Ireland and Southern United States' (2012 52 (1) *International Journal of Comparative Sociology* 3–22; Virginia Passalacqua, 'Legal Mobilization via Preliminary Reference: Insights from the Case of Migrant Rights' (2021) 58 3 *Common Market Law Review Volume* 751–76.

[14] Lehoucq and Taylor, n 1, 183.

[15] Passalacqua, n 13, 757.

[16] De Fazio, n 13, 6.

[17] Sidney Tarrow, *Power in Movement: Social Movements, Collective Action, and Politics* (Cambridge, Cambridge University Press, 2012) 33; Andersen, n 13, 70.

judicial activism in favour of certain issues may signal to social movements that a legal opportunity exists to undertake litigation'.[18] Furthermore, strategic litigants can also contribute strongly to 'shape' the structure of legal opportunities through various forms of legal mobilisation,[19] as will also be shown in the present research.

With specific regard to legal mobilisation in the EU, Lisa Conant, Andreas Hofmann, Dagmar Soennecken and Lisa Vanhala have theorised about three categories of factors that bear upon the actors engaged in (or disengaged from) litigation.[20] These are macro-level systemic factors that originate in Europe; meso-level factors that vary nationally; and micro-level factors. Macro and meso-level factors essentially refer to the legal opportunities available under EU and national law; while the micro-level factors refer to the 'agent-level characteristics that influence whether individuals, groups or companies will turn to the courts'.[21] The 'three-layers' categorisation proposed by Lisa Conant and colleagues will not be adopted in the present contribution because it is based on a rigid distinction between European and national legal opportunities, leaving little room for other legal opportunities, which may arise, for instance, from litigants' perception of the LOS.

For this reason, the present contribution will rely on a different tripartite categorisation of factors that bear upon the actors engaged in litigation. This categorisation emphasises (i) 'LOS', broadly defined, to include the national, European or international levels; (ii) 'resources'; and (iii) strategies. These last two components will be explained below. However, before moving to this explanation, it is important to clarify that the traditional procedures available under EU law to reach the CJEU (namely, the preliminary reference procedure, the action for annulment, the infringement proceeding, etc) will be considered as 'legal mobilisation pathways', not as legal opportunities. By 'legal mobilisation pathways' I refer to the procedures established under the law to obtain judicial or quasi-judicial review.[22] These 'pathways' are thus 'part of' the structure, and not legal opportunities emerging 'within' the existing structure.

This being said, if legal opportunities are defined as 'those dimensions of the legal system that increase actors' likelihood of using litigation', the concept of 'resources' has been defined in multiple ways in existing literature: from the financial resources available to the agent/litigant to the availability of in-house lawyers and/or access to networks of *pro bono* legal advice.[23] In the present research, I

[18] De Fazio, n 13, 7.

[19] Lisa Vanhala, 'Shaping the Structure of Legal Opportunities: Environmental NGOs Bringing International Environmental Procedural Rights Back Home' (2018) 40 (1) *Law & Policy* 110–27.

[20] Lisa Conant, Andreas Hofmann, Dagmar Soennecken and Lisa Vanhala, 'Mobilizing European Law' (2018) 25 (9) *Journal of European Public Policy* 1376–89.

[21] ibid, 1382.

[22] For a more comprehensive explanation, see below section II.

[23] ibid, see also Rachel A Cichowski, 'The European Court of Human Rights, Amicus Curiae and Violence Against Women' (2016) 50 (4) *Law and Society Review* 912; Lamin Khadar, *Expanding Access to Justice: An Exploration of Large Firm Pro Bono Practice across Europe* (2019) PhD dissertation, EUI. Available at: https://hdl.handle.net/1814/63004.

include within the concept of 'resources', those dimensions or characteristics of the agent or litigant that increase the likelihood of them turning to litigation.

Despite the need for further research on agents' resources,[24] these have been found to play a key role in igniting legal mobilisation. Galanter, for instance, found that 'the haves' tend to come out ahead,[25] in other words, those natural or legal persons who pursue litigation repeatedly and have the resources to pursue long-term interests ('repeat players')[26] shape the development of the law by 'playing for favourable rules-settling cases likely to produce adverse precedent and litigating cases likely to produce rules that promote their interests'.[27]

In this regard, the role of lawyers has obviously attracted significant attention. Scott Cummings has reflected extensively on the relationship between lawyers and social movements and the added value that public interest lawyers bring to the fight for social justice in the US context.[28] However, even in Europe socio-legal scholars have shed new light on some of the 'classics' of EU law (namely some of the most important rulings issued by the CJEU) and the role that 'Euro-lawyers' have played in enhancing the European integration process.[29]

Other scholars have focused on the value of legal expertise in specific types of social movements (eg the environmental movement) and even beyond the use of courts in litigation.[30] Apart from examining the role of lawyers and legal expertise, other scholars have attempted to dig into the third component I introduced in the analytical framework of the present contribution, namely 'strategies'.

The third component of the analytical framework – represented by litigants' strategies – certainly deserves further investigation on a global scale, especially in the area of environmental and climate litigation. A 'strategy' is a plan of action for achieving a given objective.[31] By the expression 'legal strategy' I thus refer to a plan of action aimed at using the law (usually in the form of litigation) to achieve

[24] Conant et al, n 20, 1383.

[25] Marc Galanter, 'Why the "Haves" Come Out Ahead: Speculations on the Limits of Legal Change' (1974) 9 (1) *Law and Society Review* 95–160.

[26] ibid, 103.

[27] Shauhin Talesh, 'How the "Haves" Come out Ahead in the Twenty-First Century' (2013) 62 *DePaul Law Review* 519.

[28] Scott Cummings, 'Law and Social Movements: Reimagining the Progressive Canon' (2018) 441 *Wisconsin Law Review* 158. See also Scott Cummings, Catherine Albiston and Richard L Abel, 'Making Public Interest Lawyers In A Time Of Crisis: An Evidence-Based Approach' (2021) 34 (2) *Georgetown Journal of Legal Ethics*, UCLA School of Law, Public Law Research Paper No 20-30, Available at SSRN: https://ssrn.com/abstract=3712664.

[29] See Antoine Vauchez, *Brokering Europe – Euro-Lawyers and the Making of a Transnational Polity* (Cambridge, CUP, 2015); Amedeo Arena, 'From an Unpaid Electricity Bill to the Primacy of EU Law: Gian Galeazzo Stendardi and the Making of Costa v. ENEL' (2019) 30(3) *European Journal of International Law* 1017–37; Tommaso Pavone, *The Ghostwriters Lawyers and the Politics behind the Judicial Construction of Europe* (Cambridge, CUP, 2022).

[30] Pola Cebulak, Marta Morvillo and Stefan Salomon, 'Strategic Litigation in EU Law: Who Does it Empower?' (2024) 25 (6) *German Law Journal* 800–21. See also the whole special issue 'Strategic Litigation in EU Law', (2024) 25 6 *German Law Journal*; Carolyn Abbot and Maria Lee, *Environmental Groups and Legal Expertise – Shaping the Brexit Process* (London, UCL Press, 2021).

[31] *Cf* https://dictionary.cambridge.org/it/dizionario/inglese/strategy.

a specific legal, political or societal objective. Conversely, by 'non-legal strategy' I refer to a plan of action which does not entail the use of the law to achieve its mobilisation objective(s). However, this book will show how legal and non-legal strategies are often combined in an 'integrated advocacy' plan intended to achieve broader mobilisation objectives, making legal mobilisation a 'fluid' concept, which can hardly be encapsulated within the rigid boundaries of litigation.

Having clarified that, when it comes to exploring litigants' strategies, scholars have studied the use of 'incrementalistic' approaches in legal mobilisation, based on the idea that change does not have to be sudden, but may be achieved more slowly, one step after the other.[32] Existing literature has also stressed the relevance of combining legal strategies with other forms of mobilisation (eg political),[33] while other scholars have highlighted the opportunity of using common 'building blocks' to create a more homogenous legal framework for transnational environmental litigation.[34]

In this regard, when it comes to strategies deployed by litigants in specific domains, scholars are increasingly deepening their analysis of the role that specific plaintiffs play in certain types of strategic litigation, such as children in climate litigation;[35] migrants in the area of migration law;[36] LGBTQ members in the area of non-discrimination law.[37]

Moreover, other scholars are exploring the relevance of the legal reasoning in strategic litigation. For instance, Thierse and Badanjak have provided a thought-provoking analysis of the legal arguments deployed by EU litigants mobilising against the Data Retention Directive,[38] while Philippe Paiement noticed that the legal reasoning and, more broadly, the legal strategies of societal actors involved

[32] See Nan D Hunter, 'In Search of Equality for Women: From Suffrage to Civil Rights' (2021) 59 *Duquesne Law Review* 155; Michael M Atkinson, 'Lindblom's Lament: Incrementalism and the Persistent Pull of the Status Quo' (2011) 30 (1) *Policy and Society* 9–18; Saul Levmore, 'Interest Groups and the Problem with Incrementalism' (2009) 501 John M. Olin Program in Law and Economics Working Paper 2.

[33] For a broader conceptualisation and discussion on the evolution of public interest litigation, see Scott Cummings and Deborah L Rhode, 'Public Interest Litigation: Insights From Theory and Practice' (2009) 36 *Fordham Urbana Law Journal* 615.

[34] Hans van Loon, 'Principles and Building Blocks for a Global Legal Framework for Transnational Civil Litigation in EnvironmentalMatters' (2018) 23 (3) *Uniform Law Review* 298–318.

[35] Elizabeth Donger, 'Children and Youth in Strategic Climate Litigation: Advancing Rights through Legal Argument and Legal Mobilization' (2022) *Transnational Environmental Law* 1–27; Larissa Parker, Juliette Mestre, Sébastien Jodoin and Margarentha Wewerinke-Singh, 'When the Kids Put Climate Change on Trial: Youth-Focused Rights-Based Climate Litigation Around the World' (2022) 13(1) *Journal of Human Rights and the Environment* 64–89.

[36] Passalacqua, n 13. From the same author, see also *Legal Mobilization for Migrant Rights – Opportunities and Barriers at the European Court of Justice* (Oxford, OUP, 2025).

[37] Gwendolyn M Leachman, 'From Protest to Perry: How Litigation Shaped the LGBT Movement's Agenda' (2013–14) 47 *UCD Law Review* 1667.

[38] Stefan Thierse and Sanja Badanjak, *Opposition in the EU Multi-Level Polity – Legal Mobilization against the Data Retention Directive* (Basingstoke, Palgrave Macmillan, 2021).

in CCL across the globe are deeply contributing to the creation of 'transnational narratives' about science and governance of climate change.[39]

Having provided the reader with the theoretical framework that will be adopted in the present contribution, in the next section I will outline my research question and explain how my research is situated within the broader literature on legal mobilisation.

II. My Research

The present contribution mainly aims at answering the following research question: how have environmental NGOs (ENGOs) deployed legal mobilisation to overcome the *Plaumann* test in environmental matters?

As will be explained in chapter one, the 'Plaumann test' is the narrow interpretation given by the CJEU to the standing requirements allowing private applicants to bring an action for annulment directly before the EU judiciary. For those readers who lack any background in EU law, I must briefly clarify that – via actions for annulment – the EU institutions, the EU Member States (MSs), as well as natural and legal persons, have the possibility to contest the legality of an EU measure intended to produce legal effects *vis-à-vis* third parties under the conditions provided under Article 263 of the Treaty on the Functioning of the European Union (TFEU).[40] However, while the EU institutions and the EU MSs are traditionally considered 'privileged' applicants who are not required to satisfy any particular test in order to be granted standing, natural and legal persons – as we will see – are considered 'non-privileged' applicants who have to meet extremely narrow conditions in order to bring an action under Article 263 of the Treaty. In this regard, ENGOs have de facto never been granted standing in actions for annulment by the CJEU outside cases concerning access to environmental information and rejections to requests for internal review under the Aarhus Regulation (AR).

[39] Phillip Paiement, 'Urgent Agenda: How Climate Litigation Builds Transnational Narratives' (2020) 11 (1) *Transnational Legal Theory* 121–43.

[40] Art 263(1), (2) and (3) TFEU: '(1) The Court of Justice of the European Union shall review the legality of legislative acts, of acts of the Council, of the Commission and of the European Central Bank, other than recommendations and opinions, and of acts of the European Parliament and of the European Council intended to produce legal effects vis-à-vis third parties. It shall also review the legality of acts of bodies, offices or agencies of the Union intended to produce legal effects vis-à-vis third parties.

(2) It shall for this purpose have jurisdiction in actions brought by a Member State, the European Parliament, the Council or the Commission on grounds of lack of competence, infringement of an essential procedural requirement, infringement of the Treaties or of any rule of law relating to their application, or misuse of powers.

(3) The Court shall have jurisdiction under the same conditions in actions brought by the Court of Auditors, by the European Central Bank and by the Committee of the Regions for the purpose of protecting their prerogatives.'

Nevertheless, ENGOs and private parties have the possibility to mobilise EU law before the CJEU also under Article 267 TFEU, through the mediation of national courts. Indeed, as will be deepened in chapter two, wherever a question over the interpretation of EU law is raised before any court of tribunal of a MS, that court or tribunal may, if it considers that a decision on the question is necessary to enable it to give judgment, request the CJEU to give a preliminary ruling thereon.[41] If the question raised by the national court actually concerns the validity of EU law, then that court *must* refer the question to the CJEU.[42]

Having briefly outlined the differences between the legal pathways available under Articles 263 and 267 TFEU, recent developments in the context of the Aarhus Convention as well as growing interest in climate change and environmental protection in the public arena, make the question of access to justice in environmental matters all the more relevant. This is demonstrated by the fact that, despite the constant rejections ENGOs have received from the CJEU, they have never stopped trying to overcome *Plaumann*. In this regard, besides the main research question outlined above, the present contribution will also attempt to address a number of sub-questions, namely:

i. Who has been actively mobilising against *Plaumann* in environmental matters? In other words, which ENGOs?
ii. Why have these actors mobilised against *Plaumann*?
iii. What kinds of mobilisation pathways and legal opportunities have ENGOs resorted to in the attempt to overcome *Plaumann*?
iv. How have ENGOs shaped the LOS in order to contest *Plaumann*?
v. What kind of resources and legal strategies have ENGOs deployed to overcome *Plaumann*?
vi. What have ENGOs achieved by mobilising against *Plaumann*?

In answering these questions, I decided to present my analysis of legal mobilisation in the European environmental context by charting its historical trajectory. Indeed, the cases I have identified were triggered across four decades (from the 1990s to the present), a long timeframe where important legal changes in the EU legal order have occurred and different actors have come into play. My research will therefore follow the evolution of the European legal landscape and provide the reader with the relevant knowledge about those legal changes, which have greatly affected environmental legal mobilisation before the CJEU.

As mentioned in the first part of this introduction, the present research seeks to provide an 'NGO perspective' to the fight against *Plaumann*, leaving outside more court-centred theories on the role of the CJEU in the European integration process.[43] In this regard, I want to stress that, by undertaking this research, I do

[41] Art 267 TFEU.
[42] ibid.
[43] See, inter alia, Joseph HH Weiler, 'The Transformation of Europe' (1991) 100 (8) *The Yale Law Journal, Symposium: International Law* 2403–83; Mark Dawson, Bruno De Witte and Elise Muir

not intend to suggest alternative interpretations of Article 263(4) TFEU or try to convince the CJEU that *Plaumann* should be abandoned. It is not *Plaumann* which is at the core of the present contribution, but rather 'the fight against *Plaumann*'.

Therefore, in the present research I consider the *Plaumann* test as a 'closure' in the LOS and as a 'static' judicial interpretation that the Court does not intend to amend. The goal is to observe 'the other side of the river', that is to describe how have interest groups 'adapted' (or not) to *Plaumann*, without taking any normative stand as to whether the Court's narrow test is right or wrong. This with the aim of contributing to advancing the literature on legal mobilisation in the European environmental and climate context. In light of this, the theoretical underpinnings of *Plaumann* will only be partially addressed – essentially for reasons of completeness – but the main focus of this research will obviously concern the legal mobilisation strategies deployed by ENGOs to actually 'overcome' *Plaumann*.

Considering the theoretical framework and the relevant literature described above, the present research is situated at the intersection between scholarship on the 'macro' dimension of LOS on the one hand, and the more 'micro' dimension of 'resources' and 'legal strategies' on the other. I argue that legal scholarship on the application of *Plaumann* in the environmental context has overlooked the potential offered by the adoption of a legal mobilisation perspective. However, considering the Court's rigidity on the interpretation of the 'individual concern' requirement, the scholarly silence on ENGOs' legal strategies in actions for annulment is not surprising. Indeed, most of the scholars who have examined EU LOS have focused, to a large extent, on the role that the preliminary reference procedure (PRP) has played in enhancing EU legal mobilisation.[44] The present contribution does not intend to diminish the relevance of the PRP in the judicial construction of Europe. Rather, I aim to shed light on the unexplored potential for EU legal mobilisation offered by Article 263(4) TFEU.[45] Indeed, I consider that the issue of access to justice under Article 263(4) TFEU is still relevant and that the efforts of the European environmental movement provide the greatest proof of just how crucial it remains for actors to overcome *Plaumann*.

In the description of the relevant literature on legal mobilisation, I referred to Sidney Tarrow's contribution stressing how important it is to have a 'flexible' conception of opportunities.[46] A conception which does not simply rely on the 'existing' legal opportunities available under a given legal system, but also on those

(eds), *Judicial Activism at the European Court of Justice* (Cheltenham, Edward Elgar Publishing Ltd, 2013); Anne-Marie Slaughter and Walter Mattli, 'Europe Before the Court: A Political Theory of Legal Integration', in Beth A Simmons and Richard H Steinberg (eds), *International Law and International Relations: An International Organization Reader (International Organization)* (Cambridge, CUP, 2007) 457–85.

[44] Arena, n 29; Passalacqua, n 13; Pavone, n 29; Jos Hoevenaars, *A People's Court? A Bottom-Up Approach to Litigation Before the Court of Justice of the European Union* (The Hague, Eleven International Publishing, 2018).

[45] A fascinating example is provided in Claire Kilpatrick, 'The EU and its Sovereign Debt Programmes: The Challenges of Liminal Legality' (2017) 70 (1) *Current Legal Problems* 337–63.

[46] Tarrow, n 17.

that are 'perceived' as being available by social movements. This contribution maintains that, despite *Plaumann*, a 'closure' in the LOS can still be 'perceived' as a viable opportunity to trigger further litigation and to produce significant impact.

On this last point, in the present research the term 'impact' must be understood in both 'subjective' and 'objective' terms. 'Subjective impact' refers to the way each ENGO or strategic litigant measures the impact produced by its own litigation on the basis of the case-specific objectives. Conversely, 'objective impact' can either be 'legal' or 'political'.[47] By 'legal impact' I refer to the effects that the case produces on the interpretation or the legality/validity of EU law or on subsequent litigation; while by 'political impact' I refer to the effects that the case produces on the political institutions of the EU, both in terms of stimulating a political debate on the lawsuit or its content or triggering legislative reform.[48]

This book thus provides an empirical and theoretical contribution to the study of legal mobilisation in the environmental and climate change domain. This research sheds light on the NGOs' understanding of the legal opportunity structure in the EU, as well as on NGOs' resources and legal strategies deployed to overcome *Plaumann*. This contribution shows the relevance of networks membership and the added value of adopting an integrated approach to advocacy, making – as mentioned above – legal mobilisation a 'fluid' concept, which can hardly be encapsulated within the rigid boundaries of strategic litigation.[49]

Furthermore, this contribution holds that, despite *Plaumann*, NGOs' achievements are remarkable. The new AR is, for instance, one of the major achievements of this long legal mobilisation journey. The new AR is expected to bring more legal mobilisation in Europe and deliver more disputes on the 'science' underlying EU environmental measures. Conversely, in the climate domain, NGOs are building what I conceptualised in terms of 'transnational incremental judicial comfort', through which climate litigants aim at setting persuasive precedents with the idea of convincing more and more judges to take innovative interpretative steps in climate adjudication. The spreading of 'judicial comfort' in the climate context casts shadows on the CJEU, which looks increasingly 'obsolete' in the eyes of climate litigants. Indeed, this research contextualises the role of the CJEU within the current judicial landscape, which sees national and international courts increasingly taking specific stands in relation to climate change adjudication, including the ECtHR. Finally, this contribution argues that there is a demand within the European environmental movement for a different kind of EU environmental justice, which does not settle for administrative review of EU acts, but that rather strives for a more substantive constitutional judicial review of EU policy measures (including legislative acts).

[47] The measurement of 'societal impact' falls outside the scope of the present book.

[48] See Miriam Smith, 'Social Movements and Judicial Empowerment: Courts, Public Policy, and Lesbian and Gay Organizing in Canada' (2005) 33 (2) Politics & Society 327–53.

[49] Pola Cebulak, Marta Morvillo and Stefan Salomon, 'Introduction to the Special Issue: "Strategic litigation in EU Law"' (2024) 25 (6) *German Law Journal* 797.

Having clarified how my research is situated within the existing literature and what its added value is, in the next section I will now turn to outline the methodology deployed in the present contribution.

III. Methodology

In terms of methods, the field of legal mobilisation asks questions that traditional doctrinal analysis of legal sources can only answer to a limited extent. For this reason, I had to rely on wider methods, including those developed in other disciplines, that will be explained in the sections below.

A. Case Selection

Considering that my research question concerns legal mobilisation against the judicial interpretation of the 'individual concern' requirement laid down under Article 263(4) TFEU, my starting point was the case law of the CJEU on *Plaumann* in environmental actions initiated by environmental organisations. While the *Plaumann* test is only applied in actions intended to contest the legality of EU law, the fight 'against' *Plaumann* is also a fight to subject EU acts to judicial review. The present research is thus based on the assumption that, every time an environmental organisation seeks to contest the legality (or validity) of an EU act, that same organisation is also de facto trying to overcome *Plaumann*. Thus, 'overcoming' refers not only to amending/softening *Plaumann*, but also to (i) circumventing the *Plaumann* test by mobilising EU law before courts other than the CJEU; (ii) creating new pathways to challenge EU law within or outside the EU, which may or may not unlock access to the Court.

Having clarified this crucial point, I can now explain in greater detail my case selection in relation to the judgments of the CJEU. I carried out a keyword search on the CURIA database relating to actions for annulment on the subject matter of the 'environment' and including the terms 'association' and 'organisation'.[50] Then, through qualitative analysis of the results, I excluded those actions for annulment brought by corporations/for-profit organisations and/or those actions triggered in the context of access to environmental information. In relation to the latter, this was because such actions are aimed at contesting the legality of the denial to grant access to the relevant information, not the legality of an EU measure stricto sensu.

On the contrary, I included those actions for annulment brought under Article 12 of the AR and I will now explain why. Although these actions are aimed at contesting the legality of the denial to carry out an internal review on an administrative act adopted by an EU institution or body, the original intention of the

[50] See: https://curia.europa.eu/juris/recherche.jsf?language=en.

complainant was precisely to challenge an EU non-legislative act and to subject the latter to administrative review. The goal pursued by an environmental organisation in seeking the internal review of an administrative act is therefore comparable to the one pursued by an ENGO contesting the legality of an EU act directly before the EU judiciary under Article 263(3) TFEU. That is to say, to obtain substantive review of an EU act having an impact on the environment.

Based on these premises, I identified 19 cases, consisting of 29 judgments in total, including judgments adopted by the Court of First Instance (CFI)/General Court (GC)[51] and then the CJEU in appeal. I excluded those actions for annulment initiated by ENGOs which did not culminate into a judgment or an order on standing of the applicant(s). For this reason, cases like *Mellifera II* (*Mellifera v Commission* (T-393/18))[52] and *ClientEarth v Commission* (T-436/17)[53] have not been considered. I list below the rulings and orders of the CJEU which have been included in my analysis.

i. Actions for Annulment

T-585/93, *Stichting Greenpeace Council (Greenpeace International) and others v Commission*, CFI (1995)
C-321/95 P, *Greenpeace and Others v Commission*, CJEU (1998)
T-142/03, *Fost Plus v Commission*, CFI (2005)
Joined cases T-236/04 and T-241/04, *EEB and Stichting Natuur en Milieu v Commission*, CFI (2005)
T-91/07, *WWF-UK v Council*, CFI (2008)
C-355/08 P, *WWF-UK v Council*, CJEU (2009)
T-600/15, *PAN Europe and Others v Commission*, GC (2016)
T-330/18, *Carvalho and Others v Parliament and Council*, GC (2019)
C-565/19 P, *Carvalho and Others v Parliament and Council*, CJEU (2021)
T-141/19, *Sabo and Others v Parliament and Council*, GC (2020)
C-297/20 P, *Sabo and Others v Parliament and Council*, C-297/20 P CJEU (2021)

ii. Actions for Annulment Brought under the Aarhus Regulation

T-338/08, *Stichting Natuur en Milieu and Pesticide Action Network Europe v Commission*, GC (2012)
Joined Cases C-404/12 P and C-405/12 P, *Council and Commission v Stichting Natuur en Milieu and Pesticide Action Network Europe*, CJEU (2015)

[51] The Court of First Instance changed its name in 'General Court' with the Treaty of Lisbon, entered into force on 1 December 2009.
[52] The case was removed from the register.
[53] No need to adjudicate.

T-396/09, *Vereniging Milieudefensie and Stichting Stop Luchtverontreiniging Utrecht v Commission*, GC (2012)
Joined Cases C-401/12 P to C-403/12 P, *Council and Others v Vereniging Milieudefensie and Stichting Stop Luchtverontreiniging Utrecht*, CJEU (2015)
T-192/12, *PAN Europe v Commission*, GC (2014)
T-168/13, *EPAW v Commission*, GC (2014)
T-19/13, *Frank Bold v Commission*, GC (2014)
T-565/14, *EEB v Commission*, GC (2015)
T-685/14, *EEB v Commission*, GC (2015)
T-177/13, *TestBioTech and Others v Commission*, GC (2016)
C-82/17 P, *TestBioTech and Others v Commission*, CJEU (2019)
T-33/16, *TestBioTech v Commission*, GC (2018)
T-12/17, *Mellifera v Commission*, GC (2018)
C-784/18 P, *Mellifera v Commission*, CJEU (2020)
T-108/17, *ClientEarth v Commission*, GC (2019)
C-458/19 P, *ClientEarth v Commission*, CJEU (2021)
T-9/19, *ClientEarth v EIB*, GC (2021)
C-212/21 P, *EIB v ClientEarth*, CJEU (2023)

In addition to these cases, I also included preliminary references on validity triggered by ENGOs before national courts[54] as well as specific rulings, findings and recommendations issued by non-EU courts and international compliance bodies.[55] Indeed, besides the actions for annulment triggered before the EU judiciary, I decided to also include cases where EU law and *Plaumann* were de facto challenged, even before non-EU courts and quasi-judicial bodies, for example *Duarte Agostinho*[56] and communication ACCC/C/2008/32 (before the Aarhus Convention Compliance Committee).[57] This by virtue of the premise highlighted above, according to which 'overcoming' *Plaumann* can be equated with enhancing opportunities to contest the legality or validity of EU law.

For the analysis of the legal arguments deployed by the ENGOs, as well as of the legal reasoning adopted by the Court, I carried out traditional doctrinal analysis of these cases. The same has been done in relation to the relevant legal provisions included in pieces of international, EU and national law, such as the ones of the Aarhus Convention and the AR.

B. Direct Observation and Semi-Structured Interviews

The volume of information I could gain access to from the use of doctrinal methods of analysis of the relevant case law in relation to my research question(s) was quite

[54] See chapter 2.
[55] For a complete overview of the case law considered, see bibliography at the end of the book.
[56] See chapter 6.
[57] See chapter 3.

limited. For this reason, I undertook an internship in the legal unit of Greenpeace International (GPI) (Amsterdam, NL), where I had the chance to observe directly from the inside the work of in-house lawyers dealing with strategic litigation in the European and global climate context. At GPI, I also had a unique opportunity to carry out semi-structured interviews with some of their in-house lawyers, who I want to warmly thank for their time and openness.

In addition to the interviews carried out at GPI, I also undertook semi-structured interviews[58] with at least one plaintiff (individual or ENGO) and one external attorney representing the plaintiff(s) before the CJEU[59] for each of the actions for annulment listed above. With regard to ENGOs, I tried to interview at least one in-house lawyer working for each ENGO. In the absence of a legal unit or of any in-house lawyer inside the ENGO, I interviewed the President or the general coordinator of the organisation.

The interviews undertaken have revealed other legal strategies pursued by ENGOs before non-EU courts, where the fight against *Plaumann* may be considered more marginal but is, I argue, still present. As a consequence, I decided to also include these ENGOs and the cases they identified within the scope of my analysis. On the basis of these criteria, below I listed the ENGOs falling within the scope of my research, followed by the number of relevant cases they have brought before the EU judiciary.

Client Earth: 2
European Platform Against Windfarms (EPAW): 1
European Environmental Bureau (EEB): 3
Fost Plus: 1
Frank Bold: 1
Greenpeace International: 1
Mellifera: 1
Pesticide Action Network (PAN): 3
Stichting Natuur en Milieu: 2
Stichting Stop Luchtverontreiniging Utrecht: 1
Testbiotech: 2
World Wide Fund for Nature-UK (WWF-UK): 1

In addition to these ENGOs, I have also included the Global Legal Action Network (GLAN) within the scope of my research. GLAN is the CSO that assisted the plaintiffs in the previously mentioned Duarte Agostinho case before the ECtHR.

[58] To sample the interviews and structure my interviews I relied on Emilia Korkea-Aho and Päivi Leino, 'Interviewing Lawyers: A Critical Self-Reflection on Expert Interviews as a Method of EU Legal Research' (2019) *SI, European Journal of Legal Studies* 17–47.

[59] By 'external attorney' I refer to those lawyers who are not 'in-house lawyers' and provide their services independently.

I contacted all these ENGOs (including GLAN) by emailing them on the addresses displayed on their official websites[60] and asking for an interview with one of their in-house lawyers or with their president. Most of them refused the interview or did not answer my request. The same request was presented to all the external attorneys representing the plaintiffs in court, with very similar results.[61] In the end, I was able to interview 19 people in total. Below you will find their names, affiliations, and the cases in which they were involved. I want to warmly thank all the people listed here below for kindly accepting to take part in the present research.

i. In-House Lawyers/Members of ENGOs

a. GPI (Plaintiff in *Greenpeace v Commission*)

1. Jasper Teulings, former General Counsel (GPI), current Director, Climate (Strategic Litigation) at Children's Investment Fund Foundation (CIFF)
2. Kristin Casper, former Senior Legal Counsel, current General Counsel (GPI)
3. Richard Harvey, Legal Counsel Campaigns (GPI)
4. Daniel Simons, Senior Legal Counsel Strategic Defense (GPI)
5. Andrea Carta, Senior Legal Strategist at Greenpeace European Union (GPEU)[62]

b. ClientEarth (Plaintiff in *ClientEarth v Commission* and *ClientEarth v EIB*; Applicant in ACCC/C/2008/32 before the ACCC)

1. Anne Friel, Lawyer, Environmental Democracy Lead (ClientEarth)
2. Ugo Taddei, Director of Nature and Health (ClientEarth)

c. EPAW (Plaintiffs in *EPAW v Commission*)

1. Pat Swords, Technical and Legal Adviser (EPAW)

d. 2Celsius (Plaintiff in *Sabo and Others v Parliament and Council*)

1. Raul Cazan, President (2Celsius)
2. In-house lawyer at ENGO (anonymous)

[60] Where the personal email address of in-house lawyers was present, I directly emailed the in-house lawyer(s).

[61] The surnames of the lawyers representing the plaintiffs before the CJEU are publicly disclosed on the judgments of the latter.

[62] This interviewee was added on the basis of snowball sampling.

e. Global Legal Action Network (GLAN)

1. Gerry Liston (in-house lawyer at GLAN)[63]

f. Individuals

1. Giorgio Elter (plaintiff in *Carvalho and Others v Parliament and Council*)

g. External Attorneys

1. Gerd Winter, Professor of public law, European law and sociology of law at Department of Law, University of Bremen (representing the plaintiffs in *Carvalho and Others v Parliament and Council*)
2. David Wolfe, QC, Barrister, of Matrix Chambers (representing the plaintiffs in *Sabo and Others v Parliament and Council*)
3. Pavel Cerny, Attorney and Partner, Frank Bold Advokáti (representing the plaintiff in *Frank Bold v Commission*)
4. Csaba Kiss, Executive Director at EMLA and in-house lawyer at Justice & Environment (representing the plaintiff in *EPAW v Commission*)
5. Jemima Stratford, Brick Court Chambers (representing the plaintiff in *ClientEarth v Commission*)[64]

h. Other Interviews[65]

1. Harriet Mackaill-Hill, EU Climate Governance and Human Rights Policy Coordinator (CAN Europe)
2. Peter Oliver, member of the Aarhus Convention Compliance Committee, Visiting Professor at Université Libre de Bruxelles

In relation to the ENGOs I have not been able to interview, as well as for other types of information I could easily find on the web, I relied on other sources (most of them publicly available) which I am going to discuss in more detail in the next section.

ii. *Other Sources*

In addition to rulings, findings and recommendations, relevant international, European and national legislation as well as direct observation, semi-structured interviews and previous scholarly contributions, I also carried out qualitative analysis of other sources, most of which were publicly available on the internet. In this regard, I had the chance to consult the application files of some of the actions for

[63] In this case, the lawyer answered via questionnaire, not in an interview.
[64] In this case, the lawyer answered via questionnaire, not in an interview.
[65] These interviewees were added on the basis of snowball sampling.

annulment listed in section III.A. In particular, I consulted the original application file submitted by the applicants in the appeal process of *Council and Commission v Stichting Natuur en Milieu and Pesticide Action Network Europe* before the CJEU.[66] Moreover, I also consulted the application files submitted by the applicants in *Carvalho and Others v Parliament and Council* before the GC; *Sabo and Others v Parliament and Council* before the GC; *Duarte Agostinho and Others v Portugal and Others* before the ECtHR. These application files were all made publicly available on the official websites created to increase the impact of the lawsuits.[67]

Furthermore, I carried out qualitative analysis of additional documents found by consulting the following sources:

- reports of the negotiations of the Aarhus Convention, which are publicly available on the UNECE website;[68]
- ENGOs public statements and reports released on their official websites;
- CJEU annual reports publicly available on the CJEU website;[69]
- official websites of the EU institutions (including consultation of legislative proposals; public consultations material and the Aarhus internal review repository of the European Commission);
- articles published on online newspapers.

Finally, I also attended the 62nd meeting of the Compliance Committee to the Aarhus Convention, (Geneva, 5–9 November 2018) as well as 13 conferences and webinars (some online, some in presence) hosting academics, practitioners and members of ENGOs working on environmental and climate litigation in Europe and across the globe.[70]

Having outlined the socio-legal methods deployed in the present research, as well as the sources consulted, I will now turn to outline the overall structure of my book.

IV. Structure

The whole analysis is divided into five distinct 'key periods', representing five crucial timeframes in the legal history of environmental legal mobilisation against *Plaumann*. These periods can be explained as follows:

1. **The 'pre-Aarhus' period:** the first period considered runs from 1996 to 2012. The case study that I chose to shed light on developments during

[66] In this regard, I want to warmly thank the law firm Van Den Biesen in Amsterdam for making such file available for legal research. See chapter 3.

[67] See chapters 6 and 7. I want to warmly thank the organisations and the lawyers involved in *Carvalho*, *Sabo* and *Duarte* for making the application files publicly available for legal research.

[68] See chapter 3.

[69] See chapter 2.

[70] See complete list in the bibliography, at the end of the book.

this timeframe is *Greenpeace*,[71] the very first environmental direct action brought by an ENGO before the EU judiciary. I chose this case because all the main arguments used by GPI's lawyers have been replicated to a large extent in the subsequent case law occurring during the same period. In this sense, GPI can be considered as a 'model case' for what I called the 'pre-Aarhus period'.

2. **The 'post-Aarhus (I)' period:** the second period considered runs from 2012 to 2017 and sees the entry into force of the AR as a first major change impacting environmental litigation before EU Courts. The case study that I chose to represent this period is *Stichting Natuur*,[72] one of the first cases brought before the EU judiciary under Article 12 AR. Once again, I chose this case because all the main arguments used by the applicants' lawyers have been reflected in following rulings on access to justice under the AR.
3. **The 'post-Aarhus (II)' period:** this timeframe runs from 2017 to 2021 (the year in which the AR was amended). This pathway refers, once again, to Article 12 AR. This section will draw attention to how ENGOs mobilised to overcome *Plaumann* after the publication – in 2017 – of the ACCC findings on EU compliance with the Aarhus Convention. I have chosen *Mellifera*[73] as a case study for this period, since this is the first case brought under the AR after the publication, in 2017, of the ACCC findings on EU compliance.
4. **The 'post-Aarhus reform' period:** this timeframe runs from 2021 to the present and refers to the use of the internal review mechanism established by the 'new' AR, after the amendment occurred in October 2021. This timeframe will provide a preliminary assessment of the novelties introduced in the AR by the EU legislator. In the analysis of this last timeframe, I included the *ClientEarth v EIB* case[74] in order to show the 'unexplored' potential for legal mobilisation of the 'old' version of the AR, compared to the 'new' one.
5. **The CCL trend:** the second timeframe runs from 2018 to the present and refers to, both, the current mobilisation of non-EU Courts by ENGOs in a bid to also influence the CJEU through CCL; the actions for annulment being triggered by ENGOs directly before the CJEU in climate-related matters. This section will particularly emphasise how the ongoing global climate change litigation (CCL) trend is affecting the arguments used by civil society organisations to overcome the *Plaumann* test. The cases I chose for this period

[71] Case T-585/93, *Stichting Greenpeace Council (Greenpeace International) and others v Commission* (1995) ECLI:EU:T:1995:147; C-321/95 P, *Greenpeace and Others v Commission* (1998) ECLI:EU:C:1998:153.

[72] T-338/08, *Stichting Natuur en Milieu and Pesticide Action Network Europe v Commission* (2012) ECLI:EU:T:2012:300; joined cases C-404/12 P and C-405/12 P, *Council and Commission v Stichting Natuur en Milieu and Pesticide Action Network Europe* (2015) ECLI:EU:C:2015:5.

[73] T-12/17, *Mellifera v Commission* (2018) ECLI:EU:T:2018:616.

[74] C-212/21 P, *EIB v ClientEarth*, CJEU (2023) ECLI:EU:C:2023:546.

are *The People v Arctic Oil*,[75] *Duarte Agostinho*[76] and *Müllner v Austria*[77] in chapter 6 on CCL before non-EU Courts; *Carvalho*[78] and *Sabo*[79] in chapter 7 on CCL before the CJEU.

It is crucial to stress that, as also seen in Figure 1, some of these periods inevitably overlap, as they explore different mobilisation pathways that have been used at the same time by ENGOs in the attempt to get access to justice before EU Courts. For instance, in 2018 while some ENGOs were trying to challenge EU climate measures directly before the CJEU, some others were seeking the internal review of EU administrative acts under the AR.

Figure 1 Timeline of key events in the history of legal mobilisation against Plaumann

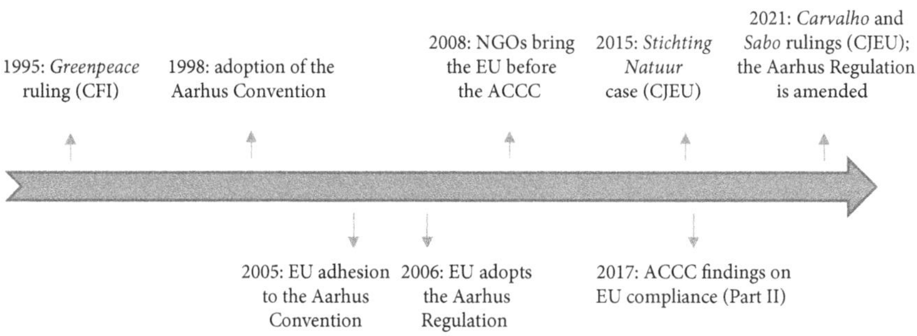

The 'pre-Aarhus' period is addressed in chapter one. This chapter will show how the *Plaumann* test constituted a 'closure' in the EU LOS, both generally and more specifically in the environmental context. The first chapter will briefly outline the relevant literature on the 'origins' of *Plaumann*, in order to provide the reader with a clearer explanation about why this test still exists. In fact, as mentioned above, the first chapter will mainly focus on the Greenpeace case[80] and will show how ENGOs have mobilised against *Plaumann* before the entry into force of the Aarhus Convention.

Chapter two represents already an exception to the other chapters, which are clearly delimited on a temporal basis. This chapter focuses on a different mobilisation pathway, namely the PRP, which has been used by environmental organisations throughout each of the five timeframes. This chapter explores the potential for EU legal mobilisation against *Plaumann* offered by the PRP on validity, laid down

[75] *The People v Arctic Oil (Nature and Youth, Greenpeace v Norway's Ministry of Petroleum and Energy)* Case Number: 18-060499ASD-BORG/03 (Norway).

[76] *Duarte Agostinho and Others v Portugal and Others*, n. 39371/20, ECtHR, 9 April 2024.

[77] *Müllner v Austria*, n. 18859/21, ECtHR (pending).

[78] T-330/18, *Carvalho and Others v Parliament and Council* (2019) ECLI:EU:T:2019:324; C-565/19 P, *Carvalho and Others v Parliament and Council* (2021) ECLI:EU:C:2021:252.

[79] T-141/19, *Sabo and Others v Parliament and Council* (2020) ECLI:EU:T:2020:179; C-297/20 P, *Sabo and Others v Parliament and Council* (2021) ECLI:EU:C:2021:24.

[80] *Greenpeace*, n 71.

under Article 267 TFEU. This chapter seeks to show how complex the LOS at national level is for ENGOs willing to mobilise national courts and what kind of additional barriers they encounter in the attempt to stimulate references on validity. Chapter two will also show how Article 267 TFEU has been used by ENGOs as a mobilisation pathway to challenge the validity of EU law and with what results.

The 'post-Aarhus (I)' period is addressed in chapter three, which deepens the analysis of this first crucial 'legal change', namely the negotiation, and subsequent conclusion and implementation, of the Aarhus Convention. This chapter will show how ENGOs contributed deeply to 'shaping' the Aarhus Convention, by taking part in the negotiation of the agreement and by proposing a compliance mechanism which was then officially adopted by the Parties to the Convention. Stressing ENGOs' participation in the Aarhus negotiation is essential to demonstrate how political mobilisation can 'shape' new legal opportunities which have then been used by other collective actors to take over the fight against *Plaumann*. The adoption of the Aarhus Convention led to the creation of a new mobilisation pathway available for ENGOs under EU law, that is the adoption of the AR, establishing an internal review mechanism of EU administrative acts. However, chapter three will also show how this apparent 'opening' in the LOS later turned into a new 'closure', because of the extremely narrow scope of the definition of 'administrative act' included in the AR. The analysis of the *Stichting Natuur* case[81] will show how the AR became a further obstacle to EU legal mobilisation in the environmental context.

Chapter four focuses on the 'post-Aarhus (II) – post findings' period, showing how ENGOs have used the compliance mechanism established under the Aarhus Convention (mechanism that they have contributed to shape) to hold the EU accountable for the narrow legal opportunities available under the EU Treaties and the AR. This chapter will equally highlight how the Aarhus Committee's findings on EU compliance were then used by ENGOs to mobilise the CJEU, in the attempt to convince the EU judiciary to broaden the legal opportunities available for ENGOs. This chapter will thus show how the findings of the Aarhus Committee were 'perceived' by environmental organisations as an 'opening' in the LOS, which spawned further litigation before the CJEU.

Conversely, the 'post-Aarhus – post reform' period is addressed in chapter five, which will show that, despite the Court's reluctance to comply with the Aarhus Committee's findings, these produced significant 'indirect effects' and greatly contributed to putting pressure on the EU institutions with regard to direct access to justice before the EU judiciary. The pressure produced by the Committee's findings unlocked opportunities for law-making, which – within four years from the findings – led to the amendment of the AR in 2021. In this regard, this chapter will also present and explore the potential for EU legal mobilisation offered by the amendment of the AR.

[81] ibid.

Chapter six inaugurates 'the CCL trend' period, running from 2018 to the present. This chapter will first show how the judicial landscape has evolved in the last decade in relation to climate adjudication. Climate change litigation (CCL) has grown enormously since 2015, the year in which the first ruling in the *Urgenda* case[82] was released. Indeed, ENGOs involved in transnational CCL are strongly contributing to build what I conceptualised in terms of 'transnational incremental judicial comfort' (TIJC), through which precedents are used as building blocks to 'incrementally' contribute to make judges feel more comfortable in taking new interpretative steps on a transnational scale. In this regard, CCL is also having an impact on legal mobilisation against *Plaumann* in the environmental context. This chapter will show how ENGOs involved in CCL are trying to challenge EU climate policy measures by litigating before non-EU courts.

Chapter seven expands 'the CCL trend' by analysing the climate cases triggered by CSOs directly before the CJEU. This final chapter will particularly focus on two lawsuits, namely *Carvalho*[83] and *Sabo*,[84] which have been rejected precisely because of *Plaumann*. Thanks to the interviews undertaken with the lawyers involved in the two cases, this chapter will reveal interesting findings on how in-house lawyers and external attorneys have constructed the lawsuits and what role *Plaumann* has played in the planning of the legal strategy. This chapter will emphasise a key shift in ENGOs' claims making across the timeframes here considered. From the project-specific lawsuits brought in the 'pre-Aarhus' period, or the substance-specific actions brought in the 'post-Aarhus I' period under the AR, legal mobilisation against the legality of EU environmental law has in more recent years shifted towards broader policy arrangements, including legislative acts and programmes, impacting the lives of all European citizens.

The final conclusions will put forward the main findings of the overall book and set the ground for future scholarly contributions.

Finally, considering my current working position, before delving into the analysis embedded in this research, I want to clarify that the views and opinions expressed in this book belong solely to the author, and do not reflect the view of the European Commission.

[82] *Urgenda Foundation v The Netherlands* [2015] HAZA C/09/00456689 (24 June 2015); aff'd (9 October 2018); aff'd (20 December 2019) (District Court of the Hague, The Hague Court of Appeal, Dutch Supreme Court).

[83] *Carvalho*, n 78.

[84] *Sabo*, n 79.

1

The *Plaumann* Test

I. Introduction

This first chapter of this book describes the manner in which the *Plaumann* test closes down direct access to the CJEU under Article 263(4), creating a 'closure' in the LOS available for environmental organisations under EU law.[1] In this regard, the first four sections will aim at clarifying *what* the *Plaumann* test is and *why* it exists. Indeed, the topic of direct access to justice for private applicants before the CJEU has been highly debated in legal scholarship. Commentators have provided insightful explanations about *why* the Court keeps reiterating its narrow formula without really engaging with alternative proposals advanced by litigants and other members of the CJEU. Although, as mentioned in the introduction to the present book, this research looks at the issue of access to justice before the CJEU by taking a legal mobilisation perspective – therefore by looking at the legal strategies deployed by ENGOs to be granted standing – I still decided to report on the relevant literature on *Plaumann*. This is in order to provide the reader with a clearer explanation about why this formula is still there and why it constitutes a 'closure' in the LOS.

Then, the analysis embedded in the following sections will focus on the cases brought by ENGOs under Article 263(4) TFEU before the AR entered into force. The first period here considered therefore runs from 1996 to 2012. The case study that I have selected to shed light on this timeframe is *Greenpeace*, the very first environmental direct action in which the *Plaumann* test found application. I chose this case because all the main arguments used by *Greenpeace*'s lawyers have been very largely replicated in the subsequent case law occurring within the same timeframe. In this respect, *Greenpeace* can be considered as a 'model case' for what I called the 'pre-Aarhus period'.

Indeed, before the entry into force of the AR, ENGOs tried on a number of occasions to challenge EU measures before the CJEU under the relevant Treaty

[1] A version of this description of the 'pre-Aarhus' period has been previously published in Mario Pagano, 'Overcoming Plaumann in EU Environmental Litigation: An Analysis of ENGOs Legal Arguments in Actions for Annulment' (2019) *Diritto e Processo* 311–60.

provisions.[2] But they never succeeded. The *Greenpeace* case[3] is thus crucial in the current analysis for a number of reasons. It is the very first direct challenge against an EU measure brought by an ENGO before the EU judiciary and it therefore also represents the very first time the *Plaumann* test found application in the environmental context. Because of this and because of the legal arguments presented before the Court, this case has been used as a point of reference by other environmental litigants in subsequent actions for annulment. Furthermore, the *Greenpeace* case has contributed to stimulating a rich theoretical debate over environmental judicial protection in the EU.[4] In the light of this, a close analysis of the main arguments deployed by ENGOs to mobilise against *Plaumann* in the 'pre-Aarhus period' will be provided. This in order to show *how* ENGOs attempted to be granted standing in actions for annulment. The concluding part will sum up the analysis in this first chapter and set the ground for the chapters that follow.

II. The *Plaumann* Test

When the first action for annulment in the environmental domain was brought before the Court of First Instance (CFI)[5] in 1993, Article 173(4) TEC was the provision establishing the conditions under which any natural or legal person could challenge the legality of an EU act before the EU judiciary. Notably, under paragraph 4

> Any natural or legal person may, under the same conditions, institute proceedings against a decision addressed to that person or against a decision which, although in the form of a regulation or a decision addressed to another person, is of direct and individual concern to the former.

The CJEU interpreted the criterion of 'individual concern' for the first time in 1963 in the *Plaumann* case.[6] In this ruling, the Court held that:

> [Persons] other than those to whom a decision is addressed may only claim to be individually concerned if that decision affects them by reason of certain attributes which are peculiar to them or by reason of circumstances in which they are differentiated from all other persons and by virtue of these factors distinguishes them individually just as in the case of the person addressed.[7]

[2] See T-142/03, *Fost Plus v Commission* (2005) ECLI:EU:T:2005:51; joined cases T-236/04 and T-241/04, *EEB and Stichting Natuur en Milieu v Commission* (2005) ECLI:EU:T:2005:426; T-91/07, *WWF-UK v Council* (2008) ECLI:EU:T:2008:170.

[3] Case T-585/93, *Stichting Greenpeace Council (Greenpeace International) and others v Commission* (1995) ECLI:EU:T:1995:147; C-321/95 P, *Greenpeace and Others v Commission* (1998) ECLI:EU:C:1998:153. Hereinafter '*Greenpeace* (CFI)' and '*Greenpeace* (CJEU)'.

[4] See below section VII.

[5] Current 'General Court' (GC).

[6] Case 25-62, *Plaumann & Co. v Commission* (1963) ECLI:EU:C:1963:17.

[7] ibid, § 9.

The criteria for standing established in this decision have since then been referred to as the '*Plaumann* test', which has traditionally been extremely difficult to satisfy in environmental litigation. This is because environmental measures are usually acts of general application and are only rarely capable of addressing specific subjects or affecting them by reason of certain attributes that are peculiar to them.[8] Such a narrow interpretation of the individual concern requirement is thus particularly problematic when environmental protection is at stake. In this regard, it is no surprise that – at present – no action for annulment brought by ENGOs has ever been deemed admissible by the EU judiciary.[9]

More broadly speaking, the subject of access to justice of private applicants before the EU judiciary has been widely discussed in EU and international legal scholarship.[10] However, the two contributions which are generally considered as being the most influential[11] in legal scholarship in trying to explain *why Plaumann* exists, are the ones authored by Eric Stein and G Joseph Vining (1976) on the one hand, and Hjalte Rasmussen (1980) on the other.[12] In addition to these contributions, I will also briefly outline the interesting claim of Matthijs van Wolferen, who devoted his PhD dissertation to explore the reasons preventing the Court from abandoning *Plaumann*.[13]

Hence, in the section below, I will now outline key aspects of some of the most important scholarly contributions on *Plaumann* in order to provide the reader with a clearer idea of why direct access of private applicants before the CJEU is considered as a 'closure' in the LOS under EU law.

III. Stein's and Vining's Contribution

Already in the 1970s, Stein and Vining carried out a comparative analysis of access to justice before the US Supreme Court and the Court of Justice of the European Economic Community of that time (CJEEC). The authors observed that one of the factors which contributed to a broadening of the standing requirements for

[8] eg EU measures setting national quotas for fishing or maximum residue levels for products.

[9] Not listing all the cases here but discussed in this and later chapters.

[10] See, inter alia, Carol Harlow, 'Towards a Theory of Access for the European Court of Justice' (1992) 12(1) *Yearbook of European Law* 213–48; Marie-Pierre Granger, 'Towards a Liberalisation of Standing Conditions for Individuals Seeking Judicial Review of Community Acts: Jégo-Quéré et Cie SA v Commission and Unión de Pequeños Agricultores v Council' (2003) 66(1) *The Modern Law Review* 124–38; Mariolina Eliantonio and Haakon Roer-Eide, 'Regional Courts and Locus Standi for Private Parties: Can the CJEU Learn Something from the Others' (2014) 13 *The Law and Practice of International Courts and Tribunals* 27–53.

[11] Matthijs van Wolferen, 'To Justifie the Wayes of God to Men – Limits to the Court's Power of Interpretation', Doctoral Thesis – University of Groningen, 2018, 16.

[12] Eric Stein and G Joseph Vining, 'Citizen Access to Judicial Review of Administrative Action in a Transnational and Federal Context' (1976) 70 *American Journal of International Law* 219–41; Hjalte Rasmussen, 'Why Is Article 173 Interpreted against Private Plaintiffs?' (1980) 5 *EL Rev* 112.

[13] van Wolferen, n 11.

private applicants in the US was the emergence of 'economic and non-economic forces and interests such as environmental and consumer protection, which have had such impact on the liberalization of the American rule'.[14]

Stein and Vining thus linked the need for wider standing requirements to the presence, inter alia, of wider regulatory powers attributed to the federal authorities. Considering the limited regulatory powers of the EEC at that time, they assumed that

> as the scope of the Community regulatory powers broadens to include other fields and affect other values, economic and non-economic – health and safety, environment, consumer protection, energy conservation – the Court may well feel called upon to broaden direct access by private complainants.[15]

IV. Rasmussen's Contribution

To this assumption (and to many others included in Stein's and Vining's article), in 1980 Rasmussen responded by stressing – and reflecting on – the peculiarities of the European Community, which, in his view, did not leave room for standing requirements in actions for annulment other than those laid down in *Plaumann*. But what peculiarities?

First, Rasmussen maintained that the Community Treaties did not establish the Court of Justice as a supreme appellate court, while in other federal experiences, such as the US and Germany, the Supreme Courts are true 'constitutional courts' called upon to assess the legality of national laws *vis-á-vis* the constitution of the State. Conversely, under Community law, the Court of Justice does not have the jurisdiction to assess the compliance of the law of the MSs with the Community Treaties, as only national constitutional courts have the power to declare the laws of a MS unconstitutional.[16] In this regard, the Court of Justice has not been empowered to receive appeals from national judges as to whether national laws are unconstitutional.[17]

Second, the US and German Supreme Courts originally had very limited powers, which have then been gradually expanded. In the US, for instance, it was initially the Congress which exercised the function of court of appeal. On the contrary, in the EEC, the Court of Justice was immediately acknowledged a very broad jurisdiction and all cases that did not fall within those expressly laid down in the Treaties were strictly excluded from its jurisdiction.[18]

[14] Stein and Vining, n 11, 234.
[15] ibid, 241.
[16] Rasmussen, n 12, 115–16. This statement should be qualified by recognising the Commission's authority to take Member States to the CJEU under the compliance procedure established by Art 258 TFEU.
[17] ibid, 116.
[18] ibid, 115.

Third, individuals inevitably bring 'facts' while the Court prefers to be a Court of 'law'. 'Assessing facts' rather than 'interpreting norms' can be more time-consuming, especially in a multi-linguistic court like the CJEU. Therefore, the EU judiciary tends to favour preliminary rulings – where the facts of the case are already well established before the national court – to direct actions (which used to take 18 months on average)[19] and where the facts of the case have to be completely assessed from scratch.[20]

Fourth, Rasmussen engaged with the 'transnational origin' of the CJEU, by what he called the 'compact among States' argument. Indeed, according to the author, the Court was created 'by the MSs for the MSs' and – presumably – these States would have rejected the idea of having private citizens having a relatively broad access before a transnational court. This seems to be confirmed even by the sentence used very often by the EU judiciary in its case law, namely 'the Court is bound by the clearly restrictive wording of Art. 173(2)'.[21]

Fifth, the author engaged with the 'sovereignty' argument, according to which the Court intends to maintain the delicate balance between the MSs and the Community. On this point, in *Alcan*,[22] AG Gand held that the Court should use 'diplomatic courtesy' and avoid limiting the MSs' discretion and sovereignty. Rasmussen showed once again scepticism and wondered how it is possible that the annulment of a Community act may lead to an intrusion into the sphere of sovereignty of a MS?[23]

Sixth, the author engaged with the 'more power, less control' argument. This point, raised by Stein and Vining in their contribution, refers to the change in the wording of the Treaties, from the ECSC to the EEC. The amendments occurred in the provisions regulating direct access of private applicants led the Court to believe that the MS wanted to restrict access to the courts of the Community (of that time). As mentioned above, standing under the ECSC Treaty – as interpreted by the Court at that time – was much broader compared to the one allowed under the TEEC (and the TFEU nowadays).[24] However, Rasmussen showed scepticism toward this argument by holding that 'it seems odd to provide less judicial protection in response to greater political powers'.[25]

Seventh, the 'political compromise argument': ensuring greater access to justice could jeopardise Community acts resulting from laborious compromise

[19] Nowadays, direct actions are mainly handled by the General Court and the average duration of legal proceedings is 16.9 months (Court of Justice of the European Union, 'The year in review – annual report 2019'. Available at: https://curia.europa.eu/jcms/upload/docs/application/pdf/2020-05/ra_pan_2019_interieur_en_final.pdf).

[20] Rasmussen, n 12, 116.

[21] ibid, 117.

[22] Opinion of AG Gand in case 69/69, *SA Alcan Aluminium Raeren and others v Commission of the European Communities* (1970) ECLI:EU:C:1970:53, 398.

[23] Rasmussen, n 12, 118–19.

[24] On this point, see Matthijs van Wolferen, 'The Limits to the CJEU's Interpretation of Locus Standi, a Theoretical Framework' (2016) 12 (4) *Journal of Contemporary European Research* 923.

[25] Rasmussen, n 12, 119.

between political forces (in particular within the Council). Rasmussen argued that especially when measures resulting from the Council's unanimity are at stake, the Court should respond by guaranteeing greater access to justice, given that no State will ever attempt to endanger strenuous negotiations by challenging that act before the CJEU (same thing for the Commission).[26]

Eighth, the 'administrative aversion against judicial review' argument: since the decision-making process presumably would be inhibited if the decision may later undergo judicial scrutiny on private initiative, the Council would oppose a broad right to judicial review'. To this argument, Rasmussen responded by basically stressing the lack of any empirical evidence supporting the hypothesis.[27]

Ninth, the argument relating to an alleged 'lack of solidarity' by powerful companies and interest groups, who would try to protect their prerogatives and freedoms by contesting any European measure, even in frivolous cases. To this claim, the author responded by emphasising the ECSC experience, where softer conditions for access to justice have not led to any significant increase in the number of cases brought before the Court.[28]

Finally, Rasmussen makes clear the main assumption of his paper, which relates to the way the Court considers itself, namely as an 'appellate court'. Although he recognises that the narrow interpretation established in *Plaumann* is most likely to be the result of a 'combination' of all the previous factors outlined by Stein and Vining (most of them criticised in his contribution), Rasmussen saw in the Court's case law the 'long term interest ... to act more as a high court of appeals of Community law', with national courts acting as courts of first instance. Therefore, in Rasmussen's interpretation of the Court's intentions, private parties should first seek relief before national judges, who should then refer the case to the Court for a preliminary ruling where an interpretation of EU law is 'desirable or required by law, or where doubt about its validity is aired before the national judge'. In the light of this, and as it will be showed in chapter 2 (dealing with the PRP pathway) if we look at the way the case law of the CJEU has evolved throughout the decades, especially in the field of environmental protection, it seems that Rasmussen's reading of the Court's jurisprudence was quite accurate.[29]

V. van Wolferen's Contribution

In his doctoral dissertation Matthijs van Wolferen criticised previous scholarship on access to justice and the CJEU's approach to standing, holding that such scholarship does not 'engage with the place that standing requirements have in a

[26] ibid, 120.
[27] ibid, 121.
[28] ibid.
[29] See chapter 2.

constitutional order'.[30] Indeed, van Wolferen drew on David Feldman's analytical framework which identifies four elements, present in common law legal orders, that shape the relationship between courts and applicants as well as the courts' 'interpretative space'.[31] These elements are:

(i) The constitutional relationship: the constitutional possibilities for legal challenges in a formal sense;
(ii) Federalism: the existence and extent of a federal system within the state;
(iii) Guiding principles: ideals set out in constitution or other documents of equal status;
(iv) Fundamental Rights: the existence of fundamental rights in the constitutional order, possibly through treaties or other international obligations.

This is not the right place for engaging with Feldman's framework and van Wolferen's application. However, on the basis of these four elements, van Wolferen concluded his analysis by claiming that the scholarly criticism toward the EU judiciary has been 'too harsh',[32] as the Court's interpretative space has not really changed since *Plaumann* was pronounced.

> For the largest period in the development of the European project, the Court of Justice did not have the interpretative space to interpret the action for annulment in any other way that it did at the time of the Plaumann case …
>
> Regarding public interest litigation, there has been no indication that any of the elements in the framework shifted to accommodate this change in legal thinking, as reflected by the changes in the [MSs] and in the Aarhus Convention. On the contrary, the Court was actively precluded from interpreting Article 263 TFEU in this manner.[33]

The author also clarified the Court's vision about an EU judicial protection system where:

> access to lower courts needs to be relatively easy for public interest litigants, so that national courts may function as a filter for issues of a constitutional nature that need to make their way to the Court of Justice. As in other federal judicial orders, the occurrence of an actual constitutional complaint is rare, and is usually only open to the individual affected by a breach of his or her constitutional rights.[34]

The author thus justified the Court's rigidity in relation to *Plaumann* and, just like the EU judiciary, maintained that, if a change in the system of direct access of private applicants to the Court should be envisioned, it should be for the EU MSs to do so through Treaty revision.[35]

[30] van Wolferen, n 24, 920.
[31] van Wolferen, n 11, 73.
[32] ibid, 297.
[33] ibid.
[34] ibid, 298.
[35] ibid, 299.

Having also briefly outlined van Wolferen's contribution, it is now time to remind the reader that, as described in the introduction of this book, the *Plaumann* test in the present research is considered in 'static' terms, as a 'closure' in the LOS currently available under EU law. It is therefore not my intention to engage with the relevant case law and literature on direct access before the Court with the aim to convince the EU judiciary to abandon (or maintain) the *Plaumann* test. The present research rather seeks to analyse the legal mobilisation strategies of ENGOs deployed to overcome *Plaumann* and contest the legality (or validity) of EU law.

In the light of this, in the next section I will now turn to describe the Greenpeace case, the first direct action in which the *Plaumann* test found application in the environmental domain.

VI. The *Greenpeace* Case

In 1991, the European Commission (the Commission) adopted Decision C(91) 440 (hereinafter 'Decision 1') granting Spain financial assistance from the European Regional Development Fund (ERDF) for the construction of two power stations in the Canary Islands. These works were to be carried out by the Spanish company 'Unelco'.

It is relevant to stress that Article 5 of Decision 1 allowed the Commission to reduce or suspend the aid granted to the operation in issue 'if an examination were to reveal an irregularity and in particular a significant change affecting the way in which it was carried out for which the Commission's approval had not been requested'.[36] Nevertheless, with Decision 1, the Commission 'promised' Spain that it would finance the project, but – as it will now be outlined – the period of time between the promise and the actual 'payment' of that aid, was characterised by a remarkable 'activism' on the part of individuals and groups concerned about the Commission's decision.[37] Indeed, a few months after the adoption of the aforementioned decision, two Spanish individuals informed the Commission by letter that they considered the works carried out on one of the islands (namely Gran Canaria) to be unlawful. This was because Unelco had, they claimed, failed to undertake an environmental impact assessment (EIA) as required by the EIA Directive.[38]

Almost a year later, in November 1992, again by letter, another individual sought the Commission's assistance on the ground that the Canary Islands Commission for Planning and the Environment (Cumac) had not issued its statements of EIA

[36] *Greenpeace* (CFI), n 3, § 2.

[37] See below.

[38] Current Directive 2011/92/EU of the European Parliament and of the Council of 13 December 2011 on the assessment of the effects of certain public and private projects on the environment, OJ L 26, 28 January 2012, pp 1–21.

with regard to Unelco's work on Gran Canaria and Tenerife in accordance with Spanish law. However, such declarations were issued by Cumac a few days later.[39]

In spite of the issuing of these declarations, in spring 1993, two local environmental associations (namely *Tagoror Ecologista Alternativo* – TEA and *Comisiòn Canaria contra la Comtaminaciòn* – CIC) lodged two different administrative actions for judicial review before the Spanish competent authorities against Cumac's declarations of EIA relating to the contested projects. The same was also done by Greenpeace Spain (GPS), an ENGO particularly active at national level.[40]

Besides the judicial proceedings brought in Spain, GPS sent a letter to the Directorate-General of the Commission for Regional Policies (current DG REGIO) asking it to confirm 'whether Community structural funds had been paid to the Regional Government of the Canary Islands for the construction of two power stations and to inform it of the timetable for the release of those funds'.[41]

DG REGIO answered by recommending that GPS read the decision containing 'details of the specific conditions to be respected by Unelco in order to obtain Community support and the financing plan'.[42] The ENGO thus asked the Commission for full disclosure of all information relating to measures it had taken with regard to the construction of the two contested power stations in accordance with Article 7 of Council Regulation n. 2052/88[43] on the tasks of the Structural Funds and their effectiveness and on coordination of their activities between themselves and with the operations of the EIB[44] and the other existing financial instruments.[45]

Under this provision,

> [measures] financed by the Funds or receiving assistance from the EIB or from another existing financial instrument shall be in keeping with the provisions of the Treaties, with the instruments adopted pursuant thereto and with EU policies, including those concerning … environmental protection.[46]

Nevertheless, the European Commission denied access to information, since the request was deemed to concern the internal decision making procedure of the Commission.[47] After a meeting in Brussels between representatives of DG REGIO and GPS, the latter – along with various individuals – decided to bring an action before the CFI seeking annulment of the decision alleged to have been taken by the Commission to disburse regional development funds to Spain (hereinafter 'Decision 2').[48] In 1995 the CFI issued its ruling, dismissing the action brought

[39] *Greenpeace* (CFI), n 3, § 4.
[40] ibid, §§ 6–7.
[41] ibid, § 8.
[42] ibid, § 9.
[43] No longer in force.
[44] European Investment Bank.
[45] *Greenpeace* (CFI), n 3, § 10.
[46] ibid.
[47] ibid, § 11.
[48] ibid, § 13.

by the applicants for lack of standing. This decision was then upheld by the CJEU three years later, in 1998. In the next section, I will outline the main arguments deployed by the applicants in Greenpeace to mobilise against the *Plaumann* test.

VII. Mobilising against *Plaumann* in the pre-Aarhus Period

In *Greenpeace*, the applicants put forward a number of legal arguments mainly aiming to support three different propositions, which were then replicated to a large extent in the subsequent environmental actions for annulment in the 'pre-Aarhus period'. The three main arguments were:

(i) The environment and ENGOs should receive special treatment: environmental protection is a peculiar kind of public interest which requires a different treatment. This special position of the environment is enshrined in EU primary law and in the case law of the CJEU. As a consequence, even ENGOs should receive special treatment when accessing EU courts.
(ii) Effective judicial protection: by denying standing to ENGOs before EU courts, there arises a judicial protection vacuum in the EU legal order.
(iii) EU law consistency: granting standing to civil society environmental organisations would be a consistent step to take having regard to EU law as well as with the case law of the CJEU in policy areas other than environmental protection.

Having outlined the main arguments referred to by ENGOs to mobilise against *Plaumann* in the 'pre-Aarhus period', I will now attempt to analyse each of these arguments more in depth and show how these – although ultimately unsuccessful – found internal support within the CJEU in the opinions of a number of AGs.

A. Treating the Environment Differently

According to the applicants in *Greenpeace*, the Court's traditional interpretation of Article 173(4) TEC should be amended in order to also take into account the peculiar characteristics of the environment. In particular, in the appeal process of this case, the applicants explained the main reason why – in their view – the environment should receive special judicial treatment. They maintained that in the area of environmental protection, the interests are, 'by their very nature, common and shared, and the rights relating to those interests are liable to be held by a potentially large number of individuals'.[49]

[49] *Greenpeace* (CJEU), n 3, § 18.

Even Advocate General (AG) Cosmas seemed to agree with the applicants on this point, as in his opinion he stated:

> For environmental protection is indeed a matter of general interest. Conservation of the environment is a legal interest theoretically shared by all natural persons; it thus has a communal dimension. Furthermore, the more significant is the intervention in or impingement on the environment, the greater is the number of persons affected thereby.[50]

In the same opinion, AG Cosmas provided an interesting overview of the position occupied by environmental protection in the EU Treaties and the Court's case law.[51] By so doing, he seemed to imply that environmental protection already had – even at that time – a special place within the EU legal order. Indeed, he recalled that in 1985 the EU judicature in *ADBHU*[52] affirmed that 'environmental protection is one of the fundamental objectives of the [EU]', a status confirmed one year later, when the European Single Act introduced a specific chapter on the environment in EU primary law.

'The general outlines of that policy – argued the AG – are elaborated in Title XVI of the Treaty [of the European Communities].'[53] That policy is to contribute, under Article 130r of the Treaty (current Article 191 TFEU), *inter alia*, to 'preserving, protecting and improving the quality of the environment, protecting human health', and 'prudent and rational utilization of natural resources'.[54] The AG further pointed out that EU primary law also establishes that 'environmental protection requirements must be integrated into the definition and implementation of other [EU] policies'. A principle testifying the 'peculiar place' of environmental policy in the EU Treaties.[55]

Despite AG Cosmas' overview, the CJEU was silent on the argument related to the 'distinctiveness' of the environment as an objective or as a policy domain. Indeed, the EU judges did not provide any answer on whether they agreed or not with the applicants and the AG. Conversely, the Court highlighted that the environmental rights invoked by the applicants under the EIA directive were judicially 'fully protected'. On this point, the Court stressed that it was the Commission's decision to build the two power stations in question which was able to affect the environmental rights arising under the EIA directive that the appellants were seeking to invoke.[56] Nevertheless, the Court concluded by holding that those rights were 'fully protected by the national courts which may, if need be, refer a question to this Court for a preliminary ruling under [Article 267] of the Treaty'.[57]

[50] Opinion AG Cosmas, *Greenpeace* (CJEU), n 3, § 102.
[51] ibid, § 51.
[52] Case 240/83, *Procureur de la République v Association de défense des brûleurs d'huiles usagées (ADBHU)* (1985) ECLI:EU:C:1985:59.
[53] Opinion AG Cosmas, *Greenpeace* (CJEU), n 3, § 51.
[54] ibid.
[55] Today the principle of integration is enshrined under Art 11 TFEU.
[56] *Greenpeace* (CFI), n 3, § 30.
[57] ibid, § 33.

The Court thus seemed to disagree with the applicants on *how* this 'special treatment' for the environment should be recognised. According to the CJEU, this should be achieved by establishing an efficient system of judicial protection for the environment at national level. According to the ENGOs, this efficient system should also include a broader access to the EU jurisdictions.

Interestingly, some years after *Greenpeace*, the applicants' argument relating to the 'communal dimension' of the environment was implicitly referred to (and enriched by) two AGs – namely Sharpston and Kokott – in two different cases dealing with access to justice in environmental matters at national level.

The first reference, by AG Sharpston, was made during the hearing of the *Trianel* case,[58] where she observed that the 'fish cannot go to Court' and added: 'the environment cannot protect itself if it is threatened or harmed. It is a public good and should be supported by public voice'.[59] By making this point, AG Sharpston alluded to a second reason why the environment should be treated differently: namely because it has no voice. Therefore, it requires someone to act on its behalf. The second reference was made by AG Kokott in her opinion for the Edwards case,[60] dealing with costs in environmental judicial proceedings in the UK. Here the Court's advisor argued that:

> Recognition of the public interest in environmental protection is especially important since there may be many cases where the legally protected interests of particular individuals are not affected or are affected only peripherally. However, the environment cannot defend itself before a court, but needs to be represented, for example by active citizens or non-governmental organisations.[61]

In this section of her opinion, AG Kokott actually put forward a third reason why the environment should be granted a special treatment by courts: because there may be cases where the environment is severely impacted while the legally protected interests of individuals are not affected at all or are affected only incidentally. Furthermore, the AG argued for an 'external' intervention in defence of the environment, which needs to be represented by civil society or ENGOs. The next section addresses this specific argument.

i. *Treating ENGOs Differently*

Because of this need for an 'external intervention', according to the plaintiffs in *Greenpeace*, distinctive judicial treatment of the environment should naturally also imply a special treatment accorded to ENGOs. Indeed,

> environmental associations should be recognised as having locus standi where their objectives concern chiefly environmental protection and one or more of their members

[58] C-115/09, *Bund für Umwelt und Naturschutz Deutschland, Landesverband Nordrhein-Westfalen* (2011) ECLI:EU:C:2011:289.

[59] AG Sharpston, hearing of *Trianel*.

[60] Opinion AG Kokott, C-260/11, *Edwards and Pallikaropoulos* (2013) ECLI:EU:C:2012:645.

[61] ibid, § 42.

> are individually concerned by the contested [EU] decision, but also where, independently, their primary objective is environmental protection and they can demonstrate a specific interest in the question at issue.[62]

In this regard, the EU judges rejected any idea of making an exception for ENGOs under Article 173(4) TEC and pointed out that the same criterion used for natural persons applies to associations which claim to have *locus standi* on the basis of the fact that the persons whom they represent are individually concerned by the contested decision.[63]

B. Effective Judicial Protection

The second main argument put forward by *Greenpeace* to justify why the *Plaumann* test should be overcome concerned the fundamental right to effective judicial protection, today enshrined under Article 47 EUCFR.

The applicants claimed that, if the individuals affected by the challenged EU measure were not granted *locus standi*, this would create a legal vacuum in the EU judicial protection system.[64] In addition, this vacuum could not be filled even by the possibility of bringing proceedings before the national courts. In fact, the plaintiffs clarified that they had already brought such proceedings in Spain, but these concerned the national authorities' failure to comply with their obligations under the EIA directive and not the legality of the contested EU measure. In other words, the illegality alleged at the EU level centred on the lawfulness under EU law of the Commission's disbursement of structural funds on the ground that that disbursement was in violation of an obligation for protecting the environment.[65]

Nonetheless, as mentioned before, the CJEU responded by simply stating that the rights which the plaintiffs claimed to be impaired by the contested EU decision were in fact 'fully protected by the national courts which may, if need be, refer a question to this Court for a preliminary ruling'.[66]

This line of reasoning was confirmed by the Court a few years later in another relevant ruling, namely *Unión de Pequeños Agricultores* (*UPA*).[67] In this case, the EU judiciary held that current Article 263 TFEU[68] should be read in a more systemic way, in accordance with Articles 267 and 277 TFEU. This since, under these provisions, the Treaty has established a

> complete system of legal remedies and procedures designed to ensure review of the legality of acts of the institutions, and has entrusted such review to the [EU] Courts.

[62] *Greenpeace* (CJEU), n 3, § 25.
[63] ibid, § 29.
[64] ibid, § 18.
[65] ibid.
[66] *Greenpeace* (CJEU), n 3, § 33.
[67] C-50/00 P, *Unión de Pequeños Agricultores v Council* (2002) ECLI:EU:C:2002:462. Hereinafter '*UPA*'.
[68] Art 173 TEC at that time.

> Under that system, where natural or legal persons cannot, by reason of the conditions for admissibility laid down in the fourth paragraph of Article 173 TEC, directly challenge [EU] measures of general application, they are able, depending on the case, either indirectly to plead the invalidity of such acts before the [EU] Courts under Article 177 TEC or to do so before the national courts and ask them, since they have no jurisdiction themselves to declare those measures invalid, to make a reference to the Court of Justice for a preliminary ruling on validity.
>
> Thus it is for the Member States to establish a system of legal remedies and procedures which ensure respect for the right to effective judicial protection.[69]

Therefore, in the Court's view, the EU judicial system should not be seen as limited to the GC and the CJEU, but as also including all the MSs' courts. Indeed, national courts contribute to 'complete' the EU judicial protection system, having the duty to apply and enforce EU law provisions and – at least in the case of courts from which there is no right of appeal – the duty to refer questions of interpretation or validity to the CJEU.[70]

However, in other cases,[71] the applicants shared the view that, in some circumstances, the PRP may not be sufficient. Indeed, they claimed that access to justice before the EU judiciary must be granted wherever no legal remedies under national law are available. In addressing this argument, the GC affirmed the sharp separation between judicial proceedings at national and EU level, and stated that 'the admissibility of an action for annulment before the [EU] courts does not depend on whether there is a remedy before a national court enabling the validity of the act being challenged to be examined'.[72] As an inevitable consequence, the argument was rejected and EU Courts never recognised a breach of the fundamental right to effective judicial protection with regard to the *Plaumann* test.[73]

C. EU Law Consistency

The third main proposition supported by ENGOs in actions for annulment before the entry into force of the AR concerns the necessity of guaranteeing *consistency* in the EU legal order. By the term *consistency*, I refer to the necessity of making sure that the interpretation provided by the Court in a given case is coherent with the overall jurisprudence of the Court as well as with EU primary and secondary law.

Indeed, according to the applicants, a more comprehensive reading of EU primary and secondary law, as well as of the jurisprudence of the CJEU, would naturally lead the latter granting standing to ENGOs in direct actions. This is for the reasons that will be outlined in the following sections.

[69] *UPA*, n 67, §§ 40–41.
[70] See chapter 2.
[71] Joined cases T-236/04 and T-241/04, *EEB and Stichting Natuur en Milieu v Commission* (2005) ECLI:EU:T:2005:426; T-541/10, *ADEDY and Others v Council* (2012) ECLI:EU:T:2012:626.
[72] ibid, *EEB*, § 67.
[73] See chapter 7.

As far as consistency with EU primary law and the CJEU's jurisprudence in environmental matters is concerned, I would like to refer the reader back to the description of AG Cosmas' arguments.[74] Conversely, the sections below will unpack the arguments used in *Greenpeace* to promote better consistency with EU secondary law on the one hand and with the case law of the CJEU in areas *other* than environmental protection on the other.

i. Consistency with EU Secondary Law

Consistency in this first sense has usually been understood by environmental litigants as consistency between the procedural rights recognised by EU primary law in the *litigation phase* and the procedural rights provided by EU secondary law in the *pre-litigation phase*. To give a clear example, in *Greenpeace* the applicants claimed that:

> special circumstances such as the role played by an association in a procedure which led to the adoption of an act within the meaning of Article 173 of the Treaty may justify holding admissible an action brought by an association whose members are not directly and individually concerned by the contested measure.[75]

In this regard, given that some of the applicants submitted complaints to the Commission in the pre-litigation phase, it was argued that the Court should grant them standing on this basis alone. The plaintiffs added that the exchange of correspondence and the meeting in Brussels between members of GP and the Commission was enough to provide them with locus standi.

In addressing these arguments, the EU judiciary sharply distinguished between the 'spontaneous participation' of private parties in the EU decision-making and 'mandatory consultation duties' provided under EU law. The CFI made clear that 'no specific procedures are provided for whereby individuals may be associated with the adoption, implementation and monitoring of decisions taken in the field of financial assistance granted by the ERDF'.[76] The Commission – continued the Court – 'was under no duty either to consult or to hear the applicants in the context of the implementation of the contested decision. Greenpeace's approaches to the Commission cannot, therefore, give it *locus standi*.'[77]

In the next section, I will now turn to analyse the ENGOs' arguments, raised in the 'pre-Aarhus period', based on a lack of consistency with the case law of the CJEU.

[74] See above section VI.A.
[75] *Greenpeace* (CFI), n 3, § 59.
[76] ibid, § 56.
[77] ibid, § 63.

ii. Consistency with the Case Law of the CJEU

In this section, I will critically engage with the arguments of the applicants in *Greenpeace* aiming to strengthen the consistency of the case law of the CJEU on standing in environmental matters on the one hand, and standing in different areas of EU law on the other hand.

In particular, the plaintiffs argued that the requirement that applicants must show that they are affected in the same way as the addressee of a decision was 'not borne out by the case-law of the Court of Justice'.[78] In this regard, the plaintiffs cited the CJEU case law in the field of State aids, 'recognizing that competitors of beneficiaries of aid have standing to bring an action under Article 173 of the Treaty although their interests are not affected in the same way as the addressee of a decision, which is the Member State concerned'.[79] The applicants sought to persuade the GC to adopt a more liberal approach, arguing that 'their *locus standi* should depend not only on purely economic interests but on their interests in the protection of the environment'.[80] In other words, the real question raised in *Greenpeace* was: why *yes* for corporations in State Aid cases and *no* for NGOs in environmental cases?

On this point, the EU judges did not provide a comprehensive answer. They limited themselves to defending the CJEU's *Plaumann* formula and maintained that this test 'remains applicable whatever the nature, economic or otherwise, of those of the applicants' interests which are affected' and that the conditions laid down in Article 173(4) TEC may not be disregarded.[81] However, despite the Court's dismissal, this argument deserves a deeper analysis, aiming to provide the reader with a clearer explanation of the Court's approach to standing in different legal areas.

Besides State Aid, other examples of economic-related cases in which the Court adopted a different approach towards standing have been outlined by legal scholars, who – on the same line of reasoning of ENGOs – have vividly questioned the double standards of the CJEU.[82] One such ruling is *Timex*, an anti-dumping law case where the Court ruled on the link between procedural guarantees in the pre-litigation and litigation phases. Nonetheless, in *WWF*[83] the Court still denied standing to the applicant and confirmed its jurisprudence providing that 'a person involved in the procedure leading to the adoption of an EU measure can be considered as being individually concerned only if the applicable [EU] legislation grants him certain procedural guarantees'.[84]

[78] *Greenpeace* (CFI), n 3, § 31.
[79] Case C-198/91, *William Cook plc v Commission* (1993) ECLI:EU:C:1993:197.
[80] *Greenpeace* (CFI), n 3, § 32.
[81] *Greenpeace* (CJEU), n 3, § 9.
[82] Ludwig Krämer, 'Access to Environmental Justice: The Double Standards of the ECJ' (2017) 14 *Journal for European Environmental & Planning Law* 175.
[83] *WWF-UK*, n 2.
[84] ibid, § 69.

Conversely, in *Timex* the final outcome was significantly different. Here the EU judiciary had to decide on the application by an undertaking which had complained to the Commission and had been heard by the Commission during the anti-dumping procedure. All these elements were found by the EU judges as being sufficient to consider the applicant as individually (and directly) concerned by the regulation which ended the anti-dumping procedure.[85] Nevertheless, in *Timex* the Court did not discuss which procedural guarantees the EU anti-dumping law gave to the complainant and yet recognised standing to the applicant for the active role played during the pre-litigation phase.

According to some commentators, documented participation of representative groups in the pre-litigation phase can be 'essential' in order to obtain standing before EU courts.[86] Indeed, participation may create procedural rights in a later stage, but *Greenpeace* proves that it must not be the result of the 'group's general activity in the field but part of the procedural requirement for the adoption of the measure'.[87]

However, if no procedural guarantees are laid down in EU law for ENGOs in the pre-litigation phase, is there a serious risk of having a double standard between environmental and State Aid/competition cases with regard to standing of private applicants in direct actions? In this regard, the Court has already been accused by legal scholars[88] and ENGOs' members[89] of favouring, in its case law, economic-oriented and corporate interests over public and shared interests. This is due to the Court's allegedly more 'liberal' approach toward standing in the aforementioned areas of State Aids and competition.

However, I would like to criticise this argument, which seems too simplistic to demonstrate the so-called 'double standard' of the Court. This is for two main reasons: (i) the EU judiciary has refused to grant standing to private corporations even in competition and State Aid cases in a significant number of rulings;[90] (ii) the CJEU is the same Court that, in 1988, qualified environmental protection as a mandatory requirement capable of justifying proportionate restrictions to free movement of goods in the internal market,[91] thus showing that the Court does not favour corporate interests over environmental interests in absolute terms.

Therefore, more cautious and elaborate explanations should be explored. A more valid description of this inconsistency in the case law of the Court, can be found in the traditional distinction between 'acts of quasi-judicial nature' and 'acts based purely on policy and discretion' – outlined for the first time by Trevor

[85] Krämer, n 82, 169.

[86] Costas Kombos, 'Locus Standi of Representative Groups in the Shadow of Plaumann: Limitations and Possible Solutions' (2006) 47 *Acta Juridica Hungarica* 403.

[87] ibid.

[88] Krämer, n 82.

[89] Anne Friel, 'People's climate case highlights lack of access to the EU courts', ClientEarth official website, available at www.clientearth.org/peoples-climate-case-highlights-lack-of-access-to-the-eu-courts/.

[90] Inter alia, C-263/02 P, *Commission v Jégo-Quéré & Cie SA* (2004) ECLI:EU:C:2004:21; C-78/03 P, *Commission v Aktionsgemeinschaft Recht und Eigentum* (2005) ECLI:EU:C:2005:761; C-287/12 P, *Ryanair v Commission* (2013) ECLI:EU:C:2013:395.

[91] C-302/86, *Commission v Denmark* (1988) ECLI:EU:C:1988:421, § 21.

Hartley in 1981.[92] In this 'classic' of EU law, Hartley points out that the reason given by the CJEU on the 'individual concern' requirement are often 'scanty and sometimes conflicting'.[93] This is why he draws a distinction (which – he clarifies – has not been adopted by the Court itself) between (i) proceedings to annul acts of a quasi-judicial nature and (ii) proceedings to annul acts based purely on policy and discretion.[94] The meaning of these categories will now be explained.

In adopting acts falling in the first category, the EU institution is 'bound by clear rules, and the final determination depends largely on questions of fact'.[95] This justifies scrupulous investigations, and a semi-judicial procedure is followed. The main cases falling into this category concern precisely competition, anti-dumping and state aids.[96]

By contrast, discretionary acts falling in the second category are usually drafted in general and broad terms. In such cases, the Court seems to have developed two different tests, depending on how the contested measure applies to a given group of persons. The first one is the 'small group' test under which measures drafted in abstract terms – in theory – affect members of an open category, but – in practice – this category consists of a small and easily identifiable group. This situation arises quite frequently and the Court almost always denies *locus standi*.[97] Conversely, the second one is the 'closed categories' test: here the measure, even if drafted in abstract terms, applies (in whole or in part) to a closed category of persons[98] and the measure at stake can either be a decision or even a regulation.[99] As is clear from *Greenpeace*, it is only when the category is closed in this way that the Court is willing to grant standing in relation to discretionary acts.

Hartley points out that, in proceedings to annul acts of a quasi-judicial nature, the Court usually adopts a much more liberal attitude than it does where the proceedings concern a discretionary act. 'Not only is the closed category test often ignored but, in the case of anti-dumping regulations, the Court does not even concern itself with the nature of the act.' This is very different from the position where discretionary acts are involved, especially when regulations are at stake. Here the measure is based on policy considerations and involves political choices that the Court is traditionally more reluctant to scrutinise. Hartley's distinction can therefore help to understand not only the Court's rigidity on *Plaumann* in the field of environmental protection, but also the so-called 'double standard' of the EU judiciary when dealing with cases in different legal domains.

Having completed the analysis of the main arguments deployed by ENGOs to mobilise against *Plaumann* in the 'pre-Aarhus period', I will now turn to describe

[92] Trevor Hartley, *The Foundations of EC Law* (Oxford, OUP, 2010) 374. The first edition of this book was published in 1981.

[93] ibid.

[94] ibid.

[95] ibid.

[96] ibid.

[97] ibid.

[98] ibid, 375.

[99] An example is the aforementioned *UPA* case.

one crucial 'proposal' for amending *Plaumann* embedded in the opinion of AG Jacobs in the *UPA* case, which drew – to a large extent – directly form the Court's ruling in *Greenpeace*.[100]

VIII. AG Jacobs and *Plaumann*

Although unsuccessful, the *Greenpeace* case generated a remarkable theoretical debate on the EU judicial protection system, as can be seen in AG Jacobs' opinion in *Unión de Pequeños Agricultores v Council (UPA)* in 2002,[101] where the AG drew directly from the Court's reasoning in *Greenpeace* to examine the 'completeness' of the EU system of legal remedies.[102]

In *Greenpeace*, the applicants were particularly 'creative' with regard to Article 173(4) TEC. Indeed, they proposed an alternative interpretation of this provision, that aimed to recognise standing for natural and legal persons able to demonstrate that they

> (i) personally suffered (or are likely personally to suffer) some actual or threatened detriment as a result of the allegedly illegal conduct of the EU institution concerned, such as a violation of his environmental rights or interference with his environmental interests; (ii) the detriment can be traced to the act challenged; iii) the detriment is capable of being redressed by a favourable judgment.[103]

This interpretation does not seem too different from the one suggested by AG Jacobs in *UPA*. Here, Jacobs maintained that a person should be regarded as individually concerned by an EU measure where, 'by reason of his particular circumstances, the measure has, or is liable to have, a substantial adverse effect on his interests'.[104] This is close to the concept of an actual or threatened detriment raised by the applicants in *Greenpeace*. However, we do not know whether the AG was influenced in this regard by the arguments put forward by *Greenpeace*, which had been ignored by the Court.

Although the EU judges ultimately rejected this alternative interpretation of the 'individual concern' requirement, the Court in *UPA* provided the applicants with a different (and richer) response from the one given in *Greenpeace*.

> Although [the individual concern requirement] must be interpreted in the light of the principle of effective judicial protection by taking account of the various circumstances

[100] Opinion AG Jacobs in C-50/00 P, *Unión de Pequeños Agricultores v Council (UPA)* (2002) ECLI:EU:C:2002:197, § 34.

[101] ibid, § 60. On this point, see Takis Tridimas and Sara Poli, 'Locus Standi of Individuals under Article 230(4): The Return of Euridice?' in Anthony Arnull, Piet Eeckhout and Takis Tridimas (eds), *Continuity and Change in EU Law: Essays in Honour of Sir Francis Jacobs* (Oxford, Oxford Scholarship Online, 2009) 74.

[102] n 100, § 34. On this point, see chapter 2.

[103] *Greenpeace* (CFI), n 3, § 30.

[104] ibid, § 60.

> that may distinguish an applicant individually …, such an interpretation cannot have the effect of setting aside the condition in question, expressly laid down in the Treaty, without going beyond the jurisdiction conferred by the Treaty on the Community Courts.
>
> While it is, admittedly, possible to envisage a system of judicial review of the legality of Community measures of general application different from that established by the founding Treaty and never amended as to its principles, it is for the Member States, if necessary, in accordance with Article 48 EU, to reform the system currently in force.[105]

In other words, in *UPA* the Court clarified that, if broader access to justice for natural and legal persons ought to be guaranteed under Treaty provisions, it should be for the MSs to amend such provisions in accordance with the procedure established under Article 48 TEU. It is this response of the Court that essentially certifies *Plaumann* as a 'closure' in the LOS. Indeed, by so arguing, the EU judiciary de facto qualified itself as a judiciary 'unresponsive' to CSOs' claims to review *Plaumann* through judicial interpretation. On the contrary, ENGOs disagreed with the CJEU, arguing that the EU judges' interpretative space[106] is 'wide' enough to allow for a different interpretation of the 'individual concern' requirement.

On the same line, some scholars[107] have criticised the Court for its response in *UPA* and compared the approach taken by the Court in 2002 in *UPA* with the one taken in 1990 in *European Parliament v Council*, concerning the capacity of the European Parliament to bring an action for annulment.[108] Indeed, at that time, the European Parliament was not included among the institutions having the right to bring an action under Article 173 TEC. However, in that case the Court recognised such a right for the European Assembly. It justified its choice on the basis of the need to maintain the institutional balance between the institutions and characterised the original approach of the Treaty-makers as giving rise to a 'procedural gap' within the Treaties.[109] Such a 'proactive' hermeneutic approach has never been replicated by the Court with regard to access to justice of ENGOs under Article 263(4) TFEU. An attitude which has exacerbated the criticisms advanced by social movements and legal scholars toward the EU judiciary. In the next section, I will draw my conclusions on the analysis undertaken throughout this first chapter.

IX. Conclusions

The present chapter intended to show *why* and *how* the *Plaumann* test turned direct access to justice for private applicants before the CJEU into a 'closure' in the LOS under EU law. The *Plaumann* test is the narrow interpretation given

[105] ibid, §§ 44–45.
[106] See above, section V.
[107] Krämer, n 82.
[108] C-70/88, *European Parliament v Council* (1990) ECLI:EU:C:1990:217.
[109] Krämer, n 82.

by the EU judiciary of the 'individual concern' requirement laid down under Article 263(4) TFEU. Since 1963, the *Plaumann* test has never been abandoned by the Court, thereby hindering any possibility for public interest litigation via actions for annulment.

In this regard, the present chapter, first, attempted to provide the reader with a clearer explanation of *why* the *Plaumann* test is there and is unlikely to be modified by the CJEU. In relation to this, legal scholarship showed that the Court's narrow interpretation of Article 263(4) TFEU is rooted in the history of the European legal integration process. Leading scholars, like Rasmussen, Vining and Stein, have already provided insightful explanations on the matter, but this book is not intended to convince the Court to abandon the *Plaumann* test. As mentioned above, the present contribution intends to focus on ENGOs' strategies rather than institutional narratives. This is by providing a legal mobilisation perspective on access to justice at EU level in the environmental context.

Second, the present chapter also aimed at showing *how* ENGOs mobilised against the *Plaumann* test in the 'pre-Aarhus period'. From the close analysis of the plaintiffs' reasoning in *Greenpeace*,[110] three main arguments emerged. The first one being that the protection of the environment represents a particular kind of public interest, deserving a special treatment in courts. The second one being that denying standing to ENGOs before EU Courts creates a legal vacuum in the EU judicial protection system. The third one being that standing of ENGOs must be ensured in order to guarantee consistency between EU primary and secondary law as well as in the case law of the CJEU in all the policy domains. However, the Court has usually been deeply unreceptive to such claims and has often avoided to fully address some of the ENGOs' arguments.[111]

Furthermore, in the 'pre-Aarhus period' ENGOs adopted a very procedural approach to *locus standi*.[112] On this point, in all the environmental actions for annulment brought to the CJEU before the entry into force of the AR, the applicants put particular emphasis on procedural participatory rights. In *Greenpeace*, the plaintiffs claimed standing on the basis of their spontaneous participation in the decision-making process. Similarly, in *WWF* – a case dealing with the Common Fisheries Policy – the plaintiff held that its membership to the North Sea Regional Advisory Council was sufficient to prove that the organisation was actually individually concerned by the contested EU measure.

Third, by simply looking at the names of the plaintiffs litigating under 173(4) TEC (now Article 263(4) TFEU) before the entry into force of the AR, we can observe that the main and most famous European (and international) ENGOs were all actively involved. The first cases brought under Article 173(4) TEC were initiated by leading organisations like *Greenpeace*, *WWF*, and the *EEB*, while – as

[110] In *Greenpeace* and in subsequent actions for annulment brought by ENGOs in the 'pre-Aarhus period'.

[111] In *Greenpeace*, the CJEU was silent on five arguments (out of 10) raised by the applicants.

[112] *Cf* with chapter 7.

it will be shown in chapter three – environmental actions for annulment initiated after the entry into force of the AR have seen different actors acting as applicants.

Lastly, from the analysis embedded in this chapter it is possible to notice that, for ENGOs, the question of access to environmental justice was a question purely internal to the EU legal order. Indeed, in the absence of an international agreement governing the matter, the plaintiffs solely referred to provisions and principles laid down in EU law. In this respect, chapters three and four will show how the EU adhesion to the Aarhus Convention as well as the adoption of the AR, changed the legal opportunities available for ENGOs and the legal understanding the these have of the question of direct access to the CJEU under the EU Treaties.

2

Circumventing *Plaumann* via National Courts

I. Introduction

The first chapter described how the *Plaumann* test has blocked access to justice before the Court of Justice of the European Union (CJEU) for environmental non-governmental organisations (ENGOs). In particular, the first chapter showed how ENGOs relied on direct actions (namely actions for annulment) to attempt to directly contest the legality of EU environmental law in the pre-Aarhus period, that is, before the EU adopted the Aarhus Regulation (AR).

Conversely, the present chapter will delve into environmental organisations' efforts to overcome *Plaumann* indirectly, more specifically by mobilising national courts. Here, my focus will be on the use of another legal avenue, that is the preliminary reference procedure (hereinafter PRP) enshrined under Article 267 Treaty on the Functioning of the European Union (TFEU). The present chapter is particularly relevant within the framework of this book, since both the Commission and the CJEU identify the PRP as being the most appropriate avenue to contest the validity of EU environmental measures as well as the true 'gap filler' between EU law and the Aarhus Convention.

The present chapter deviates from the chronological categorisation presented in the introduction to this book. This is because ENGOs have mobilised national courts through the PRP in each of the five different timeframes analysed throughout the book. Furthermore, those chronological categories were conceived in relation to (i) actions for annulment initiated directly before the CJEU; (ii) key legal 'moments' (eg the adoption of the AR or the ACCC findings on EU compliance) which affected the legal strategies and the arguments put forward by environmental organisations in actions brought under Article 263(4) TFEU. On the contrary, those same events have not produced the same impact on the strategy and the reasoning of ENGOs aiming to contest the validity of EU law through the PRP. For these reasons, the analysis embedded below cannot sensibly be presented on the basis of a temporal approach.

In the analysis below, I argue that ENGOs have been using national courts to circumvent *Plaumann* essentially in four ways, which constitute the four main sections of this chapter. These are (i) by criticising the 'complete' system of legal remedies as defined by the CJEU; (ii) by broadening standing at national level via

PRP on interpretation; (iii) by training national judges; (iv) by triggering references on validity at national level.

I will illustrate how ENGOs have, first, relied on AG Jacobs' critique of the alleged 'completeness' of the EU judicial protection system to display, with louder voice, the shortcomings embedded in the PRP. The chapter will also highlight how ENGOs have 'shaped' opportunities to engage in legal mobilisation, but this time under national law. They did so in order to increase their chances of obtaining references on validity and circumvent *Plaumann*. This being said, the shaping of legal opportunities at national level has not only taken the form of litigation. On the contrary, as it will also be observed in the next chapters, ENGOs have combined litigation with other forms of mobilisation, in an attempt to remove also other types of barriers hindering access to justice before domestic courts. More specifically, beyond litigation, the ENGOs have used the provision of judicial training to national judges and legal practitioners as a way of increasing legal opportunities. Indeed, by training national judges and lawyers in EU environmental law, ENGOs are seeking to influence the receptivity of domestic courts to arguments based on environmental law. This with the hope of obtaining not only better enforcement of EU environmental law at national level, but also more referrals to the CJEU.

The last part of this chapter will focus on the PRP on validity and the way this has concretely been used by CSOs as a tool to circumvent *Plaumann* in environmental matters. ENGOs' efforts to obtain a validity reference succeeded only in six cases. In this regard, an in-depth analysis of the relevant case law will be provided, followed by a discussion on the pertinence of the findings from a legal mobilisation perspective. Such findings will show how ENGOs, after having been granted standing at national level, encounter other barriers hindering their mobilisation efforts. One of these barriers is constituted by the limited substantive review carried out by the CJEU on EU measures *vis-à-vis* the principle of precaution.

However, this chapter will argue that the PRP on validity remains the best option for ENGOs to contest the validity of legislative acts, while the new internal review procedure established under the AR should be preferred to challenged EU regulatory acts.

II. 'Complete', Yet not Perfect

Under Article 267 TFEU, the CJEU shall have jurisdiction to give preliminary rulings concerning:

(a) the interpretation of the Treaties;
(b) the validity and interpretation of acts of the institutions, bodies, offices or agencies of the Union;

Where such a question is raised before any court or tribunal of a Member State, that court or tribunal may, if it considers that a decision on the question is necessary to enable it to give judgment, request the Court to give a ruling thereon.

The pathway laid down under Article 267 TFEU has traditionally played a key role in EU environmental litigation. Since the early 1990s, environmental organisations have mobilised national courts with the aim of enforcing EU environmental law in the EU Member States (MSs).[1] Their crucial role as 'watchdogs' of MSs' compliance with EU law and the Aarhus Convention has duly been recognised by EU institutions and legal scholars.[2] However, in an attempt to stimulate referrals to the CJEU by domestic judges, environmental organisations have commonly encountered a number of barriers (or shortcomings), creating closures in the legal opportunity structure (LOS).

AG Jacobs in his opinion in the *UPA* case carefully listed some of these 'closures' in the LOS to prove why the PRP cannot compensate for the lack of direct access to the CJEU under Article 263 TFEU.[3] This by way of response to the CJEU, which has traditionally encouraged private applicants to bring cases before national courts, so as to allow the latter to refer questions of interpretation or validity to the CJEU.[4] Environmental organisations have tried to overcome this line of reasoning in different ways, usually by referring precisely to AG Jacobs 'list of shortcomings' included in his famous opinion. Here, he claimed that:

1. National courts are not competent to declare an EU measure invalid, this is an exclusive competence of the CJEU.[5] National courts are simply empowered and sometimes required to refer questions of validity to the CJEU. The PRP should thus be seen as more useful when it comes to guaranteeing an harmonious 'interpretation' of EU law than when assessing its 'validity';
2. The vast majority of national courts may refuse to refer questions to the CJEU, since only national courts against whose decisions there is no judicial remedy under national law are required to refer questions of EU law to the CJEU;[6]
3. Access to national courts may also be hindered by a number of factors (narrow standing requirements at national level, for example prohibitive costs or absence of interim reliefs, etc);

[1] C-435/92, *Association pour la protection des animaux sauvages and Others v Préfet de Maine-et-Loire and Préfet de la Loire-Atlantique* (1994) ECLI:EU:C:1994:10.

[2] See European Commission, Science for Environment Policy, 'Wildlife law enforcement: the vital role of NGOs', July 2016, Thematic issue 56. Available at: https://ec.europa.eu/environment/integration/research/newsalert/pdf/wildlife_law_enforcement_the_vital_role_of_NGOs_56si13_en.pdf; Nicolas de Sadeleer, Gerhard Roller, Miriam Dross and Sandrine Bélier, *Access to Justice in Environmental Matters and the Role of NGOs: Empirical Findings and Legal Appraisal* (Zutphen, Europa Law Publishing, 2005); Mariachiara Alberton 'Environmental Protection in the EU Member States: Changing Institutional Scenarios and Trends' (2012) 1 (363) *L'Europe en Formation* 287–300; Andreas Hofmann, 'Left to Interest Groups? On the Prospects for Enforcing Environmental Law in the European Union' (2019) 28 (2) *Environmental Politics* 342–64.

[3] Opinion AG Jacobs, C-50/00 P, *Unión de Pequeños Agricultores v Council (UPA)* (2002) ECLI:EU:C:2002:462, § 40 and following paragraphs.

[4] See chapter 1.

[5] C-314/85, *Foto-Frost v Hauptzollamt Lübeck-Ost* (1987) ECLI:EU:C:1987:452, § 17.

[6] Except for the CILFIT exceptions, see C-283/81, *CILFIT v Ministero della Sanità* (1982) ECLI:EU:C:1982:335.

4. Under the PRP, the questions to be referred are formulated by national judges, not by the applicants;[7]
5. Certain EU acts do not require national implementing measures. In these cases, it can be very difficult to identify a challengeable act under national law. Plus, even if it would always be possible to challenge a sanction issued by a national authority in the enforcement of EU law, it is not appropriate for individuals to be required to breach the law in order to gain access to justice;
6. Preliminary references procedures give rise to extra costs and delays, while the existence of interim relief – the availability of which is often discretionary – may vary from jurisdiction to jurisdiction.[8] This might push applicants to bring cases in different MSs with the risk of having final conflicting judgments coming from different jurisdictions.

These gaps identified by AG Jacobs de facto reduce the legal opportunities available for citizens and ENGOs under EU law. ENGOs found this list extremely useful for their legal mobilisation purposes and in the next section I will show how they have often referred to it in their judicial pleadings, considering Jacobs' Opinion a trusted source of influence over the EU judiciary. Then, I will illustrate some practical implications that the PRP shortcomings highlighted by AG Jacobs have on ENGOs' legal mobilisation at national level.

III. Using AG Jacobs' Opinion

The shortcomings reported by AG Jacobs in *UPA* were used by the Court's AG to explain why a new test for the standing of private applicants, other than *Plaumann*, was needed. With the same goal in mind, ENGOs have also referred (not always explicitly)[9] to AG Jacobs' Opinion in their pleadings in direct actions under Article 263 TFEU.[10] Such references to AG Jacobs' list have also been made to show that, even inside the Court's 'golden towers' in Luxembourg, there were distinguished members of the EU judiciary who did not agree with the traditional understanding of the 'individual concern' requirement.[11] For instance, Jacobs' arguments point 6 was used in the *Fost plus* case, where the applicant argued that:

> only the Belgian Cour de cassation …, the highest court in this instance, would be obliged to make a reference to the Court of Justice for a preliminary ruling. That would involve

[7] See Urška Šadl and Anna Wallerman, 'The Referring Court Asks, in Essence: Is Reformulation of Preliminary Questions by the Court of Justice a Decision Writing Fixture or a Decision-Making Approach? (2019) 25 *European Law Journal* 416–33; Graham Butler and Urška Šadl, 'The Preliminaries of a Reference' (2018) *European Law Review* 120–28.

[8] See C-441/17, *Commission v Poland (Białowieża Forest)* (2018) ECLI:EU:C:2018:255.

[9] See paragraphs below.

[10] See T-91/07, *WWF-UK v Council* (2008) ECLI:EU:T:2008:170, § 60. See also the analysis of the *Carvalho* case in chapter 7.

[11] See also opinion of AG Bobek in C–352/19 P *Région de Bruxelles-Capitale v European Commission* (2020) ECLI:EU:C:2020:588.

> the passage of at least five years during which the applicant would continue to be exposed to such fines and to legal uncertainty as regards the validity of the recovery rates.[12]

Conversely, arguments 5 and 6 were raised in the *EEB* case,[13] where the applicants argued that:

> [the] annulment of the [contested] decisions would prevent triggering a myriad of complex, lengthy and costly authorisation procedures in various Member States. They state [the applicants] that if they had to apply to the national courts, they would have to identify authorisations … in all Member States, study the legal systems of the States where marketing authorisations have been applied for and bring proceedings before the competent national courts.

In the paragraphs just cited, the applicants highlighted what is distinctive about the procedure laid down under current Article 263(4) compared to the PRP. ENGOs stressed the added value of direct actions *vis-à-vis* the procedure established under Article 267 TFEU.[14]

First, direct actions would help achieve legal certainty and address situations of urgency more quickly. This is mainly due to the fact that actions under Article 267 TFEU can be raised at any time thereby creating the potential for delay[15] and, second, these usually require a national implementing measure for a challenge to ensue. The adoption of a national implementing measure may take time, potentially allowing for an exacerbation of environmental damage in certain circumstances (eg, hypothetically, pending the adoption of a national measure implementing a EU decision which grants derogations to the annual limit values for nitrogen dioxide, polluters may still pollute beyond what is allowed).

Third, ENGOs argued that preliminary references may lead to greater procedural inefficiency, by requiring the triggering of a number of judicial proceedings in different jurisdictions. This may result in both, costly and time-consuming judicial activities, which can be avoided by simply starting one single case before one single court.

With regard to the need to challenge a national implementing measure mentioned above, this has also been stressed by the European Commission in its report on 'European Union implementation of the Aarhus Convention in the area of access to justice in environmental matters'.[16] Indeed, it is necessary to recall that the procedure under Article 267 can, in practice due to constraints under national law, only be triggered where national implementing measures have been adopted

[12] T-142/03, *Fost Plus v Commission* (2005) ECLI:EU:T:2005:51, § 42.

[13] T-236/04, *EEB and Stichting Natuur en Milieu v Commission* (2005) ECLI:EU:T:2005:426, § 46.

[14] See another example in chapter 7, in the analysis of the *Carvalho* case.

[15] While actions under Art 263(4) TFEU may be brought only within two months of the publication of the measure.

[16] Commission Staff Working Document, Report on European Union implementation of the Aarhus Convention in the area of access to justice in environmental matters, Brussels, 10 October 2019 SWD(2019) 378 final, 15.

by the competent authorities and challenged before domestic courts. This is often the case even though as a matter of EU law, 'the issue of the validity of a Union … act without national measures can be raised under Article 267 TFEU'.[17] In noting this point, the Commission made reference to the *British American Tobacco* (*BAT*) case,[18] where the EU judiciary maintained that:

> The opportunity open to individuals to plead the invalidity of a Community act of general application before national courts is not conditional upon that act's actually having been the subject of implementing measures adopted pursuant to national law. In that respect, it is sufficient if the national court is called upon to hear a genuine dispute in which the question of the validity of such an act is raised indirectly. That condition is amply fulfilled in the circumstances of the case in the main proceedings.[19]

By so arguing, the EU judiciary granted discretion to national courts in assessing whether the question of validity is raised in a 'genuine dispute' at MS level. On the contrary, the EU judiciary did not view as relevant the question of whether judicial proceedings had been triggered by challenging a national implementing measure. However, considering that the *BAT* case arose in a common law country, the Commission wondered whether domestic courts in continental law systems would have more difficulties in raising questions of validity of EU acts not entailing implementing measures.[20]

An Irish case actually seems to contradict this reading. Indeed, we know very little about 'what if' or 'what could have been' preliminary rulings, namely domestic cases where questions of interpretation or validity were raised by the parties, but the national judge decided not to refer them to the CJEU.[21] However, we do know about one case in Ireland, namely *Friends of the Irish Environment CLG v Minister Communications, Climate Action and the Environment*,[22] where the national court

[17] ibid.

[18] C-491/01, *British American Tobacco (Investments) and Imperial Tobacco* (2002) ECLI:EU:C:2002:741.

[19] ibid, § 40.

[20] Commission Staff Working Document, n 16, 16. This point was also addressed by Christoph Sobotta in a training module on 'National judges and the EU, Aarhus Aquis – Focus on Access to Justice', organised by the Academy of European Law on 5–7 June 2019 in Warsaw (Poland). Available at: https://ec.europa.eu/environment/legal/law/11/pdf/13_Sobotta_prp.pdf. Sobotta found 'finally there are the findings of the Aarhus Compliance Committee that the EU system of judicial protection is insufficient to transpose Art. 9(3) of the Convention. In this context they rejected EU arguments that the preliminary reference could significantly contribute to compliance. But at least with regard to incidental references, resulting from actions against domestic implementing measures, this assessment appears questionable. Some legal systems, in particular Ireland and the UK, appear to go even further and allow direct actions aiming to establish the invalidity of EU acts without recourse to any implementation by the Member State.'

[21] See Karen J Alter, 'The European Union's Legal System and Domestic Policy: Spillover or Backlash?' (2000) 54 (3) *International Organization* 501; Jos Hoevenaars, *A People's Court? A Bottom-Up Approach to Litigation Before the Court of Justice of the European Union* (The Hague, Eleven International Publishing, 2018) 51.

[22] *Friends of the Irish Environment CLG v Minister Communications, Climate Action and the Environment, Ireland and the Attorney General (Shannon LNG Terminal)* [2021] IEHC 177.

refused to refer a question of validity of the list of 'projects of common interest' (PCI) adopted by the European Commission under the 'Ten-E' Regulation.[23]

In particular, the ENGO challenged the inclusion – determined by the Commission – of the 'Shannon LNG terminal' project (an electricity plant and battery storage to be located in the county of Kerry)[24] in the list of PCI. The applicant argued that the Irish State should have exercised its power of veto provided under the Ten-E Regulation to counter the inclusion of the project, which allegedly breached the State's obligations under the Climate Action and Low Carbon Development Act 2015.[25] In his ruling, Mr Justice Simons first held that no implementation at MS level was at stake, since the Irish State's (in)actions under the Ten-E Regulation could not amount to a national act implementing an EU measure. Second, the judge found that 'it was not possible to consider the merits of the applicant's argument without engaging in a collateral challenge to the assessment carried out at the EU level'.[26] For this reason, the judge paradoxically maintained that any challenge to the validity of the EU delegated act 'should have taken the form of a direct action before the General Court pursuant to Article 263 TFEU'.[27]

In other 'what if' cases started in 2017, concerned citizens and ENGOs triggered judicial proceedings in Poland and Bulgaria in the field of air quality.[28] Nevertheless, the Supreme Administrative Courts of the two countries found that the applicants lacked standing and so dismissed their actions.[29] Both courts refused to interpret domestic law in accordance with EU law and the Aarhus Convention and equally rejected the refused to refer questions of EU law to the CJEU (even though they both were courts of last instance). In the light of this, *ClientEarth* submitted a complaint to the European Commission to stimulate the opening of an infringement procedure against Poland and Bulgaria.[30] The same organisation also presented a communication to the ACCC on compliance of Poland and Bulgaria with the Aarhus Convention.[31] Again, we see blockages in the LOS, this time at national level, stimulating ENGOs to exploit different mobilisation pathways.

[23] Regulation (EU) No 347/2013 of the European Parliament and of the Council of 17 April 2013 on guidelines for trans-European energy infrastructure and repealing Decision No 1364/2006/EC and amending Regulations (EC) No 713/2009, (EC) No 714/2009 and (EC) No 715/2009 Text with EEA relevance GU L 115 of 25 April 2013, 39–75.

[24] The Irish Times, 'Government decision on Shannon LNG plant not straightforward', 24 August 2021. Available at: www.irishtimes.com/business/energy-and-resources/government-decision-on-shannon-lng-plant-not-straightforward-1.4654435.

[25] Zoe Richardson and Patrick Reilly, 'Mr Justice Simons dismisses judicial review proceedings brought by Friends of the Irish Environment', Fieldfisher, 19 April 2021. Available at: www.fieldfisher.com/en-ie/locations/ireland/ireland-blog/mr-justice-simons-dismisses-judicial-review-procee.

[26] ibid.

[27] ibid.

[28] Polish case, in Silesia (File No II OSK 3218/17, 23 January 2018).

[29] ibid; Bulgarian cases, in Sofia (ruling No 13138 on 1 November 2017) and Plovdiv (ruling No 16049 on 20 December 2018).

[30] Sebastian Bechtel, 'Poland and Bulgaria deny access to justice to citizens and NGOs fighting dirty air' ClientEarth, 26 April 2019. Available at: www.clientearth.org/projects/access-to-justice-for-a-greener-europe/updates/poland-and-bulgaria-deny-access-to-justice-to-citizens-and-ngos-fighting-dirty-air/.

[31] ibid.

These 'what if' cases just presented are extremely relevant from a legal mobilisation point of view, in particular to prove three main points. The first one is that some national courts do not treat the *BAT* case law as applicable and therefore do require a challenge against a national implementing act to indirectly question the validity of EU law.[32] The CJEU should probably clarify its interpretation in this regard, since it does not seem clear to all domestic judges whether there must be a challenge to a national implementing act for the Court to refer a question on validity to the CJEU under Article 267 TFEU.

The second main point is that raising a question of EU law before a domestic court does not automatically give rise to a preliminary reference to the CJEU. Domestic courts use their discretion to review whether the question raised by the parties is relevant and leaves reasonable doubt on what the correct interpretation of EU law should be. This being said, when the question raised before the national court concerns the conformity of national law with the Aarhus Convention, international law offers an additional tool: ENGOs can always ask the ACCC to review national legislation *vis-à-vis* the Convention.[33] Conversely, when the denial to refer comes from a last instance court, ENGOs can submit a complaint to the European Commission in order to stimulate the opening of an infringement procedure.[34]

The third main point is that national courts may have different understandings of what is the most adequate legal avenue to contest the validity or legality of EU measures. In the Irish case, the national judge clearly stated that the applicants should have contested the Commission delegated act under Article 263(4) TFEU. This creates an evident short circuit in the 'complete system of legal remedies' narrative promoted by the CJEU. While the latter pushes litigants to trigger judicial proceedings at national level, domestic courts (like the Irish one) maintain the very opposite, namely that national applicants should contest the legality of EU measures under Article 263(4) TFEU.

With regard to the other critique, according to which, an effective reference on validity requires the triggering of many proceedings in different jurisdictions, I have to disagree with environmental litigants on this point. One reference is enough to obtain a preliminary ruling by the CJEU invalidating the contested EU provision(s).[35] Furthermore, in *International Chemical Corporation*, the Court clarified the scope of a preliminary ruling on validity. The EU judiciary stated that:

> [Although] a judgment of the Court given under Article [267] of the Treaty declaring an act of an institution, in particular a Council or Commission regulation, to be void

[32] See Irish case above.

[33] See Áine Ryall, 'The Relationship between Irish Law and International Environmental Law: A Study of the Aarhus Convention' (2018) 41 (2) *Dublin University Law Journal* 163–88.

[34] See C-416/17, *Commission v France* (2018) ECLI:EU:C:2018:811.

[35] See TL Early, 'The Scope of Preliminary Rulings on the Validity of Community Law' (1980) 15 (2) *Irish Jurist* 261.

> is directly addressed only to the national court which brought the matter before the Court, it is sufficient reason for any other national court to regard that act as void for the purposes of a judgment which it has to give.[36]

As a consequence, a preliminary ruling on validity is de facto binding on all national courts. This makes unnecessary the triggering of several judicial proceedings in different MSs to achieve the goal of setting aside EU law provisions being incompatible with EU primary law.

With regard to the other shortcomings, it must be stressed that, since the late 2000s, the CJEU has greatly contributed to enforcing the Aarhus Convention in the legal orders of the EU MSs and opened new legal opportunities for ENGOs at national level.[37] The Court did so solicited by ENGOs and produced a considerable number of preliminary rulings, which have de facto supported environmental organisations in their campaigns and removed a number of obstacles in the EU MSs. Many examples can be found in the case law of the CJEU on national disputes brought under the EIA Directive.[38] I will now outline some of these cases in the sections below, in order to illustrate the second way in which ENGOs have mobilised to remove the obstacles hindering access to justice at national level and circumvent *Plaumann*, namely by using the PRP on interpretation to open new legal opportunities under national law.

IV. Opening Legal Opportunities at National Level

In the cases described below, the PRP was not only used in its traditional 'dress', as a tool created to favour judicial dialogue between national courts and the CJEU. Besides this 'classical' function, the rulings below show how ENGOs used the PRP on interpretation also as Pescatore defined it, namely as the 'citizens' infringement procedure'.[39] Indeed, these cases exemplify how the PRP can actually be used by ENGOs as a tool to contest MSs' legislation as being incompatible with EU environmental law and open legal opportunities under national law.

[36] C-66/80, *International Chemical Corporation v Amministrazione delle finanze dello Stato* (1981) ECLI:EU:C:1981:102, § 13.

[37] See, inter alia, Lisa Vanhala, 'Shaping the Structure of Legal Opportunities: Environmental NGOs Bringing International Environmental Procedural Rights Back Home' (2018) 40 (1) *Law & Policy* 110–27.

[38] Council Directive 85/337/EEC of 27 June 1985 on the assessment of the effects of certain public and private projects on the environment GU L 175 del 5 July 1985, 40–48. Repealed by Directive 2011/92/EU of the European Parliament and of the Council of 13 December 2011, Text with EEA relevance GU L 26, 28 January 2012, 1–21. Hereinafter 'EIA Directive'.

[39] Bruno De Witte, 'The Impact of Van Gend en Loos on Judicial Protection at European and National Level: Three Types of Preliminary Questions' in Antonio Tizzano, Juliane Kokottand Sacha Prechal (eds), *50th Anniversary of the Judgment in Van Gend en Loos, 1963–2013* (Luxembourg, Office des Publications de l'Union Européenne, 2013) 95.

In *Djurgården*[40] for instance, the CJEU was called upon to assess whether the requirement established under Swedish law that an ENGO had to have a certain number of members to enjoy standing was compatible with the 'old' EIA Directive, as amended by Directive 2003/35 on public participation in the environmental decision-making.[41] The CJEU found that the '2000 members' criterion established under national law was fixed at such a level to run against the Directive's objective of facilitating access to justice.[42] The Court also emphasised the importance of supporting locally based NGOs, as these may be the most likely to challenge smaller scale projects which do not have a national or regional importance but still have a significant effect on the environment.[43] Therefore this ruling opened legal opportunities for ENGOs across the MSs allowing for broader access to justice at national level.

Moreover, in *Edwards & Pallikaropoulos* the EU judges dealt with prohibitively expensive environmental judicial proceedings.[44] In this case, the House of Lords (now the Supreme Court) of the UK ordered Ms Pallikaropoulos to pay the respondents' costs of an appeal against the dismissal of an action challenging the decision of the Environment Agency approving the operation of a cement works.[45] Ms Pallikaropoulos was ordered to pay two bills for recoverable costs in the amounts of GBP 55,810 and GBP 32,290.

In answering the national court's questions, the EU judges held that potential litigants should not be 'prevented from seeking, or pursuing a claim for, a review by the courts by reason of the financial burden that might arise as a result'.[46] The CJEU also made clear that, when making an order for costs against an unsuccessful claimant in an environmental dispute, the national court 'cannot act solely on the basis of that claimant's financial situation but must also carry out an objective analysis of the amount of the costs'.[47] By doing so, the EU judiciary established a

[40] C-263/08, *Djurgården-Lilla Värtans Miljöskyddsförening* (2009) ECLI:EU:C:2009:631. See Jane Reichel, 'Judicial Control in a Globalised Legal Order – A One Way Track? An Analysis of the Case C-263/08 Djurgården-Lilla Värtan' (2010) 3 (2) *Review of European Administrative Law* 69–87; Case C-263/08, Áine Ryall, 'Djurgården-Lilla Värtans Miljöskyddsförening v. Stockholms kommun genom dess marknämnd, Judgment of the Court (Second Chamber)' (2010) 47 (5) *Common Market Law Review* 1511–21.

[41] Directive 2003/35/EC of the European Parliament and of the Council of 26 May 2003 providing for public participation in respect of the drawing up of certain plans and programmes relating to the environment and amending with regard to public participation and access to justice Council Directives 85/337/EEC and 96/61/EC – Statement by the Commission GU L 156, 25 June 2003, 17–25.

[42] *Djurgården*, n 40, § 48.

[43] ibid, § 50. See also Commission Notice on access to justice in environmental matters C/2017/2616 GU C 275, 18 August 2017, 24.

[44] C-260/11, *Edwards and Pallikaropoulos* (hereinafter '*Edwards*') (2012) ECLI:EU:C:2013:221. See Juliane Kokott and Christoph Sobotta, 'The Contribution of the Case Law of the CJEU to the Judicial Enforcement of EU Environmental Law in the UK' (2019) 16 *Journal for European Environmental & Planning Law* 109–24.

[45] *Edwards*, n 44, § 17.

[46] ibid, § 35.

[47] ibid, § 40.

positive precedent for ENGOs, aiming to avoid the danger that prohibitively high costs could prevent litigants from triggering judicial proceedings aiming to protect the environment.[48]

One final example can be found in *Trianel*.[49] In this ruling, the CJEU had to deal with the standing of ENGOs in judicial proceedings under the EIA Directive in Germany. The ENGO *Friends of the Earth* challenged the permissions issued by the district authority of Arnsberg for the construction and operation of the 'Trianel' power plant, pleading the violation of several laws protecting the environment. According to the ENGO, the project would have had a significant negative impact on a Natura 2000 site close by and thus not be in accordance with legislation derived from the Habitats Directive.[50] Under the now current Article 11 of the EIA Directive, 'what constitutes a sufficient interest and impairment of a right shall be determined by the [MSs], consistently with the objective of giving the public concerned wide access to justice'.[51] Nevertheless, the main issue was that the German 'Environmental Appeals Act' granted standing to ENGOs only in case of an impairment of an individual right, making it extremely difficult for public interest litigants to bring cases not affecting the organisation's own rights. In this regard, the Court pointed out that individuals and ENGOs do not protect the same kinds of interests, and that applying to environmental organisations the same rules laid down for individuals would go against the purpose of the EIA Directive.[52] Legal persons protecting collective interests can hardly ever meet procedural requirements making access to justice conditional on the impairment of an individual right.[53]

In addition, the Court found that the German provisions on standing prevented the ENGO from relying on EU environmental law (more specifically on the Habitats directive). The EU judiciary thus held that ENGOs, in judicial proceedings pursuant to Article 11 of the EIA Directive, shall be able to rely on rules of EU environmental law and on the rules of national law flowing from EU environmental law.[54] For this reason, the CJEU declared the German standing requirements incompatible with the EIA Directive.

Thanks to the Court's ruling in *Trianel*, the Environmental Appeals Act has been amended and now it grants standing to recognised environmental organisations 'without they having to show that their own rights are affected'.[55] Under the new

[48] Even the ACCC has been active on highly prohibitive costs of judicial proceedings. On this matter, see, inter alia, communication ACCC/C/2008/27 and findings on compliance by the United Kingdom of Great Britain and Northern Ireland with its obligations under the Convention.

[49] C-115/09, *Bund für Umwelt und Naturschutz Deutschland, Landesverband Nordrhein-Westfalen* (hereinafter '*Trianel*') (2011) ECLI:EU:C:2011:289. See European Union Agency for Fundamental Rights (FRA), *Handbook on European law relating to access to justice* (2016), 176. Available at: https://fra.europa.eu/en/publication/2016/handbook-european-law-relating-access-justice.

[50] *Trianel*, n 49, § 24.

[51] Art 11 of the EIA Directive.

[52] *Trianel*, n 49, § 46.

[53] ibid, § 47.

[54] ibid, § 58.

[55] Art 2 of the German *Umwelt-Rechtsbehelfsgesetz* (UmwRG). Available at: www.umweltbundesamt.de/en/legal-background-to-the-environmental-appeals-act.

legislation, for an ENGO it suffices to claim that the contested decision breaches environmental law.[56] Although the German legal system still presents barriers hindering access to justice in environmental matters,[57] *Trianel* perfectly exemplifies how triggering litigation at national level and calling for the attention of the CJEU on domestic provisions, can open legal opportunities at national level for ENGOs.

However, many 'closures' in the LOS are still present in many EU MSs.[58] In Ireland for instance, triggering judicial proceedings remains relatively expensive,[59] while in Eastern European countries like Poland, Romania and Hungary, ENGOs still face major issues in being granted legal standing.[60] However, domestic environmental litigation also requires 'trained' judges, meaning members of the judiciary who are familiar with the law of the Union and who know how to make wise use of the remedies available under the EU Treaties.[61] For this reason, the next section will dig into the third way in which ENGOs have mobilised to remove the obstacles hindering access to justice at national level and circumvent *Plaumann*, namely by training judges and legal practitioners.

V. Training National Judges and Practitioners

On top of the shortcomings described by AG Jacobs in his opinion in *UPA*,[62] which have often prevented citizens from securing adequate access to justice at national level, there are also other factors influencing national courts' decision to

[56] ibid.

[57] Mariolina Eliantonio and Franziska Grashof, 'Wir müssen reden! – We Need to Have a Serious Talk! The Interaction between the Infringement Proceedings and the Preliminary Reference Procedure in Ensuring Compliance with EU Environmental Standards: A Case Study of Trianel, Altrip and Commission v Germany (2016) 13 *Journal for European Environmental & Planning Law* 340–41. According to the authors, German law still raises questions of compatibility with EU law, for instance with regard to the requirement that 'environmental organisations need to be officially recognised according to the criteria listed in § 3 UmwRG before being able to access courts'.

[58] Hofmann, n 2, 357.

[59] ibid.

[60] Communication from the Commission to the European Parliament, the Council, the European Economic and Social Committee and the Committee of the Regions, 'Environmental Implementation Review 2019: A Europe That Protects Its Citizens And Enhances Their Quality Of Life', Brussels, 4 April 2019 Com(2019) 149 Final, 14. For a more comprehensive analysis of the structural barriers hindering access to justice in environmental matters in the EU MSs, please see Jan Darpö, 'Effective Justice? Synthesis report of the study on the Implementation of Articles 9.3 and 9.4 of the Aarhus Convention in the Member States of the European Union', 2013-10-11/Final. Available at: https://ec.europa.eu/environment/aarhus/pdf/synthesis%20report%20on%20access%20to%20justice.pdf.

[61] See Monika Glavina, 'The Reality of National Judges as EU Law Judges: Knowledge, Experiences and Attitudes of Lower Court Judges in Slovenia and Croatia' (2021) 17 *Croatian Yearbook of European Law and Policy* 1; Jasper Krommendijk, *National Courts and Preliminary References to the Court of Justice* (Cheltenham, Edward Elgar, 2021) 74. In this book, Jasper Krommendijk confirms that 'a judge's attitude to referring is closely related to his or her amount of knowledge'. However, the author also argues that '[at] a certain point, too much knowledge of EU law can also be a factor that can discourage references. This seems to be the case for the UK Supreme Court, whose judges are often 'confident' to interpret EU law themselves because they think that they understand the case law'.

[62] See section I.

refer questions of EU law to the CJEU.[63] These factors are crucial from a litigant's perspective since they can *de facto* make preliminary references more unlikely to occur. Official statistics on the PRP only consider EU law questions that are actually referred.[64] But what about all those 'what if' questions mentioned before, namely all those EU law questions raised in a dispute at national level but which do not make it to Luxembourg?

Recent socio-legal inquiries have shed light on the 'context' in which the referral of a question of EU law is decided. For instance, Monika Glavina found that, on a more micro-level, having judges feeling more pro/anti EU integration, can make the difference when it is time to refer to the CJEU.[65] In this respect, even public support for EU membership in a given MS can contribute to explaining the (un)willingness of local judges to refer questions under Article 267 TFEU.[66]

On a more practical level, another aspect making the difference is the availability to judges of an EU law research unit at the respective court.[67] 'The existence of such a unit saves the time and effort a judge has to invest in doing research on the issue', as Glavina has found.[68] An additional factor is the familiarity that judges have with EU law: more expertise has been proven to bring a higher probability of referring.[69] This 'expertise' can be seen as including both an adequate EU law education at university as well as experience in dealing with cases falling within the scope of EU law. Both of these factors contribute to an increase in the probability of referral.[70]

Moreover, legal scholarship at the intersection with historical and archival research has also demonstrated that even lawyers' expertise in the field of EU law matters a great deal.[71] Indeed, some of the most iconic EU law cases (which happen to be preliminary rulings)[72] were often examples of strategic legal mobilisation, that is, pieces of a broader 'strategy' put forward by specific 'Euro-lawyers',

[63] See Krommendijk, n 61.

[64] In 2020, the CJEU received 556 preliminary references, source: 2020 annual report of the Court. Available at: https://curia.europa.eu/jcms/upload/docs/application/pdf/2021-04/ra_pan_2020_en.pdf.

[65] Monika Glavina, '"To Refer or Not to Refer, That Is the (Preliminary) Question": Exploring Factors Which Influence the Participation of National Judges in the Preliminary Ruling Procedure' (2020) 16(1) *Croatian Yearbook of European Law & Policy* 35.

[66] Clifford J Carrubba and Lacey Murrah, 'Legal Integration and Use of the Preliminary Ruling Process in the European Union' (2005) 59 *International Organization* 399.

[67] Glavina, n 65, 38.

[68] ibid.

[69] ibid, 47. See also Juan A Mayoral, Urszula Jaremba and Tobias Nowak, 'Creating EU Law Judges: the Role of Generational Differences, Legal Education and Judicial Career Paths in National Judges' Assessment regarding EU Law Knowledge' (2014) 21 *Journal of European Public Policy* 1136.

[70] ibid, 48.

[71] Amedeo Arena, 'From an Unpaid Electricity Bill to the Primacy of EU Law: Gian Galeazzo Stendardi and the Making of Costa v. ENEL' (2019) 30(3) European Journal of International Law 1017–37; Virginia Passalacqua, 'Legal Mobilization via Preliminary Reference: Insights from the Case of Migrant Rights' (2021) 58(3) *Common Market Law Review* 768.

[72] Eg C-26/62, *Van Gend en Loos/Administratie der Belastingen* (1963) ECLI:EU:C:1963:1; C-6/64, *Costa v ENEL* (1964) ECLI:EU:C:1964:66; C-6/90, *Francovich and Bonifaci v Italy* (1991) ECLI:EU:C:1991:428.

using EU law and the PRP to achieve societal change and/or political goals.[73] These 'euro-lawyers' can either trigger litigation, for instance, to push courts to provide a different interpretation of a given provision or to indirectly call the attention of governments on sensitive issues.[74]

Indeed, expertise and familiarity with EU law matters. In this regard, there is an institutional 'will' to improve the enforcement of EU environmental law across the Union. This is confirmed, for instance, by the different forms of cooperation taking place between the Commission and national judges.[75] In 2008, DG ENV outsourced the organisation of a number of judicial training activities to the European Institute of Public Administration (EIPA) on various topics of EU environmental law (including workshops and seminars focusing on implementation).[76] Today, the Commission works with Judicial Training Centres[77] and provides 'training materials in a way which allows their up-date and adaptation to the needs at the national level'.[78]

Since 2012 the Commission has provided further training modules through the Academy of European Law (ERA) in Trier (Germany) where national judges have the possibility to directly contribute to the programme design through questionnaires.[79] In addition, judges' professional associations like the 'EU Forum of Judges for the Environment', the 'Association of the Councils of State' and the 'European Association of Administrative Judges' are represented in the programme's Steering Committee and in the Plenary Assembly.[80]

These training modules touched upon different EU environmental law-related topics, ranging from the enforcement of the EIA directive, nature protection, waste and water management, general principles of EU environmental law and environmental crimes.[81] According to the European Commission, the seminars organised were 'attended by more than 400 judges and prosecutors, from the courts of first instance to the Supreme Courts from 27 Member States'.[82]

Furthermore, the Commission also funded projects targeting the improvement of access to justice at national level through the 'Life programme', the EU's funding instrument for the environment and climate action created in 1992.[83] In particular,

[73] Arena, n 71. In this article, Arena proves how the Italian lawyer Gian Galeazzo Stendardi 'designed' the *Costa v Enel* case in the attempt to prevent the advancement of socialism in Italy. See also Antoine Vauchez, *Brokering Europe – Euro-Lawyers and the Making of a Transnational Polity* (Cambridge, CUP, 2015) 124. In this book, Vauchez emphasises the role played by specific 'Euro-lawyers' in pushing further the advancement of the European integration project via litigation.

[74] See Tommaso Pavone, *The Ghostwriters Lawyers and the Politics behind the Judicial Construction of Europe* (Cambridge, CUP, 2022).

[75] See https://ec.europa.eu/environment/legal/law/judges.htm.

[76] ibid.

[77] These are established in any EU MS, for a complete list please see: www.ejtn.eu/About-us/Members/.

[78] ibid.

[79] ibid.

[80] ibid.

[81] ibid.

[82] ibid.

[83] See https://cinea.ec.europa.eu/life_it.

in 2017, the ENGOs Justice & Environment and ClientEarth were awarded around €680,000 from the European Commission to perform the 'A2J EARL' (Education and Awareness Raising of Legal Professionals on Access to Justice) project, aiming to raise awareness about the legal possibilities available for citizens and ENGOs to help protect the environment through access to justice.[84] The beneficiaries essentially served as trainers on the ground to build expertise, share good practises and open up opportunities for access to justice in a number of MSs.[85]

The project took place from 1 July 2017 to 31 December 2020 in eight different MSs, namely Austria, Estonia, France, Germany, Hungary, Poland, Slovakia and Spain. The initiative contributed to the training of around 1000 practitioners on access to justice issues in 48 workshops and seminars held in different locations in the MSs concerned or via 12 webinars. The project also gathered approximately 120 people to share their experience and knowledge at a virtual conference on the topic held in October 2020.[86] At least 80 per cent of the target audience accessing project materials or attending events, 'found that they will have a better understanding of the specific challenges and obstacles to proper access to justice on environmental matters'.[87]

Figure 2 A2J EARL project, training in Berlin (3 June 2019). By gracious permission of the Independent Institute for Environmental Issues (*UfU e.V.*). Available at: www.ufu.de/en/

The project website outlines the different initiatives that have been put into place by the beneficiaries throughout the three years of the program. In particular, they set up: a monthly newsletter about the latest updates on access to justice;[88] a guide on access to justice EU procedural rules and case law and the Aarhus Convention

[84] See https://webgate.ec.europa.eu/life/publicWebsite/index.cfm?fuseaction=search.dspPage&n_proj_id=6323.

[85] See www.clientearth.org/projects/access-to-justice-for-a-greener-europe/.

[86] See www.clientearth.org/projects/access-to-justice-for-a-greener-europe/events/virtual-conference-on-access-to-justice-in-environmental-matters/.

[87] See www.ufu.de/en/projekt/a2j-earl/.

[88] See www.clientearth.org/projects/access-to-justice-for-a-greener-europe/newletters/.

equivalents;[89] national toolkits on access to justice in the eight MSs concerned;[90] a digital information platform with an 'ask a lawyer function';[91] a public-interest lawyer database regrouping lawyers active in the field of environmental law;[92] a series of webinars held in different locations in the eight MSs;[93] an EU wide conference held in Brussels.[94]

Especially the national toolkits on access to justice were written in the local languages and framed on the basis of the domestic legal system. In this respect, ClientEarth specified that 'they are meant to ensure that all the relevant stakeholders – judges, public authorities, public interest lawyers and NGOs – are aware of the existing legal opportunities but also obstacles and insufficiencies of the national legal framework'.[95]

Anne Friel, in-house lawyer at ClientEarth, described with these words the level of satisfaction of the ENGO in relation to the A2J EARL project:

> We were very happy with the engagement actually … We covered eight MSs, we had to do around 800 trainings overall. It's kind of worrying to know whether people were really engaged in it, whether we pitched the right level of expertise, etc. But we were very pleased because there was a lot of engagement, there was a lot of interest and in some of the MSs there was a lot interest also coming from public authorities (eg ombudsman offices, etc). What stakeholders wanted to reach turned to be very difficult, namely the judiciary. So we did manage in some countries to engage with them but mostly they weren't so receptive to go in seminars and trainings provided by ENGOs but by in large we have already seen some concrete results, in France for example. Quite small ENGOs there now are engaging with litigation at national level on pesticides. I'm not saying … that it was because of our project, sometimes it's just a 'happy coincidence'! Because sometimes they were thinking about triggering litigation while coming to the training and then thanks to the training they managed to interact with some people who are already doing this kind of litigation and then all brings to 'more action'. For example we had an Irish judgement which came out recently where they invited *ClientEarth* and *Justice & Environment* to join the case as interveners because it was going to make a preliminary reference so he said it would be a good idea if we have some European level NGOs involved, 'I heard of these trainings, so maybe they're appropriate!'. They see some kind of concrete results, which is very nice. Yeah so, we were very happy with the project and the Commission was as well.[96]

The award of the A2J EARL project can be used to illustrate two main points. The first refers to the EU institutional understanding of the EU judicial protection system. The European Commission is de facto executing what the CJEU has favoured in its case law, that is, promoting the necessity to open up opportunities

[89] See www.clientearth.org/latest/documents/guide-on-access-to-justice-in-european-union-law/.
[90] See www.clientearth.org/latest/documents/country-toolkits-on-access-to-justice/.
[91] See www.clientearth.org/latest/documents/interactive-platform-on-access-to-justice/.
[92] See www.clientearth.org/latest/documents/access-to-justice-lawyer-database/.
[93] See www.clientearth.org/latest/documents/webinars-on-access-to-justice-replays/.
[94] See above, n 86. The conference was postponed to October 2020 and ultimately held online because of the Covid-19 pandemic.
[95] See www.clientearth.org/latest/documents/country-toolkits-on-access-to-justice/.
[96] ibid.

for access to justice at national level and to make sure that national courts refer cases to the CJEU. This is not only intended to bring the national legal systems into compliance with EU environmental law, but also to contest the validity of EU law via the PRP. In other words, this project contributes to the implementation of the EU judicial protection system that the Court has always advocated for, that is the one relying on a more systematic use of Article 267 TFEU.[97]

The second point concerns the role of civil society in EU environmental governance and the relevance of this project for legal mobilisation. Indeed, by having taken part in a call for EU funding for a project on access to justice, ENGOs proved their 'proactive' attitude when dealing with MSs' non-compliance with EU environmental law. Rather than waiting for the Commission to open infringement proceedings or for national judiciaries to train their own judges on the enforcement of EU law, CSOs decided to combine, once again, legal with non-legal strategies,[98] and turn themselves into 'trainers' and provide judges and practitioners with the relevant know-how on environmental justice. This is also relevant from a legal mobilisation perspective, as this can be seen as a further endeavour of ENGOs to open legal opportunities at national level by seeking to increase judicial receptivity in domestic courts.[99] Indeed, these organisations are trying to change the 'landscape' in which national courts operate, by acting on some of the more 'hidden' barriers (such as judges' familiarity with EU law) hindering the enforcement of EU law and preventing referrals from happening. ENGOs have invested in human capital which they believe will be extremely beneficial not only for EU institutions but for environmental litigants too: these have provided judges with an expertise which increases the likelihood of more and higher quality referrals by national courts under the PRP.[100]

Having provided a broad overview of the first three ways through which ENGOs have mobilised to remove the obstacles hindering access to justice at national level and circumvent *Plaumann*, it is now time to look more specifically at the last tool, namely the PRP on validity.

VI. ENGOs and the PRP on Validity

Preliminary references represent the vast majority of the cases received by the CJEU.[101] Indeed, in the last nine years, 5409 cases out of 8081 (66,9 per cent)

[97] C-263/02 P, *Commission v Jégo-Quéré* (2004) ECLI:EU:C:2004:210, § 30.

[98] See definition in the introduction to the present book.

[99] In chapters 6 and 7 I will show how ENGOs are trying to increase judicial receptivity by other means, namely by building 'transnational incremental comfort' across jurisdictions in the climate litigation context.

[100] Interview with Anne Friel and Ugo Taddei, respectively Lawyer at Environmental Democracy and Director of Nature and Health at ClientEarth (Brussels office), 19 July 2021.

[101] CJEU, Annual Reports 2019 and 2024 – Judicial Activity, 214. This data refers to the period going from 2015 to 2024.

were preliminary references. Of these 5409 preliminary rulings, 202 concerned environmental protection,[102] and of these 202, only 46 – originating from 15 MSs – were triggered by ENGOs or private citizens (Figure 3).[103]

Figure 3 Preliminary rulings in environmental matters in cases triggered by ENGOs or private citizens (2015–2024)

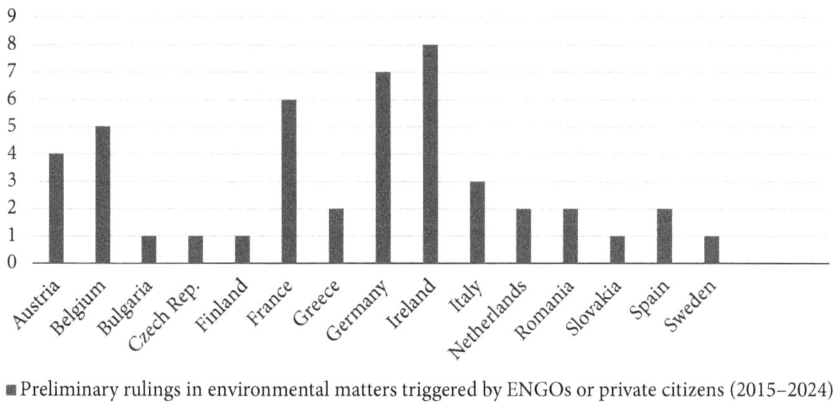

If we narrow the analysis down to include only references on validity brought in environmental matters, the figure is much smaller. From 1981 to 2020, it is possible to identify only 28 references on validity concerning environmental protection, originating in eight MSs.[104]

'The contribution of this piece of the puzzle [the validity reference] to date has thus been minimal' found Ioanna Hadjiyianni.[105] According to this scholar, of these 28 cases, eight were EU ETS-related, while the CJEU annulled the contested EU act only 'in a handful of them'.[106] 'Most validity references were initiated by economic operators, which generally have a better chance of directly accessing the CJEU', the same author found.[107]

[102] This data (referring to both, PRPs on interpretation and validity) is based on a search on the CURIA database relating to preliminary references on the subject matter of the 'environment' in a timeframe going from 1 January 2015 to 31 December 2024.

[103] This data (referring to both, PRPs on interpretation and validity) is based on a keyword search on the CURIA database relating to preliminary references on the subject matter of the 'environment' and including the term 'association'. This yielded 76 results and the false positives were eliminated through qualitative analysis. This does not necessarily capture every single preliminary ruling relating to environmental matters, since many rulings are still not available in English. As a consequence, it was not possible to identify the word 'association' in the text of such rulings. Eg C-323/17, *People Over Wind and Sweetman* (2018) ECLI:EU:C:2018:244 is not part of these results for the reason just explained.

[104] Ioanna Hadjiyianni, 'Judicial Protection and the Environment in the EU Legal Order: Missing Pieces For A Complete Puzzle Of Legal Remedies' (2021) 58 *Common Market Law Review* 806.

[105] ibid.

[106] ibid, 807.

[107] ibid.

This data is confirmed by the European Commission, which in 2019 argued that 'validity references represent a small sub-set of cases brought under Article 267 – and validity references related to the environment have been very rare'.[108] Up to 2024, I identified only six[109] references on validity originating in lawsuits triggered by ENGOs before national courts, five unsuccessful and one successful. These references will now be described in the sections here below. Indeed, I will examine part of these cases in turn and, for each case, I will mostly analyse the arguments presented by environmental organisations to mobilise the CJEU and reflect on the potential for legal mobilisation offered by the PRP on validity. I decided not to include the *Confédération Paysanne* ruling in the present analysis, since the Court ultimately did not scrutinize the question of validity raised in the case.[110] I equally decided not to also analyse the *Friends of the Irish Environment* case for space constraint reasons.[111] My reflections on the legal mobilisation dimension stemming from the description of each case will be collected in a specific section, at the end of the case law examination.

A. The *Associazione Italia Nostra* Case

In one of the few validity references triggered by CSOs, the ENGO Associazione Italia Nostra Onlus started judicial proceedings in Italy and contested the validity of a legislative act, that is Article 3(3) of the Strategic Environmental Assessment (SEA) Directive,[112] *vis-à-vis* Articles 191 TFEU and 37 of the EUCFR.[113] According to the association, the SEA Directive provision should be declared invalid in so far as it allows for the exclusion of an environmental assessment for plans and programmes to be undertaken in 'small areas at local level', where the MSs determine that such plans are not likely to have 'significant environmental effects'.[114]

The case was referred to the CJEU for a preliminary ruling, which recalled that Article 191 TFEU requires the EU to adopt policy measures aiming – *inter alia* – at a 'high level of protection' of the environment while taking into account the diversity of situations in the various regions of the Union. However, when pursuing these objectives – recalled the Court – the EU shall enjoy broad discretion, in view of the need to strike a balance between the objectives and principles governing

[108] Commission Staff Working, n 16.
[109] C-444/15, C-78/16, C-281/16, C-528/16, C-616/17, C-330/22.
[110] C-528/16, *Confédération paysanne and Others* (2018) ECLI:EU:C:2018:583, § 83.
[111] C-330/22, *Friends of the Irish Environment* (2024) ECLI:EU:C:2024:19.
[112] Directive 2001/42/EC of the European Parliament and of the Council of 27 June 2001 on the assessment of the effects of certain plans and programmes on the environment OJ L 197, 21 July 2001, 30–37.
[113] C-444/15, *Associazione Italia Nostra Onlus v Comune di Venezia and Others* (2016) ECLI:EU:C:2016:978.
[114] ibid, § 11.

the EU environmental action and the complexity of the implementation of such criteria.[115] As a consequence, the Court's review must necessarily be limited to the question of whether the EU legislator, by adopting the contested provision, committed a 'manifest error of appraisal'.[116]

In carrying out its review, the CJEU did not find that the institutional assessment made by the EU legislator in granting discretion to the MSs, could be deemed as being 'unreasonable'[117] or manifestly wrong. Indeed, the EU judiciary argued that it should be for the competent authorities at national level to determine whether a given plan or programme is likely to have significant environmental effects.[118] In this respect, the Court recalled that:

> it is for the [MSs] to take, within the sphere of their competence, all the general or particular measures necessary to ensure that all plans or programmes likely to have significant environmental effects within the meaning of that directive are subject, before adoption, to an environmental assessment in accordance with the procedural requirements and the criteria laid down by that directive.

Regarding Article 37 of the EUCFR, the Court pointed out that, as is apparent from the explanations relating to the Charter in connection with that provision, the 'principles set out in [Article 37] have been based on Articles 2, 6 and 174 [EC], which have now been replaced by Article 3(3) [TEU] and Articles 11 and 191 [TFEU]'.[119] Considering that the EU judiciary did not find anything capable of leading to a declaration of invalidity of Article 3(3) of the SEA Directive *vis-à-vis* Article 191 TFEU, the Court equally found 'nothing which could affect its validity in the light of Article 37 of the Charter'.[120] As a consequence, the Court deemed that there was no ground to declare the Directive's provision invalid.

B. The *Xylella* Case

A similar outcome also resulted from another reference on validity which originated – once again – from Italy in 2015. Since 2013, the Apulian region (Southern Italy) has been facing a tremendous phytosanitary emergency caused by a plant pathogen called *Xylella fastidiosa* (hereinafter 'Xylella'), which invades the host plants' xylem vessels and blocks the transportation of water and soluble mineral

[115] ibid, § 46.
[116] ibid.
[117] ibid, § 27. The applicant in the case at stake also claimed that the contested provision infringed the 'principle of reasonableness', given the 'inappropriate and insufficient level of protection which that provision provides in view of the objectives pursued by the Habitats Directive and by the, purely quantitative, reference criterion of the size of the area concerned by the plans or programmes coming under that provision'.
[118] ibid, § 58.
[119] ibid, § 62.
[120] *ibid.*

nutrients, causing plants to wilt, dry up and die.[121] In eight years, the pathogen has killed around four million[122] olive trees in Apulia, with a huge impact on the Italian and European olive oil industry.[123] In order to counter the spread of the pathogen to other regions, inside and outside Italy, in 2015 the Commission ordered – inter alia – the eradication of all infected plants and of the healthy plants within a radius of 100 metres around the infected ones, provided that this measure is proportionate to the objective pursued.[124]

Local growers and environmental associations contested this specific provision before domestic courts, claiming, in particular, that the eradication measures were invalid in light of the precautionary and proportionality principles.[125] The Administrative Tribunal of Lazio referred the case to the CJEU for a preliminary ruling on validity.[126]

Even in this case, the EU judiciary found that, when taking decisions in conditions of scientific uncertainty, the EU executive should enjoy broad discretion. This is because such procedures entail 'political choices' and complex assessments on the part of the Commission, which has to strike a balance between the different interests at stake.[127] The Court also re-affirmed that 'the validity of a measure adopted in that area can be affected only if the measure is manifestly inappropriate'.[128]

This point is particularly relevant when EU environmental measures are concerned, since these can often be qualified as 'risk management measures', that is, measures adopted in conditions of scientific uncertainty to minimise the risks arising from a current or potential threat. In *Xylella*, the Court made clear that – in such conditions – 'the validity of an EU measure must be assessed on the basis of the facts and the law as they stood at the time when that measure was adopted and cannot therefore depend on retrospective assessments of its efficacy'.[129] Moreover, the EU judiciary added:

> Where the EU legislature is obliged to assess the future effects of rules to be adopted and those effects cannot be accurately foreseen, its assessment is open to criticism only if it

[121] European Commission, 'What is *Xylella fastidiosa*?'. Available at: https://ec.europa.eu/food/plants/plant-health-and-biosecurity/legislation/control-measures/xylella-fastidiosa_en.

[122] Italia Olivicola, 'Lo studio: 4 milioni di alberi morti e improduttivi, 50mila ettari desertificati, perso il 10% dell'olio italiano'. Available at: www.italiaolivicola.it/news/comunicati-stampa/xylella-lo-studio-4-milioni-di-alberi-morti-e-improduttivi-50mila-ettari-desertificati-perso-il-10-dellolio-italiano/.

[123] ibid. According to the European Commission, Xylella has the 'potential of causing in the EU, an annual production loss of 5.5 billion euros, affecting 70% of the EU production value of older olive trees (over 30 years old), and 35% value of younger ones'.

[124] Art 6(2), Commission Implementing Decision (EU) 2015/789 of 18 May 2015 as regards measures to prevent the introduction into and the spread within the Union of Xylella fastidiosa (Wells and others) (notified under document C (2015) 3415), OJ L 125, [2015], 36–53. Hereinafter 'Decision 2014/789'.

[125] C-78/16, *Pesce and Others* (2016) ECLI:EU:C:2016:428, § 21.

[126] ibid.

[127] ibid, § 49.

[128] ibid.

[129] ibid, § 50.

> appears manifestly incorrect in the light of the information available to it at the time of the adoption of the rules in question.[130]

In this respect, in *Xylella*, the Court used the scientific opinion issued by EFSA[131] on the risk to plant health posed by the pathogen, as a benchmark to review the exercise of the Commission's discretion.[132] The EU judiciary found that, in adopting the contested provision requiring the eradication of all infected plants and of the healthy plants within a radius of 100 meters around the infected ones, the Commission did not make any manifest error of assessment, as this was justified by the relevant scientific evidence.[133] Hence, the Court found that the EU act at stake was not invalid *vis-à-vis* the principles of precaution and proportionality.

C. The *Blaise* Case

Another relevant reference on validity in the environmental context can be found in *Blaise*.[134] This case concerned Mr Mathieu Blaise and 20 other individuals (hereinafter 'the Defendants') who, in 2016, entered three shops and damaged cans containing glyphosate as well as glass display cases. Glyphosate is a weed killer whose carcinogenicity is still highly debated within the scientific community: it has been classified as a 'potential carcinogen' by IARC in 2015, and – on the opposite – as a substance 'unlikely to pose carcinogenic hazard to humans' by EFSA in the same year.[135] Glyphosate is currently approved for use in the EU until 15 December 2033.[136]

The Defendants' acts led to criminal proceedings being brought against the defendants in the Criminal Court of Foix (France), on charges of 'defacing or damaging the property of another, while acting in concert with others'.[137] The Defendants based their defence on grounds of necessity and precaution, claiming that their actions were intended to inform the shops concerned and their customers about the risks associated with selling glyphosate without sufficient warnings.[138]

[130] ibid.
[131] European Food Safety Authority, Panel on Plant Health (PLH), 'Scientific Opinion on the risk to plant health posed by *Xylella fastidiosa* in the EU territory, with the identification and evaluation of risk reduction options' (2015) 13 (1) *EFSA Journal* 3989.
[132] *Pesce*, n 126, § 65.
[133] ibid, § 81.
[134] C-616/17, *Blaise and Others* (2019) ECLI:EU:C:2019:800.
[135] GM Williams, M Aardema, J Acquavella, et al, 'A Review of the Carcinogenic Potential of Glyphosate by Four Independent Expert Panels and Comparison to the IARC Assessment' (2016) 46(sup1) *Critical Reviews in Toxicology* 2–3. Erratum in: *Critical Reviews in Toxicology* 2018 Nov 30: 1–2. The position of EFSA was also confirmed by the European Chemicals Agency (ECHA) in 2017.
[136] See www.efsa.europa.eu/en/topics/topic/glyphosate#:~:text=Glyphosate%20is%20currently%20approved%20for,authorities%20following%20a%20safety%20evaluation.
[137] Alessandra Donati, 'The Glyphosate Saga, A Further but Not a Final Step: The CJEU Confirms the Validity of the Regulation on Plant Protection Products in Light of the Precautionary Principle' (2020) 11 *European Journal of Risk Regulation* 149.
[138] ibid.

The French Criminal Court decided to stay proceedings and to refer questions for a preliminary ruling to the CJEU on the validity of Regulation n. 1107/2009,[139] concerning the placing of plant protection products (including glyphosate) on the market (hereinafter 'the PPP Regulation').[140]

In particular, the referring court asked the CJEU – inter alia – whether the imprecise definition of 'active substance', as well as the requirement according to which the tests, analyses and evaluations necessary for investigating the dossier have to be conducted by the applicants alone, were compatible with the precautionary principle.[141] Considering that the Regulation at stake was based on the precautionary principle, in her opinion AG Sharpston pointed out that it covered a 'technically and scientifically complex area of law'.[142] As a result, the EU institutions enjoy a 'particularly wide discretion' in regulating that field, making their acts susceptible to be annulled only where 'they are manifestly inappropriate or where the institutions have committed manifest errors in the light of the objective sought to be achieved'.[143] AG Sharpston also found that the submission of a complete dossier of data, along with the application for an active substance, and the review of the latter carried out by the MS rapporteur, addressed the concerns of the referring court. Indeed, the Court's advisor argued that 'the PPP Regulation [imposes] objective requirements on the quality of data to be submitted'.[144] In the light of this, AG Sharpston proposed that the validity of the contested EU measures was to be upheld.[145]

In its preliminary ruling, the EU judiciary followed to a large extent Sharpston's line of reasoning and held that the Regulation at stake could not be deemed invalid due to the precautionary principle.[146] Apart from the limited intensity of judicial review on precautionary measures, which was confirmed even in *Blaise*, this case is also relevant in the present analysis as regards the granting of standing to the defendants. In her opinion, AG Sharpston briefly referred to the unequal treatment granted to corporations and ENGOs in actions for annulment under Article 263(4) TFEU:[147]

> Whereas the former are presumed to be directly and individually concerned by an act that affects their activities, the latter's concern for the environment or public health does not suffice to demonstrate locus standi.[148]

[139] Regulation (EC) No 1107/2009 of the European Parliament and of the Council of 21 October 2009 concerning the placing of plant protection products on the market and repealing Council Directives 79/117/EEC and 91/414/EEC OJ L 309, 24 November 2009, 1–50.
[140] ibid.
[141] *Blaise*, n 135, § 30.
[142] Opinion of AG Sharpston in *Blaise*, n 135, § 52.
[143] ibid.
[144] ibid, § 65.
[145] ibid, § 84.
[146] *Blaise*, n 135, § 117.
[147] Opinion of AG Sharpston in *Blaise*, n 135, § 49.
[148] Antoine Bailleux, 'Don't Judge a Case by its Cover: The Pesticides Regulation Survives Judicial Scrutiny But Is Given New Teeth: Blaise' (2020) 57 *Common Market Law Review* 870.

From a legal mobilisation perspective, this triggers the questions of whether the Defendants in *Blaise* (i) breached the law in order to get access to justice; (ii) could really contest the validity of the PPP Regulation by other means. The people arrested in France were active members of the 'Voluntary Reapers of GMOs' group.[149] This is relevant from a legal mobilisation point of view, as the Defendants were active members of an organised group fighting against GMOs.[150]

In her opinion, Sharpston revealed that '[at] one of the shops, they distributed leaflets with the headline "Roundup and Co, we can't and won't stand this any longer"'.[151] Some members of the 'Voluntary Reapers' informed the police that their intention was to 'hammer home the point' that 'the rules requiring products containing glyphosate to be kept locked in glass cabinets and to be accompanied by the vendor's warning that glyphosate was carcinogenic were being broken'.[152]

This suggests that the Defendants, being part of an organised national group with access to legal expertise, were aware of the relevant national provisions.[153] In addition, Sharpston clarified that '[at] a hearing before the referring court on 17 August 2017, the defendants requested that that French Criminal Court referred questions to EU judiciary under Article 267 TFEU'.[154] Therefore, referring those questions to the CJEU for a preliminary ruling was the object of a specific request advanced by the Defendants and endorsed by the Criminal Court of Foix. This seems to confirm the hypothesis according to which the Defendants put themselves into the position of being arrested with the intention of contesting the validity of the PPP Regulation through the national courts.

Antoine Bailleux, a French scholar, stressed that breaching the law was probably the only way the Defendants could actually challenge the validity of the EU measure at stake.[155] Indeed, 'they could have sought the annulment of the French authorization of glyphosate before domestic administrative courts. But the time limit for such an action had probably elapsed at the time of the offence'.[156] Hence, Bailleux added, 'it is safe to say that [getting arrested was] probably the most straightforward way for the accused to obtain such a wide-ranging ruling on the validity of Regulation 1107/2009'.[157] This reading was also confirmed by Andrea Carta, Senior Legal Strategist at Greenpeace EU, who argued that *Blaise* perfectly demonstrates why the PRP cannot compensate for the justice gap experienced under Article 263(4) TFEU. Indeed, in *Blaise* 'the activists had to breach the law

[149] Opinion of AG Sharpston in *Blaise*, n 135, § 32.
[150] See https://aseed.net/french-voluntary-reapers-remove-70-gm-vines-2/: '[the] reapers are doing their actions without violence, recognizable, without covering their faces, and they take full responsibility'.
[151] ibid.
[152] ibid.
[153] This shows, once again, the legal mobilisation dimension and the relevance of this case in the present analysis.
[154] ibid, § 33.
[155] Bailleux, n 149.
[156] ibid.
[157] ibid.

in order to be able to contest the validity of an EU measure. This is completely unacceptable.'[158]

D. The *Vereniging Hoekschewaards Landschap* Case

In 2013, the Netherlands proposed to the European Commission that it remove the polder of Leenheeren from the Haringvliet 'site of Community interest' (SCI), established under the Habitats Directive.[159] The Netherlands had decided to abandon its plan of 'depolderisation', initially aiming to convert such areas into natural sites 'under tidal influence to develop its potential'.[160] In this respect, the Dutch State found that the 'Leenheerenpolder' had 'no ecological assets' and so asked for its removal from the SCI.[161]

The Commission agreed on the exclusion and argued that the initial inclusion of the polder in the SCI was due to a 'scientific error'. Hence, despite maintaining the Haringvliet site on the list, the Commission removed the Leenheerenpolder from that same site by adopting Implementing Decision 2015/72.[162] The local environmental association 'Vereniging Hoekschewaards Landschap' (VHL) contested the implementing decision before the national judiciary, which referred the case to the CJEU for a preliminary ruling. In essence, the domestic court asked whether the reduction in the size of the SCI, on the ground that the initial inclusion of the polder in the same site was due to a scientific error, was valid.[163]

To answer this question, the CJEU referred to the opinion of AG Kokott, who noticed that 'the inclusion of a site in the list gives rise to the presumption that it is relevant in its entirety from the point of view of the Habitats Directive's objective of conserving natural habitats and wild fauna and flora'.[164] Therefore:

> a proposal by a [MS] to reduce the size of a site placed on that list requires proof that the areas in question do not have a substantial interest in achieving that objective at national level. In addition, the Commission may accept and implement the proposal only if it concludes that those areas are also not necessary from the perspective of the entire European Union.[165]

In light of this, the Court found that, on the one hand, the Netherlands had not invoked the existence of a 'scientific error' at the time it presented its proposal to the Commission; on the other hand, the Commission had not provided to the

[158] Interview to Andrea Carta, Senior Legal Strategist at Greenpeace EU, Amsterdam, 25 February 2020. On this point, see also *Commission v Jégo-Quéré*, n 98, § 45.
[159] C-281/16, *Vereniging Hoekschewaards Landschap* (2017) ECLI:EU:C:2017:774, § 16.
[160] ibid, § 14.
[161] ibid, § 18.
[162] ibid, § 20.
[163] ibid, § 25.
[164] ibid, § 36.
[165] ibid.

EU judiciary any scientific evidence demonstrating that such an error had vitiated the initial proposal to reduce the size of the natural site.[166] Given this, the CJEU deemed that the exclusion of the polder from the SCI was not duly justified and that, as a consequence, the Commission implementing decision was invalid.[167]

Having presented all the references on validity promoted by ENGOs, I will now draw my conclusions on the case law just outlined from a legal mobilisation perspective.

E. Preliminary Conclusions on ENGOs and the PRP on Validity

The limited number of preliminary rulings on validity obtained in references triggered by ENGOs already provides evidence of the 'closures' experienced by CSOs at national level.[168] Furthermore, even the legal impact[169] of ENGOs' legal mobilisation is severely hampered in references on validity. This is for the reasons that will be analysed below.

Indeed, legal scholarship has extensively attempted to make sense of the case law of the CJEU on the justiciability of the precautionary principle.[170] The rulings presented above seem to confirm what Giulia Claudia Leonelli found in her research.[171] Indeed, the type of procedure seems to matter in relation to the intensity of the Court's scrutiny, as do the grounds of review presented by the applicants. In this regard, Leonelli highlighted that in references on validity of EU precautionary measures, the review by the CJEU of 'a breach or misapplication of the precautionary principle is always absorbed in the … review of the proportionality of the final measures'.[172] Furthermore, this seems to occur 'regardless of whether specific questions on manifest errors or the precautionary principle have been referred and regardless of whether legislative or regulatory acts are at stake'.[173]

Nevertheless, in cases where the violation of the principle of proportionality was not contested by the applicants (eg *Blaise*), the Court limited its scrutiny to assess whether the EU institutions made a manifest error of assessment in the adoption of the measure at stake (ie the PPP Regulation). This in order to preserve the

[166] ibid, § 39.
[167] ibid, § 41.
[168] See above, section I.
[169] See definition in the introduction to the present book.
[170] See, inter alia, Elizabeth Fisher, 'Is the Precautionary Principle Justiciable?' (2011) 13 (3) *Journal of Environmental Law* 315–34; Ragnar Lofstedt, 'The Precautionary Principle in the EU: Why a Formal Review Is Long Overdue' (2014) 16 (3) *Risk Management* 137–63; Kenisha Garnett and David J Parsons, 'Multi-Case Review of the Application of the Precautionary Principle in European Union Law and Case Law' (2017) 37 *Risk Analysis* 502–16.
[171] Giulia Claudia Leonelli, 'Acknowledging the Centrality of the Precautionary Principle in Judicial Review of EU Risk Regulation: Why It Matters' (2020) 57 (6) *Common Market Law Review* 1794.
[172] ibid.
[173] ibid.

political discretion that the EU decision-makers enjoy in the adoption of specific environmental policy measures. It goes without saying that the acknowledgement of this political space to the Commission reduces the spectrum of justiciable principles available for legal mobilisation. Indeed, the 'manifest error of appraisal' test de facto constrains legal mobilisation of ENGOs, limiting the extent to which environmental organisations can invoke general principles of EU environmental law before the Court. This occurs precisely in relation to the principle of precaution, which is frequently invoked in environmental references on validity.

In this respect, even in cases where ENGOs are granted standing at national level and domestic courts refer questions of validity under Article 267 TFEU, the intensity of the Court's judicial review on precautionary measures prevents the EU judiciary from fully examining the scientific evidence and the cost-benefit analysis on which the policy measure is based.[174] This is because the Court cannot balance the different interests at stake in the place of decision-makers and has to preserve their political prerogatives. Obviously, the margin of discretion recognised to the EU institutions (and especially to the EU executive) is not fixed and predetermined, but dynamic and contextual: the intensity of judicial review varies depending on the degree of scientific uncertainty: 'the greater the scientific uncertainty, the greater the margin of appreciation of the authority'.[175]

However, if in references on validity the Court's review of a breach of the precautionary principle is usually 'absorbed' in the proportionality test, the same does not occur in direct actions.[176] Indeed, when dealing with precautionary measures challenged under Article 263(4) TFEU, the Court's review draws 'a clear connection between administrative discretion and precautionary risk management, and [interprets] the notion of a manifest error of assessment in light of the precautionary principle'.[177] In other words, the Court's review of precautionary measures challenged in direct actions, is not absorbed in the proportionality test, but is subject to a different scrutiny, based on a more intense 'procedural review' of those same measures.[178] This approach seems to value the role of the precautionary principle and safeguard its true 'scientific' nature.[179]

Indeed, the application of the precautionary principle triggers a number of procedural obligations that the EU decision-maker on risk has to fulfil and duly justify in its act.[180] Therefore, 'the review of the legality of the decision-makers' action becomes a review of the procedural implications triggered by the

[174] This since the Court does not hold the relevant scientific expertise, which is actually held by EFSA (especially in the field of food safety).

[175] Opinion of AG Mischo, C-192/01, *Commission v Denmark* (2002) ECLI:EU:C:2002:760.

[176] Leonelli, n 172, 1791.

[177] ibid.

[178] ibid.

[179] ibid, 1816.

[180] C-326/05 P, *Industrias Químicas del Vallés v Commission* (2007) ECLI:EU:C:2007:443. § 76: 'However, the exercise of that discretion is not excluded from review by the Court. The Court has consistently held that in the context of such a review the Community judicature must verify whether the relevant procedural rules have been complied with, whether the facts admitted by the Commission

precautionary principle'.[181] Some scholars have argued that, in fact, by verifying that the authorities have complied with their procedural obligations, the Court de facto carries out a more 'substantive' (or quasi-substantive)[182] scrutiny on the contested EU precautionary measure.[183] This is because it examines whether 'the elements of fact and law on which the exercise of the discretionary power depends are present, and therefore whether the precautionary principle has been correctly applied'.[184] In other words, the Court's assessment is based on a delicate analysis aiming, on the one hand, to verify whether the precautionary principle has been properly observed, and, on the other hand, preserve the risk manager's prerogatives and apply its consolidated judicial self-restraint. By limiting its judicial review only to a procedural control, which might reveal manifest errors of assessment, the Court attempts to preserve the scientific nature of the precautionary principle while protecting a political space reserved to the EU executive, especially when the Commission operates in conditions of uncertainty and unpredictability.[185]

This different (and more intense) standard of 'procedural' judicial review does not seem to be applicable in most references on validity, where – as previously mentioned – the Court's review does not do justice to the 'key role of precaution'.[186] My explanation for the Court's different standard is that the raison d'être of the latter is to be found in the different procedural implications stemming from Article 267 and Article 263(4) TFEU. Indeed, the review of the precautionary principle entails the evaluation of a broad range of complex factual and technical evidence.[187] The PRP traditionally focuses on questions of 'law', while the action for annulment is also a procedure of 'facts'.[188] As a consequence, even the types of dossiers filed by the parties in the two procedures are not the same. Plaintiffs in the PRP should have submitted their evidence already before the national court referring the questions, as the Court's rules of procedure do not encompass the

have been accurately stated and whether there has been a manifest error of appraisal or a misuse of powers.'

[181] Alessandra Donati, 'The Precautionary Principle under European Union Law' (2021) 49 *Hitotsubashi Journal of Law and Politics* 59.

[182] Leonelli, n 172, 1775.

[183] Paul Craig, *EU Administrative Law* (Oxford, OUP, 2018) 721; Alessandra Donati, *Le principe de précaution en droit de l'Union européenne* (Bruxelles, Larcier, 2021) 24.

[184] Donati, n 184. See also Joanne Scott and Susan P Sturm, 'Courts as Catalysts: Rethinking the Judicial Role in New Governance' (2007) 13 *Columbia Journal of European Law*. In this article, Joanne Scott and Susan Sturm claimed that the CJEU considers itself an 'information catalyst', meaning that, within the traditional perimeter of its limited review of legality, the Court verifies that the decision-makers hold the right scientific information to adopt decisions which comply with the law and the objective pursued.

[185] Giulia Claudia Leonelli, 'Judicial Review of Compliance with the Precautionary Principle from *Paraquat* to *Blaise*: "Quantitative Thresholds" Risk Assessment, and the Gap Between Regulation and Regulatory Implementation' (2021) 22 *German Law Journal* 185.

[186] Leonelli, n 172, 1795.

[187] Ellen Vos, 'The European Court of Justice in the Face of Scientific Uncertainty and Complexity' in Mark Dawson, Bruno De Witte and Elise Muir (eds), *Judicial Activism at the European Court of Justice* (Cheltenham, Edward Elgar Publishing Limited, 2013) 154.

[188] This point was also raised by Rasmussen's analysis of the *Plaumann* test, see chapter 1.

possibility to file any evidence in requests submitted under Article 267 TFEU.[189] On the contrary, dossiers filed under Article 263(4) TFEU can also include 'any evidence',[190] where appropriate, including 'scientific evidence' which has not eventually been considered by the EU risk manager. In the light of this, I argue that the possibility to submit scientific evidence in direct actions against precautionary measures expands the scope of the Court's review, allowing the EU judiciary to provide a more 'substantive' – although procedural – analysis of the measure at stake, keeping always in mind that the EU institutions enjoy 'broad discretion' when adopting precautionary measures.

But what are the consequences of this different standard of judicial review on access to justice and the choice of the most adequate legal mobilisation avenue? With regard to regulatory acts, as will be shown in chapter five, the new AR allows for the internal review of administrative acts of general scope, regardless of whether these entail implementing measures. This implies that, in principle, even an administrative/regulatory act entailing implementing measures at national level can be contested under the internal review mechanism (post-amendment), which also enables ENGOs to file scientific evidence in support of their requests.[191] The new AR is thus expected to also have an impact on challenges against environmental regulatory acts based on precautionary grounds.[192] This would obviously discourage ENGOs from triggering validity references against EU regulatory acts at national level, making the internal review procedure under the AR a more appropriate avenue to contest EU regulatory acts. This also in view of the fact that the internal review mechanism has a clear timeframe that EU administrative bodies have to respect.[193]

With regard to actions against legislative acts, these would still need to be brought under Article 263(4) TFEU – since these are excluded from the scope of the AR – and therefore *Plaumann* would apply. As discussed above, direct challenges promoted by ENGOs against legislative acts on precautionary grounds could enjoy a more intense judicial review, based on a procedural check of the EU decision-making leading to the adoption of the contested act. However, *Plaumann* makes any ruling on the merit of a direct challenge de facto impossible. In this regard, references on validity against legislative acts have certainly been characterised by judicial deference toward the EU political institutions, in particular in relation to political judgments abouts the level of environmental protection that the Union should pursue.[194] Nevertheless, in validity references against legislative acts, ENGOs and natural persons have still succeeded in gaining standing before national courts and received judgments on the merit of the case, which is

[189] Rules of procedure of the CJEU, Art 94.
[190] ibid, Art 120.
[191] On this point, see chapter 5.
[192] ibid.
[193] ibid.
[194] Leonelli, n 186, 200.

something environmental organisations have never been able to achieve in direct actions for annulment. This leads me to conclude that, from a legal mobilisation perspective, ENGOs should prefer the internal review procedure under the AR to challenge EU regulatory acts; while – *rebus sic stantibus* – ENGOs should prefer the PRP to challenge the validity of legislative acts.

This chapter has shown that plaintiffs aiming to contest the validity or legality of EU measures walk on a slippery path. Indeed, they do not only have to consider the timeframe laid down under the EU Treaties to initiate an action for annulment, that is, two months,[195] since when these two months have already expired, plaintiffs may be seeking to contest the validity of the EU measure at stake via PRP. However, under these circumstances, ENGOs and activists also have to take into account another timeframe, that is the one established under national law to contest a national act implementing the disputed EU measure. Nonetheless, when even this second timeframe has expired, not many options are left. The *Blaise* case demonstrates that, in an effort to obtain a more straightforward access to domestic courts, litigants can be forced to breach national law.

Nevertheless, where there is a national implementing measure, I argue that litigants could be forced to breach national law to get access to justice only if they neglect procedures and deadlines laid down under national law. An ENGO having a well-functioning legal unit should be able to anticipate the expiry of the deadline for challenging the national measure implementing the relevant EU act. The other three references on validity here presented, namely *Associazione Italia Nostra*, *Xylella* and *VHL*,[196] demonstrate that claiming that ENGOs and activists need to breach the law to be granted standing before domestic courts is false and misleading, at least where there is an implementing act in existence. Even though much still needs to be done to broaden access to justice in several MSs, the majority of the EU MSs (including France) do grant standing to ENGOs to bring legal challenges on environmental issues.[197] In many EU countries there is therefore no need for environmental organisations to breach the law to be granted standing before domestic courts.

Having discussed the relevant references on validity triggered by ENGOs, I will now draw my conclusions on the overall analysis outlined in this chapter.

VII. Conclusions

The present chapter has showed how ENGOs have mobilised national courts in an attempt to circumvent *Plaumann*. I have argued that ENGOs have done so in four

[195] Art 263(6) TFEU lays down a time limit of two months from the publication of the measure, or from its notification to the plaintiff to initiate an action for annulment.

[196] The same also applies to the Friends of the Irish Environment case (C-330/22).

[197] Environmental Implementation Review 2019, n 60.

main ways: (i) by criticising the 'complete' system of legal remedies as defined by the CJEU; (ii) by broadening standing at national level via PRP on interpretation; (iii) by training national judges; (iv) by triggering references on validity at national level. Having access to national courts to contest the validity of EU law is crucial, also for the sake of this research, since the PRP is traditionally considered by the EU Commission and the EU judiciary as the 'gap filler' between the lack of direct access to the CJEU in actions for annulment and the necessity to comply with the Aarhus Convention.

In the light of this, first the present chapter described how ENGOs joined the 'choir' of criticism surrounding the PRP by using in their pleadings some of the arguments presented by AG Jacobs in his opinion in *UPA*. Indeed, the PRP presents a number of shortcomings that ENGOs have to face when trying to stimulate preliminary references to the CJEU. However, when facing 'closures' in the LOS at national level (eg narrow standing requirements, prohibitively expensive judicial proceedings, etc), ENGOs can rely on the strong cooperation guaranteed by the EU institutions, in particular the CJEU and the European Commission. Indeed, the EU judiciary has proven on several occasions to be more than willing to review MSs' legislation *vis-à-vis* the Aarhus Convention,[198] while the Commission has also demonstrated a willingness to open infringement proceedings against those MSs which do not guarantee effective judicial protection.[199]

Despite the Court's and the Commission's efforts, many ENGOs also have to face many additional barriers, for example, national courts' unfamiliarity with EU law, lack of research units in their premises, and so on. Aware of such additional obstacles, the Commission decided to provide training for judges and practitioners, sometimes even by outsourcing (and funding) responsibility for training to ENGOs in a number of MSs. By doing so, this chapter argues that ENGOs are trying to open new legal opportunities for legal mobilisation by increasing the receptivity of domestic courts. Indeed, by providing training and a more solid EU law background to national judges, lawyers and other organisations, ENGOs are trying to 'reshape' the context in which national courts operate and to ensure that more and more judges will refer cases to the CJEU. Increasing referrals will also likely increase the number of references concerning the validity of EU law.[200]

In this regard, ENGOs have tried to contest the validity of EU environmental measures via the PRP, but with scarce results. Only six cases have made it to the CJEU, while the exact figure of those cases that did not make it to the Court is hard to identify. Of these six cases, only one was successful. These preliminary rulings

[198] Áine Ryall, 'The Aarhus Convention: Standards for Access to Justice in Environmental Matters' in Stephen J Turner, Dinah L Shelton, Jona Razzaque, Owen McIntyre and James R May (eds), *Environmental Rights: The Development of Standards* (Cambridge, Cambridge University Press, 2019) 146.

[199] *Commission v France*, n 25.

[200] See above, section IV.

show the additional obstacles faced by ENGOs once standing has been granted at national level. Indeed, in most of these cases, the Court's traditional judicial restraint when dealing with precautionary measures constrained the possibilities for environmental litigants to obtain deep scrutiny of the contested EU acts. However, the analysis of the case law of the CJEU also revealed that (i) the Court is willing to accept references on validity, even when these are raised in cases where their relevance at national level is highly disputed;[201] (ii) in references on validity, the CJEU is placed in the position of being required to give a ruling on the merits of the case.

Besides the well-known shortcoming of the PRP, the Commission has suggested that the PRP on validity is a tool that is deeply underexploited by ENGOs.[202] The question is therefore whether ENGOs could be more daring in using the mobilisation pathway that is constituted by the PRP validity. Assuming that the scarce number of validity references is not due to national courts' unwillingness to refer, it must be pointed out that leading environmental organisations have already proven to be more than aware of the functioning of the EU judicial protection system and of the systems of its MSs. As outlined above, ENGOs have raised many questions of interpretation of EU law at national level, which have been referred to the Court and opened legal opportunities in many jurisdictions.[203] Then, why should it be different for questions of validity? Indeed, questions of validity are probably harder to identify, but are they also more difficult to refer? After all, the CJEU has stressed that questions of validity *shall* be referred by *all* national courts[204] and many national courts across Europe have already proven to be more than willing to refer questions of interpretation raised precisely by ENGOs.[205]

My conclusion is thus that, as highlighted by the ACCC, the PRP is – for the time being – inadequate to fill the access to justice gap created by Article 263(4) TFEU, especially for small and understaffed organisations. This is because there are too many hurdles making the likelihood of obtaining a validity reference extremely hard to predict. Nevertheless, if ENGOs are serious about challenging EU environmental measures not granting an adequate level of protection, then all avenues should be exploited, including increasing redress to the PRP on validity. This is especially the case as concerns legislative acts, which cannot de facto be challenged – for the time being – under Article 263(4) TFEU and are also excluded from the internal review established under the AR.[206] As for challenges against regulatory acts, I argue that the internal review mechanism offers

[201] See above, *Blaise*, n 135.
[202] Commission Staff Working Document, n 16, 17.
[203] See section II.D. See also C-240/09, *Lesoochranárske zoskupenie* (2011) ECLI:EU:C:2011:125; C-243/15, *Lesoochranárske zoskupenie VLK* (2016) ECLI:EU:C:2016:838.
[204] Opinion of AG Bobek in C-561/19, *Consorzio Italian Management and Catania Multiservizi* (2021) ECLI:EU:C:2021:291, § 44.
[205] See above, section III.
[206] See chapter 7.

more opportunities than the PRP on validity. This is because the new AR establishes a clear timeframe for the EU administration to respond and ENGOs are also allowed to submit scientific evidence in support of their files. An opportunity which – in substance – is excluded under the PRP, this being a procedure focusing on questions of 'law' rather than 'facts'. The more intense standard of judicial review applied by the Court on precautionary measures challenged under Article 263(4) TFEU suggests that ENGOs are correct to consider that it is preferable to shift judicial scrutiny of EU precautionary measures from the national level via the PRP to the EU level via actions for annulment.

3

Shaping the Aarhus Convention

I. Introduction

The first two chapters described how the *Plaumann* test has blocked access to justice before the Court of Justice of the European Union (CJEU) for environmental non-governmental organisations (ENGOs) and how these have tried to overcome *Plaumann* through direct and indirect actions, under Articles 263(4) and 267 Treaty on the Functioning of the European Union (TFEU). The present chapter seeks to shed light on the turning point constituted by the EU accession to the Aarhus Convention, as well as on the 'post-Aarhus (I)' period, which runs from 2012 to 2018.

Indeed, while the *Greenpeace* case described in the first chapter was pending before the CJEU, a coalition of ENGOs was already actively contributing to negotiations for a new international convention, that is, the Aarhus Convention, providing citizens and environmental organisations with procedural rights in the environmental domain. The Aarhus Convention has seen the involvement of ENGOs in every stage of its 'legal life' (conception, implementation and enforcement). In light of this, the present chapter will, first, provide the reader with a general overview of the Aarhus Convention, including its scope and objectives. Second, the chapter will highlight how CSOs have contributed to 'shaping' the Convention and to broadening its legal scope. Third, this chapter will focus on the EU's adhesion to the Aarhus Convention, which occurred in 2005 and changed the legal opportunities available for European ENGOs. Fourth, this chapter will focus on the adoption of the AR and show how this piece of EU legislation constrained environmental litigation before the CJEU. In the final part of the chapter, I will draw my conclusions on the analysis presented.

II. The Aarhus Convention

The Aarhus Convention can be seen as a major contribution to fostering environmental democracy at the global level.[1] The need for legislation enhancing citizen

[1] For a definition of 'environmental democracy', please see Principle 10 of the 1992 Rio Declaration here below. See also Emily Barritt, *The Foundations of the Aarhus Convention: Environmental Democracy, Rights and Stewardship* (Oxford, Hart Publishing, 2020) 73.

participation in the environmental context was already advanced in the 1992 Rio Declaration, where principle 10 stated that:

> Environmental issues are best handled with participation of all concerned citizens, at the relevant level. At the national level, each individual shall have appropriate access to information concerning the environment that is held by public authorities, including information on hazardous materials and activities in their communities, and the opportunity to participate in decision-making processes. States shall facilitate and encourage public awareness and participation by making information widely available. Effective access to judicial and administrative proceedings, including redress and remedy, shall be provided.[2]

Principle 10 may therefore be considered as the provision paving the way for a more solid operationalisation of the idea of 'environmental democracy', which Emily Barritt wrote as having multiple 'facets' that cannot be reduced to one simple definition.[3] However, one essential marker of any definition of 'environmental democracy' seems to refer to the value that participatory rights have in any democracy, and therefore even in an 'environmental democracy'.[4] These rights applied in the environmental context have the power to enhance citizens' stewardship in relation to the protection of nature and wildlife,[5] but also – inter alia – to improve the legitimacy of environmental decisions by holding decision-makers accountable.[6] Hence, it is through such lenses that the participatory rights enshrined under the Aarhus Convention should be read. These are: (i) the right to access to environmental information, (ii) the right to participate in the environmental decision-making and (iii) the right to access to justice.[7]

The Aarhus Convention moves precisely in this direction. The rights just mentioned represent the three 'Aarhus pillars' and their enshrinement under the Convention grants a new role to individuals and organisations in the protection of the environment along with legislatures and administrations.[8] Although all the Parties to the Aarhus Convention geographically belong to the European region,[9] the Convention is now open to every UN Member State, making it a potential global 'role model agreement' for participatory rights in the environmental context.[10]

[2] Principle 10 of the Rio Declaration on Environment and Development, 1992.

[3] Barritt, n 1, 72.

[4] ibid, 63.

[5] ibid.

[6] ibid, 61.

[7] Definition also confirmed by the Environmental Democracy Index (EDI) of the World Resources Institute. Available at: www.wri.org/our-work/project/environmental-democracy-index.

[8] See Jacqueline Peel, 'Giving the Public a Voice in the Protection of the Global Environment: Print Avenues for Participation by NGOs in Dispute Resolution at the European Court of Justice and World Trade Organization', (2001) 12 *Colorado Journal of International Environmental Law and Policy* 47; Ludwig Krämer, 'Public Interest Litigation in Environmental Matters before European Courts' (1996) 8 *Journal of Environmental Law* 1.

[9] Map of Parties to the Aarhus Convention, UNECE official website. Available at: www.unece.org/env/pp/aarhus/map.html#:~:text=Aarhus%20Convention%20has%2047%20Parties,European%20Union%20(ratified%20on%2017.2.

[10] On 4 March 2018, the Latin American and Caribbean region adopted the Regional Agreement on Access to Information, Public Participation and Justice in Environmental Matters in Latin America and the Caribbean, at Escazú, Costa Rica, which was profoundly inspired by the Aarhus Convention.

With regard to access to justice, the rationale for the Convention lies in a loosening of the standing requirements, leading to a broadening of the possibilities of challenging administrative measures having a negative impact on the environment. Just to give a concrete example, under Article 9(2) of the Convention, dealing with access to justice in the public participation context:

> Each Party shall, within the framework of its national legislation, ensure that members of the public concerned
>
> (a) Having a sufficient interest or, alternatively,
> (b) Maintaining impairment of a right, where the administrative procedural law of a Party requires this as a precondition,
>
> have access to a review procedure before a court of law and/or another independent and impartial body established by law, to challenge the substantive and procedural legality of any decision, act or omission subject to the provisions of article 6 and, where so provided for under national law and without prejudice to paragraph 3 below, of other relevant provisions of this Convention.

This provision deals with two different (and consolidated) approaches to standing, namely the 'sufficient interest' (or 'individual interest') approach and the 'individual right' approach, respectively belonging to the French and German legal traditions.[11] Therefore, the Convention, by ensuring a right to impartial review of non-legislative acts (by a judicial or administrative body) for the members of the public concerned (i) having a sufficient interest or (ii) maintaining impairment of a right, de facto considerably expands opportunities for public interest litigation (PIL) in the jurisdictions adhering to the Convention.

But what does 'public interest' stand for? This question has no easy answer. In the mid-70s, a team of American social scientists led by Burton A Weisbroad defined public interest law as meaning an 'activity that is undertaken by an organization in the voluntary sector; which provides fuller representation of underrepresented interests; and involves the use of law instruments, primarily litigation'.[12]

In particular, the authors of this study identified 11 subject areas that represented the vast majority of public interest law activities: civil liberties, environmental protection, consumer protection, employment, education, media reform, healthcare, welfare benefits, housing, voting and occupational health and safety.[13]

As a consequence, by relying on a broadening of the standing requirements in such areas, CSOs were able to increase the frequency and scope of judicial review

[11] See, inter alia, André de Laubadère, Jean-Claude Venezia and Yves Gaudemet, *Traité de droit administratif*, Tome I, 14th edn (Paris, LGDJ, 1996) 306; Florian Becker, 'The Development of German Administrative Law' (2017) 24 (2) *George Mason Law Review* 453.

[12] Burton A Weisbrod, 'Conceptual Perspective on the Public Interest: An Economic Analysis', in *Public Interest Law: An Economic and Institutional Analysis* (Berkeley, University of California Press, 1978) 22.

[13] Ann Southworth, 'What Is Public Interest Law? Empirical Perspectives on an Old Question' (2013) 62 *DePaul Law Review* 494.

of administrative action, strengthening the power of judges and third parties intervening in the decision-making process.[14]

From an historical perspective, PIL has its roots in the US legal tradition, where it emerged during the 1960s and 1970s as a result of strategic litigation pursued by liberal lawyers using the judiciary as a way to drive political change for African Americans.[15] In this regard, PIL facilitated the promotion of the interests of minorities who – at that time in the US – were marginalised from traditional channels of political decision making.[16]

A quest for broader use of PIL had to be followed by an expansion of the standing requirements, which was made possible thanks to an enlargement of the traditional model of protection to new classes of interests.[17] In fact, this enlargement process was a response to bigger concerns and pressures triggered by the growth of the government's role in society.[18] In the first half of the twentieth century, administrative regulation of the economy in the US rapidly increased in order to protect new interests belonging to significant parts of the population and secure fundamental societal objectives.[19]

Nevertheless, this growth in the role of the executive and its agencies often provoked unchecked and abusive intrusions into private liberty and property interests.[20] As a consequence, administrative law could no longer be limited to the protection of small classes of citizens against unauthorised governmental intrusions, but assumed far more ambitious responsibilities, namely the protection of a broader set of interests pertaining to bigger classes of persons or the general public.[21] Another relevant element to stress concerns the role of the US judiciary, which was extremely open in providing a wider legal shelter to these new interests in its case law.[22] Moreover, even the Congress reacted positively to civil society's claims and, since the early 1970s, vigorously backed the expansion of standing rules in particular in the environmental and consumer protection domains.[23]

In fact, according to some scholars, this *liaison dangereuse* between the US judiciary and the Congress could be explained in terms of a better use of the 'checks and balances' system.[24] Considering that, in the US, the executive branch is not elected by the legislature, the latter seemed to use judicial adjudication as an

[14] Michael S Greve, 'The Non-Reformation of Administrative Law: Standing to Sue and Public Interest Litigation in West German Environmental Law' (1989) 22 (2) *Cornell International Law Journal* 229.

[15] Scott Cummings and Louise G Trubek, 'Globalizing Public Interest Law' (2008) 13 *UCLA Journal of International Law and Foreign Affairs* 1–53.

[16] ibid.

[17] Richard B Stewart, 'The Reformation of American Administrative Law' (1975) 88 *Harvard Law Review* 1685.

[18] ibid.

[19] ibid.

[20] ibid, 3.

[21] ibid.

[22] Greve, n 14, 229.

[23] eg Consumer Product Safety Act, 15 USC, 1972 and the Magnuson Moss Act of 1975, 15 USC, 1975.

[24] Greve, n 14, 230.

instrument of control over government agencies and to increase its power over the executive.[25]

Besides the political context in which it was conceived, the 'public interest' approach has found breeding ground even in European legal systems and has been adopted in many different jurisdictions (in some of them even before the adoption of the Aarhus Convention, such as in France and Italy).[26] The protection of the public interest (including the environment) based on citizens' participation, therefore represents a relatively recent approach and it constitutes the foundation of the Aarhus Convention and the legal culture embedded therein.[27]

In this regard, what has the Aarhus Convention added to the pre-existing European legal culture?[28] It has certainly promulgated values which are today at the core of EU administrative and environmental law, such as the openness and transparency of the public administration, co-decision and accountability in environmental decision-making, environmental awareness among citizens and effectiveness through judicial review.[29] Nonetheless, the Convention has 'not yet shaped a single, solid and unified common attitude or behaviour towards public participation in environmental decision-making'.[30] This is also due to the fact that no specific EU directive was adopted to harmonise the conditions governing access to environmental justice in the different Member States (MSs).[31] A missing piece which has (improperly) led many national legislators to consider that their domestic legal systems were already sufficiently compliant with the obligations stemming from the Convention.[32] In the next section, I will now turn to describe how ENGOs deeply contributed to the negotiations of the Aarhus Convention in the 1990s.

III. ENGOs and the Aarhus Negotiation

The peculiarities of the Aarhus Convention lie not only in its legal scope and objectives, but also in the way it was negotiated and conceived in the first place. Indeed, what makes this piece of international law so special is also that, 'consistently with the idea to promote bottom up democracy, ENGOs were already involved in the

[25] ibid.

[26] See *Loi n. 76-663 du 19 juillet 1976 relative aux installations classées pour la protection de l'environnement*; *Legge 8 luglio 1986, n. 349 – Istituzione del Ministero dell'ambiente e norme in materia di danno ambientale.*

[27] Barritt, n 1, 72.

[28] By 'legal culture' I refer to 'ideas, attitudes, opinions, and expectations with regard to the legal system' (see Lawrence M Friedman, 'The Place of Legal Culture in the Sociology of Law' in Michael Freeman (ed), *Law and Sociology* (Oxford, OUP, 2006) 189.

[29] Anna Gerbrandy and Laurens van Kreij, 'The Impact of the Convention of Aarhus on the Emerging European Legal Culture' in Roberto Caranta, Anna Gerbrandy and Bilun Muller (eds), *The Making of a New European Legal Culture: The Aarhus Convention* (Zutphen, Europa Law Publishing, 2018) 447–48.

[30] ibid, 452.

[31] A proposal for an EU directive was presented by the Commission in 2003, but this was then withdrawn in 2014 for lack of political consensus within the Council. See section III below.

[32] Gerbrandy and van Kreij, n 29, 452.

drafting of the Convention'.[33] Indeed, the negotiations saw the participation of the European Environmental Citizens' Organizations (ECO) Forum, an open coalition of environmental organisations, acting in the UNECE region.[34] The ECO Forum was established in preparation for the Lucerne Ministerial Conference (1993), under the name of the 'Pan-European NGO Coalition' and, since that time, the Forum has continued to coordinate NGOs' participation and involvement to the 'Environment for Europe' (EfE) processes.[35]

The UNECE official website describes the EfE process as a:

> [Partnership] of Member States within the UNECE region, organizations of the United Nations system represented in the region, other intergovernmental organizations, regional environmental centres, non-governmental organizations, the private sector and other major groups.[36] The process and its Ministerial Conferences provide a high-level platform for stakeholders to discuss, decide and join efforts in addressing environmental priorities across the 56 countries of the UNECE region, and is a regional pillar of sustainable development.[37]

In this regard, ENGOs – especially those involved in the EfE process – were welcomed by the UNECE Committee during the negotiation of the Aarhus Convention.[38] Indeed, the ECE Environment and Human Settlements Division believed that the participation of civil society would strengthen the agreement.[39]

Carol Day, Senior Planning Officer and Solicitor at WWF-UK at that time, reported that the Working Group (WG) 'met ten times between June 1996 and March 1998' and that 'NGOs were invited to form a 'coalition' and take seats at the negotiating table. Different scholars have described the negotiation of the Aarhus Convention as a 'special moment' for civil society in the history of multilateral environmental agreements (MEAs).[40] A representative of the European Commission stated that ENGOs 'had an enormous impact on the negotiations'.[41] This since the ENGOs taking part in the process were given their own flag of identification at the table and the right to request the floor and provide their insights at each stage of the negotiations.[42] Environmental organisations were able to lobby governmental

[33] ibid, 410. See also Tom Delreux, 'The EU in Environmental Negotiations in UNECE: An Analysis of its Role in the Aarhus Convention and the SEA Protocol Negotiations' (2009) 18 (3) *RECIEL* 328–37; Lisa Vanhala, 'Shaping the Structure of Legal Opportunities: Environmental NGOs Bringing International Environmental Procedural Rights Back Home' (2018) 40 (1) *Law & Policy* 110–27.

[34] European ECO Forum, 'What is the Aarhus Convention?', November 2010. Available at: www.unece.org/fileadmin/DAM/env/pp/Media/citizens_rights_under_Conv_e.pdf.

[35] ibid.

[36] UNECE official website. Available at: www.unece.org/env/efe/welcome.html.

[37] ibid.

[38] Carol Day, 'NGOs and the Negotiation of the Convention' in Charles Banner (ed), *The Aarhus Convention: A Guide for UK Lawyers* (Oxford, Hart Publishing, 2015) 182.

[39] ibid.

[40] ibid. see also Delreux, n 33; Lalanath de Silva, 'Public Participation in International Negotiation and Compliance' in Shawkat Alam, Atapattu Sumudu, Carmen G Gonzalez and Jona Razzaque (eds), *International Environmental Law and the Global South* (Cambridge, Cambridge University Press, 2021) 586.

[41] Delreux, n 33.

[42] ibid.

delegates in the hosting premises (mainly in corridors and coffee shops) and put forward amendments and drafts of possible provisions to be included, some of which were accepted by the delegates from participating countries.[43]

Other organisations were regularly represented throughout the process including ICEL, REC and IUCN.[44] ENGOs apparently took the most maximalist positions at the international level, together with Norway and Poland[45] and lobbied strongly for gaining high standards of protection for the three rights enshrined under the Convention.[46]

Since the Convention was qualified as a mixed agreement, both the EU and its MSs had to be represented during the negotiation.[47] However, during the first part of the negotiating process, the EU MSs negotiated on their own behalf, without adhering to any EU line and making the Commission's role extremely marginal.[48] Indeed, the Commission received a clear mandate from the Council only starting from the fourth day of the eighth negotiation session.[49] The mandate allowed the Commission to negotiate – on behalf of the MSs – all articles falling under EU competence.[50] Environmental protection is included among the shared competences listed in Article 4 TFEU. As far as shared competences are concerned, the EU MSs retain the competence to conclude an agreement in so far as the EU has not 'occupied the field', in other words, it has not made use of its own competence.[51]

In this regard, the Aarhus articles covered by EU legislation included the Convention's provisions falling under the first two pillars, namely access to environmental information and participation in environmental decision-making. This since the EU had already exercised its powers by issuing two directives on such matters,[52] both adopted under the environmental chapter of the Treaty (today Articles 191, 192 and 193 TFEU). Conversely, the third pillar on 'access to justice' was only later introduced to the Convention, starting from the fifth meeting.[53] EU

[43] ibid.
[44] ibid.
[45] ibid.
[46] ibid.
[47] Piet Eeckhout, *EU External Relations Law* 2nd edn (Oxford, Oxford University Press, 2011) 255.
[48] ibid.
[49] ibid.
[50] Ludwig Krämer, 'The Aarhus Convention and the European Union', in Charles Banner (ed), *The Aarhus Convention – A Guide for UK Lawyers* (Oxford, Hart publishing, 2015) 79.
[51] Eeckhout, n 47, 214.
[52] Directive 2003/4/EC of the European Parliament and of the Council of 28 January 2003 on public access to environmental information and repealing Council Directive 90/313/EEC OJ L 41, 14 February 2003, 26–32; Directive 2003/35/EC of the European Parliament and of the Council of 26 May 2003 providing for public participation in respect of the drawing up of certain plans and programmes relating to the environment and amending with regard to public participation and access to justice Council Directives 85/337/EEC and 96/61/EC – Statement by the Commission OJ L 156, 25 June 2003, 17–25.
[53] Economic Commission for Europe, Committee on Environmental Policy, Working Group for the preparation of a draft Convention on Access to Environmental Information and public Participation in environmental decision-making, Report of the fifth session, 7 July 1997. Available at: www.unece.org/fileadmin//DAM/env/pp/adwg.htm.

exclusive competence for this pillar was excluded because the EU had not (and still has not) 'occupied the field' by adopting an EU binding measure,[54] leaving the MSs free to negotiate all the 'access to justice' provisions in their own capacities as UNECE members, without having to follow any EU common line.[55]

IV. The Introduction of the 'Justice' Pillar

The introduction of a 'justice' pillar was strongly advocated by the ENGOs' coalition. An informal meeting on 'access to justice' took place after the fourth session of the negotiations and ENGOs made sure that their voice was adequately heard even in that context.[56] It was during this 'informal meeting' that the Parties came up with the first draft of current Article 9 of the Convention on access to justice.[57] In particular, the ENGOs coalition requested that such provisions should also 'extend to individuals without impairment of their financial interests or health'.[58] A proposal that was later officially included in the text of the Convention,[59] despite the opposition of countries like Turkey, which expressed reservations on the subjects to be included among the 'members of the public'.[60]

Environmental organisations truly promoted a broad idea of 'standing', completely detached from the impairment of citizens' financial or health rights and to be interpreted as including not only ENGOs, but also 'individuals' among the 'members of the public' as defined under the Convention.

During the sixth session of the negotiating process, ENGOs also presented a proposal for a compliance mechanism (current Article 15 of the Convention).[61] Interestingly, this proposal was not immediately accepted by the Parties, which introduced in Article 15 an 'open clause' as to the type of review of compliance mechanism to be adopted, as proposed by the UK.[62] Indeed, in the text of the Convention, the Parties simply specified that the Meeting of the Parties (MOP) shall

[54] A proposal for an EU directive on access to justice in environmental matters was actually put forward by the European Commission in 2003, but it was then withdrawn in 2014 for lack of political consensus within the Council.

[55] Delreux, n 33, 332.

[56] Report of the fifth session, n 53, 11.

[57] ibid.

[58] ibid.

[59] Article 2(4) of the Aarhus Convention: '"The public" means one or more natural or legal persons, and, in accordance with national legislation or practice, their associations, organizations or groups'.

[60] Economic Commission for Europe, Committee on Environmental Policy, Working Group for the preparation of a draft Convention on Access to Environmental Information and public Participation in environmental decision-making, Report of the eight session, 17 December 1997, 5. Available at: www.unece.org/fileadmin//DAM/env/pp/adwg.htm.

[61] Economic Commission for Europe, Committee on Environmental Policy, Working Group for the preparation of a draft Convention on Access to Environmental Information and public Participation in environmental decision-making, Report of the sixth session, 7 July 1997, annex IV. Available at: www.unece.org/fileadmin//DAM/env/pp/adwg.htm.

[62] ibid.

'establish, on a consensus basis, optional arrangements of a non-confrontational, non-judicial and consultative nature for reviewing compliance with the provisions of this Convention'.[63]

As will be outlined in the next chapter, such a compliance mechanism was concretely established only in 2002 (during the first MOP under the Convention)[64] and it was, to a large extent, modelled on the basis of the proposal submitted by the ENGO coalition in the course of the negotiations. It is thus possible to conclude that this coalition deeply affected not only the way standing for natural and legal persons was constructed under the Convention, but also – at a later stage – the type of mechanism for review of compliance set up by the MOP. Such a mechanism was then extensively used by environmental organisations as a mobilisation tool, to spread the 'Aarhus model' and its legal culture across all the adhering jurisdictions.[65] In the light of this, we can clearly notice how ENGOs mobilised during the negotiations of the Aarhus Convention to 'shape' an additional mobilisation pathway under international law.[66] This pathway was then used by environmental organisations to hold national and EU institutions accountable for environmental protection.[67]

Nevertheless, ENGOs were not satisfied by the final version of the Convention. They strongly contested the final text of the agreement in relation to the parts on genetically modified organisms (GMOs)[68] and expressed the wish for CSOs to enjoy, in the Meeting of the Parties (MOPs),[69] the same level of participation they were granted during the negotiation process. Carol Day also reported that ENGOs 'lobbied actively to make sure that the required minimum number of 16 ratifications for the Convention resulted in its entry into force just three years later in October 2001'.[70] ENGOs' mobilisation was therefore constant in every phase of the process, even to make sure that the Convention actually entered into force. As the Convention is also open to accession by regional economic integration organisations,[71] the EU decided to join the Aarhus Convention in 2005. In the next section, I will now focus on this key moment.

[63] Art 15 of the Aarhus Convention.

[64] See sections II and II.A.

[65] Jerzy Jendroska, member of the ACCC, presentation during the virtual conference on 'access to justice in environmental matters: obstacles, impacts and ways forward', 15–16 October 2020, panel on 'Session 3: How to promote access rights?'. Available at: https://app.livestorm.co/clientearth/clientearth-virtual-conference-session-3-how-to-promote-access-rights/live?s=5369ef0b-338a-487c-bac0-f7bb0f08b94b#/chat.

[66] Vanhala, n 33, 116.

[67] ibid; see also sections here below and chapter 4.

[68] Art 6(11) of the Aarhus Convention states that 'Each Party shall, within the framework of its national law, apply, to the extent feasible and appropriate, provisions of this article to decisions on whether to permit the deliberate release of genetically modified organisms into the environment.'

[69] Day, n 38, 184.

[70] ibid.

[71] Art 19(2) of the Aarhus Convention.

V. The EU Adhesion to the Aarhus Convention

In 2005, the EU adhered to the Aarhus Convention by adopting Council decision 2005/370/EC.[72] Upon approval, the EU explicitly declared that:

> the legal instruments in force do not cover fully the implementation of the obligations resulting from Article 9(3) of the Convention as they relate to administrative and judicial procedures to challenge acts and omissions by private persons and public authorities other than the institutions of the European Community as covered by Article 2 (2) (d) of the Convention, and that, consequently, its Member States are responsible for the performance of these obligations at the time of approval of the Convention by the European Community and will remain so unless and until the Community, in the exercise of its powers under the EC Treaty, adopts provisions of Community law covering the implementation of those obligations.[73]

Already in this declaration, the EU seemed to have a very 'MSs-based' understanding of Article 9(3) of the Convention. The Union referred to obligations imposed on the MSs, until the moment the EU itself adopts measures harmonising the conditions allowing for access to justice at national level. No clear reference is made to access to justice in environmental matters at EU level. This said, the EU also reiterated its declaration made upon signing of the Convention, namely that the EU institutions:

> will apply the Convention within the framework of their existing and future rules on access to documents and other relevant rules of Community law in the field covered by the Convention. The European Community is responsible for the performance of those obligations resulting from the Convention which are covered by Community law in force.[74]

Here we can read the intention of the EU institutions to limit the scope of application of the Convention. The latter – according to the EU – should not be applied 'as it is' but 'within the framework' of their existing and future (relevant) rules of EU law 'in the field covered by the Convention'. A statement that brings us to the 'autonomy of the EU' argument, which will be briefly discussed in the next chapter.

However, at the end of the paragraph above, the EU also declared itself to be ultimately responsible for 'the performance of those obligations resulting from the Convention which are covered by [EU law] in force'. Considering this sentence, how should the first and second part be read in order to be given a coherent interpretation? In my view, the reading of this declaration should be that the EU will apply the Convention within the relevant legal framework established under EU law. Nevertheless, in case of incompatibility between existing EU provisions and

[72] Council Decision of 17 February 2005 on the conclusion, on behalf of the European Community, of the Convention on access to information, public participation in decision-making and access to justice in environmental matters OJ L 124, 17 May 2005, pp 1–3.

[73] EU declaration upon approval of the Aarhus Convention, 25 June 1998. Available at: https://treaties.un.org/Pages/ViewDetails.aspx?src=IND&mtdsg_no=XXVII-3&chapter=27&clang=_en#EndDec.

[74] ibid.

the Convention, the EU remains responsible in case of violation of the obligations stemming from the Convention. This point is extremely relevant. Indeed, the EU considered itself responsible for the obligations covered by EU law, and not responsible for the obligations not covered by EU law.[75] Since the EU had not adopted legislation on the 'access to justice' pillar, the Union made clear that it would apply the Convention 'within the EU framework', which entails (i) that as long as the EU does not 'pre-empt' the field, the MSs remain responsible for the obligations stemming from the access to justice pillar; (ii) that direct access before the CJEU is not to be changed.[76]

In the light of this, in the next section I will now focus on another key moment of this legal mobilisation 'journey' against *Plaumann*, that is the adoption of the Aarhus Regulation (AR). This Regulation opened a new mobilisation pathway to challenge the legality of EU measures, which will be outlined more in detail in the section below.

A. The Aarhus Regulation

In 2006, one year after its adhesion to the Convention, the EU adopted the so-called AR – namely Regulation n. 1367/2006[77] – which binds the EU institutions, bodies and agencies to respect the obligations stemming from the Aarhus Convention. Indeed, the AR aims – inter alia – to grant access to justice in environmental matters at EU level under the conditions laid down by the Regulation. Article 10 of the Regulation provides a procedure for internal review of administrative acts which is available to any ENGO meeting the criteria set out in Article 11:

> Any non-governmental organisation which meets the criteria set out in Article 11 is entitled to make a request for internal review to the Community institution or body that has adopted an administrative act under environmental law or, in case of an alleged administrative omission, should have adopted such an act.[78]

The request for internal review of EU administrative acts has to be made in writing and within a time limit not exceeding six weeks[79] after the administrative act was

[75] Report of the Compliance Committee, findings and recommendations with regard to communication ACCC/C/2008/32 (Part I) concerning compliance by the European Union, 14 April 2011, § 58.

[76] Recital 18 of the AR: 'Article 9(3) of the Aarhus Convention provides for access to judicial or other review procedures for challenging acts and omissions by private persons and public authorities which contravene provisions of law relating to the environment. Provisions on access to justice should be consistent with the [EC] Treaty. It is appropriate in this context that this Regulation address only acts and omissions by public authorities.'

[77] Regulation (EC) n. 1367/2006 of the European Parliament and of the Council of 6 September 2006 on the application of the provisions of the Aarhus Convention on Access to Information, Public Participation in Decision-making and Access to Justice in Environmental Matters to Community institutions and bodies OJ L 264, 25 September 2006, pp 13–19.

[78] These criteria have been amended in 2021 (see chapter 5).

[79] This timeframe has been amended in 2021 (see chapter 5).

adopted, notified or published. Plus, in case the EU institution addressed rejects the request or stays silent, the ENGO may institute proceedings before the EU Courts 'in accordance with the relevant provisions of the Treaty'.[80]

It is worth noting that, since the entry into force of the AR, ENGOs have usually brought actions for annulment via the internal review procedure established under the AR. At present,[81] CSOs have submitted 104 requests to the Commission under Article 10 AR and only 10 of these have been found admissible, while for nine of these the Commission's reply is pending.

Under the old AR, the Commission received 48 requests for internal review.[82] Eighteen out of these 48 requests ended up in court proceedings. In seven of these proceedings the applicants withdrew their applications before adjudication, while in one case the Court issued a decision not to prosecute. The other 10 cases were concluded with a final ruling/order issued by the EU judiciary.[83] Conversely, under the new AR, there are currently 18 cases pending before the CJEU.[84] However, as the reader can imagine, such figures can easily change.

These data show that ENGOs saw the internal review mechanism established under the AR as an effective alternative to direct access under Article 263(4) TFEU. Indeed, environmental organisations, which had significantly mobilised the EU judiciary under the relevant Treaty provisions in the 'pre-Aarhus' period,[85] shifted their mobilisation efforts toward the internal review procedure in the post-Aarhus I period. However, their hopes were soon dented by another 'closure' in the EU LOS, a closure that will be examined in more in detail in the sections below.

To highlight the new obstacles that ENGOs encountered when mobilising under the AR, I will now examine the *Stichting Natuur* case, the ruling that I chose to

[80] Regulation (EC) n. 1367/2006, n 77, Art 12.

[81] 22 March 2025.

[82] Repository of requests for internal review lodged with the European Commission pursuant to Article 10 of Regulation (EC) No 1367/2006 ('Aarhus Regulation'). Available at: https://ec.europa.eu/environment/aarhus/requests.htm.

[83] ibid. It should be noted, however, that other EU bodies can – and do – also receive requests for internal review under the AR. Here the lists of requests which ended up in court proceedings: T-338/08, *Stichting Natuur en Milieu and Pesticide Action Network Europe v Commission* (2012) ECLI:EU:T:2012:300; T-574/12, *PAN Europe and Stichting Natuur en Milieu v Commission* (2015) ECLI:EU:T:2015:541; T-396/09, *Vereniging Milieudefensie and Stichting Stop Luchtverontreiniging Utrecht v Commission* (2012) ECLI:EU:T:2012:301; T-232/11, *Stichting Greenpeace Nederland and PAN Europe v Commission* (2015) ECLI:EU:T:2015:342; T-192/12, *PAN Europe v Commission* (2014) ECLI:EU:T:2014:152; T-458/12, *Générations futures v. Commission* (2015) ECLI:EU:T:2015:155; T-168/13, *EPAW v Commission* (2014) ECLI:EU:T:2014:47; T-177/13, *TestBioTech and Others v Commission* (2016) ECLI:EU:T:2016:736; T-8/13, *ClientEarth and Others v Commission* (2015) ECLI:EU:T:2015:348; T-19/13, *Frank Bold v Commission* (2015) ECLI:EU:T:2015:520; T-462/14, *EEB v Commission* (2015) ECLI:EU:T:2015:327; T-565/14, *EEB v Commission* (2015) ECLI:EU:T:2015:559; T-685/14, *EEB v Commission* (2015) ECLI:EU:T:2015:560; T-33/16, *TestBioTech v Commission* (2018) ECLI:EU:T:2018:135; T-108/17, *ClientEarth v Commission* (2019) ECLI:EU:T:2019:215; T-12/17, *Mellifera v Commission* (2018) ECLI:EU:T:2018:616; T-436/17, *ClientEarth and Others v Commission* (2021) ECLI:EU:T:2021:320; T-393/18, *Mellifera v Commission* (2020) ECLI:EU:T:2020:639.

[84] Mario Pagano, 'Climate Legal Mobilization Under the New Aarhus Regulation' (2024) 25 (6) *German Law Journal* 921.

[85] See chapter 1.

represent the 'post-Aarhus (I)' period, running from 2012 to 2018. As mentioned in the introduction to this book, this timeframe sees the entry into force of the AR as a first major change impacting environmental litigation before EU Courts. I chose *Stichting Natuur* since this is one of the first cases brought before the EU judiciary under Article 10 AR and all the main arguments used by the applicants' lawyers in this lawsuit have been reflected in following rulings on access to justice under the AR.

VI. Mobilising against *Plaumann* in the 'Post-Aarhus (I)' Period

The *Stichting Natuur* case[86] was brought by two ENGOs founded under Dutch law, namely Stichting Natuur en Milieu, set up in 1978 and established in Utrecht, whose object is the protection of the environment, and Pesticide Action Network Europe (PAN Europe), set up in 2003 and now based in Brussels, whose purpose is to campaign against the use of chemical pesticides.[87]

In 2008, these ENGOs submitted two requests under Article 10 AR to the Commission for an internal review of Regulation n. 149/2008[88] amending Regulation n. 396/2005 of the European Parliament and of the Council on maximum residue levels (MRLs) of pesticides in or on food and feed of plant and animal origin.

Article 2(1)(g) AR defined the concept of an 'administrative act' as meaning 'any measure of individual scope under environmental law, taken by a Community institution or body, and having legally binding and external effects'. On the basis of this, the Commission rejected the applicants' requests presented under Article 10 by holding that 'a request for internal review shall comply with certain conditions, including the nature of the administrative act, which has to fall under the definition given in Article 2(1)(g) of the same Regulation'.[89] The Commission did not consider that the contested measures constituted administrative acts within the meaning of the AR. In the light of this rejection, in 2008 the two ENGOs instituted proceedings before the GC and sought the annulment of both the Commission's decision rejecting the requests as well as of the initial Regulation which had formed the subject matter of the ENGOs' internal review demand.

[86] T-338/08, *Stichting Natuur en Milieu and Pesticide Action Network Europe v Commission* (2012) ECLI:EU:T:2012:300; joined cases C-404/12 P and C-405/12 P, *Council and Commission v Stichting Natuur en Milieu and Pesticide Action Network Europe* (2015) ECLI:EU:C:2015:5. Hereinafter '*Stichting Natuur* (GC)' and '*Sitchting Natuur* (CJEU)'.

[87] Both ENGOs do not seem to have a strong presence of in-house lawyers in their respective staffs. Indeed, their official websites reveal that, at present, Stichting Natuur has only one in-house lawyer (with expertise in private law), while PAN Europe has no specific member in charge of this position.

[88] Commission Regulation (EC) No 149/2008 of 29 January 2008 amending Regulation (EC) No 396/2005 of the European Parliament and of the Council by establishing Annexes II, III and IV setting maximum residue levels for products covered by Annex I thereto (Text with EEA relevance) OJ L 58, 1 March 2008, pp 1–398.

[89] *Stichting Natuur* (GC), n 86, § 4.

At the end of the judicial proceedings, the applicants' arguments prevailed before the GC, which found the *Fediol* and *Nakajima* case law to be applicable, as it will be outlined more in depth in the sections below. The Court thus annulled the two contested measures, namely the initial Regulation (object of the internal review request) and the Commission's decision rejecting the requests of the ENGOs. The GC's judgment was then appealed by the Council and the Commission, and the case was finally decided by the CJEU in 2015.

VII. The Arguments of the Applicants in *Stichting Natuur*

By contrast with *Greenpeace*, in the drafting of this section I have had the advantage of gaining access to the original application file[90] submitted by the applicants in the appeal process of *Stichting Natuur* before the CJEU.[91] In seeking the annulment of the two EU measures, the applicants in *Stichting Natuur* put forward a number of legal arguments, mainly aimed at supporting two different arguments, each an alternative to the other:

A. An act of 'individual scope': the act for which the internal review under Article 10 AR was requested (the original contested act) is an administrative act, having individual scope;
B. Compliance with international environmental law: Article 2(1)(g) AR is not in compliance with Article 9(3) of the Aarhus Convention. Plus, the latter can be invoked in order to assess the legality of the AR.

A. An Act of 'Individual Scope'

The EU's adoption of the AR immediately provoked an interesting change in EU environmental litigation. While in previous actions for annulment ENGOs had struggled to show that they were 'individually concerned' by the contested EU act, the real challenge under the AR related to the quality of 'challengeable act'. In this respect, in *Stichting Natuur* the applicants were required to prove that the act in relation to which they submitted a request for internal review was an administrative act having 'individual scope'. However, all their arguments were firmly rejected by the EU judiciary.

The case law of the CJEU does not offer any definition of 'act of individual scope' but it does provide a definition of its opposite, namely an 'act of general scope' under EU law. Indeed, in the *UCDV* case, the CJEU ruled that a measure is regarded as being of general application if it applies to 'objectively determined

[90] ibid, application file (hereinafter 'AF').
[91] In this regard, I warmly thank the law firm *Van Den Biesen* in Amsterdam for making such file available for legal research.

situations and entails legal effects for categories of persons envisaged generally and in the abstract'.[92]

In the case at stake here, the applicants claimed that the Commission wrongly found that the challenged Regulation could not be considered to be an act of 'individual scope'.[93] The plaintiffs maintained that the contested EU measure represented a specific application of the general standards laid down in Regulation n. 396/2005[94] and applied only to specific activities.[95] In addition, Directive 91/414/EEC on the placing of plant protection products on the market grants the possibility to submit to the Commission a separate application for establishment or modification of each temporary MRL. For this reason, the applicants argued that the contested measure had to be considered as a 'bundle of individual decisions'.[96]

On such points, the GC found that the contested Regulation set out the list of active substances for plant protection products evaluated under EU law for which no MRLs were required.[97] Thus, the EU judges held that – in view of its purpose and content – the contested Regulation had to be qualified as an 'act of general scope'.[98] This was because it applied to 'objectively determined situations' and entailed 'legal effects for categories of persons envisaged generally and in the abstract; that is to say, economic operators who are manufacturers, growers, importers or producers of products covered by the annexes to Regulation n. 396/2005'.[99]

Being an 'act of general scope', the fact that the contested Regulation applied to a clearly defined group of products and substances to which no other substance could be added at a later stage was thus for the Court 'not relevant for the purposes of identifying the scope of that regulation'.[100]

Furthermore, with regard to the 'bundle of individual decisions' argument advanced by the applicants, the GC recalled the *International Fruit Company* case law,[101] according to which 'a contested measure adopted in the guise of a measure of general application is deemed to constitute a bundle of individual decisions if it has been adopted in order to respond to individual claims, so that the contested measure affects the legal position of each claimant'.[102] Since the MRLs established by the challenged EU act were not adopted in response to individual claims, the Court concluded that the applicants' argument had to be rejected.[103]

[92] C-244/88, *UCDV v Commission* (1989) ECLI:EU:C:1989:588, § 13.
[93] *Stichting Natuur* (GC), n 86, § 27.
[94] ibid, § 41.
[95] ibid, § 42.
[96] ibid, § 27.
[97] ibid, § 38.
[98] ibid.
[99] ibid.
[100] ibid, § 44.
[101] Joined cases 41/70 to 44/70, *NV International Fruit Company and others v Commission of the European Communities* (1971) ECLI:EU:C:1971:53.
[102] *Stichting Natuur* (GC), n 86, § 45.
[103] ibid. Because of the 'individual scope' requirement, the only requests for internal review which were deemed admissible on procedural grounds were those against authorisations on substances or GMOs. See for instance, *Testbiotech I* and *II*, respectively cases T-177/13 and T-33/16, where the Commission did not contest that the act at issue was an act of 'individual scope'.

B. Compliance with International Environmental Law

In *Stichting Natuur*, the applicants also invoked a plea of illegality before the GC: if the latter did not find the contested measure to be an 'act of individual scope', the Court ought then to recognise Article 9(3) of the Aarhus Convention as having direct effect and review the legality of Article 10 AR *vis-à-vis* such a provision. Article 9(3) of the Convention represents the 'heart' of the Aarhus third pillar and reads as follows:

> Each Party shall ensure that, where they meet the criteria, if any, laid down in its national law, members of the public have access to administrative or judicial procedures to challenge acts and omissions by private persons and public authorities which contravene provisions of its national law relating to the environment.

Therefore, in the applicants' view, an internal review procedure limited to administrative acts of 'individual scope', was not compatible with the wording of Article 9(3). By so arguing, the applicants raised the crucial question of whether provisions of an international agreement, to which the EU is a party, can be relied on in support of an action for annulment of an act of secondary EU legislation.[104] According to the CJEU's *Intertanko*[105] and *FIAMM*[106] jurisprudence, applicants may rely on such provisions when 'first, the nature and the broad logic of that agreement do not preclude it and, secondly, those provisions appear, as regards their content, to be unconditional and sufficiently precise'[107] (in other words, have direct effect).

However, in the case at issue here, the GC recalled that where the EU has intended to

> implement a particular obligation assumed under an international agreement, or where the measure makes an express *renvoi* to particular provisions of that agreement, it is for the Court to review the legality of the measure in question in the light of the rules laid down in that agreement.[108]

In this regard, the EU judges found the so-called *Fediol*[109] and *Nakajima*[110] 'exceptions' applicable in relation to the contested measures.

[104] See Katja Rath, 'The EU Aarhus Regulation and EU Administrative Acts Based on the Aarhus Regulation: The Withdrawal of the CJEU from the Aarhus Convention' in Christina Voigt (ed), *International Judicial Practice on the Environment: Questions of Legitimacy (Studies on International Courts and Tribunals)* (Cambridge, Cambridge University Press, 2019) 52–73.

[105] C-308/06, *Intertanko and Others* (2008) ECLI:EU:C:2008:312.

[106] C-120/06 P *FIAMM and Others v Council and Commission* (2008) ECLI:EU:C:2008:476.

[107] ibid, §§ 110–120.

[108] *Stichting Natuur* (GC), n 86, § 54.

[109] Case 79/87 *Fédération de l'industrie de l'huilerie de la CEE (Fediol) v Commission of the European Communities* (1989) ECLI:EU:C:1989:254.

[110] C-69/89 *Nakajima All Precision Co Ltd v Council of the European Communities* (1991) ECLI:EU:C:1991:186.

In those cases the Court recognised its competence to review the legality of the EU act at issue, and the acts adopted for its implementation, in the light of the rules of the World Trade Organization (WTO) agreements where (i) the EU intends to implement a particular obligation concluded in the context of the WTO (*Nakajima* exception);[111] or (ii) where the EU act at issue refers explicitly to specific provisions of those agreements (*Fediol* exception).[112]

The GC dismissed the plaintiffs' argument on direct effect of Article 9(3) based on the *Slovak bear*[113] case law, where the CJEU held that Article 9(3) of the Aarhus Convention does not contain 'any unconditional and sufficiently precise obligation capable of directly regulating the legal position of individuals and therefore does not meet those conditions'.[114]

Nonetheless, the GC found that the AR 'implemented' the relevant international agreement, as it was adopted to meet 'the European Union's international obligations under Article 9(3) of the Aarhus Convention'. By carrying out its review, the GC pointed out that the Convention does not provide any definition of the term 'acts',[115] and an internal review procedure covering only measures of individual scope would be very limited, 'since acts adopted in the field of the environment are mostly acts of general application'.[116] The GC thus found the internal review procedure laid down under Article 10 AR incompatible with the Convention and annulled the contested measures.[117] A moment of great success for the ENGOs seeking to mobilise against *Plaumann*.

The GC's decision was then appealed by the Council and the Commission, which maintained that the Court erred in law in finding the two exceptions to be applicable.[118] On the opposite side, the ENGOs argued that the Court also erred in law by denying the direct effect of Article 9(3) of the Convention.[119] This latter point deserves a closer reading. Indeed, in their pleadings the ENGOs strongly emphasised that the *Slovak bear* and *Stichting Natuur* cases focused on very different matters.[120] *Slovak bear* dealt with the 'procedure' under which national ENGOs could be granted access to justice in Slovakia, while the present case dealt with the 'object' of the internal review procedure, namely the notion of 'administrative act' as laid down in the AR.[121]

In other words, the ENGOs seemed to argue that Article 9(3) could be denied direct effect with regard to standing at national level, but that provision should be

[111] ibid, § 31.
[112] *Fediol*, n 109, § 19.
[113] C-240/09 *Lesoochranárske zoskupenie* (2011) ECLI:EU:C:2011:125.
[114] *Sitchting Natuur* (CJEU), n 86, § 47.
[115] *Stichting Natuur* (GC), n 86, § 72.
[116] ibid, § 76.
[117] ibid, § 84.
[118] *Sitchting Natuur* (CJEU), n 86, § 33.
[119] ibid, § 15.
[120] *Stichting Natuur*, n. 86, AF, 9.
[121] ibid.

regarded as sufficiently clear and precise to set aside EU legislation limiting the object of a judicial or administrative review to environmental administrative acts of individual scope.

In spite of the ENGOs' arguments, the CJEU confirmed what was stated in *Slovak bear* and denied the direct effect of Article 9(3) of the Aarhus Convention. Moreover, the Court dismissed the applicability of the *Fediol* and *Nakajima* exceptions on the basis that they were 'justified solely by the particularities of the agreements that led to their application'.[122] As to the *Fediol* exception, it did not apply to the cases at issue since Article 10 AR does not directly refer to any specific provisions of the Aarhus Convention, nor does it explicitly confer a right on individuals. As to the *Nakajima* exception, the factual and legal background of *Nakajima* had to be distinguished from the case at hand.[123] In *Nakajima* the dispute centred on an EU implementing act linked to the anti-dumping system, which was, according to the Grand Chamber, 'extremely dense in its design and application, in the sense that it provides for measures in respect of undertakings accused of dumping practices'.[124] As a consequence, the CJEU concluded that no implementation was at stake in the *Stichting Natuur* case.[125]

Furthermore, by adopting the AR, which concerns only EU institutions and only one of the remedies available to private citizens for ensuring compliance with EU environmental law, the EU had not intended to implement the obligations deriving from Article 9(3) of the Convention, within the meaning of the *Fediol* and *Nakajima* case law.[126] According to the Court's reasoning, those obligations 'fall primarily within the scope of Member States law', as previously stated in the *Slovak bear* case, confirming the EU institutional understanding of the relationship between the Aarhus Convention and the EU legal order.[127] As a consequence, the CJEU dismissed the cross-appeal and set aside the GC's ruling.[128]

Having examined the key parts of the Court's ruling in *Stichting Natuur*, in the next section I will now draw my conclusions on the analysis carried out throughout the chapter.

VIII. Conclusions

This chapter intended to demonstrate how ENGOs have contributed significantly to shaping the UNECE Aarhus Convention, enshrining the rights to access to

[122] *Stichting Natuur* (CJEU), n 86, § 49.
[123] Hendrik Schoukens, 'Access to Justice in Environmental Cases after the Rulings of the Court of Justice of 13 January 2015: Kafka Revisited?' (2015) 31 (81) *Utrecht Journal of International and European Law* 58.
[124] *Stichting Natuur* (CJEU), n 86, § 51.
[125] Schoukens, n 123.
[126] *Stichting Natuur* (CJEU), n 86, § 52.
[127] See above, section IV.
[128] ibid, § 54.

environmental information, public participation in the environmental decision-making and access to justice in environmental matters. Indeed, this piece of international law has permeated the legal systems of the Parties to the Convention (including the EU) with its own innovative legal culture, based on openness, transparency and participation of the civil society.

CSOs have, first, actively taken part in the negotiation process leading to the Aarhus Convention. This by submitting provisions drafts and amendments, by lobbying national delegates in the corridors of the negotiation premises and by contesting some parts of the final text on which they disagreed. From a legal mobilisation perspective, ENGOs were crucial in shaping new legal opportunities and even a new mobilisation pathway under international law, enabling them to hold national and EU authorities accountable for environmental protection. In particular, environmental organisations played a key role in drafting the access to justice provisions of the Convention and strongly advocated for the establishment of a compliance mechanism. This was concretely achieved in 2002, one year after the Convention entered into force.

The EU adhered to the Aarhus Convention in 2005, making very clear – already at the moment of the signature – its intention to limit the scope of application of the Convention in the Union. This by declaring that the EU will apply the Convention 'within the framework of their existing and future rules … of Community law in the field covered by the Convention'. A crucial declaration, to which the Commission also referred in the 'Aarhus v EU' saga before the Aarhus Convention Compliance Committee (ACCC).[129]

However, in order to comply with the obligations stemming from the Convention, the EU in 2006 adopted the AR, establishing an internal review mechanism allowing ENGOs to ask the EU institutions to review their administrative acts of individual scope adopted under environmental law. The AR seemed to provide new legal opportunities for ENGOs for challenging EU administrative acts. However, the definition of 'administrative act' laid down under Article 2(1)(g) AR soon turned into the major bone of contention between the EU and ENGOs, and this for more than a decade. Indeed, this definition represented a further 'closure' in the LOS available under EU law, which, in the *Stichting Natuur* case, showed all its pervasiveness in further constraining environmental litigation before the CJEU.

Indeed, the final outcome of *Stichting Natuur*, which anticipated many similar unsuccessful rulings,[130] leads to the conclusion that the entry into force of the AR in the EU legal order has brought small 'procedural' changes but no 'substantive' improvements with regard to access to environmental justice before EU courts.[131]

[129] See the next chapter.

[130] See above, n 83.

[131] Hendrik Schoukens, 'Articles 9(3) and 9(4) of the Aarhus Convention and Access to Justice before EU Courts in Environmental Cases: Balancing On or Over the Edge of Non-Compliance?' (2016) 25 (6) *European Energy and Environmental Law Review* 178; Marc Pallemaerts, 'Access to Environmental Justice at EU Level: Has "the Aarhus Regulation" Improved the Situation?' in Marc Pallemaerts, *The Aarhus Convention at Ten: Interactions and Tensions between Conventional International Law and*

The internal review procedure laid down under Article 10 AR could be seen – initially – as a new tool, to be used by CSOs to push the EU institutions to reconsider their administrative decisions taken in the field of the environment. However, the narrow scope of the review provided under the Regulation made it extremely difficult for ENGOs' requests to be deemed admissible by the addressed institution.[132]

In particular, accessing EU courts under the AR made the 'object' of the procedure, namely the character of the legal act, the main obstacle on the ENGOs' path toward judicial review. Furthermore, the AR increased the use of the plea of illegality in EU environmental litigation. Indeed, ENGOs usually invoked the remedy available under Article 277 TFEU to contest the legality of the AR in actions for annulment. This shows how ENGOs resorted to any possible remedy available under EU law to challenge the legality of the AR. Such illegality has generally been based on the alleged non-compliance of the AR with the Aarhus Convention.

This aspect probably highlights the most interesting change that the AR brought in the EU legal order. From being a purely internal issue – to be solved only through the provisions available under EU law – the question of access to environmental justice suddenly became a matter of 'EU external relations' and compliance with the Aarhus Convention. In other words, if in the pre-Aarhus period the question of access to justice was a matter of 'EU law *versus* EU law', after Aarhus the same question became a matter of 'EU law *versus* international law'.[133] An important shift, which brought also the Aarhus Committee to take position on this matter.[134]

One last interesting aspect worthy of consideration concerns the 'new' litigants who emerged after the entry into force of the AR. In addition to some of the ENGOs already litigating in the pre-Aarhus period (such as Greenpeace, EEB and Stichting Natuur), the (potential) opportunities offered by the procedure laid down under Article 10 AR attracted a number of smaller and highly specialised ENGOs. These include organisations like Testbiotech, focusing on risks deriving from genetical engineering;)[135] or Mellifera, focusing on bees' protection,[136] as will be reported in the next chapter.

EU Environmental Law (Zutphen, Europa Law Publishing, 2011) 271; Jan H Jans and G Harryvan, 'Internal Review of EU Environmental Measures. It's True: Baron Van Munchausen Doesn't Exist! Some Remarks on the Application of the So-Called Aarhus Regulation' (2010) 3 (2) *Review of European and Administrative Law* 55.

[132] On this point, see the amendment of the AR included in chapter 4.

[133] I acknowledge that this is not entirely correct, since international agreements to which the EU is a party become an integral part of EU law.

[134] See the next chapter.

[135] From Testbiotech official website, available at: www.testbiotech.org/en/testbiotech.

[136] From Mellifera e. V. official website, available at: www.mellifera.de/ueber-uns/.

4

Using the Aarhus Convention against *Plaumann*

I. Introduction

This chapter shows how environmental non-governmental organisations (ENGOs), after having contributed to the shaping of the Aarhus Convention in the negotiation process and experiencing failures in relation to the Aarhus Regulation (AR), made strategic use of the compliance mechanism established under the Convention to bring the legal systems of the Parties (including the EU) into compliance with the Convention itself. More specifically, this chapter intends to deepen our understanding of how ENGOs used the Compliance Committee established under the Aarhus Convention as a mobilisation pathway to exert pressure on the EU institutions in a bid to overcome the *Plaumann* test.

In the analysis in the sections below, I will focus on what I called the 'post-Aarhus (II) – post findings' period, running from 17 March 2017 – the day on which the Aarhus Convention Compliance Committee (ACCC) released its findings on compliance of the EU with the Aarhus Convention – to 2021, the year in which the AR was amended.

In terms of structure, the present chapter will first describe the role and composition of the ACCC. Emphasis will be put on the intensity of its scrutiny of the law of the Parties as well as on the controversial 'non-binding character' of its findings and recommendations. From a more general examination of the key features of the Aarhus Committee, the analysis will then turn to look more closely at the findings on EU compliance that the ACCC issued in 2011 and 2017. Indeed, such findings have been crucial in creating new legal opportunities for ENGOs and in re-orienting the EU approach to access to justice in environmental matters. This is because the ACCC findings on EU compliance had a domino effect on the EU decision-making, which ultimately led to the revision of the AR in 2021, that will be deepened in the next chapter. Each step of this 'chain' of events will be carefully described.

Subsequently, I will show how ENGOs have mobilised under the 'old' AR, prior to its amendment, and emphasise how in-house lawyers working for environmental organisations deployed their legal imagination in litigation to expand the legal opportunities available even under the old AR. My conclusions at the end of the chapter will sum up the findings of the analysis embedded in the sections below.

II. The Role of the ACCC

Having illustrated in the previous chapter the role played by ENGOs in the making of the Aarhus Convention, the next sections will examine the functioning of the Compliance Committee established under the Convention. It will consider how the Committee's members are appointed, what specific functions the Committee has, and how intensive and effective its scrutiny is.

A. Composition and Functions

Article 15 of the Aarhus Convention established a mechanism for compliance review which aims at guaranteeing that the legal and administrative framework of each Party fulfils the requirements laid down in the Convention itself. On the basis of this provision, at its first session (Lucca, October 2002) the MOP adopted Decision I/7 on review of compliance that created the ACCC.[1] Decision I/7 specifies that review of a specific Party's compliance with the Convention may be triggered, inter alia, by a communication concerning a Party's compliance with the Convention submitted by members of the public. This fact makes the Aarhus compliance mechanism one of the few international mechanisms that grant members of the public the opportunity to communicate their concerns about a Party's compliance directly to a board of independent experts.[2]

The Committee 'is composed of nine members with recognised competence in the field of the Convention. The Committee may not include more than one national from the same State'.[3] Decision I/7 specifies that it shall be composed of 'nationals of the Parties and Signatories to the Convention who shall be persons of high moral character and recognized competence in the fields to which the Convention relates, including persons having legal experience'.[4] In order to ensure competence and the presence of experienced members in the Committee, the members are elected on a rotation scheme, meaning that at each ordinary session, the Meeting of the Parties (MOP) elects four or five members, as appropriate.[5]

As reported in Decision I/7, the Compliance Committee has the function of:

- Considering any submission, referral or communication made under the relevant conditions;
- Preparing, at the request of the MOP, a report on compliance with or implementation of the provisions of the Convention;

[1] United Nations Economic Commission for Europe, The Aarhus Convention: An Implementation Guide, II edition (2014), 223. Available at: www.unece.org/env/pp/implementation_guide.html.

[2] Decision I/7, Annex, 3.

[3] I personally participated as an external observer in the 62nd meeting of the Compliance Committee from 5 to 9 November 2018 at the *Palais des Nations* in Geneva. Hereinafter the 'Aarhus EXP'.

[4] Decision I/7, Annex, 2.

[5] ibid.

- Monitoring, assessing and facilitating the implementation of and compliance with the relevant reporting requirements laid down in the Convention.[6]

The MOP may, upon consideration of a report and any recommendations of the Committee, decide upon appropriate measures to bring about full compliance with the Convention.[7] The MOP may, depending on the particular question before it and taking into account the cause, degree and frequency of the non-compliance, decide to take one or more of the following measures:

- Provide advice and facilitate assistance to individual Parties regarding the implementation of the Convention.
- Make recommendations to the Party concerned.
- Request the Party concerned to submit a strategy, including a time schedule, to the Compliance Committee regarding the achievement of compliance with the Convention and to report on the implementation of this strategy.
- In cases of communications from the public, make recommendations to the Party concerned on specific measures to address the matter raised by the member of the public.
- Issue declarations of non-compliance.
- Issue cautions.
- Suspend, in accordance with the applicable rules of international law concerning the suspension of the operation of a treaty, the special rights and privileges accorded to the Party concerned under the Convention.
- Take such other non-confrontational, non-judicial and consultative measures as may be appropriate.
- Having clarified functions and powers of the Compliance Committee as well as of the MOP, in the next section, I will shed light on the type of scrutiny undertaken by the Compliance Committee established under the Aarhus Convention.

B. The Scrutiny of the Compliance Committee

Although 'non-judicial' in its character, as provided under Article 15 of the Convention,[8] the ACCC traditionally carries out an intensive scrutiny of national legislative and administrative frameworks allegedly not in compliance with the Convention.[9] The Committee strictly assesses the way national administrative and

[6] ibid, 7.
[7] ibid.
[8] Art 15 of the Aarhus Convention reads as follows: 'The Meeting of the Parties shall establish, on a consensus basis, optional arrangements of a non-confrontational, non-judicial and consultative nature for reviewing compliance with the provisions of this Convention. These arrangements shall allow for appropriate public involvement and may include the option of considering communications from members of the public on matters related to this Convention.'
[9] Direct observation of the 62nd meeting of the ACCC, Geneva, 5–9 November 2018.

judicial authorities implement or interpret the national provisions at stake in a given case. This is mainly due to the 'procedural' nature of the Aarhus Convention, which often requires the members of the Committee to put complex local administrative procedures and practices 'under the microscope'. This in order to assess whether – de facto – such practices prevent members of the public from effectively relying on the rights enshrined under the Convention.[10]

An example of this can be found in the ACCC findings and recommendations on communication ACCC/C/2010/50, concerning compliance by the Czech Republic.[11] In this case, the Committee was called upon to assess whether the restrictive definition of who may be party in the environmental decision-making,[12] due to the so called 'impairment of rights doctrine' established under Czech law, was compatible with Article 9(2) of the Convention.

One of the issues arising in the case was whether the comments provided by citizens or organisations during the EIA procedure were concretely taken into account in the subsequent decision-making phases. In order to answer this question, it was necessary for the ACCC to examine the public participation safeguards granted at each stage of the EIA procedure (as required under Article 6(3) of the Convention).[13]

In particular, the Committee found that

> Czech law limits the rights of NGOs to participate after the EIA stage, and individuals may only participate if their property rights are directly affected. This means that individuals who do not have any property rights, but may be affected by the decision, are excluded.[14]

For this reason, the UN compliance body recommended the Party concerned to undertake the necessary regulatory measures to ensure that, inter alia, the 'members of the public concerned, including tenants and NGOs fulfilling the requirements of article 2, paragraph 5, are allowed to effectively participate and submit comments throughout the decision-making procedure subject to article 6'.[15]

The intensity of the Committee's scrutiny was also confirmed in Communication ACCC/C/2008/32 on EU compliance with the Aarhus Convention.[16] In the next

[10] ibid.

[11] Findings and recommendations with regard to communication ACCC/C/2010/50 concerning compliance by the Czech Republic, prepared by the Compliance Committee and adopted on 29 June 2012.

[12] In this context, being a party in the environmental decision-making has to be interpreted as provided under Art 6 of the Aarhus Convention. In other words, being a party holding a 'right to participate' entails a number of procedural rights, in particular (i) the right to be informed about the commencement of a procedure having an impact on the environment, about its characteristics, its development and its conclusion; (ii) the right to submit, in writing or, as appropriate, at a public hearing or inquiry with the applicant, any comments, information, analyses or opinions that it considers relevant to the proposed activity; (iii) the right to have such comments, information, analysis or opinions duly taken into account in the outcome of the public participation.

[13] ibid, § 68.

[14] ibid, § 70.

[15] ibid, § 90.

[16] See below, section III.

section, I will now turn to present the charity ClientEarth, which – along with other CSOs – submitted the communication on EU compliance to the Committee.

III. ClientEarth as a 'Legal ENGO'

A key role in this legal mobilisation 'journey' before the ACCC was played by the ENGO ClientEarth, an environmental charity focusing on the strategic use of the 'law' as a tool to protect 'life on Earth'.[17] ClientEarth counts eight offices in eight different countries around the world. More specifically, its offices are based in London, Brussels, Warsaw, Madrid, Berlin, Beijing, Santa Monica (US) and Luxembourg.[18] Despite its physical presence in these cities, ClientEarth's professional reach extends to more than 50 countries around the globe, where they have more than 140 active environmental cases.[19] The peculiarity of ClientEarth lies in its dominant legal 'soul'. Its founder, James Thornton, worked for many years as an environmental lawyer in the US at the Natural Resources Defense Council (NRDC) for whom he set up the 'Citizens' Enforcement Project' focusing on the Clean Water Act.[20] ClientEarth's approach to bottom-up legal enforcement strongly resonates with Thornton's vision about the role of citizens – and public interest lawyers in particular in protecting the environment. As he notes:

> If you are going to make the law that exist work, you really need citizens to have the ability to enforce the laws when the government doesn't do so. Without that, there isn't a constituency. These are very complex issues, and citizens don't have any information. They are not going to demand the government enforce the laws, because they won't even know the laws are being violated.
>
> This is what sets legal environmental law groups apart from environmental campaigning organisations. They have the expertise to analyse the science, understand the law, and actually force implementation and enforcement where it isn't being done.[21]

At the moment ClientEarth has more than 300 staff members, half of whom are legally trained.[22] In-house lawyers at ClientEarth have very diverse legal backgrounds, ranging from traditional environmental/regulatory law to climate finance and corporate accountability law.[23] This diversity stretches ClientEarth's legal imagination across the domains, allowing the organisation to use different legal tools to protect the environment and hold public authorities and private actors accountable.[24]

[17] See www.clientearth.org/.
[18] See www.clientearth.org/about/who-we-are/transparency/#offices.
[19] See www.clientearth.org/about/who-we-are/.
[20] James Thornton and Martin Goodman, *Client Earth* (London, Scribe, 2018) 24.
[21] ibid, 28.
[22] See above, n 19.
[23] See www.clientearth.org/about/who-we-are/our-team/experts/.
[24] For an example, see below the *ClientEarth v EIB* case (C-212/21 P).

With specific regard to *Plaumann*, since the opening of its Brussels office in 2008, the question of access to justice before the CJEU was proven to be crucial for ClientEarth.[25] As Thornton notes:

> The courts of the European Union have worked hard to deny citizens standing. They have dipped into logic that would make sense only to medieval theologians. The test for standing in the treaty is that you must have a direct and individual concern. This should be read broadly so as to allow citizens to test actions of the EU for legality. The way the EU courts interpret 'individual concern' is that it must be a unique concern.[26]

It was inevitable that ClientEarth's conception of environmental protection as a collective effort – which sees citizens and public authorities cooperating in the enforcement of environmental laws – would collide with the CJEU's narrow interpretation of the standing requirements laid down under the Treaties. In the light of this, in the next section I will now describe how ClientEarth – at the head of a coalition of ENGOs – triggered a key legal fight against *Plaumann* before the Aarhus Committee.

IV. ACCC/C/2008/32

In 2008, ClientEarth, along with a group of other ENGOs, submitted a Communication[27] to the Committee concerning compliance by the EU with the Aarhus Convention. In particular, the ENGO complained about the *Plaumann* test and the alleged incompatibility between the internal review procedure laid down under the AR and the Aarhus Convention.

With regard to the *Plaumann* test, the ACCC pointed out that Article 263(4) Treaty on the Functioning of the European Union (TFEU) – on which the EU judges have based their strict position on standing – is 'drafted in a way that could be interpreted so as to provide standing for qualified individuals and civil society organizations in a way that would meet the standard of Article 9(3) of the Convention'.[28]

In this regard, in their communication, the ENGOs argued that, to be individually concerned, according to the CJEU, 'the legal situation of the person must be affected because of a factual situation that differentiates him or her from all other persons'.[29] Thus, private citizens cannot be individually concerned if the decision or regulation takes effect by virtue of an objective legal or factual situation.[30] The

[25] See next section.
[26] Thornton and Goodman, n 20, 155.
[27] Communication ACCC/C/2008/30.
[28] Report of the Compliance Committee, findings and recommendations with regard to communication ACCC/C/2008/32 (Part I) concerning compliance by the European Union, 14 April 2011, § 86. Hereinafter 'Part I'.
[29] ibid.
[30] ibid.

consequences of applying the *Plaumann* test to environmental and health issues is that in effect no member of the public is ever able to challenge a decision or a regulation in such case before the CJEU.[31]

The ACCC thus concluded that 'without having to analyse further in detail all the cases referred to, it is clear to the Committee that this jurisprudence established by the [CJEU] is too strict to meet the criteria of the Convention'.[32]

With regard to the internal review procedure laid down under the AR, it is necessary to highlight that, at the time of the ACCC review, the *Stichting Natuur* case (presented in the previous chapter) was still pending before the CJEU. For this reason, the Committee refrained from examining whether the AR or any other relevant internal administrative review procedure of the EU met the Convention's requirements on access to justice.

Therefore, on 14 April 2011, the ACCC released only a first part of its findings and simply concluded with regard to access to justice by members of the public that:

> [if] the jurisprudence of the EU Courts, as evidenced by the cases examined, were to continue, unless fully compensated for by adequate administrative review procedures, the Party concerned would fail to comply with Article 9, paragraphs 3 and 4, of the Convention.[33]

Hence, in the first part of its findings, the ACCC – while waiting for a decision in *Stichting Natuur* – held back from observing a clear incompatibility between the *Plaumann* test and the Aarhus Convention.[34]

The second part of the ACCC findings was published almost a decade later, on 17 March 2017,[35] two years after *Stichting Natuur* was decided. The Committee found that Article 2(1)(g) AR, defining the concept of an 'administrative act' as 'any measure of individual scope adopted under environment law', was in breach of the obligations stemming from Article 9(3) of the Convention which covers 'any act under any law' which contravenes law relating to the environment.[36]

Plus, the Committee maintained that even the scope of the formulation 'acts adopted under environmental law' is too narrow, as Article 2(1)(f) AR intends 'environmental law' as including any EU legislation which, irrespective of its legal basis, contributes to the pursuit of the objectives of the EU policy on the environment as set out in Article 191 TFEU.[37] The definition laid down under

[31] ibid.
[32] ibid, § 87.
[33] ibid, § 94.
[34] ibid, § 86.
[35] Report of the Compliance Committee, findings and recommendations with regard to communication ACCC/C/2008/32 (Part II) concerning compliance by the European Union, 17 March 2017. Hereinafter 'Part II'.
[36] ibid, § 99.
[37] ibid, § 96.

Article 2(1)(f) AR thus seemed to require an act having a link with the goals of EU environmental policy. Conversely, the scope of Article 9(3) of the Convention – held the ACCC – is broader than that, since it is clear that, under the Aarhus Convention, 'an act may contravene laws relating to the environment without being adopted under environmental law' within the meaning of the AR.[38] Furthermore, the Committee found that the Treaty of Lisbon – amending the fourth paragraph of Article 263(4) TFEU – did not improve the conditions for access to justice at EU level of ENGOs.[39]

The ACCC's final assessment identified an instance of non-compliance with Article 9(3) and (4) of the Convention with regard to 'access to justice by members of the public because neither the [AR], nor the jurisprudence of the CJEU, implements or complies with the obligations arising under those paragraphs'.[40] In conclusion, the Committee recommended the EU to amend the AR and invited the CJEU to review its jurisprudence on Article 263(4) TFEU.[41]

The Committee's findings concerning EU compliance with the Convention confirm the intensity of the Committee's scrutiny. Indeed, in Communication ACCC/C/2008/32, the UN compliance body carried out a close review of the *Plaumann* jurisprudence, as well as of the case law dealing with the AR.[42] The interesting aspect is that – although non-judicial in its character – the Committee provided its own interpretation of EU law, in direct contradiction with what established by the jurisprudence of the EU judiciary.[43] This raises the crucial question as to whether the ACCC findings may still have an 'impact' despite their 'non-binding' nature.[44] However, this point will be addressed later in this chapter.

Having described how ENGOs used the ACCC to identify a broad incompatibility between EU law rules on access to justice and the Aarhus Convention, the next sections will shed light on the aftermath of the Aarhus Committee's findings and will emphasise the legal and political impact[45] that such findings have produced on the case law of the CJEU as well as on the EU decision-making. More specifically, the next section will show how the ACCC findings created the 'perception' of new legal opportunities for ENGOs under EU law.

[38] ibid, § 98.
[39] ibid, § 120.
[40] ibid, § 123.
[41] ibid; see also Matthijs van Wolferen and Mariolina Eliantonio, 'Access to Justice in Environmental Matters: The EU's Difficult Road Towards Non-Compliance With the Aarhus Convention' in M Peeters and M Eliantonio, *Research Handbook on EU Environmental Law* (Cheltenham, Edward Elgar, 2019).
[42] See chapters 1 and 3.
[43] ibid.
[44] On this point, see Jutta Brunnée and Stephen J Toope, 'An Interactional Theory of International Legal Obligation' in *Legitimacy and Legality in International Law: An Interactional Account* (Cambridge, CUP, 2010) 20–55. Brunnée and Toope hold that it is 'obligation that constitutes law's added value, not form, and that a sense of obligation will only arise when states and other actors perceive lawmaking to be legitimate' (55).
[45] See definition in the introduction to this book.

V. Mobilising against *Plaumann* in the 'Post-Aarhus (II)' Period

The opportunity to strategically 'use' the findings on EU compliance released by the ACCC in 2017 to mobilise the CJEU was soon seized by environmental organisations. Indeed, the first action for annulment brought by an ENGO under the AR after the ACCC findings is *Mellifera.*[46]

The factual background in *Mellifera* is very similar to the one in *Stichting Natuur.* 'Mellifera eV' is a German environmental association which aims at preserving bees' health. Mellifera seems not to count any lawyer among the members of its staff.[47] The association asked the Commission to review – under Article 10 AR – Implementing Regulation 2016/1056,[48] extending the approval period of the active substance glyphosate. The European executive rejected *Mellifera*'s request on the ground that such a measure did not constitute a challengeable EU administrative act as outlined in Article 2(1)(g) AR. As a consequence, in January 2017 the association decided to contest the legality of the Commission's decision rejecting its request before the EU GC.

Apart from the arguments advanced by the applicant to demonstrate that the contested measure was an administrative act having 'individual scope', what is extremely worth considering in *Mellifera* is the explicit invitation made to the Court to take into account the ACCC findings and modify the jurisprudence on the 'act of individual scope' requirement.[49] In addition, the association invited the EU judges to provide an interpretation of Article 10 AR which is consistent with the Aarhus Convention, in order to bring the EU closer to achieving full compliance with this international agreement.[50]

As showed in chapter three, in *Stichting Natuur* the GC proved to be more willing than the CJEU to review conformity of EU secondary law with the Aarhus Convention. In that case, the GC actually declared Article 10 AR incompatible with the Convention and it annulled the EU measures challenged by the applicants. However, such a 'progressive' interpretation of the AR was already abandoned by the GC in *Frank Bold*[51] in 2015, where it aligned its case law with the jurisprudence of the CJEU on Article 10 AR. Such consistency in the case law has been confirmed by the GC also in *Mellifera*, where, in spite of the applicant's invitation to take into account the ACCC findings, the Court dismissed the action brought by the association.

In this regard, the applicant in *Mellifera* recalled that the Aarhus Convention is binding on the EU and that Article 9(3) guarantees the broadest access to

[46] T-12/17, *Mellifera v Commission* (2018) ECLI:EU:T:2018:616.

[47] See www.mellifera.de/kontakt/.

[48] Commission Implementing Regulation (EU) 2016/1056 of 29 June 2016 amending Implementing Regulation (EU) No 540/2011 as regards the extension of the approval period of the active substance glyphosate (Text with EEA relevance) C/2016/4152 OJ L 173, 30 June 2016, 52–54.

[49] *Mellifera*, n 46, § 78.

[50] ibid, § 79.

[51] T-19/13, *Frank Bold v Commission* (2015) ECLI:EU:T:2015:520.

justice possible which is not limited to acts of 'individual scope'.[52] In addition, the applicant stressed that, in spite of the lack of direct effect of Article 9(3) of the Convention – strongly affirmed in *Stichting natuur* and *Slovak bear*[53] – the Court has a duty to interpret EU secondary law to be consistent with international agreements to which the EU is a party. This meant that, according to *Mellifera*, the Court had to interpret – where possible – Article 10 AR in a manner which is compatible with Article 9(3) of the Aarhus Convention.[54]

Nevertheless, the GC rejected all the applicant's arguments. First, it denied once again that Article 9(3) may have direct effect in the EU legal order.[55] Second, regarding the invitation to follow the ACCC findings, the EU judges answered that even assuming that such findings had binding force, these are nothing more than a 'draft', not officially adopted by the MOP and released on 17 March 2017, therefore after the contested Implementing Regulation had already been adopted by the Commission (in 2016).[56]

Regarding the duty of consistent interpretation with international agreements to which the EU is a Party, the Court held that this is possible only where the wording of the concerned legislation allows for such an interpretation and this does not lead to an interpretation *contra legem*.[57] On this point, the EU judges noted that, since the wording of the AR is very clear in limiting the types of challengeable measures to administrative acts having an 'individual scope', a consistent interpretation of such a regulation must be excluded, especially in the case at stake, since the Court had already qualified the contested implementing regulation 2016/1056 as a measure of 'general scope'.[58] For these reasons, the Court rejected all the pleas advanced by the association and dismissed its action.[59] The GC's decision was then upheld by the CJEU in 2020.[60]

Therefore, in *Mellifera*, the EU judiciary clearly refused to directly engage with the ACCC findings. The Court qualified the findings as a simple 'draft', lacking any binding character. In this respect, the 'impact' of such findings on the case law of the EU judiciary was essentially non-existent. However, as it will be highlighted for other cases here below, the ACCC findings were 'perceived' by ENGOs as creating a new legal opportunity, capable of increasing the CJEU's judicial receptivity in relation to the AR's compliance with the Aarhus Convention.

As a prelude, in the next section I will now turn to examine to what extent the ACCC's findings lack any binding character and what have legal scholars suggested on this specific aspect.

[52] *Mellifera*, n 46, § 78.
[53] See chapter 2.
[54] ibid, § 79.
[55] ibid, § 95.
[56] ibid, § 86.
[57] ibid, § 87. See also C-106/89, *Marleasing v Comercial Internacional de Alimentación* (1990) ECLI:EU:C:1990:395.
[58] ibid.
[59] ibid, § 88.
[60] C-784/18 P, *Mellifera v Commission* (2020) ECLI:EU:C:2020:630.

A. The Non-Binding Character of the ACCC's Findings

If we go back to the actual wording of Article 15 of the Convention, we notice that this provision actually makes clear that the compliance mechanism to be established by the MOP shall have a 'non-confrontational, non-judicial and consultative nature'. It therefore goes without saying that the Aarhus Committee may not be considered as a court or tribunal, but rather as a 'quasi-judicial' body, as it was not created to settle disputes.[61] For this reason, it is formally correct to point out that the ACCC decisions may not produce per se any legally binding effect.[62]

However, the relationship between the MOP and the Committee should also be taken into account. Indeed, the Committee has a 'functional' connection to the MOP and has only limited powers to proceed on its own initiative.[63] On this point, paragraph 13(b) of Annex to Decision I/7, states that the Committee has to '[prepare], at the request of the [MOP], a report on compliance with or implementation of the provisions of the Convention'.[64]

Furthermore, paragraph 35 of the same Annex establishes that the ACCC 'shall report on its activities at each ordinary [MOP] and make such recommendations as it considers appropriate'.[65] Conversely, paragraph 36 provides that '[pending] consideration by the [MOP], with a view to addressing compliance issues without delay, the Compliance Committee' may:

i) in consultation with the Party concerned, provide advice and facilitate assistance to individual Parties regarding the implementation of the Convention;[66]
ii) subject to agreement with the Party concerned,
   - make recommendations to the Party concerned;
   - request the Party concerned to submit a strategy, including a time schedule, to the Compliance Committee regarding the achievement of compliance with the Convention and to report on the implementation of this strategy;
   - in cases of communications from the public, make recommendations to the Party concerned on specific measures to address the matter raised by the member of the public.[67]

By reading these provisions, it seems clear that 'nothing the Committee does by itself may be legally binding'.[68] Nevertheless, some commentators have pointed out

[61] Elena Fasoli and Alistair McGlone, 'The Non-Compliance Mechanism Under the Aarhus Convention as 'Soft' Enforcement of International Environmental Law: Not So Soft After All!' (2018) 65 *Netherlands International Law Review* 35.
[62] ibid.
[63] ibid, 36.
[64] Annex to Decision I/7, § 13(b).
[65] ibid, § 35.
[66] ibid, § 36(a).
[67] ibid, § 36(b).
[68] Fasoli and McGlone, n 61, 36.

that when the findings and the recommendations of the ACCC are endorsed by the MOP, MOP decisions may produce legally binding effects.[69]

In particular, these scholars claim that the MOP's endorsement of the Committee's findings 'may constitute a subsequent agreement between the parties regarding the interpretation of the treaty or the application of its provisions' in accordance with Article 31(3)(a) of the Vienna Convention on the Law of Treaties (VCLT).[70] This provision states that, in the interpretation of a treaty, 'there shall be taken into account, together with the context: (a) any subsequent agreement between the parties regarding the interpretation of the treaty or the application of its provisions'. Consolidated legal scholarship seems to agree on the fact that, in order to find this 'agreement', there is no need for a further 'treaty' and such consensus may also take 'various forms', including being in the form of a 'decision'.[71]

As a consequence, by endorsing the findings of the Committee, the MOP 'may be agreeing on an authoritative interpretation of the Aarhus Convention and, as such, the decision may have legal effect'.[72] This seems to be a truly viable reading of the VCLT and – at first glance – even the case law of the EU's first instance court seems to confirm this interpretation. Indeed, as reported above, in *Mellifera*, the GC – when called upon to bring its case law in compliance with the ACCC findings – answered that even assuming that such findings had binding force, these are nothing more than a simple 'draft', not officially adopted by the MOP, as specified in the Aarhus Convention implementation guide.[73] By putting forward such an answer, the Court seemed to leave an open door for a different consideration of the Committee's findings if these had already been endorsed by the MOP.[74]

That said, it is important to bear in mind that the CJEU is very protective of the autonomy of the EU legal order and of its interpretative monopoly in relation to EU law.[75] Even if MOP Decisions are binding on the EU as a matter of public international law, the CJEU would consequently not consider itself to be bound by the ACCC's interpretation of EU law as opposed to the Convention itself. Hence, in so far as the Committee's findings are premised upon an interpretation of EU law with which the Court disagrees, it is unlikely to accept recommendations even when these have been endorsed by the MOP.

[69] ibid.

[70] Veit Koester, 'The Aarhus Convention Compliance Mechanism and Proceedings before Its Compliance Committee' in Charles Banner (ed), *The Aarhus Convention: A Guide for UK Lawyers* (Oxford, Hart Publishing, 2015) 201–16. See also Gor Samvel, 'Non-Judicial, Advisory, Yet Impactful? The Aarhus Convention Compliance Committee as a Gateway to Environmental Justice' (2020) 9(2) *Transnational Environmental Law* 211–38.

[71] Anthony Aust, *Modern Treaty Law and Practice*, 2nd edn (Cambridge, Cambridge University Press, 2007) 213.

[72] Fasoli and McGlone, n 61, 39.

[73] T-12/17, *Mellifera v Commission* [2018] ECLI:EU:T:2018:616, § 86.

[74] This endorsement was received in 2021 at the 7th session of the Aarhus MOP, see Decision VII/8f concerning compliance by the European Union with its obligations under the Convention, 3.

[75] See, inter alia, Marcus Klamert, 'The Autonomy of the EU (and of EU Law): Through the Kaleidoscope' (2017) 42 (6) *EL Rev* 7; case Opinion 2/13, accession of the EU to the ECHR – Compatibility of the draft agreement with the EU and FEU Treaties (2014) ECLI:EU:C:2014:2454.

This being said, despite the Court's 'judicial unresponsiveness', along with the non-binding character of the ACCC findings, some scholars argue that these may still produce significant impact on the legal systems of the Parties to the Aarhus Convention. My research confirms this conclusion. Indeed, as it will be shown in relation to the EU, the Committee's intervention has de facto unlocked the EU decision-making and made sure this proceeded on the right track. The next section will briefly outline the existing scholarship on the (general) capacity of the ACCC to trigger legislative change *beyond* the binding character of its findings and recommendations.

B. The Impact of the ACCC Findings

It is by no means straightforward to 'measure' the impact of the Aarhus Committee's 'case law'. Interesting work in this regard has been produced by Gor Samvel, who carried out a qualitative and quantitative impact evaluation of the Compliance Committee's jurisprudence on Article 9 of the Convention.[76] Samvel defined the Committee's quantitative impact as being the positive difference between the number of recommendations issued and the number of recommendations complied with.[77] Conversely, Samvel's qualitative analysis is based on existing literature on access to environmental justice, which is 'indicative of an emerging and consistent practice of access to justice across the UNECE region'.[78]

The conclusions reached by Samvel are extremely interesting. He stressed the 'soft law' character of the Committee's acts and 'resized' their impact on the basis of empirical evidence. On this point, he maintained that 'it is still too early to declare the internalization of the access to justice provisions by the parties to the Convention'. This since

> despite the more recent claims that portray the Committee as a more judicialized institution and its rulings as binding, … the role of normative characteristics of the Committee and its rulings should not be exaggerated in the process of ensuring compliance by parties with their obligations under the Aarhus Convention.[79]

Samvel also argued that, in the end, the findings of the Aarhus Committee face challenges which are similar to those faced by other jurisdictions and compliance bodies in international law. Specifically, the author referred to the traditional 'lack of enforcement' of judgments and decisions adopted under international law. With regard to the jurisprudence of the ECtHR for instance, the 11th Annual Report of the Committee of Ministers of the Council of Europe stated that, 'as of 2017,

[76] Samvel, n 70.
[77] ibid, 218. 'Respectively, a four-degree index is applied for the impact evaluation: (i) no impact/compliance; (ii) minor impact/compliance; (iii) partial impact/compliance; and (iv) full impact/compliance.'
[78] ibid, 226.
[79] ibid, 235.

nearly half of the judgments rendered by the ECtHR since its inception 60 years ago' remain unenforced.[80] This highlights a common (and long-standing) trend in international human rights law,[81] which may well be extended to the impact of the Aarhus Committee's work.

Despite the importance of assessing the legal impact of the ACCC's recommendations and MOP decisions, the Aarhus Committee has certainly played a relevant role which has favoured ENGOs with regard to access to justice before the CJEU. Indeed, the action of the UN compliance body significantly contributed, on the one hand, to stimulating ENGOs' legal mobilisation efforts *vis-à-vis* the EU judiciary; on the other hand, to putting 'pressure' on the EU institutions, pressure that ultimately led to the amendment of the AR, as will be shown in the following sections.

VI. The Impact of the ACCC's Findings on EU Decision-Making

A few months after the UN Committee released its findings in March 2017, ENGOs took part in informal meetings at the EU Council along with the Commission and strongly criticised the latter.[82] This was because in its draft decision VI/8f on compliance by the EU, the Commission submitted to the Council a version suggesting that the MOP should not 'endorse' the Committee's findings, but simply 'take note' of them.[83] After the Council's approval, this position was then officially presented at the sixth session of the MOP, which took place in Budva (Montenegro) on 11–13 September 2017.

On this occasion, the position of the EU was vigorously contested by representatives of the ENGOs (in particular by ClientEarth) and some of the other Parties to the Convention, namely Georgia, Norway, Switzerland and Ukraine.[84]

[80] ibid, 233.

[81] On this point, see Diana Panke, 'The European Court of Human Rights Under Scrutiny: Explaining Variation in Non-Compliance Judgments' (2020) 18 *Comparative European Politics* 151–70; Alastair Mowbray, 'Faltering Steps on the Path to Reform of the Strasbourg Enforcement System' (2007) 7(3) *Human Rights Law Review* 609–18; Élisabeth Lambert Abdelgawad, 'The Enforcement of ECtHR Judgments' in András Jakab and Dimitry Kochenov (eds), *The Enforcement of EU Law and Values: Ensuring Member States' Compliance* (Oxford, Oxford University Press, 2017).

[82] Bluebook traineeship at DG ENV (Unit E2), from 1 March 2017 to 31 July 2017 (hereinafter 'Bluebook').

[83] European Parliament, 'Implementing the Aarhus Convention – Access to justice in environmental matters', briefing, October 2017. Available at: www.europarl.europa.eu/RegData/etudes/BRIE/2017/608753/EPRS_BRI(2017)608753_EN.pdf.

[84] Inter alia, Georgia and Switzerland. From Meeting of the Parties to the Convention on Access to Information, Public Participation in Decision-making and Access to Justice in Environmental Matters, Sixth session, Budva, Montenegro, 11–13 September 2017 – Report of the sixth session of the Meeting of the Parties, 13. Available at: www.unece.org/fileadmin/DAM/env/pp/mop6/English/ECE_MP.PP_2017_2_E.pdf.

Because of these strong protests, the MOP – 'considering the exceptional circumstances' (consisting, more specifically, of the impossibility to reach consensus on the adoption of Decision VI/8f) – decided to 'postpone the decision-making on draft Decision VI/8f concerning the EU to the next ordinary session of the [MOP] to be held in 2021'.[85] On the other side, the EU recalled its 'willingness to continue exploring ways and means to comply with the Convention in a way that is compatible with the fundamental principles of the Union legal order and with its system of judicial review'.[86]

Such a final outcome of the sixth session of the MOP was – once again – highly criticised by CSOs, which accused the EU of 'hypocrisy' and invited the latter, without delay, to start the process of 'revising the [AR] which up to now, in combination with the jurisprudence of the [CJEU], has effectively prevented NGOs from seeking access to justice in defence of the environment at the EU level in all but access to documents cases'.[87]

As mentioned above, the ACCC findings have produced significant 'indirect effects' on the EU institutions and the EU decision-making. Here below I will summarise how the Committee's findings have been received by the European Parliament (hereinafter 'the EP'), the Council of the EU (hereinafter 'the Council') and the European Economic and Social Committee (hereinafter 'the EESC'), which have all taken clear positions with regard to EU compliance with the Aarhus Convention.

First, the EP on 15 November 2017 adopted a resolution on an 'Action Plan for nature, people and the economy'.[88] In this document the EP emphasised 'the role of civil society in ensuring better implementation of Union nature protection legislation, and the importance of the provisions of the AC in this regard'.[89] In addition, and most importantly, the European co-legislator called on the Commission to:

> come forward with a new legislative proposal on minimum standards for access to judicial review, and a revision of the Aarhus Regulation implementing the Convention as regards Union action in order to take account of the recent recommendation from the Aarhus Convention Compliance Committee.[90]

[85] See www.ukhumanrightsblog.com/2017/09/23/the-biter-bit-eu-does-not-like-being-criticised-by-aarhus-body.

[86] Full Summary of the Budva Meetings – Sixth Session of the Meeting of the Parties to the Aarhus Convention. Available at: www.unece.org/environmental-policy/conventions/public-participation/aarhus-convention/tfwg/envppmop/envppmop6mopp3highlights/full-summary-of-budva-meetings.html.

[87] European Eco Forum statement on the role of the European Union in relation to the finding that it is in non-compliance with the Aarhus Convention, Budva, Montenegro, Thursday 14 September 2017. See www.wecf.eu/download/2017/09-September/EuropeanECOForumStatementNon-ComplianceEU.pdf.

[88] European Parliament resolution of 15 November 2017 on an Action Plan for nature, people and the economy (2017/2819(RSP)).

[89] ibid, § 15.

[90] ibid, § 16.

Second, the EESC – in its opinion[91] adopted on 7 December 2017 on the Commission's notice on access to justice in environmental matters[92] – highlighted the limitations inherent in that notice in 'failing to include the findings of the independent Compliance Committee of the Aarhus Convention (ACCC)'.[93]

Furthermore, the EESC expressed its full support for 'the Aarhus Convention and its full implementation by and within the EU' and added '[it] is therefore essential that the findings on compliance of the ACCC, appointed by the Parties, are fully endorsed by the Parties'.[94]

Third, with respect to this matter, the Council decided on 11 June 2018 to trigger the procedure under Article 241 TFEU, which has rarely been used in the EU legal history. This Treaty provision allows the Council, acting by a simple majority, to:

> request the Commission to undertake any studies the Council considers desirable for the attainment of the common objectives, and to submit to it any appropriate proposals. If the Commission does not submit a proposal, it shall inform the Council of the reasons.[95]

In its decision triggering the procedure, the Council took into serious consideration the ACCC findings. In this regard, I want to stress that, at this point, in June 2018, the MOP had still not endorsed the Aarhus Committee's findings on EU compliance. This while, a few months later (in September 2018) the GC, in dismissing the action of *Mellifera*, stated that these findings were 'only a draft'.[96] In spite of this, the Council still decided to explicitly refer to such findings in its decision and to ask the Commission – under Article 241 TFEU – to complete, by 30 September 2019, a study to 'explore ways and means to comply with the Aarhus Convention in a way that is compatible with the fundamental principles of the Union legal order and with its system of judicial review'.[97] Furthermore, the Council stated that, if changes to the AR are considered appropriate in view of the outcomes of the study, the Commission should prepare a proposal for an amendment of the regulation by 30 September 2020.[98]

Therefore, the decision of the Council – explicitly referring to the ACCC findings – essentially triggered the process which led to the revision of the AR. This by obliging the Commission to, first, present a study on EU compliance with the

[91] EESC opinion on Communication from the Commission of 28 April 2017 'Commission Notice on Access to Justice in Environmental Matters' [C(2017) 2616 final].

[92] Commission Notice on access to justice in environmental matters, C/2017/2616, OJ C 275, 18 August 2017, pp 1–39.

[93] EESC opinion, n 91, § 1.12.

[94] ibid, § 1.13.

[95] Council decision requesting the Commission to submit a study on the Union's options for addressing the findings of the Aarhus Convention Compliance Committee in case ACCC/C/2008/32 and, if appropriate in view of the outcomes of the study, a proposal for a Regulation of the European Parliament and of the Council amending Regulation (EC) No 1367/2006.

[96] See above, section V.

[97] ibid, 7.

[98] ibid, Art 1.

Aarhus Convention; then, eventually submit a proposal for amending the AR. The next sections will address these two key steps taken by the European Commission after the European Council's decision to trigger Article 241 TFEU, which have then led to the final amendment of the AR. The goal is to show (i) the content of the public debate generated by ENGOs' legal mobilisation activities before the CJEU and the ACCC; (ii) the concrete 'achievements' obtained by ENGOs via legislative action. Indeed, I will now turn to describe (i) the outcome of the study outsourced by the European Commission exploring 'ways and means' to bring the EU in compliance with the Aarhus Convention; (ii) the key amendments introduced in the 'new' AR.

A. The Commission's Study and Report

This section will highlight how the legal mobilisation efforts of environmental organisations have opened broader opportunities for public participation in the EU environmental decision making.

After the Council asked the Commission to complete its study on ways and means to comply with the Convention by the end of September 2019, the Commission published a roadmap to 'evaluate the current situation and assess options to address compliance, to underpin possible decision-making'.[99] In spring 2018, the roadmap was opened for external feedback and received 53 comments in total, mostly from environmental organisations and citizens.

Figure 4 Categories of respondents to the 2019 Commission roadmap

Total of valid feedback instances received: 53

The number of feedback instances shown includes only the valid ones, respecting the feedback rules. The data is regularly updated.

By category of respondent

- Non-governmental organisation (NGO): 24 (45.28%)
- EU citizen: 12 (22.64%)
- Environmental organisation: 8 (15.09%)
- Company/business organisation: 5 (9.43%)
- Business association: 2 (3.77%)
- Other: 1 (1.89%)
- Academic/research Institution: 1 (1.89%)

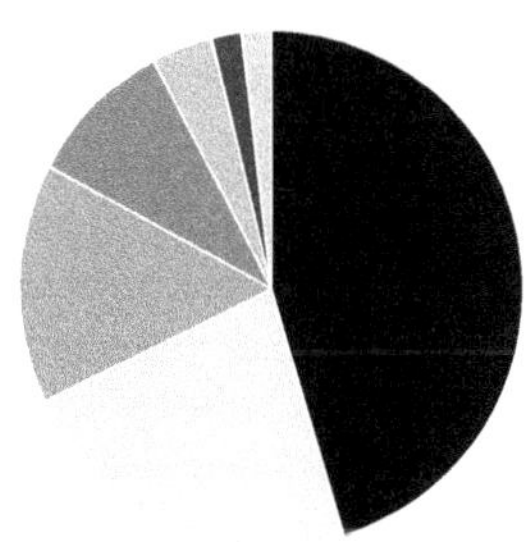

Source: https://ec.europa.eu/info/law/better-regulation.

[99] Commission roadmap on 'EU implementation of the Aarhus Convention in the area of access to justice in environmental matters', Inception impact assessment – Ares(2018)2432060, available at: https://ec.europa.eu/info/law/better-regulation/have-your-say/initiatives/1743-EU-implementation-of-the-Aarhus-Convention-in-the-area-of-access-to-justice-in-environmental-matters_en.

Outside the realm of litigation, this was a further opportunity for environmental organisations to make the EU executive aware of their views and opinions on access to environmental justice before EU courts. The solution mostly referred to by ENGOs in the consultation on the Commission's roadmap, was the amendment of the AR. Indeed, according to many organisations, the definition of 'administrative act'[100] had to be modified as to also include administrative acts of 'general scope'.

On this specific point, ClientEarth stressed that:

> amendment of the [AR] is the only mean available to the EU legislature to bring the EU into compliance with its international law obligations. … Over the last years, the CJEU has further consolidated its case law in claims brought by NGOs, thereby clarifying that members of the public have no standing under Article 263 TFEU to challenge acts and omissions of EU institutions that are not addressed directly to them. The Aarhus Regulation is the only remaining avenue for the public but it remains unduly restrictive in its current form.
>
> … The situation is therefore clear: (1) The EU is a party to the Aarhus Convention in its own right; it therefore constitutes an integral part of the EU legal order. (2) The EU is in non-compliance with the Convention and therefore violates international law and primary EU law. (3) Based on one of the fundamental principles of the international legal order (article 27 of the Vienna Convention of the Law of Treaties), the EU cannot avoid performing its obligations by invoking its internal law. (4) The only option open to the Commission to remedy this violation of international law is to propose an amendment of the Aarhus Regulation.[101]

In addition, PAN, GPEU and WWF Italy put forward very similar lines of reasoning with regard to the AR. The Czech Frank Bold Society further criticised the solution advanced by the Commission and the CJEU to address the 'access to justice conundrum' (ie by enhancing the use of the PRP on validity) and held that 'rather than being "already complete" as stated in the Roadmap, the EU system of remedies suffers from considerable shortcomings. The preliminary reference system under Article 267 TFEU does not meet the requirements of Article 9(3) of the Convention.'[102]

Nevertheless, different stakeholders took also part in the consultation by submitting feedback showing the 'other side of the coin'. For example, the *Federation of Austrian Industries*, highlighted that:

> [a] recent study by the Institute of Industrial Science on the consequences of Aarhus judgements by the European Court of Justice shows that 86% of the companies surveyed expect significant legal uncertainty. Equally it should be contestable to carry over proceedings, as this could lead to a huge lack of investment. Therefore, the Federation of Austrian Industry warns against a super derogatory transposition, as such would be in contradiction to the principle of proportionality and Art. 173 TFEU. The EU

[100] See chapter 3.

[101] ClientEarth feedback to the European Commission's public consultation on the 'EU implementation of the Aarhus Convention in the area of access to justice in environmental matters' roadmap, 8 May 2018–5 June 2018 (hereinafter '2018 roadmap PC'). Available at: https://ec.europa.eu/info/law/better-regulation/have-your-say/initiatives/1743-EU-implementation-of-the-Aarhus-Convention-in-the-area-of-access-to-justice-in-environmental-matters_en.

[102] Frank Bold Society feedback to the 2018 roadmap PC.

> should not disproportionately transpose (gold plate) guidelines specified by the Aarhus Convention. The existing consultation should cover the scope of the Aarhus Convention, which covers environmental law, such as in Article 9(3) of the Aarhus Convention.[103]

The Commission's public consultation held in spring 2018 was thus a first opportunity to gather diverse views on access to justice before the CJEU in environmental matters. However, it was with the publication of the study on EU implementation of the Aarhus Convention that the necessity to amend the AR emerged more clearly. The study provided 'an assessment of the relevant aspects of the current application of access to justice in environmental matters governed by EU law at EU level and the national courts'.[104] It was conducted by an external contractor, namely *Milieu Consulting*, an independent private sector consultancy based in Brussels which specialises – inter alia – in EU environmental regulation.[105]

The study commissioned by the EU executive provided (inter alia): a detailed analysis of the current redress mechanisms available in EU law and of the challenges by reference to typology of acts and Commission services; an overview of experiences to date with judicial review under Articles 263(4), 267 and 277 TFEU as well as of decisions on requests for internal review under the AR. Furthermore, as mentioned in the above section, the study provided an overview of the stakeholder perspectives on the legal issues therein described.

Figure 5 General overview of the current redress mechanisms in environmental matters

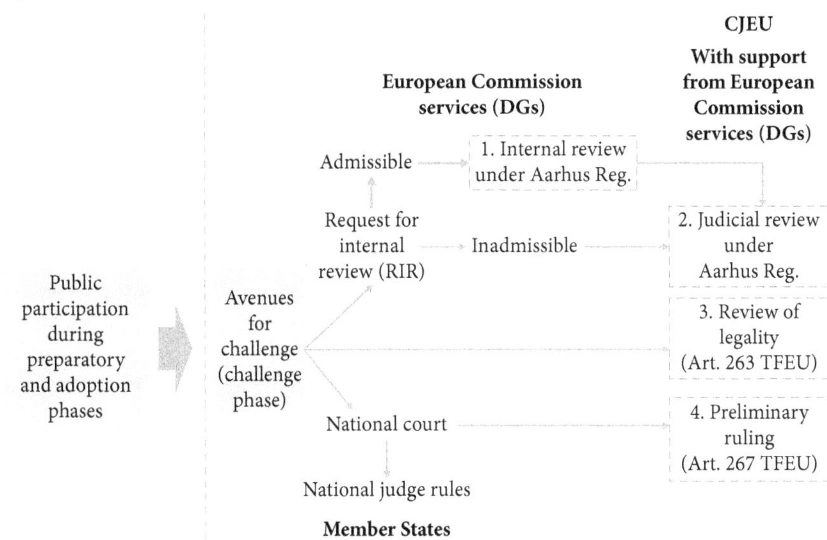

Source: Final study of the European Commission on EU implementation of the Aarhus Convention in the area of access to justice in environmental matters.

[103] Federation of Austrian Industries feedback to the 2018 roadmap PC.
[104] Final study on EU implementation of the Aarhus Convention in the area of access to justice in environmental matters (carried out by 'Milieu'). Available at: https://ec.europa.eu/environment/aarhus/pdf/Final_study_EU_implemention_environmental_matters_2019.pdf.
[105] See www.milieu.be/company-overview/what-we-stand-for/.

With regard to the general overview on the current redress mechanisms, the study essentially confirmed the major barriers to access to justice at EU level already described in chapters one and three.[106] Conversely, with regard to the stakeholder perspectives, the study gathered the opinions of those who took part in the open public consultation (OPC), opinions which are worth briefly outlining here below.

With regard to access to justice under Article 263(4) TFEU, many citizens and ENGOs obviously criticised the Court's rigidity on *Plaumann*. This is how the study summarised some of these views:

> Questions were [also] raised about the compatibility of Article 263(4) TFEU with Article 9 of the Aarhus Convention and Article 47 of the European Charter on Fundamental Rights, suggesting that Article 263(4) TFEU does not guarantee the right to access to justice when it should, and that the public interest is deprived of protection as a result.[107]

On a similar note, industry stakeholders reported their own difficulties in obtaining standing.[108] They also shared the difficulty of meeting the direct and individual concern requirements under the first limb of Article 263(4) where an act is not directly addressed to them.[109]

In addition, the same stakeholders pointed to a number of cases where the CJEU dismissed actions brought by business associations because they were considered 'representatives of a category of operators and not individually concerned by a measure affecting the general interests of that category'.[110]

Because of these obstacles in challenging EU acts of general application, the study highlighted that corporations and trade associations (much like ENGOs) believed that the only plausible option to actually subject those acts to judicial review is to trigger proceedings at national level.[111] In order to do so, private applicants shall contest MSs' measures implementing EU law and ask the local court to refer the question to the CJEU for a preliminary ruling.[112]

In this respect, the jurisprudence of the CJEU has certainly facilitated access to justice at national level in environmental matters for members of the public.[113] Nevertheless, the EU executive itself acknowledged that 'environmental NGOs and individuals can still face significant hurdles in using national courts, thereby limiting possible recourse to validity references under Article 267 TFEU to challenge EU-level acts'.[114]

[106] Final study, n 104, 65–71.
[107] ibid, 74.
[108] ibid, 77.
[109] ibid.
[110] ibid.
[111] ibid.
[112] ibid.
[113] Commission notice, n 92. See also chapter 2.
[114] Commission Report published on EU implementation of the Aarhus Convention in the area of access to justice in environmental matters, 28. Available at: https://ec.europa.eu/environment/aarhus/

Finally, the study of the Commission presented a number of possible non-legislative and legislative measures to remedy the EU non-compliance with the Aarhus Convention.[115] The non-legislative measures consisted of raising awareness with regard to use of the AR and the PRP on validity; whilst, the legislative measures referred to the amendment of the AR 'to enlarge the category of acts that can be made subject to administrative review and extending the time-frames governing review applications and handling'.[116]

After the publication of a second roadmap, followed by another public consultation,[117] the Commission presented a formal proposal for amending the AR in October 2020.[118] The proposal explicitly mentioned the ACCC findings on EU compliance and the EU institutional response to the latter.[119] This is crucial from a legal mobilisation perspective to show, once again, the impact on the EU decision-making of ENGOs' litigation before the ACCC.

The proposal went through the legislative process in a relatively short time and was officially approved one year later, in October 2021.[120] The next chapter will deepen such novelties and offer a first assessment of their potential for legal mobilisation in Europe. Nonetheless, before delving into the analysis of the 'new' Aarhus Regulation, I believe it is worth digging into the case law of the CJEU on the 'old' Aarhus internal review mechanism, to show the unexplored potential offered by the latter even before its amendment in 2021. In this regard, below I will analyse and provide a critical appraisal of the key *ClientEarth v EIB* case.

VII. The *ClientEarth v EIB* Case

The case law of the CJEU on the use of the internal review mechanism showed the unexplored potential for legal mobilisation that even the old version of the AR

pdf/Commission_report_2019.pdf. These hurdles in the use of the preliminary reference mechanism will be deepened in the following chapter.

[115] ibid, 29.

[116] ibid.

[117] Roadmap published on access to justice in environmental law, outlining the Commission's plans to work towards a proposal for a revised Aarhus Regulation, as well as an accompanying Communication. Ref. Ares(2020)1406501–06/03/2020. Available at: https://ec.europa.eu/info/law/better-regulation/have-your-say/initiatives/12165-Access-to-Justice-in-Environmental-matters.

[118] Proposal for a Regulation of the European Parliament and of the Council on amending Regulation (EC) n. 1367/2006 of the European Parliament and of the Council of 6 September 2006 on the application of the provisions of the Aarhus Convention on Access to Information, Public Participation in Decision-making and Access to Justice in Environmental Matters to Community institutions and bodies, COM/2020/642 final, 2–3.

[119] ibid.

[120] Regulation (EU) 2021/1767 of the European Parliament and of the Council of 6 October 2021 amending Regulation (EC) No 1367/2006 on the application of the provisions of the Aarhus Convention on Access to Information, Public Participation in Decision-making and Access to Justice in Environmental Matters to Community institutions and bodies PE/63/2021/REV/1 OJ L 356, 8 October 2021, 1–7.

could offer. Indeed, in 2018 – before the amendment to the AR – ClientEarth relied on the internal review mechanism outside the regulatory context on substances and/or emissions where this mechanism was usually triggered. More specifically, the ENGO sought a review of the Resolution of the European Investment Bank (EIB)'s Board of Directors of 12 April 2018, by which the Board approved for €60 million for the financing of a biomass power generation plant in Galicia (Northern Spain).[121] The ENGO's lawyers considered that 'the loan breaches the bank's financing criteria for responsible investment in renewable energy generation and that numerous errors were made in the assessment of financing for the project'.[122] In October 2018, the EIB rejected ClientEarth's request for internal review, claiming that the act at stake did not constitute an 'administrative act' within the scope of the AR. As a consequence, the ENGO decided to challenge the EIB's denial before the GC.[123]

In this case, the Court had to deal with two main arguments raised by the EIB in its reply to ClientEarth's request: (i) that the EIB's decision did not have any legally binding external effects; (ii) that the same decision had not been taken 'under environmental law', as required under Article 2(1)(g) AR. On the contrary, the ENGO claimed that the original contested decision had to be considered as an 'administrative act' within the scope of the AR, and that the EIB – by not adequately explaining why it did not consider the original contested act an 'administrative act' – had breached the obligation to give adequate reasons, laid down under Article 296 TFEU.[124]

In relation to this last point, the EIB maintained that the Resolution at stake was a purely internal act, which was 'required for the signature of the corresponding finance contract, but which did not necessarily lead to the contract being signed, or create any right for the counterparty to demand that it be signed'.[125] In its answer, the Court made a clear distinction between the *procedural* and *substantive* value of the duty to state reasons. Indeed, the EU judiciary found that – from a purely procedural point of view – the explanation provided by the EIB as to why ClientEarth's request had to be rejected, was sufficient to put the ENGO in the conditions to contest the merit of the Bank's rejection.[126]

Therefore, the Court passed to examine the first plea put forward by the applicant, namely that by rejecting the request for internal review, the EIB wrongly

[121] See www.clientearth.org/clientearth-takes-eib-to-court-over-failure-to-review-financing/.

[122] ibid.

[123] T-9/19, *ClientEarth v EIB* (2021) ECLI:EU:T:2021:42.

[124] ibid, § 77.

[125] ibid, § 59; Art 296 TFEU (1)(2): 'Where the Treaties do not specify the type of act to be adopted, the institutions shall select it on a case-by-case basis, in compliance with the applicable procedures and with the principle of proportionality. Legal acts shall state the reasons on which they are based and shall refer to any proposals, initiatives, recommendations, requests or opinions required by the Treaties.'

[126] ibid, § 102.

interpreted Article 2(1)(g) AR, thereby making a clear error of assessment.[127] The GC started its assessment on this point by considering whether the contested Resolution had been taken 'under environmental law'. The Court recalled that the notion of an 'administrative act' laid down in the AR must be interpreted very broadly.[128] Indeed, the possibility to contest EU administrative acts cannot be limited to measures adopted on the basis of Article 191 TFEU, as this would run against the objective of providing the public concerned with 'wide access to justice' in environmental matters, as enshrined under the AR.[129] The GC thus held that Article 2(1)(g) AR should be interpreted as covering 'any measure of individual scope subject to requirements under secondary EU law which, regardless of their legal basis, are directly aimed at achieving the objectives of EU policy on the environment'.[130]

The GC then stressed that the financing Resolution approved by the EIB's Board of Directors aimed at providing funding for a project concerning the production of renewable energy and contributing to the 'security of energy supply and the achievement of environmental objectives'.[131] Furthermore, the project also contributed to 'the prevention of forest fires and to the sustainability of forestry in the Galicia region'.[132] In light of this, the EU judiciary concluded that the original Resolution contributed to the achievement of the objectives pursued by EU environmental policy and could thus be considered as adopted under environmental law.[133]

The GC turned to a different point, assessing whether the Resolution at issue had any 'legally binding external effect'. The European Bank claimed that the measure was merely a 'mandatory stage in the EIB's internal decision-making process', and was neither capable of creating 'any obligation for the EIB to grant the land to the special purpose vehicle for the … project' nor of 'confer[ring] any right on the promoter of the project or alter its legal position'.[134]

In addressing this argument, the GC adopted a *substantive* rather than a *formal* approach in accordance with the established case law of the CJEU.[135] According to this, even acts that *formally* do not seem to produce any legally binding external effect *vis-à-vis* third parties can still be deemed de facto to produce such effects.[136] In order to assess whether this was the case for the contested Resolution, the Court carried out a meticulous examination of the *substance* of the measure at issue and

[127] ibid, § 105.
[128] ibid, § 120.
[129] ibid, § 126.
[130] ibid.
[131] ibid, § 129.
[132] ibid.
[133] ibid, § 138.
[134] ibid, § 146.
[135] C-163/06 P, Finland v Commission (2007) ECLI:EU:C:2007:371.
[136] ibid.

the relevant 'context' in which this was adopted.[137] The Court ultimately found that:

> even if the resolution at issue was not, as the EIB maintains …, a legal commitment to grant the loan to the special purpose vehicle, in so far as other technical, economic and financial aspects of the project were still to be appraised, it nevertheless produced certain definitive legally binding effects [*vis-à-vis*] third parties, in particular as regards the promoter of that project, in that it stated the eligibility of that project for EIB financing with regard to its environmental and social aspects, thus enabling the promoter to take the next steps needed to formalise the loan.[138]

Thus, the EU judiciary found that the Resolution did produce certain legally binding external effects and that, as a consequence, the measure at stake could be considered an 'administrative act' within the scope of Article 2(1)(g) AR. This led the GC, first,[139] and the CJEU, then,[140] to annul the contested decision by which the EIB had rejected ClientEarth's request for internal review.

A. Comment on the *ClientEarth v EIB* Case

The *ClientEarth v EIB* case shows how ENGOs have been resorting to the AR as a tool to broaden access to justice before the EU judiciary but also for holding EU bodies accountable in relation to the EUs climate change goals.[141] This judgment demonstrates how CSOs could have mobilised EU law under the pre-amendment AR by targeting acts which did not, on the face of it, have binding character or constitute part of EU environmental law. By persuading the EU judiciary to adopt an expansive definition of the concept of an administrative act, ClientEarth started down a new road of seeking to expand the type and range of measures that could be subject to internal review. While the GC clarified that the expression 'under environmental law' can include any measure which aims directly to achieve the EU's environmental policy objectives, the EU legislator amended the AR precisely in the direction indicated by the EU judicature.[142] The same was done in relation to the removal of the word 'binding' from the new definition of 'administrative act'.[143] The case under discussion here shows that, despite the clear constraints established under the old AR, ClientEarth's lawyers saw a new potential in the pre-amendment internal review mechanism. As it will be shown in the next chapter,

[137] T-9/19, *ClientEarth v EIB*, n 123.

[138] ibid, § 170.

[139] ibid, § 173.

[140] C-212/21 P, *EIB v ClientEarth* (2023) ECLI:EU:C:2023:546.

[141] Interestingly, this case was initiated when the 'individual scope' requirement was still laid down in the original AR, but surprisingly this was not an issue in the lawsuit. The 'individual scope' of the financing resolution at stake was clearly evident, as this was intended to provide funding for one specific biomass power generation plant to be located in the north of Spain.

[142] See chapter 5.

[143] ibid.

the 2021 amendment creates new legal opportunities for environmental organisations to challenge EU environmental measures. In the next section, I will now set out my conclusions on the analysis embedded in the present chapter.

VIII. Conclusions

This chapter focused on European ENGOs' capacity to 'shape' legal opportunities under international and EU law and their strategic use in relation to access to justice before the CJEU. Indeed, the communications submitted by ENGOs to the compliance mechanism established under the Aarhus Convention constitute an additional mobilisation pathway to keep 'shaping' legal opportunities under EU law. However, ENGOs have also contributed to shaping the Aarhus Committee itself. Since the negotiations of the Convention, CSOs strongly advocated for the introduction of a compliance mechanism, which was concretely established in Geneva a few years later, in 2001. The ACCC today seeks to guarantee that the legislation of the Parties to the Convention is in compliance with the provisions laid down in the Convention itself. In 2008, the EU was brought before the Aarhus Committee by a coalition of ENGOs led by ClientEarth, which asked the UN compliance body to check whether certain provisions of EU law were compatible with the Convention. The review carried out by the Committee was not finalised until nine years later (in 2017) and found major non-compliance by the EU with the Convention, particularly as far as the *Plaumann* test and the internal review procedure established under the AR were concerned. The findings and recommendations on EU compliance triggered, once again, the question of whether such findings may have any legally binding force. Some scholars have argued that the Committee's findings may acquire binding character once these are endorsed by the MOP, in accordance with Article 31(3)(a) of the VCLT. Nevertheless, in 2017 in Budva (Montenegro) the MOP failed to reach consensus and the discussion on the decision on compliance by the EU was postponed until the next ordinary session of the MOP in 2021, when the MOP did ultimately endorse the Committee's findings on EU compliance.[144]

In terms of binding character and impact of the Committee's findings, legal scholarship demonstrated that the ACCC's faces challenges which are similar to those faced by other jurisdictions and compliance bodies in international law, namely the traditional 'lack of enforcement' of judgments and decisions adopted under international law. However, at least in the EU countries which are also Parties to the Convention, the enforcement of the latter is facilitated by the infringement procedures of the European Commission as well as by the judicial review of national legislation which is carried out both by the CJEU and national courts. In particular, the EU judiciary has produced a vast case law aiming to bring the

[144] See above, n 74.

legislation of the MSs into compliance with the Aarhus Convention.[145] This case law has also been collected by the Commission in 2017 in a 'Communication' aiming to provide local courts with guidance when dealing with matters falling under the scope of the Convention.[146] With specific regard to EU compliance, the ACCC's findings have been crucial in unlocking the EU decision-making process. Indeed, beside their marginal legal impact on the case law of the CJEU (eg *Mellifera*) the ACCC findings on EU compliance undoubtedly produced other remarkable indirect effects and led to the adoption of concrete measures by the EU institutions. In June 2018 the Council exceptionally triggered the procedure established under Article 241 TFEU and asked the Commission to carry out a study on the Union's options for addressing the findings of the Aarhus Committee and 'explore ways and means to comply with the Aarhus Convention in a way that is compatible with the fundamental principles of the Union legal order and with its system of judicial review'.[147] The Council added that, if changes to the AR are considered appropriate in view of the outcomes of the study, the Commission should prepare a proposal for an amendment of the regulation by 30 September 2020.[148] The decision of a few ENGOs to bring the EU before the Aarhus Committee has therefore de facto forced the EU institutions to take action on the matter. Because of the Council's decision to trigger Article 241 TFEU, the Commission issued a first roadmap in 2018 and launched a public consultation, which provided citizens and ENGOs with a further opportunity for mobilising the European Commission in relation to direct access to justice in environmental matters. The consultation collected a broad variety of critical voices and concerns, which contributed to feed the Commission's study published in October 2019, along with a report acknowledging the well-known inconsistencies between EU law and the Aarhus Convention. The study laid down five options for the EU to comply with the Convention, the most feasible being the amendment of the AR. In this regard, in October 2020 the Commission presented a formal proposal for amending the AR, explicitly mentioning the ACCC findings on EU compliance. The Commission's proposal and the new AR will be analysed more deeply in the next chapter.

However, the present chapter also intended to show how, even under the old text of the AR, ENGOs have managed to obtain favourable rulings, rewarding their legal mobilisation efforts. As shown here above, in *ClientEarth v EIB*, the ENGO resorted to the internal review procedure outside the traditional regulatory framework on substances and/or emissions in which the procedure is usually triggered. This with the intention of holding EU financial bodies accountable for environmental protection. The 'substantive' approach taken by the EU judiciary in relation to the legal effects produced by the contested act vis-à-vis third parties,

[145] See chapter 2.
[146] Commission notice, n 92.
[147] See above, n 95.
[148] ibid.

could – even under the pre-amendment AR – already be considered as a relevant 'building block' for future mobilisation. This proves the key value of legal expertise and legal imagination in legal mobilisation, capable of 'unlocking' legal opportunities even where there seems to be a clear closure in the LOS. Legal expertise, combined with the deployment of effective non-legal strategies – as will be shown in the next chapter – can lead to crucial legislative change. Indeed, the 'binding' requirement included in the old version of the AR has now been removed, in line with the ACCC's demands and the CJEU case law, leaving wider space to ENGOs for challenging EU administrative acts.[149]

[149] See the next chapter.

5

The New Aarhus Regulation

I. Introduction

In the present chapter, I will first describe how environmental non-governmental organisations (ENGOs) combined legal and non-legal strategies in order to shape the new Aarhus Regulation (AR) and show the role played by the Aarhus Convention Compliance Committee (ACCC) in this intricated legal mobilisation process. Then, I will move to examine the main amendments introduced in the AR, which have entered into force since October 2021. These amendments are crucial to (i) identify the main achievements of the environmental movement in this legal mobilisation journey under the Aarhus Convention; (ii) show how ENGOs keep 'shaping' the legal opportunities available under EU law by combining legal and non-legal strategies of mobilisation; (iii) provide a preliminary assessment of the new legal opportunities available under EU law. The amendments reported here mainly refer to (i) the new definition of 'administrative act' laid down under Article 2(g)(1) AR; (ii) the possibility for 'other' members of the public to submit a request for internal review; (iii) the broader timeframe acknowledged to complainants and EU administrative bodies dealing with requests for internal review.

After the analysis of the key changes that occurred in the new AR, I will, first, provide my own assessment of what this reform entails for EU legal mobilisation in the environmental context; then, I will outline the assessment of the Aarhus amendment given by some of the leading European ENGOs and set out my concluding remarks.

II. Shaping the New Aarhus Regulation

A few months after the entry into force of the new AR, ENGOs started to 'test' the amended version of the Regulation, in order to check its potential for present and future legal mobilisation. At the moment of the entry into force of the amended regulation, the overall assessment of the new AR given by leading European environmental organisations was positive, as they considered the new rules introduced in 2021 as a relevant 'step forward' on the road that brings the EU into compliance with the Aarhus Convention.[1]

[1] For ClientEarth, see www.clientearth.org/latest/press-office/press/eu-pulls-down-barriers-for-public-to-challenge-environmental-wrongdoing-in-court/; interview with Harriet Mackaill-Hill, former EU

A crucial role in this regard was played – once again – by the ACCC, which, at the request of the Meeting of Parties (MOP), took steps to monitor the EU's progress in complying with the Convention, in a procedure where the Commission as well as the relevant ENGOs were all involved.[2] After an exchange of feedback on the Commission's proposal for amending the AR,[3] the ACCC provided its own assessment of the proposal and advised the Union to:

- Ensure that access to review procedures to challenge acts and omissions by institutions and bodies of the European Union which contravene EU law relating to the environment is provided not only to NGOs, but also to other members of the public, even if subject to certain criteria in accordance with the Convention;[4]
- Remove the word 'binding' from the proposed amendment so the relevant wording would state 'has legal and external effects' only;[5]
- Amend the proposed exception from the scope of review of those provisions of an act for which Union law explicitly requires implementing measures at Member State level so that such provisions are indeed immediately open to review (the Committee does not expect administrative review under the Aarhus Regulation to cover the implementing measures taken by Member States).[6]

It is interesting to note that three out of three of the ACCC's recommendations were actually followed in the final text of the AR.[7] Indeed, the word 'binding' was removed from the definition of administrative act, which now should 'only' produce 'legal and external effects'. This since – as it will be argued below – even acts that *formally* would not have any 'binding character' could still de facto be able to produce legal effects and 'bind' third parties.[8]

Furthermore, as anticipated, even the 'entailing implementing measures' requirement was removed from the final text of the AR, since this would have impeded review of numerous regulatory acts which do require implementing measures at EU and national level.[9]

Finally, the EU also ultimately followed the ACCC's suggestion to broaden the internal review procedure so as to include requests submitted by individuals

Climate Governance and Human Rights Policy Coordinator at CAN Europe, 21 January 2022; interview with Csaba Kiss, in-house lawyer at Justice & Environment, 11 January 2022.

[2] Advice by the Aarhus Convention Compliance Committee to the European Union concerning the implementation of request ACCC/M/2017/3, § 53. Available at: https://unece.org/sites/default/files/2021-02/M3_EU_advice_12.02.2021.pdf.

[3] ibid, § 7 ss.

[4] ibid, § 71(a).

[5] ibid, § 71(b).

[6] ibid, § 71(c).

[7] It is also interesting to highlight that the ACCC's critiques mirrored to a large extent those put forward earlier by ClientEarth. On this point, see Anne Friel, 'The Aarhus Regulation Amendment: Cause for cautious celebration', 6 November 2020. Available at: www.clientearth.org/projects/access-to-justice-for-a-greener-europe/updates/the-aarhus-regulation-amendment-cause-for-cautious-celebration/.

[8] See below, section IV.A.

[9] Advice by the Aarhus Convention Compliance Committee, n 2, § 64.

and other members of the public. Initially, the Commission was against the introduction of this change. Indeed, in its report presenting the amendment proposal, the EU executive explained this choice by mainly specifying that (i) 'opening up administrative review to all individuals would amount to a situation similar to that described by the [ACCC] as *actio popularis*, which is not required under the Convention';[10] (ii) even the Aarhus Convention 'recognises that NGOs should enjoy privileged access to justice as compared to individuals', since 'NGOs are often best positioned to effectively represent public interest and civil society concerns in this area with professional, well-founded and substantiated argumentation'.[11] Things changed precisely once the European Parliament had the opportunity to intervene on the text of the proposal.[12] Indeed, the EU Parliament's intervention also contained 'amendments providing standing rights for individuals'.[13]

The final provision included in the new AR is not entirely satisfactory for environmental organisations, since requests for internal review submitted by individuals or groups of individuals now require ENGO or lawyer representation. An 'unnecessary restriction on the right of access to justice', constituting an 'additional costs barrier, particularly in the absence of any kind of legal aid scheme at EU level', wrote Alison Hough from the Environmental Justice Network Ireland.[14]

Apart from this, there are mainly two other aspects of the Aarhus amendment which have left European ENGOs dissatisfied. The first one is the explicit exclusion of State Aid decisions from the scope of the Regulation, which cannot thus be internally reviewed by the European Commission.[15] Thanks to the contribution of the ACCC, important developments are expected in this regard, showing once again the key role of ENGOs in shaping new legal opportunities by mobilising EU institutions and international quasi-judicial bodies.[16] Indeed, in 2025 the European Commission launched a public consultation on the 'draft amendments to State aid Implementing Regulation and State aid Best Practices Code as regards access to justice in environmental matters' aiming to bring EU State aid rules in

[10] Proposal for a Regulation of the European Parliament and of the Council on amending Regulation (EC) n. 1367/2006 of the European Parliament and of the Council of 6 September 2006 on the application of the provisions of the Aarhus Convention on Access to Information, Public Participation in Decision-making and Access to Justice in Environmental Matters to Community institutions and bodies, COM/2020/642 final, 7. Hereinafter 'Commission proposal'.

[11] ibid.

[12] Alison Hough, 'Analysis of the Revised Proposal to Amend the Aarhus Regulation', (2021) EJNI Access to Justice Observatory, Final Report, 3. Available at: https://ejni.net/resources/access-to-justice-observatory-old/.

[13] ibid.

[14] ibid, 4.

[15] Art 2(2)(a) AR.

[16] On this point, see findings and recommendations with regard to communication ACCC/C/2015/128 concerning compliance by the European Union Adopted by the Compliance Committee on 17 March 2021.

compliance with the Aarhus Convention.[17] At the time of writing,[18] the public consultation has just been closed and the decision-making process will now move forward. However, it is important to stress that, without the additional input of the ACCC, this ongoing reform would have not been conceived. Empowering civil society to also challenge administrative acts in the domain of State aid is deemed crucial by environmental organisations, as State Aid measures can have major consequences for the environment (eg state subsidies to fossil fuel industries).[19]

The second aspect triggering ENGOs' disappointment following the AR reform – which will be discussed more in depth here below – is the impossibility to subject to judicial review the original administrative act for which internal review was sought before the competent EU administrative body.[20]

More generally, it is important to underline the key role played by the Aarhus Committee. Indeed, the recommendations put forward by the ACCC show the crucial role of this UN body in 'shaping' the EU framework on access to justice in environmental matters. Although non-binding, ENGOs use the ACCC's findings and recommendations in litigation before the Court of Justice of the European Union (CJEU)[21] and advocacy before the EU institutions.[22] This is in order to obtain broader access to justice before the EU judiciary, which would enable them to have wider possibilities for contesting the legality of EU measures having a negative impact on the environment. On the crucial role played by the ACCC, Anne Friel, in-house lawyer at ClientEarth clearly stated:

> We worked very very hard on that for sure [on the amendment of the AR], but I think what was also very helpful was the advice of the ACCC. That advice was really clear as to what the EU needed to change. And, for example, the Parliament really engaged with that, there was a real push among the big political groups. They all agreed that bringing the EU into compliance with international law was the most important thing and they worked very constructively together. It was a difficult process but they managed to find some sort of solution and I think that that [ie the support of the Parliament] put a lot of pressure on the Council. When one institution is saying very clearly 'this is what's needed to comply' there is a moral obligation to do that. That was very powerful on the Council I think.[23]

From Anne Friel's words, it is possible to infer that the fact that the ACCC's intervention was met with agreement by the European Parliament bolstered the

[17] European Commission, Consultation on the draft amendments to State aid Implementing Regulation and State aid Best Practices Code as regards access to justice in environmental matters. Available at: https://competition-policy.ec.europa.eu/public-consultations/2025-state-aid-environmental-matters_en.

[18] 23 March 2025.

[19] *EEB, ClientEarth* and *Justice & Environment*, 'Letter to Environmental Ministers regarding the Commission's proposal on the Aarhus Regulation', 19 November 2020. Available at: https://eeb.org/library/letter-to-environmental-ministers-regarding-the-commissions-proposal-on-the-aarhus-convention/.

[20] See below, section IV.

[21] See, for instance, the *Mellifera* case (analysis in chapter 4).

[22] Interview with Anne Friel, Lawyer at Environmental Democracy at *ClientEarth* (Brussels office), 19 July 2021.

[23] ibid.

legal mobilisation efforts of the ENGOs.[24] The ACCC created an opportunity for ENGOs to be 'taken seriously' by the EU institutions, but the political receptivity of the latter allowed for the proposal to move forward on a specific track. Obviously, the ENGOs' mobilisation efforts alone could have not achieved what they were striving for: the Parliament, first, and the Council, then, did the rest.

The Aarhus Committee thus served not only – in Galanter's terms – as a 'catalyst', allowing ENGOs to have a stronger bargaining power *vis-à-vis* the EU institutions, but also as an external monitoring body, supervising the EU decision-making process. Indeed, its preliminary assessment of the EU proposal for amending the AR was crucial in serving to orient the text toward a more Aarhus-compliant (and ENGO-friendly) direction. In this respect, the role played by the ACCC is all the more relevant if we consider, as reported in the first part of this chapter, that the proposal for creating a compliance committee under the Aarhus Convention came from the coalition of ENGOs which attended the Aarhus negotiations in the 1990s. Needless to say that environmental organisations have also played a key role at a later time, by mobilising the ACCC through their communications.

It is thus possible to affirm that, in the 1990s, ENGOs strongly mobilised to create a further mobilisation pathway outside the EU legal order, that is the possibility to submit communications to the ACCC. A pathway offering additional legal opportunities under international law (ie the Aarhus Convention). Then, they strategically used this pathway for their own legal mobilisation initiatives, at national and EU level, with the intention to – inter alia – overcome *Plaumann*, broaden access to justice before national courts and the CJEU and expand the range of challengeable acts having an impact on the environment.

Having concluded my analysis of how ENGOs mobilised against *Plaumann* through the ACCC, and achieved the significant amendment of the AR, in the next section I will outline how the AR was concretely amended.

III. The New Definition of 'Administrative Act'[25]

The amendment of the AR, the solution mostly referred to by ENGOs in the public consultation to fill the gap between the lack of access to justice before the EU judiciary and the Aarhus Convention, entered into force in October 2021. In this section, I will now describe the main amendments introduced in the AR, starting probably from the most relevant one, that is the new definition of 'administrative act' under the Regulation. Below are the old and new version of such definition, laid down under Article 2(g)(1) AR.

[24] This is also confirmed by Hough, n 12.

[25] A version of this description of the novelties introduced with the reform of the Aarhus Regulation has been previously published in Mario Pagano, 'Climate Legal Mobilization Under the New Aarhus Regulation' (2024) 25 (6) *German Law Journal* 919–34.

> Old version: 'administrative act' means 'any measure of individual scope under environmental law, taken by a Community institution or body, and having legally binding and external effects'.
>
> New version: 'administrative act' means 'any non-legislative act adopted by a Union institution or body, which has legal and external effects and contains provisions that may contravene environmental law within the meaning of point (f) of Article 2(1)'.

In light of the new definition, the 'administrative acts' which can now be contested through the internal review procedure established under the AR, are 'regulatory acts', namely non-legislative acts of general application. This amendment can significantly influence ENGOs' legal mobilisation strategies, as will be discussed later in this chapter.[26]

Furthermore, under the 'old' version of the AR, 'administrative acts' were non-legislative acts adopted 'under' environmental law, which seemed to imply – as stressed by the ACCC in its findings[27] – 'having Article 191 TFEU as a legal basis'.[28] On the contrary, the new definition specifies that the administrative acts and omissions covered by the internal review mechanism are those that 'contravene provisions of environmental law', regardless of their legal basis. Another important novelty for the environmental movement, which is expected to broaden legal mobilisation against EU regulatory acts having an impact on the environment.

Even the word 'binding' has been removed from the definition of administrative act, which now are required 'only' to produce 'legal and external effects'. This is since even acts that *formally* would not have any 'binding character' could still de facto be able to produce legal effects and 'bind' third parties.[29] The removal of the word 'binding' should thus encourage the adoption of a more *substantive* hermeneutic approach (*i.e.* based on the content rather than the pure form of the act) by the EU judiciary.[30]

Another key aspect which is worth stressing is the lack of any reference to the presence of implementing measures. Indeed, even the current text of Article 2(1)(g) AR does not make any reference to implementing measures, suggesting that even regulatory acts entailing implementing measures (at national or EU level) can be subject to an internal review by the competent EU administrative body or institution. In this regard, it is worth reminding that the original proposal presented by the European Commission explicitly excluded from the scope of the internal

[26] See below, section IV.

[27] Report of the Compliance Committee, findings and recommendations with regard to communication ACCC/C/2008/32 (Part II) concerning compliance by the European Union, 17 March 2017, § 100. Hereinafter 'Part II'.

[28] In fact, the EU judiciary already clarified this aspect in *Testbiotech* II (T-33/16) where a GMO authorisation adopted on the basis of Regulation No 1829/2003 was contested through the internal review procedure. Despite the Regulation being adopted on the basis of Arts 43, 114 and 168(4)(b) TFEU, the GC found that the contested EU administrative act still contributed to pursue the objectives of EU environmental policy enshrined under Art 191 TFEU.

[29] See below, section IV.A.

[30] Advice by the ACCC, n 2.

review those provisions of an administrative act 'for which Union law explicitly requires implementing measures at Union or national level'.[31] As mentioned above, this point was heavily contested by ENGOs,[32] which knew that this amendment would have further constrained their legal opportunities under EU law, so they strongly advocated during the decision-making process and succeeded in having that specific part of the proposal removed from the text of the Regulation.[33] This point is significant from a legal mobilisation perspective, as it shows how leading European environmental organisations, like ClientEarth, EEB and CAN Europe, keep 'shaping' the legal opportunities available under EU law by not settling for litigation, but by rather combining the latter with other advocacy tools, in order to make their overall mobilisation tactic more effective.

The final outcome is that the internal review mechanism under the AR can now be sought for regulatory acts entailing (or not entailing) implementing measures *and* contravening provisions of environmental law. On the contrary, regulatory acts contravening provisions *other* than environmental law can be challenged only under Article 263(4) Treaty on the Functioning of the European Union (TFEU) and only if such acts do not entail implementing measures.[34] In the next section I will outline the other main novelties introduced in the AR.

A. Other Main Amendments

Crucial novelties have also been introduced in relation to the subjects who can present a request for internal review to the relevant EU administrative bodies. Indeed, under the new Article 11(a) a request for internal review can now be presented not only by ENGOs, but also by 'other' members of the public, subject to certain conditions.[35] Individuals can now submit a request by showing the impairment of a right caused by the alleged contravention of EU environmental law by the relevant EU administrative body and that they are directly affected by such contravention in comparison to the public at large.[36] Moreover, even a group of individuals demonstrating 'sufficient public interest' can now submit a request for internal review, which must be supported by at least 4000 members of the public residing or established in at least five Member States (MSs), with

[31] Commission proposal, n 10, 16.

[32] EEB, ClientEarth and Justice & Environment, n 19.

[33] Interview with Harriet Mackaill-Hill, EU Climate Governance and Human Rights Policy Coordinator at CAN Europe, 21 January 2022.

[34] See below section IV.

[35] Regulation (EU) 2021/1767 of the European Parliament and of the Council of 6 October 2021 amending Regulation (EC) No 1367/2006 on the application of the provisions of the Aarhus Convention on Access to Information, Public Participation in Decision-making and Access to Justice in Environmental Matters to Community institutions and bodies PE/63/2021/REV/1 OJ L 356, 8 October 2021, pp 1–7, Art 1(3).

[36] ibid.

at least 250 members of the public coming from each of those MSs.[37] However, in both scenarios, the members of the public shall be represented by an NGO or by a lawyer authorised to practise before a court of a MS.[38] The new AR further requires that that NGO or lawyer 'shall cooperate with the Union institution or body concerned' in order to establish that the quantitative conditions mentioned above are met, where applicable, and shall provide further evidence thereof upon request.[39]

Finally, the new text of the AR also presents a different timeframe for submitting requests for internal review under Article 10, which has now been extended from six to eight weeks (same in case of an alleged omission).[40] More time is also for EU administrative bodies to give their answer, namely from the 'old' 12 to the 'new' 16 weeks after the expiry of the aforementioned eight weeks deadline, and in no case beyond 22 weeks from that same deadline.[41] In this regard, the new timeframe(s) should favour both, ENGOs seeking the internal review of EU administrative acts, as well as EU administrative authorities called upon to respond.

Having outlined the main novelties introduced in the AR, it is now time to reflect on how the internal review procedure laid down under the new AR should be coordinated with actions for annulment brought under the last limb of Article 263(4) TFEU from a legal mobilisation perspective. In other words, how should ENGOs mobilise against EU regulatory acts after the amendment of the AR? Considering that the goal put forward by the Commission was to amend the AR in a way that is also consistent with the changes to the TFEU brought by the Lisbon Treaty, what remedies would be available against a regulatory act falling under the AR, in one case, and a regulatory act falling outside the scope of the AR, in a second case? In the next section, I will discuss these different mobilisation scenarios.

IV. Contesting EU Regulatory Acts: Where Do We Go?

As mentioned above, the 'administrative acts' which can now be contested through the internal review procedure established under the AR are 'regulatory acts', namely non-legislative acts of general application, which could also be challenged via Article 263(4) TFEU. This provided that the administrative/regulatory acts contested under the AR satisfy also the other conditions laid down under Article 2(1)(g) AR. More specifically, the new 'administrative act' is a non-legislative act of general application (i) producing legal effects; (ii) adopted under no matter which legal basis; (iii) contravening provisions of environmental law.[42]

[37] ibid.
[38] ibid.
[39] ibid. For an 'ENGO assessment' of this amendment, see above section II.
[40] Art 10 AR (amended version).
[41] ibid.
[42] See above, section II.

In this regard, I believe that in order to fully understand the relevance of this amendment and its implications for legal mobilisation in the environmental context it is necessary to underline how Article 263(4) TFEU was amended by the Lisbon Treaty. Indeed, the last limb of Article 263(4) TFEU now allows any natural or legal person to institute proceedings 'against a regulatory act which is of direct concern to them and does not entail implementing measures'. This is the result of the Lisbon Treaty which entered into force in 2009. The goal of this 'new' limb was to soften the conditions allowing for access to justice of private applicants before the EU judiciary, as challenges against regulatory acts do not require natural and legal persons to prove that they are actually 'individually concerned' by the contested EU measure.[43]

Nevertheless, de facto, not much has changed for private applicants seeking access to justice in Luxembourg under the last limb of Article 263(4) TFEU. This is because most of the applicants either struggle to satisfy the 'direct concern' criterion[44] or they are encouraged by the Commission to challenge national implementing measures at national level, making domestic courts the relevant *fora* for (indirectly) contesting the validity of EU acts.

This being said, when it comes to clarifying what a 'regulatory act' actually is under EU law, it is necessary to recall that in the *Inuit* judgment the CJEU stated that the concept of a 'regulatory act' includes an 'act of general application other than a legislative act'.[45] This definition contains a substantive and a procedural dimension.[46] The former dimension refers to the actual content of the act, which has to be of 'general application', meaning that it has to apply to 'objectively determined situations' and entail 'legal effects for categories of persons regarded generally and in the abstract'.[47] The procedural dimension refers to the non-legislative nature of the measure, meaning that 'regulatory acts' shall not have been adopted by following ordinary or special legislative procedure.[48]

[43] Erica Szyszczak, 'Article 263(4) TFEU and the Impossibility of Challenging Recovery Decisions in State Aid: Annotation on the Judgments of the General Court of 15 September 2016 in T-219/13 Pietro Ferracci v European Commission and T-220/13 Scuola Elementare Maria Montessori v European Commission' (2016) 15(4) European *State Aid Law Quarterly* 638.

[44] The EU judiciary defines the 'direct concern' requirement as follows: '[the] "direct concern" condition requires that the contested measure must directly affect the legal situation of the individual and that it must leave no discretion to the addressees of the measure, who are entrusted with the task of implementing it, such implementation being purely automatic and resulting solely from the contested rules without the application of other intermediate rules. The same applies where the possibility for addressees not to give effect to the EU measure is purely theoretical and their intention to act in conformity with it is not in doubt.' (T-849/16, *PGNiG Supply & Trading v Commission* (2017) ECLI:EU:T:2017:924, § 4).

[45] C-583/11 P, *Inuit Tapiriit Kanatami and Others v European Parliament and Council of the European Union* (2013) ECLI:EU:C:2013:625, § 60.

[46] Alexander Kornezov, 'Shaping the New Architecture of the EU System of Judicial Remedies: Comment on Inuit' (2014) 39(2) *European Law Review* 5.

[47] Case C-171/00 P, *Alain Libéros v Commission* (2002) ECLI:EU:C:2002:17, § 28.

[48] Korzenov, n 46.

The scope of the last limb of Article 263(4) TFEU was further clarified by the CJEU in *Montessori*.[49] Here the Court was called upon to rule in an action for annulment challenging a Commission's decision dealing with State Aid to non-commercial entities in Italy.[50] In this case, the EU executive argued that there were 'non-legislative acts of general application' which fell outside the scope of 'regulatory acts' as spelt out in Article 263(4). The Court countered this argument by agreeing with AG Wathelet, who pointed out that consistency among the different limbs of Article 263(4) should be preserved.[51] In other words, if an act is deemed to be of 'general application' under certain criteria under the first two limbs of the Treaty provision, why should those criteria be different under the third limb of the same provision?

As a consequence, EU measures are considered as being of 'general application' if they apply to 'objectively determined situations' and entail 'legal effects for categories of persons regarded generally and in the abstract' (as mentioned above), these criteria should be respected also as far as regulatory acts are concerned.[52] The EU judiciary thus gave a very broad interpretation of 'regulatory acts', basically referring to 'any non-legislative act of general application'. The new AR is based on this same reasoning.

This being said, what kind of consequences can this amendment have on EU legal mobilisation? My reading of the new AR leads me to draw the following two key conclusions, both stemming from the new definition of 'administrative act'. First, the new definition has already led to a crucial shift in environmental legal mobilisation in Europe.[53] If under the 'old' AR requests for internal review were usually rejected on admissibility grounds, as these often aimed at challenging EU administrative acts of *general* scope, while the old internal review mechanism was limited to administrative acts of *individual* scope, internal review requests brought under the new AR will not face this same issue. Indeed, current internal review requests are actually targeting not only administrative acts of general applications, but also – indirectly – broader policy arrangements, often having the form of legislative acts.[54] The real hurdle for ENGOs is now on the 'substance' of the policy measure. The new AR is expected to finally deliver a more substantive review of EU administrative acts, which – under the old AR – have rarely been reviewed on the merits, including an appraisal of the scientific underpinnings of EU environmental and climate policy. In this regard, under the new AR, ENGOs and EU institutions are expected to agree or disagree on technical evaluations and scientific assessments, on which environmental policy measures are usually based. The Commission

[49] C-622/16 P, *Scuola Elementare Maria Montessori v Commission* (2018) ECLI:EU:C:2018:873.
[50] ibid, § 11.
[51] ibid, § 32.
[52] ibid.
[53] See Pagano, n 25.
[54] ibid.

and the other EU institutions must provide answers on such grounds, along with comprehensive justifications to their policy choices to the requests they receive from civil society.[55] Seen through such lenses, in my opinion the AR reform – even after only a few years – has already brought two key positive elements to the table: a more constructive democratic debate over the adoption of EU environmental administrative acts, as well as more transparency over the EU decision making in a number of crucial EU policy areas, such as agriculture, energy, environmental protection and climate change.[56] Only time and future scholarship on the subject will tell us if this more democratic and transparent internal review will also increase the quality of the EU decision making on the environment and the success of ENGOs' legal mobilisation efforts.

The second key conclusion on the potential for legal mobilisation offered under the new AR relates to the necessary distinction that now must be made between, on the one hand, regulatory acts contravening provisions of EU environmental law and, on the other hand, regulatory acts contravening other provisions of non-environmental EU law. Regulatory acts in the first scenario would fall within the scope of the AR. Therefore, before initiating an action for annulment under the relevant Treaty provisions, members of the public may seek internal review of the regulatory act at stake and then contest any denial before the EU Courts. Conversely, regulatory acts in the second scenario would fall outside the scope of the AR. As a consequence, in order to challenge these regulatory acts, members of the public will only be able to trigger legal proceedings under the last limb of Article 263(4) TFEU, bearing in mind that they have to be directly concerned by the contested EU measure. The illustration here below will attempt to provide a brief recap of the mobilisation pathways available for ENGOs.

Figure 6 Remedies available (at EU level) against EU regulatory acts

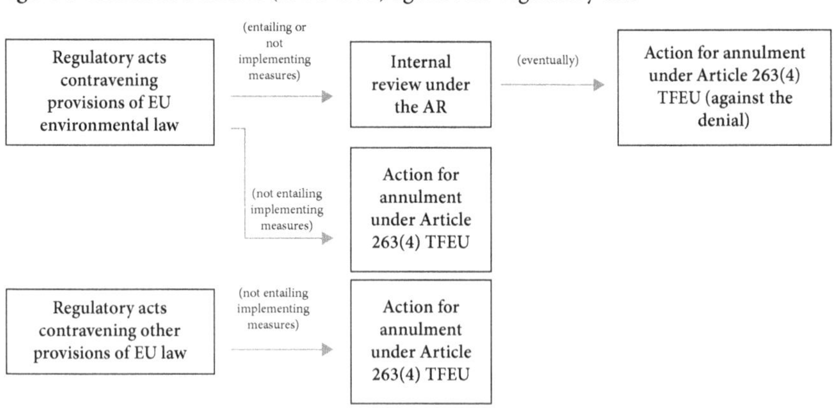

[55] See https://environment.ec.europa.eu/law-and-governance/aarhus/requests-internal-review_en.
[56] On this point, see Pagano, n 25.

Therefore, in the environmental domain there would be an additional remedy against EU regulatory acts, a remedy that is not available in other legal areas, namely the internal review procedure laid down under the AR. However, the two 'types' of actions for annulment should not be considered as equally effective for the following reasons. Actions for annulment falling within the first scenario (that is only once a request for internal review has already been rejected) are not brought against the original administrative/regulatory act, but rather against the subsequent decision by which the relevant EU administrative body or institution rejects the request of the public.[57]

This implies that the Court may not review any procedural or substantive aspect of the original EU measure which was supposed to be subject to the internal review. Indeed, the EU judiciary may only review the procedural and substantive aspects[58] of the decision rejecting the request and eventually require the relevant EU body to carry the internal review that was denied.

On the opposite side, in actions for annulment challenging the original regulatory act, the Court is able to review procedural and substantive aspects of the actual contested act. The EU judiciary has the power to annul the original contested act, without having to require any other EU body or institution to further review the contested measure.[59] This being said, the strategic choice of the 'most effective' remedy shall also take into account: (i) the standing requirements established under the Treaty; (ii) whether the regulatory act at stake entails implementing measures.[60]

In relation to the first point, under Article 263(4) TFEU ENGOs are still required to be directly concerned by the contested EU regulatory act, while this requirement is not required under Article 10 of the AR.

This basically presents potential applicants with a difficult choice between 'softer standing conditions', on the one hand, and the 'effectiveness of the remedy', on the other. Indeed, potential applicants seeking justice against a regulatory act breaching EU environmental law provisions face softer conditions for seeking an internal review. Nevertheless, such conditions are 'counterbalanced' by the impossibility to contest the original act before the Court. On the other hand, the harder

[57] Interview to Andrea Carta, Senior Legal Strategist at Greenpeace EU (25 February 2020); Anais Berthier, Senior Lawyer/Juriste, Head of Environmental Democracy/EU Litigation Specialist at ClientEarth, presentation during the virtual conference on 'access to justice in environmental matters: obstacles, impacts and ways forward', 15–16 October 2020, panel on 'Strategic litigation to make the green transition happen'. Available at: https://app.livestorm.co/clientearth/clientearth-virtual-conference-session-1-strategic-litigation-to-make-the-green-transition-happen?utm_source=Livestorm+company+page.

[58] Always within the limits established by the jurisprudence of the CJEU.

[59] Art 263(1) TFEU: 'The Court of Justice of the European Union shall review the legality of legislative acts, of acts of the Council, of the Commission and of the European Central Bank, other than recommendations and opinions, and of acts of the European Parliament and of the European Council intended to produce legal effects vis-à-vis third parties. It shall also review the legality of acts of bodies, offices or agencies of the Union intended to produce legal effects vis-à-vis third parties.'

[60] See also chapter 2.

conditions to be met in order to be granted access to justice under the last limb of Article 263(4) TFEU are 'counterbalanced' by the more intense judicial review that the Court may apply on the contested regulatory act. In the next section, I will analyse a case showing how ENGOs, already in 2017, mobilised the CJEU in order to close the gap between the two procedures and obtain a substantive review of the original administrative act also in actions for annulment brought under Article 12 of the AR.

A. The *ClientEarth v Commission* Case

The point relating to the difficulty of challenging the initial EU act once administrative internal review has already been sought, was precisely addressed by the GC in a case brought by ClientEarth in 2017 against the European Commission.[61] The ruling was then upheld by the CJEU in 2021.[62] This case shed some light on whether ENGOs may contest before the EU judiciary not only the decision by which the EU administrative body rejects a request for internal review, but also the initial administrative act allegedly breaching provisions of EU environmental law.

In 2016, ClientEarth requested the Commission to carry out an internal review of a decision authorising the use of bis(2-ethylhexyl) phthalate (DEHP) under the REACH Regulation.[63] Following the Commission's rejection of the ENGO's request, ClientEarth challenged the legality of the Commission's negative answer along with the initial authorisation issued under the REACH. In this regard, the EU executive claimed that the initial authorisation was not the subject matter of the case and that the applicant lacked standing under the last limb of Article 263(4) TFEU.[64]

To this claim, ClientEarth responded that 'it was not directly challenging the authorisation decision as it did not regard itself as having the necessary standing to bring an action based on Article 263 TFEU directed against that decision'.[65] However, 'the logical consequence of annulment of the decision on the request for internal review is that the authorisation decision must itself also be annulled'.[66] The organisation also argued that Article 266(1) TFEU[67] provided the EU judiciary

[61] T-108/17, *ClientEarth v Commission* (2019) ECLI:EU:T:2019:215.

[62] C-458/19 P, *ClientEarth v Commission* (2021) ECLI:EU:C:2021:802.

[63] Regulation (EC) No 1907/2006 of the European Parliament and of the Council of 18 December 2006 concerning the Registration, Evaluation, Authorisation and Restriction of Chemicals (REACH), establishing a European Chemicals Agency, amending Directive 1999/45/EC and repealing Council Regulation (EEC) No 793/93 and Commission Regulation (EC) No 1488/94 as well as Council Directive 76/769/EEC and Commission Directives 91/155/EEC, 93/67/EEC, 93/105/EC and 2000/21/EC (Text with EEA relevance).

[64] *ClientEarth v Commission*, n 62, § 25.

[65] ibid, §§ 26–27.

[66] ibid.

[67] Art 266(1) TFEU: 'The institution whose act has been declared void or whose failure to act has been declared contrary to the Treaties shall be required to take the necessary measures to comply with the judgment of the Court of Justice of the European Union.'

with the power to require, 'as a measure necessary to give effect to the judgment in the present proceedings, that the Commission "revoke"[68] the authorisation decision'.[69] In other words, the plaintiff argued that, as a consequence of the annulment of the Commission's denial to carry out the internal review of the initial administrative act, the Court had the power to require the Commission – by virtue of Article 266(1) TFEU – to 'revoke' the initial contested act.

On the opposite side, the Commission objected to some of the arguments put forward by ClientEarth, since these had not been raised in the initial request for internal review.[70] Indeed, according to the CJEU, there must be consistency between the arguments raised by the complainant in the original request for internal review and those raised by the applicant challenging the administrative denial under Article 263(4) TFEU.[71] New arguments cannot be presented for the first time before the Court.

To the reasoning of the parties, the EU judiciary first answered by arguing that the applicant had 'misinterpreted' the meaning of Article 266(1) TFEU. The Court held that the annulment of the initial authorisation has 'nothing to do with a possible revocation by the Commission of that decision'.[72]

Second, that provision does not confer on the Court 'any power that would go beyond the jurisdiction expressly laid down in the Treaties'.[73] According to the EU Court, Article 266(1) TFEU requires the institution whose act has been declared void by the Court, to 'take the necessary measures to comply with the annulling judgment'.[74] This since the Court is 'not entitled, when exercising judicial review of legality, to issue directions to the institutions or to assume the role assigned to them'.[75]

Third, the Court did find some of the arguments presented by the ENGO as having been raised for the first time before the GC, and not previously included in the initial request for internal review.[76] The Court found such arguments inadmissible. In the light of all of the above, the Court rejected the ENGO's action as 'manifestly inadmissible' and maintained that only the Commission could revoke the contested act annulled by the judicature. Jemima Stratford, the barrister representing ClientEarth before the CJEU in this case, used these words about the final outcome of the dispute: 'my clients were disappointed in the result, but the reasoning of the Court was quite long and detailed so on this occasion it is difficult to say that the reasoning was too short'.[77]

[68] This is a concept that has not really been conceptualised under EU law.
[69] *ClientEarth v Commission*, n 62, § 29.
[70] ibid, § 41.
[71] ibid, § 53.
[72] ibid, § 30.
[73] ibid.
[74] ibid.
[75] ibid.
[76] ibid, § 85 and § 200.
[77] Answer to the questionnaire given by Jemima Stratford, barrister at Brick Court Chambers, 2022.

This case showed how ClientEarth tried to use the law to create an indirect pathway to contest the legality of the original administrative act. This even by raising new arguments, which had not been presented in the initial request for internal review. Although unsuccessful, *ClientEarth v Commission* put this further 'closure' in the LOS under the spotlight: from the lack of standing under Article 263(4) TFEU to the impossibility to contest the initial act. *Sic stantibus rebus*, there is not much ENGOs can do to *directly* contest the legality of EU regulatory acts. This even after the reform, as will be discussed in the next section. Indeed, in their attempts to mobilise the Court to bring its case law into compliance with the Aarhus Convention, environmental organisations cannot rely on the action for annulment to challenge the legality of the initial act allegedly contravening provisions of EU environmental law. The interpretation provided by the Court of Article 266(1) TFEU, along with the narrow standing requirements laid down under Article 263(4), make it essentially impossible for ENGOs to achieve their strategic litigation objectives. The greatest achievement would rather be to obtain an annulment of the decision rejecting the original request for internal review, which would force the EU institution or body which adopted the initial contested administrative act to review that same act internally (and potentially revoke it).

Having outlined the main novelties introduced in the AR and discussed their potential for legal mobilisation in the environmental domain, I will now set out my concluding remarks on the analysis embedded in this chapter.[78]

V. Conclusions

This chapter confirmed European ENGOs' capacity to keep shaping legal opportunities under international and EU law and their strategic use in relation to access to justice before the CJEU.

Since its first formulation, the Commission proposal to reform the AR intended to broaden the scope of the definition of 'administrative act' laid down under Article 2(1)(g). However, this was not enough for environmental organisations, which still strongly criticised the proposal for a number of reasons. The main ones referred to (i) the possibility of seeking the internal review only for administrative acts not entailing implementing measures at national or EU level; (ii) the exclusion of State Aid decisions from the scope of the Regulation; (iii) the impossibility to contest via action for annulment not only the EU administrative body's denial but also the original act for which the internal review was sought.

For the time being, only one of these three points was addressed by the EU, which reached final political agreement between the European Parliament and

[78] For a more comprehensive analysis of how the internal review mechanism established under the AR has been deployed by ENGOs to mobilise EU climate policy measures, see Pagano, n 25.

the Council in July 2021.[79] Crucial in driving this change forward was the advice provided by the ACCC, which made an assessment of the Commission's amending proposal *vis-à-vis* the Aarhus Convention. The Committee's advice on the proposal found the political support of the European Parliament, which then intervened on the text of the Commission's proposal by advancing amendments in line with the new Aarhus findings. Indeed, ENGOs used the latter to advocate for additional changes to the proposal. This by combining legal with non-legal tactics (*e.g.* advocacy) in order to achieve their mobilisation objectives. In light of this, the reference to the 'implementing measures' was removed, along with the reference to the 'binding' character of the administrative act, while the points on the exclusion of State Aid decisions from the scope of the Regulation as well as the one on the impossibility of challenging the original contested act, were not modified by the EU legislator, despite of the fact that a key reform in this regard is currently ongoing.[80]

In this regard, this chapter has shown the crucial role of the ACCC in monitoring EU law including the proposal to amend the AR. The Aarhus Committee was strategically used by ENGOs against the EU in a twofold sense: (i) as an 'external supervisor' monitoring the development of the EU legal framework on access to justice in environmental matters; (ii) as a 'catalyst', increasing the bargaining power and the credibility of the ENGOs *vis-à-vis* the EU institutions to claim more in the decision-making.

The new AR was deemed by environmental organisations as a positive 'step forward' on the road that brings the EU into full compliance with the Aarhus Convention. The new definition of 'administrative act' aligns the AR with the case law of the CJEU on 'regulatory acts', as laid down under Article 263(4) TFEU. 'Administrative acts' for which the internal review can be sought under the AR have to be 'regulatory acts', namely 'non-legislative acts of general scope'. Considering this, the reform is now expected to bring more transparency over the technical and scientific assessments underlying EU environmental administrative acts, giving the possibility to civil society to require EU institutions and administrative bodies to provide adequate justifications to their policy choices in a number of key policy areas, such as agriculture, energy, environmental protection and climate change.

In addition, the new definition of 'administrative act' under the AR also raises questions on the relationship between the internal review mechanism and the action for annulment against regulatory acts established under the last limb of Article 263(4) TFEU. My analysis has shown that ENGOs face a trade-off between 'softer standing requirement' under the AR and a 'more substantive judicial review' of the contested regulatory act under Article 263(4) TFEU.

Indeed, ENGOs may still initiate legal proceedings under Article 263(4) TFEU once their request for internal review has been rejected. However, they may do so

[79] Hough, n 12, 1.
[80] See above, section II.

only against the second decision rejecting their request, not against the initial act which was supposed to be subject to the internal review. This impossibility has also been confirmed by the EU judiciary in the *ClientEarth v Commission* case. In this case, the ENGO mobilised the Court to try to close the gap between the internal review procedure and Article 263(4) TFEU. This in a bid to obtain substantive review of the original administrative act also in actions for annulment brought under Article 12 of the AR.

Having outlined how ENGOs have deeply mobilised to shape and use the legal opportunities now available under the new AR, the next chapter will now show how environmental organisations have mobilised non-EU Courts in the 'CCL trend' period in order to circumvent the *Plaumann* test.

6

Plaumann and Climate Change before Non-EU Courts

I. Introduction

In the previous chapters I explored how environmental non-governmental organisations (ENGOs) have been strategically using the remedies available under EU law (ie Article 263 Treaty on the Functioning of the European Union (TFEU) and the Aarhus Regulation (AR)) and international law (ie the Aarhus Convention Compliance Committee (ACCC)) with the aim of acquiring standing in actions for annulment and pushing the Court of Justice for the European Union (CJEU) to abandon the *Plaumann* test. The previous chapters have focused on four main time-frames which I identified as: the pre-Aarhus period; the post-Aarhus (I) period; the post-Aarhus (II) – post findings period and the post-Aarhus reform period.

Conversely, in the present chapter I intend to address legal mobilisation in the final and current timeframe, which is the 'CCL trend' period. Indeed, the present analysis shows how the ongoing climate litigation trend is impacting ENGOs seeking to contest the legality of EU law. Indeed, the famous *Urgenda* case has inspired many civil society organisations (CSOs) across the globe, which are now turning to courts in different jurisdictions in order to hold governments and corporations accountable for the negative impact of climate change on citizens' human rights and biodiversity. This chapter does not intend to delve into the flourishing literature on climate litigation,[1] but rather to continue the analysis of how ENGOs are trying to push the CJEU to abandon the *Plaumann* formula.

In this chapter, I will show how ENGOs – especially those active in the field of climate change litigation (CCL) – understand the legal opportunity structure (LOS) in flexible terms, which cannot be limited to the legal opportunities geographically and legally available in the EU. On this point, the present chapter will illustrate how environmental organisations are not only using remedies available under EU law, but also remedies available outside the EU legal order, to achieve their goals. The peculiarity of this chapter therefore lies in the non-EU reach of its analysis. The fight against *Plaumann* has become part of broader litigation campaigns that on their face have nothing to do with EU law. However, this chapter intends to

[1] See Francesco Sindico and Kate McKenzie (eds), *Research Handbook on Climate Change Litigation* (Cheltenham, Edward Elgar, 2024); Joana Setzer and Lisa Vanhala, 'Climate Change Litigation: A Review of Research on Courts and Litigants in Climate Governance' (2019) 10 (3) *WIREs Clim Change* e580.

demonstrate that the objective of gaining direct access to justice before the CJEU in order to challenge EU law is not only pursued by CSOs using EU-law means. A strategy predicated on looking beyond the EU was already introduced in chapter 4, in the description of the ACCC findings on EU compliance with the Aarhus Convention. However, in the ensuing discussion the connection with *Plaumann* – although still present – is looser. The focus is not on overcoming *Plaumann* in the sense of undermining it but rather on creating different, non-EU, opportunities to contest EU law. The ENGOs are seeking to overcome *Plaumann* by circumventing it by turning to other courts. They also hope that by so doing they will bring indirect pressure to bear on the CJEU to re-think the restrictive *Plaumann* test. Indeed, this is one of the most important and novel findings of this book.

In terms of structure, this chapter will start by providing the reader with the 'big picture', namely the ongoing climate litigation trend, that is affecting an increasing number of countries, inside and outside the EU. This trend, accelerated by *Urgenda*, sees different actors being sued (mainly governments and corporations) using a wide variety of legal arguments (eg constitutional claims, general principles, human rights claims, tort law, etc). This before a remarkable variety of courts; not only domestic but also regional/international courts.

The present chapter will focus on two main organisations, namely *Greenpeace International (GPI)* and the *Global Legal Action Network (GLAN)*, which are trying to 'indirectly' contest EU climate law before non-EU courts.[2] This contribution will thus present the organisations, their statutory goals as well as their dominant legal expertise. In presenting the NGOs, I will try to provide the reader with an understanding of how these specific organisations conceive and rely on the three key elements presented in the introduction to the present contribution, namely (i) LOS, (ii) resources, (iii) strategies. On the latter, I will delve into the actual legal strategies deployed by these organisations to achieve their goals and illustrate the case where such strategies have been used. In doing so, I try to extrapolate the EU law dimension of the case and its relevance from a legal mobilisation perspective.

Then, I reflect critically on my findings, which have been identified by mixing traditional doctrinal methods with qualitative analysis of NGOs' public statements, EU parliamentary questions as well as with interviews with some of the in-house lawyers working for the organisations involved. This discussion seeks to build theoretical foundations for the strategies and the arguments deployed by the organisations, in order to illustrate what these may entail for EU law.

In the preliminary conclusions presented after the description of each NGO and the analysis of the case(s) in which the organisation has been involved, I summarise the main findings of the previous analysis and outline what the case has achieved in terms of 'legal' and 'political' impact, as defined in the introduction to the present contribution.

The findings of the overall doctrinal and qualitative analysis will be outlined in the final conclusions to this chapter.

[2] For a deeper explanation about the selected NGOs I refer the reader to the methodology section included in the introduction to the book.

II. The Global Climate Litigation Trend

The famous *Urgenda* case,[3] ultimately decided by the Dutch Supreme Court on 20 December 2019, played a crucial role in igniting a new wave of climate cases promoted by individuals and CSOs worldwide.[4] *Urgenda* – constructed as a tort law case – was initiated by the Urgenda Foundation, an ENGO based in the Netherlands which pursues the objective of a 'fast transition towards a sustainable society, with a focus on the transition towards a circular economy using only renewable energy'.[5] In this case, three different courts (namely the District Court of the Hague first, and then the Hague Court of Appeal as well as the Dutch Supreme Court) essentially found that the Dutch State has a duty of care under the European Convention on Human Rights (ECHR) to protect the rights of the current generation of Dutch citizens.[6] In the light of this, the State was required to reduce its emissions by at least 25 per cent by the end of 2020, since its existing climate targets were not ambitious enough considering the scientific evidence put forward by the applicants.[7]

Figure 7 Number of climate litigation cases within and outside the US, 1986–2023

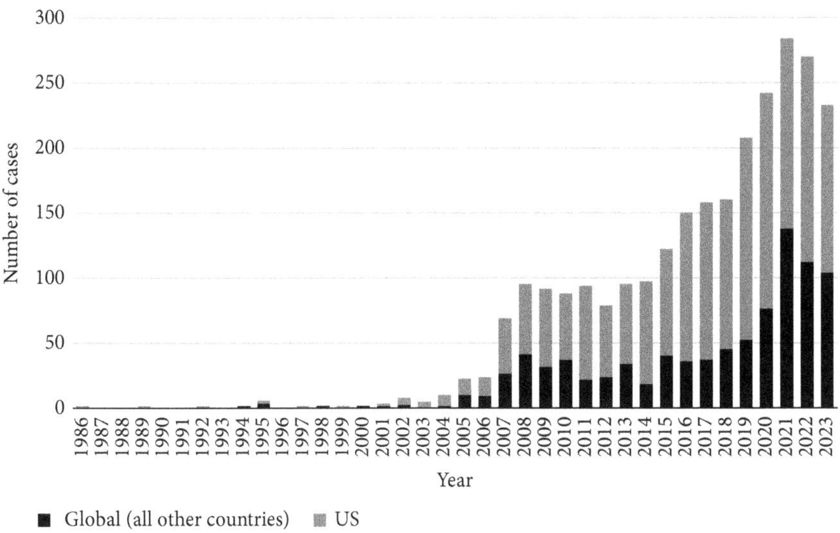

Source: Joana Setzer and Catherine Higham (2024) Global Trends in Climate Change Litigation: 2024 Snapshot. London: Grantham Research Institute on Climate Change and the Environment, London School of Economics and Political Science.

[3] *Urgenda Foundation v The Netherlands* [2015] HAZA C/09/00456689 (24 June 2015); aff'd (9 October 2018); aff'd (20 December 2019) (District Court of the Hague, The Hague Court of Appeal, Dutch Supreme Court).

[4] See below, n 9.

[5] From the 'Urgenda Foundation's official website. Available at: www.urgenda.nl/en/home-en/.

[6] *Urgenda* (The Hague Court of Appeal ruling), n 3, § 76.

[7] ibid.

Figure 7 above shows how the total number of climate cases brought inside and outside the US has increased after 2007 (year of *Massachusetts v EPA*)[8] and even more after 2015 (year of the first ruling in *Urgenda*). This graph demonstrates a correlation between *Urgenda* and climate litigation after 2015. *Urgenda* inspired several litigants in different countries (inside and outside the EU)[9] to start lawsuits against States and corporations, in order to hold them accountable for the negative effects that climate change has on present and future generations' human rights and the environment. To achieve this goal, climate litigants across the globe have framed their cases in different ways, on the basis of the local legal context and the remedies available in the selected jurisdiction where they decided to trigger litigation. In this regard, the graph below indicates the different grounds of review used in pro-climate-commitment cases[10] against governments, precisely since 2015.

Figure 8 Grounds of review in third-wave, pro-climate-commitment cases against governments (since 2015)

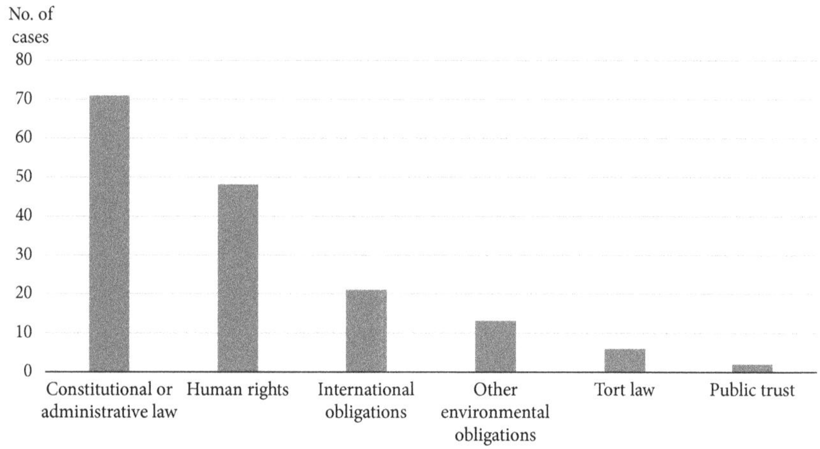

Source: Joana Setzer and Catherine Higham (2021) Global Trends in Climate Change Litigation: 2021 Snapshot. London: Grantham Research Institute on Climate Change and the Environment, London School of Economics and Political Science.

[8] *Massachusetts v EPA*, 549 US 497 (2007).

[9] Eg *Notre Affaire à Tous and Others v France* (France, decided on 3 February 2021); *Plan B Earth and Others v The Secretary of State for Business, Energy, and Industrial Strategy* (United Kingdom, decided on 20 January 2019); *The People v Arctic Oil (Nature and Youth, Greenpeace v Norway's Ministry of Petroleum and Energy Borgarting* (Norway, Supreme Court decided on 20 December 2020); *Thomson v Minister for Climate Change Issues* (New Zealand, decided on 2 November 2017). Data available on http://climatecasechart.com. To deepen the topic, see Jennifer Huang and Maria Antonia Tigre, 'Trends in Climate Justice Litigation: The Dutch Case and Global Repercussions' in Randall S Abate (eds) *Climate Justice: Case Studies in Global and Regional Governance Challenges* (Washington, D.C., Environmental Law Institute, 2016).

[10] In other words, in cases aiming to increase the level of ambition in fighting against climate change.

Constitutional and administrative law-based arguments represent the most frequently deployed set of arguments in 'pro-climate-commitment' litigation. However, human rights-based arguments are also very frequently used. On this point, since a few years already, leading scholars have pointed toward a clear 'rights turn' in CCL,[11] meaning that an increasing number of climate litigants rely on human rights enshrined under international, European or national human rights law to promote the accountability of State. In particular, the use of human rights greatly facilitates the transplantation of legal strategies from one jurisdiction to another, as will be shown in the next sections.

In the EU, we see a number of cases brought before national courts to push governments to set more ambitious climate targets at domestic level. For instance, in 2020, the ENGO Friends of the Irish Environment won a case before the Supreme Court of Ireland against the Irish government, after its applications had been refused by the High Court in Appeal.[12] In this lawsuit, the environmental organisation claimed that the National Mitigation Plan (the Plan) – adopted in 2017 – was in breach of the 'Irish Climate Action and Low Carbon Development Act' (2015, the Act), of the Constitution as well as of human rights obligations stemming from national, international and EU law.[13] In its judgment, the Supreme Court found that the ENGO did not have standing to raise the asserted breach of human rights stemming from national and international law.[14] Nonetheless, the judiciary deemed that the contested national measure fell 'well short of the level of specificity required to provide … transparency and to comply with the provisions of the 2015 Act'.[15] In the light of this, even though the Supreme Court denied the possibility to derive a right to a healthy environment from the national Constitution, it still quashed the government's Plan *vis-à-vis* the Irish Climate Act.[16]

Similarly, in France, four ENGOs (namely Greenpeace France, Oxfam, Notre affaire à tous and the Fondation pour la nature et l'homme) sought to obtain recognition of the French State's failure to adequately tackle climate change.[17] The French case also known as *L'affaire du siècle* ('The case of the century') like *Urgenda* was constructed as a tort law case, by relying upon Article 1246 of the French Civil Code, concerning 'ecological damage'.[18] The four ENGOs asked the French

[11] Jacqueline Peel and Hari M Osofsky, 'A Rights Turn in Climate Change Litigation?' (2018) 7 (1) *Transnational Environmental Law* 37–67.

[12] *Friends of the Irish Environment v The Government of Ireland & Others*, [2019] IEHC 747, § 46.

[13] ibid, [2020] IESC 49.

[14] ibid, § 6.49.

[15] ibid, § 9.3.

[16] bid, § 9.5.

[17] *Notre Affaire à Tous and Others v France*, n 1904967, 1904968, 1904972, 1904976/4-1, Paris Administrative Court (3 February 2021). See Gibson Dunn, 'The Case of the Century – The French Administrative Court Issues a Groundbreaking Ruling on State Responsibility for Climate Change', 26 February 2021. Available at: www.gibsondunn.com/the-case-of-the-century-the-french-administrative-court-issues-a-groundbreaking-ruling-on-state-responsibility-for-climate-change/.

[18] ibid.

State to repair the ecological damage it had caused by compensating them with the symbolic amount of €1.[19] The competent administrative court in Paris found that the damage claimed by the plaintiffs had been demonstrated and that the French State had contributed to it, breaching its obligations laid down under international law (ie the Paris Agreement) as well as under EU and national law.[20]

The ruling of the Administrative Court of Paris was issued just a few weeks before another important climate case in the EU, namely *Neubauer and Others v Germany*, brought by nine young people between the ages of 15 and 32 from different regions of Germany before the German Federal Constitutional Court (FCC).[21] In a decision published on 29 April 2021, the FCC ruled that Germany's Climate Protection Act of December 2019 is not sufficiently ambitious to meet Germany's climate targets *vis-à-vis* the principle of sustainable development.[22] In particular, the German FCC stressed the inter-generational dimension embedded in this principle, which is also laid down in Article 20a of the German Grundgesetz.[23] The constitutional judges found that:

> One generation must not be allowed to consume large portions of the CO2 budget while bearing a relatively minor share of the reduction effort if this would involve leaving subsequent generations with a drastic reduction burden and expose their lives to comprehensive losses of freedom. At some point in the future, even serious losses of freedom may be deemed proportionate and justified under constitutional law in order to prevent climate change. This is precisely what gives rise to the risk of having to accept considerable losses of freedom.[24]

These cases represent just a small fraction of the much bigger European (and global) climate litigation landscape illustrated above. In the last five years alone,[25] significant victories occurred in the Netherlands, France, Ireland, Belgium and Germany showing that there is a 'momentum' underpinning climate litigants in Europe. As mentioned above, *Urgenda* inspired environmental organisations and individual plaintiffs to be more daring in the climate policy arena, in their attempts to put pressure on European governments and force them to set more ambitious climate targets.

However, climate litigation in Europe is also relevant for access to justice before the CJEU for the reasons that will be unpacked in the sections below. Indeed – as it will be shown in the next chapter – some ENGOs are trying to contest the

[19] ibid.

[20] ibid.

[21] *Neubauer and others v Germany* (BvR 2656/18/1 BvR 78/20/1 BvR 96/20/1 BvR 288/20).

[22] Jelena Bäumler, 'Sustainable Development made justiciable: The German Constitutional Court's climate ruling on intra- and inter-generational equity', EJIL:Talk!, 8 June 2021. Available at: www.ejiltalk.org/sustainable-development-made-justiciable-the-german-constitutional-courts-climate-ruling-on-intra-and-inter-generational-equity/.

[23] Art 20a of the German Constitution (Protection of the natural foundations of life and animals): 'Mindful also of its responsibility towards future generations, the state shall protect the natural foundations of life and animals by legislation and, in accordance with law and justice, by executive and judicial action, all within the framework of the constitutional order.'

[24] *Neubauer and others v Germany*, n 21, § 192.

[25] Between 2019 and 2024.

legality of EU climate policy measures directly before the CJEU, while some other organisations are trying to do the same by more 'indirect' means, that is, by litigating before other courts, even outside the EU. They do so with the primary goal of holding national governments and corporations accountable for climate change but their litigation, I argue, is capable of, and intended to, indirectly influence the CJEU to amend its interpretation on *Plaumann*.

Courts are not isolated from each other. On the contrary, judges look at each other and derive confidence and 'comfort' from the reasoning adopted by other judges.[26] GPI is aware of this and relies on it in its bid to influence the reasoning of the EU judiciary. Conversely, GLAN, a non-profit organisation that pursues transnational legal actions challenging states and other actors involved with human rights violations,[27] is more blatant in its attempt to contest EU law before the European Court of Human Rights (ECtHR).

In the next section, I will thus first look into GPI's legal strategies and introduce the key concepts of 'judicial comfort' and 'building blocks', as formulated by in-house lawyers at GPI, and explain how these concepts can be used as parts of a legal strategy which aims at mobilising courts across the globe, including the CJEU. Then, I will turn to GLAN's strategy to mobilise the ECtHR by focusing specifically on the *Duarte Agostinho* case and the *Müllner v. Austria* case, which is currently pending in Strasbourg. With specific regard to the latter case, I will analyse its potential impact on EU law and what it might entail for the 'legality' of EU climate targets. In the final part, I will draw my conclusion on the overall analysis.

III. Understanding Strategic Litigation at GPI

GPI's legal unit comprises 15 people, mainly having an international environmental and human rights law background.[28] Fifteen lawyers out of a staff of 260 people working for GPI (5.77 per cent of the overall staff).[29] Indeed, unlike ClientEarth, GPI's approach to advocacy is much less focused on the use of the law as a way to achieve societal change. Being a 'campaigning' organisation, GPI considers litigation as 'a tool in a toolbox', one of the many instruments that can be deployed by ENGOs to pursue their statutory goals.[30]

Before digging into GPI's legal mobilisation, I want to clarify that my observations about GPI's litigation strategy are essentially based on the interviews carried

[26] See below section IV.

[27] Available at www.glanlaw.org/.

[28] Internship in the Legal Unit of *GPI*, January – May 2020; see also GPI Legal Unit official website, available at: www.greenpeace.org/international/explore/about/legal/.

[29] See www.greenpeace.org/international/about/structure/.

[30] Interview with Jasper Teulings, former General Counsel at GPI, current Strategic Advisor at Climate Litigation Network, 9 April 2020; interview with Daniel Simons, Senior Legal Counsel Strategic Defense, attorney-at-law (New York), 16 June 2020.

out in Amsterdam as well as on the five-month period of my internship there and the cases I worked on during that time.[31] Moreover, GPI is a coordinating and supporting organisation for national and regional Greenpeace offices. This means that their litigation strategy is not fixed in stone, but it necessarily varies in response to the requirements of the communities those offices serve.[32]

By going through Greenpeace's 'Global Programme Plan 2020–2022' it is possible to notice that the ENGO aims – inter alia – to tell powerful stories that are capable of changing the world.[33] This means that any campaign undertaken at Greenpeace[34] will have to be framed in such terms and contribute to the pursuit of three global objectives, namely (i) transforming people's relationship to the climate crisis; (ii) 'toxifying' the presence of fossil fuels interests in society; (iii) working for the creation of more climate-friendly and people-centred cities. GPI's litigation strategy has to be aligned with these global goals and it is through such lenses that we should look at cases if we want to understand rulings and legal avenues from a litigant's perspective.

Before initiating a lawsuit, any ENGO has to check whether it has the potential to contribute to its goals and fits well within the campaigns undertaken by the organisation.[35] Then, in the 'brainstorming' phase of a legal case, in-house lawyers at GPI, first check whether litigation is truly necessary to achieve the goals of the campaign (eg stopping plastic pollution or protecting the North Sea). Second, the legal unit assesses what kind of case-specific objectives the lawsuit intends to pursue. In other words, what kind of goals does the case have to achieve in order to have 'impact'. This can mean different things depending on the case-specific objective(s) to be achieved. For instance, 'impact'[36] could include obtaining a favourable judgment; providing a platform to validate certain scientific evidence; forcing the defendant to take a position in public or mobilising a given community on a particular issue.[37]

Depending on such case-specific goal(s),[38] the lawsuit will have to be framed accordingly, so as to maximise its 'impact', which therefore does not necessarily depend on winning the case in court.[39] This is one of the reasons why ENGOs like GPI tend to opt for what Kim Bouwer has called 'holy grail' cases, namely 'grand, "aspirational" or newsworthy climate change cases, including but not strictly limited to large scale primary liability cases against big corporations or

[31] See methodology section in the introduction to the present book.

[32] Interview with Richard Harvey, Legal Counsel Campaigns at GPI, 18 June 2020.

[33] Greenpeace Global Programme Plan 2020–2022, 2.

[34] The terms 'GPI' and 'Greenpeace' are used as synonyms.

[35] Carolyn Abbot and Maria Lee, *Environmental Groups and Legal Expertise – Shaping the Brexit Process* (London, UCLPress, 2021) 101.

[36] Here I am referring to 'subjective' impact. On this point, see theoretical framework description in the introduction to the present book.

[37] Internship at GPI, n 28.

[38] This since a lawsuit can be strategically planned to achieve a set of different goals.

[39] Interview with Richard Harvey, n 32: '"Winning" is changing people's mindsets, disrupting business-as-usual attitudes to polluters and proving that science-based evidence beats corporate greed. "Winning" in that sense is crucial. Winning by getting the judge to make order you asked for is great but not as important as winning in the court of public opinion.'

governments'.[40] Indeed, for organisations in which 'impact' is measured on the basis of the ENGO's capacity to cause systemic shifts or empower indigenous communities, it is inevitable that they will seek to strike a balance between the 'direct' (legal) effects produced by the ruling of the court and the 'indirect' non-legal effects produced by the case.[41]

However, this should not lead the reader to the impulsive conclusion that 'winning' cases is not relevant for Greenpeace. On the contrary, the importance attached to winning cases helps us understand why Greenpeace has stopped litigating before the CJEU in actions for annulment. This is precisely because there is virtually no prospect of winning. As one in-house lawyer said, '[we] don't like being "smashed"! We don't bring cases for losing them. In fact, we keep bringing actions for annulment but only in the context of access to information'.[42] This is how Andrea Carta, Senior Legal Strategist at GPEU, responded to my question on why Greenpeace stopped litigating before the CJEU under Article 263(4) TFEU.[43] Another in-house lawyer at GPI confirmed that *Plaumann* is the main reason why Greenpeace has not brought new actions for annulment since the 1990s,[44] more specifically, because of 'the inability in most of the cases we campaign on, to identify an individual concern'.[45] The fight for access to justice before EU Courts has thus become a secondary fight for GPI, still important, but to be conducted by 'indirect' means: namely by litigating before other courts with the aim of building 'judicial comfort', as will be outlined in the next section.

Read in these terms, the manner in which ENGOs like GPI conceive strategic litigation strongly resonates with the interpretation of judicial bodies given by Galanter, who – in 1983 – wrote about the 'radiating effect of courts'.[46] As mentioned in the introduction to this book, Galanter emphasised how courts can be seen not only in their traditional dress as dispute-settlement agencies, but also as bargaining forums, where judges contribute in important ways to 'the dissemination of messages rather than the pronouncement of authoritative decisions and application of sanctions'.[47] The manner in which Greenpeace uses strategic litigation demonstrates that this organisation is perfectly aware of the 'radiating effect' of courts and that judiciaries can really work as 'catalysts' capable of producing remarkable indirect effects.[48]

[40] Kim Bouwer, 'The Unsexy Future of Climate Change Litigation' (2018) 30 *Journal of Environmental Law* 484–85.

[41] Eg the 'indirect' effect of raising awareness on a given issue or empowering an indigenous community.

[42] Interview with Andrea Carta, Senior Legal Strategist at Greenpeace EU (GPEU), 25 February 2020.

[43] ibid. This despite the fact that GPI and GPEU are two different organisations, each pursuing its goals autonomously.

[44] Apart from those in the context of access to environmental information.

[45] Interview with Jasper Teulings, n 30.

[46] Marc Galanter, 'The Radiating Effects of Courts' in Keith O Boyum and Lynn Mather (eds), *Empirical Theories About Courts* (London, Longman Inc, 1983) 135.

[47] ibid. We have also seen this in chapter 3, in relation to the findings of the ACCC.

[48] Gerald Rosenberg, *The Hollow Hope: Can Courts Bring About Social Change?* 2nd edn (Chicago, University of Chicago Press, 2008) 25.

Having discussed how strategic litigation is situated within GPI advocacy tactics, in the sections below I am going to delve into the practice of strategic litigation at Greenpeace, by unpacking how its in-house lawyers are trying to set precedents across a wide range of courts across the globe, including the CJEU, by building what they call 'judicial comfort'.

IV. Framing 'Judicial Comfort'

The idea of 'judicial comfort' was introduced to me by Jasper Teulings, General Counsel at GPI at the time of the interview. He expressed it as follows:

> We know that in this dynamic field, politically charged, courts and judges looked at what other courts have done even abroad in finding comfort in pushing the boundaries. Judges derived comfort from seeing other judges taking the steps that have been asked to them. There is 'safety in numbers', it acts more at the psychological level … Judges derived great 'comfort' from other rulings, other jurisdictions, even if they have no direct precedent value and they cannot really invoke them but it makes them feeling that they are not alone or crazy, that they are not overly politically vulnerable if they would go in the same direction and I think this is also affected in the consideration of the Urgenda case.[49]

In light of Jasper Teulings' words, I would thus define 'judicial comfort' as the sense of safety and support that judges derive from seeing other judges taking new interpretative steps, leading a judge to diverge from the established case law on a given subject matter. Indeed, courts do not only require 'political' support from political institutions for their interpretations, but also other forms of support, coming for instance from citizens and other courts.[50] Indeed, to the 'political' and 'social' support that courts derive from political institutions and civil society, we should also add the 'judicial' support that judges derive from the rulings of other judges, inside and outside their jurisdiction.

These forms of 'mutual encouragement' among courts are not new in legal scholarship and are built on solid theoretical foundations. On this point, Joseph Weiler and Doreen Lustig wrote about 'judicial borrowing', conceived as 'a collective action between courts that operates to encourage courts in different jurisdictions to exercise their power of judicial review'.[51] Interpreted in these terms, 'judicial borrowing' takes the form of 'intentional' encouragement by courts which consciously aim to influence other courts and to stimulate judicial review in other jurisdictions. Conversely, the concept of 'judicial comfort' highlighted by Teulings seems to operate at a more 'unconscious' level: judges 'derive' comfort by looking

[49] Interview with Jasper Teulings, n 30.
[50] Susanne K Schmidt, *The European Court of Justice and the Policy Process: The Shadow of Case Law* (Oxford, OUP, 2018) 3. See also Rosenberg, n 48, 31.
[51] Doreen Lustig and JHH Weiler, 'Judicial Review in the Contemporary World – Retrospective and Prospective' (2018) 16 (2) *International Journal of Constitutional Law* 336.

at what other judges have done in similar cases (in Teulings' words). This probably is the 'greatest legacy' of the *Urgenda* case, namely its capacity to influence judges across the globe with regard to climate adjudication.[52]

Nonetheless, 'judicial comfort' appears to facilitate the transplantation (or migration) of constitutional ideas from one jurisdiction to another, allowing for what scholars have labelled as 'trans-judicial dialogue'[53] or 'interjudicial cooperation'.[54] Vicky Jackson described this process as follows:

> An increasingly transnational constitutional discourse has developed in recent years … Increasingly constitutional courts refer to the decisions and reasoning of other constitutional courts – not always to agree but rather to refine and sharpen understandings, in contemporary contexts, of such basic concepts as human dignity, equality, and freedom.[55]

In Jackson's words, constitutional courts are thus 'conversing' with each other, in order to find a common understanding of certain key concepts, shared by many countries in different jurisdictions. According to Eyal Benvenisti, courts cooperate by 'exchanging information' embedded in their judicial reasoning and final outcomes.[56] Benvenisti argues that 'both positive and negative messages can be communicated in this framework'.[57] In particular:

> Cooperative courts will be cited with approval and approbation by their counterparts, whereas courts that step out of line either by refusing to give force to a new standard or by setting a different standard will be criticized, sometimes quite severely, by others. Thus, one court's decisions function as signals to other courts about the former's commitment to cooperation. These signals can embolden the other courts or weaken their resolve in the face of the same dilemmas.[58]

Positive or negative citation can therefore signal the approval or disapproval of other courts' behaviour, but such forms of judicial cooperation are only made possible by judges' reliance on similar legal sources, facilitating this transplantation of constitutional ideas and new standards of judicial protection.[59] Indeed, in his research, Benvenisti clearly shows that courts willing to converse with each other must use a common 'language', which can be understood by all the actors involved. This language is usually found in comparative law (mainly comparative constitutional law) as well as in international law and, more specifically, in international human rights law.[60] These kinds of texts appear more accessible to

[52] Interview with Jasper Teulings, n 28.
[53] ibid.
[54] Eyal Benvenisti, 'Reclaiming Democracy: The Strategic Uses of Foreign and International Law by National Courts' (2008) 102 (2) The *American Journal of International Law* 251.
[55] Vicky Jackson, 'Comparative Constitutional Federalism and Transnational Judicial Discourse' (2004) 2 *International Journal of Constitutional Law* 91.
[56] Benvenisti, n 54.
[57] ibid.
[58] ibid.
[59] ibid. See also Eyal Benvenisti and George Downs, *Between Fragmentation and Democracy: The Role of National and International Courts* (Cambridge, Cambridge University Press, 2017) 119.
[60] Benvenisti, n 54.

judges belonging to different legal traditions and this for reasons that can be easily grasped. First, constitutional texts, especially when it comes to fundamental rights, such as the right to life, the right to health and due process, are often framed in similar terms.[61] Second, international law and international human rights law are binding on the parties ratifying the international legal instrument at stake (eg the Aarhus Convention, the ECHR or the Paris Agreement). This implies that the same legal norms can be invoked before different courts that may look at each other's rulings in the interpretation of those norms, or comply with the case law of a supranational court eventually established under that specific international agreement (eg the ECtHR under the ECHR). Therefore, relying 'on the same or similar legal norms … serves to facilitate harmonization among courts'.[62]

Obviously, each legal order has its own peculiarities and applying the same norms does not entail the same legal effects everywhere. For instance, some countries approach the relationship between domestic and international law in 'monist' terms, while some others in 'dualist' terms.[63] In the latter case, the national measure giving effect to the norms of international law may also have amended some of the relevant treaty provisions. Hence, ENGOs have to take these aspects into account when planning strategic litigation in a given jurisdiction.

However, although similar in some aspects (eg the use of common legal texts), 'judicial comfort' in GPI's terms looks different from both, 'judicial borrowing' as theorised by Weiler and Lustig, and 'interjudicial coordination' as theorised by Benvenisti. Considered from the perspective of strategic litigants and interest groups rather than judges, 'judicial comfort' does not necessarily rely on judges' willingness to 'encourage' other judges to exercise their power of judicial review as in judicial borrowing, or to 'cooperate' with each other as in interjudicial coordination. Conversely, as mentioned above, for judges, 'judicial comfort' operates on a much more psychological and unconscious level, while nonetheless being 'consciously' hinted by strategic litigants. The idea that judges' behaviour in a given jurisdiction could be influenced by what other judges might have decided on a similar matter in another jurisdiction requires additional research in areas other than law. In this regard, there is indeed a vast literature in social psychology and political science on the impact of peer influence in individual decision-making.[64] This has been studied especially among young adults,[65] but also with

[61] ibid, 252.

[62] ibid.

[63] This even though legal scholars seem to have overcome this dichotomy. On this point, see Armin von Bogdandy, 'Pluralism, Direct Effect, and the Ultimate Say: On the Relationship Between International and Domestic Constitutional Law' (2008) 6 (3–4) *International Journal of Constitutional Law* 397–413.

[64] Literature reported in the next footnotes.

[65] See, inter alia, Daniel Kangwa, Mgambi Msambwa Msafiri, Xiulan Wan and Antony Fute, 'Predictors of Cheating in Online Exams Among Business Students During the Covid Pandemic: Testing the Theory of Planned Behaviour' (2022) 20 (3) *International Journal of Management Education* 100713; Jorien van Hoorn, Andrew J Fuligni, Eveline A Crone and Adriana Galván, 'Peer Influence Effects on Risk-Taking and Prosocial Decision-Making in Adolescence: Insights from Neuroimaging Studies' (2016) 10 *Current Opinion in Behavioral Sciences* 59–64; Jasmin Maya Bautista,

specific regard to judges' social circles and judicial behaviour.[66] Further research is certainly necessary to explore whether peer pressure on judges is impactful (i) even among judges belonging to different jurisdictions; (ii) with specific regard to climate change adjudication. What is relevant in the present context, however, is that a leading global ENGO, deeply involved in legal mobilisation, believes that there is peer pressure exerted by judges onto other judges – even in other jurisdictions – and that this is taken into account in conceiving strategic litigation. This is already remarkable from a legal mobilisation perspective.

Litigants have realised that judges feel more comfortable in taking unprecedented interpretative steps when they see similar interpretative patterns emerging elsewhere. Judicial comfort operates as a continuous cycle, building momentum as more and more points of comfort appear.

The next section will examine how judicial comfort can be included as part of a legal strategy which aims at mobilizing courts and achieving political and/or societal change. It will also show how it has been included in GPI's legal strategy in particular.

V. Building Blocks and 'Incrementalism'

A simple definition of a 'building block' would be that of a 'favourable precedent'. This does not necessarily have to be represented by a case won in its entirety. It could equally be represented by a single 'won argument' in a case where all the remaining pleas have been rejected. This is how Kristin Casper, Senior Legal Counsel at GPI at the time of the interview, talked about their strategy of 'setting precedents' in climate litigation:

> Every claim brought by GPI must be 'meritorious' meaning that it has a likelihood of winning and will set a precedent in that jurisdiction.[67] Even if in a given jurisdiction judicial precedents does not have any binding force on subsequent similar cases, we do notice that courts look at each other in different jurisdictions and interpret how they are going to apply the law.[68]

In other words, winning a 'meritorious claim' entails the establishment of a favourable precedent in a given jurisdiction. Therefore, regardless of the final outcome of the overall case where the single winning claim has been included, the latter could

Emmanuel Paciano Mabulay, 'An In-Depth Exploration of How Young Adults' Decision-Making Is Influenced by Peer Pressure and Conformity' (2023) *A Journal Analysis presented as a final requirement For Social Psychology* SOCP311.

[66] Ozkan Eren, Naci Mocan, 'Judge Peer Effects in the Courthouse' (2020) 13937 *IZA DP*, available at: www.iza.org/publications/dp/13937/judge-peer-effects-in-the-courthouse; Jeffrey A Segal, 'Judicial Behavior' in Robert Goodin (ed), *The Oxford Handbook of Political Science* (Oxford, Oxford University Press, 2011; online edn, Oxford Academic, 5 September 2013); Lawrence Baum, *Judges and Their Audiences: A Perspective on Judicial Behaviour* (Princeton, Princeton University Press, 2006).

[67] This regardless of whether that specific jurisdiction applies the *stare decisis* doctrine or not.

[68] Interview with Kristin Casper, former Senior Legal Counsel, current General Counsel at GPI, 13 May 2020.

be re-used in another case before another court, in the same or in another jurisdiction. If a new case is brought before a court in a different jurisdiction, obviously the argument won in the previous case will have to be adapted to the local legal framework.[69] The plaintiff will thus cite the favourable precedent in its judicial pleadings, signalling to the court that other judges – in another jurisdiction, but on a similar subject matter – have adopted that specific legal reasoning.[70] As Casper expresses it:

> A case, in a particular country, an outcome, a ruling, would have several components and we identify those components and then we extract them to the extent that they are relevant in our jurisdiction. So, while there are obviously plenty of differences between various jurisdictions, there are also, perhaps even more so, a lot of commonalities. And that means that certain concepts (or 'building blocks') can be identified and transposed elsewhere.[71]

This 'incrementalistic' approach to strategic litigation, based on using precedents as 'building blocks' to advance the legal status quo, is well known in legal scholarship. We can find examples of 'incrementalistic' public interest litigation for gender equality[72] and disability rights[73] in the US. But how do 'building blocks' work in practice in climate litigation? In the next section, I will now try to provide a practical example of how 'building blocks' have formed part of an 'incrementalistic' legal strategy in a litigation campaign undertaken by GPI.

A. The *People v Arctic Oil* Case

In the *People v Arctic Oil* case, the plaintiffs (two ENGOs – including GPI – and six individuals) challenged the legality of licences granted by the Norwegian government to explore the Barents Sea in search of petroleum.[74] The applicants claimed that the licenses had to be revoked – inter alia – on the basis of Section 112 of the Norwegian Constitution, which reads:

> Every person has the right to an environment that is conducive to health and to a natural environment whose productivity and diversity are maintained. Natural resources shall be managed on the basis of comprehensive long-term considerations which will safeguard this right for future generations as well.

[69] ibid. See also Hans van Loon, 'Principles and Building Blocks for a Global Legal Framework for Transnational Civil Litigation in Environmental Matters' (2018) 23 (3) *Uniform Law Review* 298–318.

[70] ibid.

[71] Interview with Jasper Teulings, n 30.

[72] Nan D Hunter, 'In Search of Equality for Women: From Suffrage to Civil Rights' (2021) 59 *Duquesne Law Review* 155.

[73] Saul Levmore, 'Interest Groups and the Problem with Incrementalism' (2009) 501 John M Olin Program in Law and Economics Working Paper, 2.

[74] *The People v Arctic Oil (Nature and Youth, Greenpeace v Norway's Ministry of Petroleum and Energy)* Case Number: 18-060499ASD-BORG/03.

The plaintiffs argued that this Section of the Norwegian Constitution should be interpreted as a right-bearing provision. This entailed that it could thus be enforced by citizens against the government. Moreover, the plaintiffs claimed that Section 112 could also be applied to emissions of CO_2 produced abroad, from oil and gas exported from Norway. The case was lost at first instance, (before the Oslo District Court), second instance (before the Appeals Court) and last instance (before the Supreme Court), with particular regard to the most important claim, namely that the licenses to explore the Barents Sea had to be revoked.[75] However, the first instance District Court did recognise that Section 112 of the Constitution was a right-bearing clause. On this point, Jasper Teulings (former General Counsel at GPI) commented:

> That was the first time that was held, so from a strategic litigation perspective that was a win, even if the case was a loss. It was also a win in the sense that it gave a platform for public campaigning and it raised awareness in Norway and beyond about the strange situation in which the Norway government finds itself. In appeal, this has recently even be strengthened by another key building block, namely something that was hardly contested by the defendant (the government): the Court has found that Norway is in principle responsible for scope 3 emissions.[76] It's a key building block, I'm not aware of any other ruling where this has been established.[77]

Hence, according to GPI, the *People v Arctic Oil* case had the potential to contribute to stopping oil drilling in many different jurisdictions across the globe by setting a crucial precedent.[78] Although the case was ultimately lost, in-house lawyers at Greenpeace still saw the won argument on the nature of Section 112 as a positive outcome, as a 'building block', which could then be used before other courts, to continue the pursuit of the ENGO's campaign. Furthermore, under the 'building blocks' strategy, environmental litigants can also rely on the blocks 'built' by other organisations, even in other jurisdictions. For instance, the successful use of tort law in the *Urgenda* case has become the starting 'building block' for a number of ENGOs litigating in the climate context.[79] The same can be said with regard to the principle of 'common but differentiated responsibilities', also reasserted in *Urgenda*.[80] On this last point, a significant contribution to stimulating the advancement of 'judicial comfort' in the *People v Arctic Oil* case was given by David Boyd, UN Special Rapporteur on HRs and the Environment, who – along

[75] The case is currently pending before the ECtHR.

[76] Scope 3 emissions include indirect emissions occurring in a company's value chain. For more details, see www.carbontrust.com/.

[77] Interview with Jasper Teulings, n 30. The interview was made before the Supreme Court's decision (issued in December 2020) rejecting the plaintiffs' argument according to which Norway had to held responsible for the impact from emissions of GHG after combustion of exported oil and gas.

[78] GPI, 'Climate crisis hits the Supreme Court of Norway'. Available at: www.greenpeace.org/international/press-release/45579/climate-crisis-hits-the-supreme-court-of-norway/.

[79] eg in the French case '*L'affaire du siècle*' or in the lawsuit brought against the Italian government, which is currently pending. Available at: https://giudiziouniversale.eu/la-causa-legale/.

[80] *Urgenda*, n 3 (Dutch Supreme Court ruling), § 5.7.3.

with other organisations – submitted an *amicus curiae* brief to the Norwegian Supreme Court when the case was still pending.[81]

In his brief, the UN Special Rapporteur signalled to the highest judicial authority in Norway some of the principles applied by the Dutch Supreme Court in *Urgenda*, such as – precisely – the principle of 'common but differentiated responsibilities' and the way in which the Dutch judiciary had interpreted it in 2019.[82] By doing so, David Boyd attempted to stimulate the aforementioned 'transplantation of legal ideas' from one jurisdiction to another and facilitate a more uniform interpretation of the right to a healthy environment and the general principles of international climate change law.[83]

The 'systemic' character of the *People v Arctic Oil* case is demonstrated by a number of elements. First, the case attempted to tackle the issue of mitigating emissions 'at source', by targeting petroleum extraction in a key jurisdiction such as Norway, the tenth biggest exporter of petroleum in the world.[84] Second, the case tried to set a crucial precedent, to be used before other judges worldwide, namely that the right to a healthy environment should be interpreted to prevent countries from extracting and exporting petroleum. An interpretation having enormous potential for further litigation against other states undertaking oil drilling. Third, the case was able to catch the attention of important personalities capable of exercising influence on the judiciary, namely the UN Special Rapporteurs on HRs and the Environment and Toxics and HRs, respectively David Boyd and Marcos Orellana.[85] In the next section, I will now reflect on GPI's building block strategy and discuss its potential in relation to the *Plaumann* test.

VI. Preliminary Conclusions on GPI: An 'Obsolete' Court

GPI's strategies show that the 'impact' of a case is not necessarily linked to its final outcome. A lost case can still have a major 'impact' in both legal and societal terms. Indeed, lawsuits can serve multiple purposes, such as preventing the export of petroleum but also catching the attention of the media and mobilising indigenous communities. In terms of legal strategies, GPI intends to actively influence courts across the world (including the CJEU) and try to change the global

[81] *Amicus Curiae* Brief of the United Nations Special Rapporteur on Human Rights and the Environment and the United Nations Special Rapporteur on Toxics and Human Rights (Case No. 20-051052SIV-HRET). Hereinafter '*Amicus Curiae* Brief'. Available at: www.ohchr.org/Documents/Issues/Environment/SREnvironment/Norwegian_climate_change_case.pdf.

[82] ibid, 18.

[83] ibid, 5.

[84] Daniel Workman, 'Crude Oil Exports by Country', World Top Exports. Available at www.worldstopexports.com/worlds-top-oil-exports-country/.

[85] *Amicus Curiae* Brief, n 78.

'context' in which the judicial function is exercised. This is by using 'building blocks' stemming from precedents (established by GPI or other ENGOs) and by building 'judicial comfort' across jurisdictions. In this regard, the combination of these two intertwined strategies can be conceptualised in terms of building 'transnational incremental judicial comfort' (TIJC): precedents are used as building blocks to 'incrementally' contribute to make judges feel more comfortable in taking new interpretative steps on a transnational scale. The building blocks strategy is pursued with the concrete aim of pushing more and more courts to rule in favour of ENGOs trying to hold governments and corporations accountable for the negative impact of climate change on biodiversity; and to protect the human rights of present and future generations.

Conceived in such terms, the building of TIJC turns into a legal strategy deployed to shape new legal opportunities, in a structure with no definite borders: litigation of GPI before a court is able to increase the judicial receptivity of another court, even in another jurisdiction. The geographical scope of a litigation strategy intended to build TIJC (and therefore new legal opportunities) is, precisely, 'global' and potentially encompasses any court in any country. This implies that even the CJEU is not excluded from the reach of GPI's litigation strategy. This proves how broad and flexible Greenpeace's understanding of the LOS actually is.

Indeed, the EU matters to Greenpeace,[86] but the *Plaumann* test does not make the CJEU a viable forum for GPI's legal mobilisation.[87] Hence, other mobilisation pathways and legal opportunities must be tried. Beside the non-legal strategies deployed by GPI in relation to *Plaumann*,[88] this ENGO looks at the broader picture and includes the CJEU within the reach of its tactics.

The spread of TIJC across jurisdictions – as de facto implemented by GPI – will not necessarily affect the judicial receptivity of the EU judiciary[89] but it might have a detrimental effect on that same court, especially because of *Plaumann*. It is therefore conceivable that over times, the CJEU may feel greater pressure to relax its standing rules. As its own reputation declines, it may reassess the appropriateness of leaving any change to the *Plaumann* formula to the EU political institutions. In a European judicial context where more and more supreme and federal constitutional courts feel increasingly comfortable in taking bold interpretative steps[90] in relation to their domestic legislation, a court like the CJEU may start to appear as quite 'obsolete' in the eyes of environmental and climate litigants. This even more so in the eyes of Greenpeace, which is redirecting its efforts toward other European fora, such as domestic courts but also the ECtHR and the European Committee on

[86] Interview with Daniel Simons, n 30.

[87] ibid.

[88] ibid.

[89] This also in view of the fact that the CJEU has clearly stated that, if another system of judicial remedies is to be adopted in the EU, it would be for the MSs to change it. On this point, see chapter 1.

[90] See above section II.

Social Rights.[91] In this regard, the spreading of judicial comfort across the globe is de facto producing a sense of judicial dis-comfort *vis-à-vis* the CJEU. Indeed, the 'obsolescence' of the CJEU and its standing rules is emerging in a particularly clear guise in these days. Furthermore, its desuetude will be even more apparent if this is to emerge as one of the last European courts still denying standing to ENGOs in direct actions and refusing to review national law (in this case EU law) *vis-à-vis* international legal obligations stemming from climate and HRs agreements.[92]

This being said, building transnational judicial comfort is not the only strategy pursued in litigation before non-EU courts which might affect the *Plaumann* test. In this regard, in the next section I will describe which other organisations are trying to 'circumvent' *Plaumann* – with the aim to *indirectly* contest the legality of EU law – by triggering CCL before courts other than the CJEU.

VII. Understanding Strategic Litigation at GLAN

GLAN is a non-profit organisation that pursues transnational legal actions challenging states and other actors involved in human rights violations.[93] Its peculiarity lies in the fact that it brings together legal practitioners with investigative journalists and academics.[94]

GLAN's Legal Action Committee includes 16 lawyers, mainly specialising in the areas of international criminal law and international human rights law.[95] This committee is responsible for providing legal advice and technical expertise on GLAN's legal actions.[96] However, it is GLAN's Executive Team that carries out the strategic and legal activities.[97] This includes nine lawyers, mainly specialising in the areas of international law, international climate change law, international HRs law and domestic criminal, public and commercial law.[98]

By looking at GLAN's mission and its dominant legal expertise, it is possible to observe the vast scope of its activities. GLAN's work seems to be predominantly based on using strategic legal action to achieve legal, political and societal change.[99] In this regard, its legal action is diversified, being pursued through litigation before domestic and international courts, as well as through the use of administrative bodies.[100] The human rights-centred expertise of the organisation

[91] Interview with Kristin Casper, n 65: 'I think we've seen other opportunities in Europe to do more litigation, mainly using the ECtHR. So, we're likely to be one of the bigger players before the European Court of HRs as the climate cases that we're bringing are moving forward into that arena.'

[92] On this point, see below conclusions on the *Duarte* case.

[93] Available at www.glanlaw.org/.

[94] ibid.

[95] Available at www.glanlaw.org/legal-action-committee.

[96] See above, n 90.

[97] ibid; information acquired also through the questionnaire filled out by Gerry Liston, Legal Officer at GLAN, 14 September 2022.

[98] Available at: www.glanlaw.org/executive-members.

[99] Available at: www.glanlaw.org/what-we-do.

[100] ibid.

is due to their primary goals, which refer to empowering indigenous communities, amplifying their voices, and challenging powerful actors involved in human rights violations and 'systemic injustice'.[101] The 'raising awareness' component of GLAN's work is also crucial, since it aims at seeking 'more than success in a courtroom' and disseminating legal analyses.[102]

The focus on HRs violations makes environmental protection one of the areas in which GLAN operates, but its operating range is much broader than this. For instance, GLAN has triggered legal action by submitting complaints to UN bodies relating to the Israeli-Palestinian conflict,[103] abuses on migrants in Italy[104] and the Irish Tax Policy.[105]

Despite the broad range of legal actions, GLAN's activities are relevant to this contribution mainly because of the Duarte Agostinho case, which was decided by the ECtHR on 9 April 2024. Indeed, GLAN crowd-funded and provided legal assistance to support the case, even though this was formally brought by six individuals.[106] In the next section, I will thus outline this case and show how GLAN is trying to circumvent *Plaumann* by indirectly challenging EU climate change law before the ECtHR.

A. The *Duarte Agostinho* Case

While GLAN was considering the question whether a climate case at the regional or international level against multiple States might be appropriate, wildfires broke out in Portugal, first in 2017 and then in 2018.[107] On the plaintiffs' selection, Gerry Liston – Legal Officer at GLAN – reported that a colleague at that time was from one of those Portuguese regions worst affected by the fires.[108]

> [He] told us that many of her friends and family wanted to do something about the climate crisis as a result of these terrible events. It was through this colleague that we were introduced the children and young adults who are today the applicants.[109]

The case was ultimately initiated in September 2020. Six Portuguese children and young citizens,[110] assisted by GLAN, sued 33 MSs of the Council of Europe

[101] ibid.
[102] ibid.
[103] Available at: www.glanlaw.org/single-post/2018/02/08/robust-methodology-key-to-success-of-un-database-of-businesses-involved-in-israels-settle.
[104] Available at: www.glanlaw.org/nivincase.
[105] Available at: www.glanlaw.org/irish-tax-policies-child-rights.
[106] Available at: www.crowdjustice.com/case/youth4climatejustice/.
[107] The wildfires occurred in Portugal in 2018 were crucial in prompting the *Carvalho* case. On this point, see chapter 7.
[108] Questionnaire filled out by Gerry Liston, n 97.
[109] ibid.
[110] For a broader analysis of children's HRs-based climate change litigation, see Elizabeth Donger, 'Children and Youth in Strategic Climate Litigation: Advancing Rights through Legal Argument and Legal Mobilization' (2022) *Transnational Environmental Law* 1–27.

(hereinafter 'the Respondent States') before the ECtHR.[111] The case was brought against all the 27 EU MSs, in addition to Norway, Turkey, Russia, Switzerland, Ukraine and the UK.[112] The case was then dropped against Ukraine because of the ongoing war.[113] Interestingly, the lawsuit was initiated directly before the ECtHR, without exhausting all domestic means of redress, as is normally required under the Convention. The applicants justified this choice by putting forward a number of different reasons. First, this was because it would be practically impossible for them to exhaust all domestic remedies in all the 33 Respondent States.[114] Second, this was because even if all domestic courts were to follow the Dutch judiciary's reasoning adopted in *Urgenda*, and require a reduction by the lowest amount in the ranges applicable to both developed and developing countries, 'this would not be sufficient to maintain global warming at the level (ie no more than 2°C) to which these ranges relate'.[115] Third, this is because most European countries have not provided adequate judicial remedies with regard to their respective contributions to global emissions. In particular, according to the plaintiffs, national courts have often misapplied the 'margin of appreciation' doctrine established by the ECtHR.[116] Fourth, because – as acknowledged also by the UN – children and young people experience more difficulties in pursuing remedies for violations of their human rights.[117]

The lawsuit aimed at checking whether the Respondents' contribution to global GHG emissions is violating (and may violate) the plaintiffs' human rights protected under the Convention. In particular, the applicants claimed that the Respondent States breached Articles 2 and 8 (right to life and right to private life, to be read in the context of the Paris Agreement), as well as Article 14 (prohibition of discrimination) of the ECHR, claiming that their generation will suffer the negative impact of climate change more severely compared to older generations.[118] However, when the Strasbourg Court communicated the case, it asked the parties – in the light of the *iura novit curia* principle[119] – to also comment on the alleged violation of

[111] *Duarte Agostinho and Others v Portugal and Others*, n. 39371/20, ECtHR, 9 April 2024. Hereinafter 'Duarte Agostinho'.

[112] ibid, application file (hereinafter 'AF').

[113] *Duarte Agostinho*, n 111, § 231.

[114] Paul Clark, Gerry Liston and Ioannis Kalpouzos, 'Climate Change and the European Court of Human Rights: The Portuguese Youth Case', EJIL: Talk!, 6 October 2020. Available at: www.ejiltalk.org/climate-change-and-the-european-court-of-human-rights-the-portuguese-youth-case/.

[115] *Duarte Agostinho*, application file, § 37. Available at: https://youth4climatejustice.org/wp-content/uploads/2020/11/GLAN-ECtHR-Application.pdf. Hereinafter 'Duarte Agostinho – AF'.

[116] Clark and others, n 110.

[117] *Duarte Agostinho* – AF, n 115, § 40.

[118] Corina Heri, 'The ECtHR's Pending Climate Change Case: What's Ill-Treatment Got To Do With It?', *EJIL: Talk!*, 22 December 2020. Available at: www.ejiltalk.org/the-ecthrs-pending-climate-change-case-whats-ill-treatment-got-to-do-with-it/.

[119] Aaron X. Fellmeth and Maurice Horwitz, *Guide to Latin in International Law* (Oxford, OUP, 2011) (online version). Available at: www.oxfordreference.com/view/10.1093/acref/9780195369380.001.0001/acref-9780195369380-e-1075. In this guide, the authors defined the principle as follows: '"The court knows the laws." A doctrine providing that, because a tribunal is presumed to know and apply the law, the parties to a dispute are not required to invoke all applicable legal rules explicitly or to convince the tribunal of the law's content. A major implication of this doctrine is that a judicial or arbitral tribunal is not bound by the construction of the law or a legal instrument proposed by any of the parties to the dispute'.

Article 3 (prohibition of torture) and Article 1 of Protocol n. 1 to the Convention (right to property).[120]

The case was given priority by the ECtHR, meaning that the case was considered particularly 'serious' and the Court could, therefore, take a decision more rapidly.[121] This was because the case had been deemed to have the potential to trigger a wide number of new lawsuits.[122] In June 2022, the competent Chamber relinquished jurisdiction in favour of the Grand Chamber of the ECtHR.[123]

This being said, what is striking from a 'legal mobilisation against Plaumann' perspective, is that, first, the case has been brought against all the EU MSs, indirectly prompting the question of whether the applicants used the Strasbourg Court to circumvent *Plaumann* and challenge the EU climate targets *vis-à-vis* the ECHR. On this point, Gerry Liston stated:

> We also sued six States who are not EU Member States. We never intended to bring a case to the CJEU in part because of Plaumann but for other reasons too. The main reason for there being multiple Respondents in our case is to demonstrate to the Court, through their observations and expert evidence, that it is not possible to ensure the effective protection of the right to be free from harms caused by climate when all Respondents pursue self-serving interpretations of their 'fair share' of the required global emissions reductions, as they do. The force of this argument isn't, we believe, so apparent in a case against a single State. And in climate change litigation terms, a case against the EU to the CJEU is just like a case against a single State as it is concerned with one entity's (2030) target.[124]

Litigation directly before the CJEU was thus excluded in part because of *Plaumann* and in part for increasing the effectiveness of the case in relation to the right to be free from harms applied in the climate context. However, the intention to indirectly contest EU climate targets *vis-à-vis* the ECHR was still present in the lawsuit. On this point, Gerry Liston argued:

> We have made detailed submissions as to why the EU's 2030 target and the studies underpinning it are not compliant with ECHR obligations as this is relevant to whether all Respondents who purely follow EU targets are in breach.[125]

This is also borne out by the words of Gerd Winter, one of the lawyers indirectly involved in the case,[126] who explicitly argued that the ECtHR is an alternative pathway to hold the EU accountable for climate change.[127]

[120] ibid.
[121] ibid.
[122] ibid.
[123] ECtHR, Press Release, ECHR 226 (2022). Available at: https://hudoc.echr.coe.int/fre{%22itemid%22:[%22003-7374717-10079435%22]}.
[124] Questionnaire filled out by Gerry Liston, n 97.
[125] ibid.
[126] Gerd Winter submitted, along with other lawyers, an amicus brief to the ECHR on behalf of CAN Europe.
[127] Interview with Gerd Winter, Research Professor of environmental law at the Research Center for European Environmental Law (FEU) of the University of Bremen, 13 December 2021.

Second, the inadequacy of EU climate change law *vis-à-vis* international law was explicitly called into question by the plaintiffs in their application file.[128] Indeed, in this file the plaintiffs maintained that the Court of Strasbourg, in reviewing the case, should make use of the approach taken by the 'Climate Action Tracker' (CAT), that is, 'an independent scientific analysis that tracks government climate action and measures it against the globally agreed [goal of the] Paris Agreement' in order to evaluate the adequacy of countries' mitigation measures.[129] The applicants explained that the CAT intends to build a 'fair share range' to measure the adequacy of a given country's mitigation policy. Such 'range' is then divided into three categories: 'insufficient', '2°C compatible' and '1.5°C compatible'. Under the CAT, EU targets were deemed to be 'insufficient' and even the 2030 reduction target of 55 per cent was considered not to be 'enough to reach a Paris Agreement compatible emissions pathway.'[130] The adequacy of EU climate measures *vis-à-vis* human rights and the Paris Agreements was all the more relevant in Duarte Agostinho, especially if we consider that EU climate targets are also intertwined with emission reductions in other non-EU countries included among the Respondent States. In particular, Switzerland, which linked its emissions trading system to the EU ETS, and Norway, which is also subject to the EU ETS.[131]

However, on 9 April 2024, the ECtHR dismissed the Duarte Agostinho case, in a wave of three climate judgments involving, beside *Duarte Agostinho*, two more cases, namely *KlimaSeniorinnen v Switzerland* and *Carême v France*.[132] Out of the three cases, only *KlimaSeniorinnen* resulted in a court win. In the light of this and taking into consideration the explicit reference to the EU climate targets made by the applicants in *Duarte Agostinho*, in the next section I will engage with the Court's reasoning in the *Duarte Agostinho* judgment and discuss its potential implications for EU legal mobilisation against *Plaumann*.

B. The Court's Judgment in *Duarte Agostinho*

It is necessary to clarify that the legality of EU law had not been 'directly' called into question in this case and no reference to any specific piece of EU legislation had been put forward in *Duarte Agostinho*, at least not in the application file submitted by the plaintiffs. As mentioned above, generic references had only been made in relation to the EU climate targets to be achieved by 2030. However, as mentioned above, the case was also triggered to indirectly contest the legality of EU emission reduction targets *vis-à-vis* the ECHR rather than EU law.[133] For this

[128] *Duarte Agostinho* – AF, n 112, § 37.
[129] ibid, § 31.
[130] ibid, § 37.
[131] Available at: https://ec.europa.eu/clima/eu-action/eu-emissions-trading-system-eu-ets_en.
[132] *Verein Klimaseniorinnen Schweiz and others v Switzerland*, Application no 53600/20, ECtHR, 9 April 2024; *Carême v France*, application no 7189/21, ECtHR, 9 April 2024. Hereinafter 'Klimaseniorinnen'.
[133] Questionnaire filled out by Gerry Liston, n 97.

reason, the *Duarte Agostinho* case can still be considered as a case triggered to indirectly overcome *Plaumann* and challenge the legality of EU climate law.[134]

As mentioned above, the six applicants were all from Portugal. As a consequence, the claim was territorial against Portugal, while it was extraterritorial against the others. One of the main questions in the case was thus whether the respondent States other than Portugal could be held responsible for the climate-related impacts that their emissions contributed to, but that were felt overseas.[135] The Court referred to its previous case law on migration, particularly *M.N. and Others v Belgium*,[136] which concerned visa applications submitted at embassies abroad. In doing so, it acknowledged the applicants' argument according to which their case did not align with the Court's frameworks for establishing extraterritorial jurisdiction under Article 1 of the ECHR. Typically, jurisdiction is limited to a State's own territory, except in specific circumstances: (i) when a State exercises 'effective control' beyond its borders, (ii) when its agents exert authority over an individual in another country, or (iii) in rare cases, where procedural aspects of the case justify an exception.[137]

The Court then considered the applicants' request to establish a new 'test', based on fundamental principles and the exceptional nature of the case. Indeed, in one of the other climate cases, *KlimaSeniorinnen*, the Court had shown a certain willingness to adapt its approach to victim status in response to the specific challenges posed by climate change, introducing a distinct framework with more innovative criteria for both, individuals and NGOs.[138] Given this precedent, the Court examined whether a similarly tailored approach was necessary for establishing extraterritorial jurisdiction in this case.

In its reasoning, the Court agreed with several arguments raised by the applicants, such as the fact that climate change presents unique characteristics;[139] that States exercise ultimate control over public and private emissions within their territories;[140] that emissions negatively affect individuals beyond national borders, placing them outside the reach of a given State's democratic processes;[141] and that climate change constitutes an existential threat to humanity, distinguishing it from other cause-and-effect scenarios.[142]

[134] On this point, see also Piet Eeckhout, 'From Strasbourg to Luxembourg?: The KlimaSeniorinnen judgment and EU remedies' (2024) *VerfBlog*. Available at: https://verfassungsblog.de/from-strasbourg-to-luxembourg/.

[135] On this case, see the comment of Corina Heri, 'On the Duarte Agostinho Decision' (2024) VerfBlog. Available at: https://verfassungsblog.de/on-the-duarte-agostinho-decision/.

[136] *MN and Others v Belgium*, n 3599/18, ECtHR, 5 March 2020.

[137] *Duarte Agostinho*, n 111, § 171.

[138] On this point, see Mario Pagano, 'Legal Standing in Climate Litigation before the ECtHR and the CJEU' (2024) EU Law Live. Available at: https://eulawlive.com/op-ed-legal-standing-in-climate-litigation-before-the-ecthr-and-the-cjeu-by-mario-pagano/.

[139] *Duarte Agostinho*, n 111, § 191.

[140] ibid, § 192.

[141] ibid, § 193.

[142] ibid, § 194.

Despite recognising these factors, the Court ultimately declined to amend its well-established approach to extraterritorial jurisdiction and dismissed several of the applicants' arguments. More specifically, the Court of Strasbourg first held that jurisdiction should be assessed independently from the substantive merits of the case.[143] Second, apart from Portugal, no special connection to any respondent State had been demonstrated,[144] and the mere capacity to affect rights beyond national borders was insufficient to establish jurisdiction.[145] Furthermore, the Court also held that EU citizenship was not relevant to the jurisdictional question;[146] that the ECHR was not intended as a general instrument for environmental protection,[147] and that its scope is grounded in the principles of territoriality and subsidiarity.[148]

The Court thus rejected the proposal for a new legal test, based on control over Convention interests, enjoyment of rights, or the source of harm. Referring to an extensive and consolidated case law, the judiciary reaffirmed that jurisdiction requires direct control over an individual rather than over their interests.[149] Any deviation from this standard – the Court stated – would undermine legal predictability and open the door for claims from 'anyone adversely affected by climate change, regardless of where they experience its effects'.[150]

The Court of Strasbourg was also concerned by the fact that, by following the applicants' reasoning, the Convention would basically be transformed into an international climate change treaty.[151] It deemed this outcome untenable and declined to follow the more expansive interpretations of jurisdiction adopted by other human rights bodies, such as the Inter-American Court of Human Rights and the UN Committee on the Rights of the Child in *Sacchi et al v Argentina et al*, on the grounds that they were based on a fundamentally different conception of jurisdiction.[152] Furthermore, the Court noted that the conceptual expansion of the jurisdiction sought by the applicants could not fall within the Convention's legal framework, and it therefore ruled that all claims raised by the applicants against the respondent States, except Portugal, were inadmissible.[153]

Although the Strasbourg Court determined that it had jurisdiction over the claims against Portugal, it ultimately dismissed the case on procedural grounds, finding that the applicants had not exhausted available domestic remedies.[154] The Court reaffirmed its well-established case law, emphasising its subsidiary role and

[143] ibid, § 197.
[144] ibid, § 198.
[145] ibid, § 199.
[146] ibid, § 200.
[147] ibid, § 201.
[148] ibid.
[149] ibid, § 205.
[150] ibid, § 206.
[151] ibid, § 208.
[152] ibid, § 212.
[153] ibid, § 214.
[154] ibid, § 217.

clarifying that it does not function as a court of first instance.[155] While applicants are not required to pursue remedies that are ineffective, futile, or inadequate, and some flexibility is permitted in this regard, mere doubts about a remedy's effectiveness are insufficient to bypass the exhaustion requirement.[156]

Applying these principles, the Court held that the applicants should have pursued legal remedies within the Portuguese judicial system. The judges stressed that Portugal explicitly recognizes a constitutional right to a healthy environment and provides additional remedies, such as an *actio popularis* for environmental claims. Triggering domestic litigation first, would have allowed Portuguese courts to evaluate the case and provide the ECtHR with a more informed basis for assessing both, the facts and the legal issues at stake. The Court also reiterated the significance of exhausting domestic remedies in the section on 'victim status', emphasising that the absence of a domestic scrutiny deprived it of a clear understanding of the applicants' individual situations and their legal standing. For these reasons, the Court ultimately dismissed the case. Here below my critical appraisal on the ruling.

C. Comment on the *Duarte Agostinho* Case

A clearer picture of the European LOS in the aftermath of the *Duarte Agostinho* case is to be identified – in my view – through a common reading of the *Duarte Agostinho* case, along with the ECtHR's judgment in *Klimaseniorinnen*. In this regard, in the latter case, the ECtHR accepted to give an evolving and dynamic interpretation to the victim status requirements for NGOs, read in the light of the Aarhus Convention and based on the specific features of climate change.[157] According to the ECtHR, to be considered when assessing the standing of CSOs in the climate context, the association in question must be: (i) lawfully established in the jurisdiction concerned or have standing to act there; (ii) able to demonstrate that it pursues a dedicated purpose in accordance with its statutory objectives in the defence of the human rights of its members or other affected individuals within the jurisdiction concerned, whether limited to or including collective action for the protection of those rights against the threats arising from climate change; and (iii) able to demonstrate that it can be regarded as genuinely qualified and representative to act on behalf of members or other affected individuals within the jurisdiction who are subject to specific threats or adverse effects of climate change on their lives, health or well-being as protected under the Convention.[158]

Therefore, in *Duarte Agostinho* the ECtHR accepted the claims brought by the applicants against Portugal (the State where all the applicants were from) and

[155] ibid, § 228.
[156] ibid, § 225.
[157] *Klimaseniorinnen*, n 132, § 486.
[158] ibid, § 502.

reiterated the significance of exhausting domestic remedies as a necessary precondition for bringing a case to Strasbourg. On the other side, in *Klimaseniorinnen* the ECtHR, after having checked whether the applicants had exhausted their domestic remedies, it reviewed its standing criteria for NGOs in the climate context, following a lengthy and comprehensive discussion.[159] After having granted standing to the association – but not to the individual plaintiffs along[160] – the Court then moved to examine the substance of the case and ultimately found the Swiss State in breach of the obligations stemming from the Convention.[161] From a climate legal mobilisation perspective, the reasoning of the Court in the two cases implies that, the ECtHR will probably favour collective qualified actions brought by NGOs rather than actions triggered by individuals.[162] Indeed, the Strasbourg Court in *Klimaseniorinnen* emphasised the special role that associations and NGOs play in modern-day societies.[163] In addition, before the ECtHR, ENGOs will not be able to trigger cases targeting a vast amount of States – as GLAN attempted in *Duarte Agostinho* – but they will rather have to challenge individual national policies on climate change, going 'State after State' and only after having exhausted the domestic remedies in each jurisdiction. It is clear that, at least for cases triggered against EU MSs, overcoming *Plaumann* and being able to initiate litigation at EU level directly before the CJEU would save an enormous amount of time and resources. This especially if the goal of the applicants is not to simply challenge national measures implementing EU climate policy, but EU climate policy in itself. At the moment, this possibility is de facto precluded, before both, the ECtHR (since the EU has not adhered to the Convention) and the CJEU, because of the *Plaumann* test. To this remarkable obstacle, there seem to be three possible alternatives. The first one refers to the possibility of challenging the validity of EU law through the preliminary reference procedure.[164] The second one, refers to the possibility of challenging climate-related EU administrative acts under the new internal review mechanism established under the AR.[165] The third one, refers to the possibility of challenging the domestic climate policy of an EU MS before the ECtHR and try to rebound the Bosphorus presumption.[166] At the time of writing, this third scenario is actually a reality, currently pending before the ECtHR, and will be discussed in the following section.

[159] ibid, § 478.
[160] ibid, § 535.
[161] ibid, § 573.
[162] On this point, see also Gerd Winter, 'Climate Protection before the European Court of Human Rights: The KlimaSeniorinnen and Duarte Agostinho Cases in Perspective' (2024) 84 *Zeitschrift für ausländisches öffentliches Recht und Völkerrecht / Heidelberg Journal of International Law* 495.
[163] *Klimaseniorinnen*, n 132, § 489: 'when citizens are confronted with particularly complex administrative decisions, recourse to collective bodies such as associations is one of the accessible means, sometimes the only means, available to them whereby they can defend their particular interests effectively'.
[164] See chapter 2.
[165] See chapter 5.
[166] See the next section.

D. The *Müllner v Austria* Case

In the present section, I will briefly outline the *Müllner v Austria* case[167] and discuss the potential application of the Bosphorus presumption and what it may entail for EU climate law and the EU system of judicial protection *vis-à-vis* the ECHR.[168]

The *Müllner v Austria* case concerns complaints about Austria's alleged failure to mitigate the impacts of climate change, in particular global warming, by taking effective measures to reduce its greenhouse gas emissions and to limit the increase in the global average temperature to 1.5°C above pre-industrial levels.[169] The applicant suffers from multiple sclerosis. He claims that his symptoms worsen with the increase of external temperatures, leading to temporary paralysis and restricted mobility, an effect known as Uhthoff's Syndrome.[170]

On 20 February 2020, the applicant, along with other individuals, filed a complaint to the Austrian Constitutional Court under Articles 139 and 140 of the Federal Constitution (Bundes-Verfassungsgesetz).[171] The complaint challenged the constitutionality of certain provisions in the Value Added Tax Act (Umsatzsteuergesetz), the Mineral Oil Tax Act (Mineralölsteuergesetz) and the Aviation Benefits Regulation (Luftfahrtbegünstigungsverordnung).[172] The applicant argued that these provisions, which granted tax benefits and exemptions to the aviation industry while excluding railway companies, encouraged the use of the most environmentally harmful mode of transportation.[173] He claimed that this directly affected him as a consumer, as he had to bear the financial burden of the tax and faced a disadvantage due to his preference for travelling by train.[174] Additionally, he contended that these provisions violated the State's positive obligations under Articles 2 and 8 of the Convention by failing to protect him from the harmful effects of the climate crisis on his life and health.[175]

On 30 September 2020, the Constitutional Court dismissed the complaint as inadmissible. It reasoned that the applicant was not directly subject to the provisions governing tax benefits for businesses and that these measures did not interfere with his legal interests.[176] The Court further noted that, since the applicant stated he travelled by train rather than by air, he was not personally affected by the aviation-related tax benefits.[177]

[167] *Müllner v Austria*, n 18859/21, ECtHR (pending).
[168] See also the comment of Janine Prantl, 'After Switzerland Comes Austria: Why the ECtHR could soon grant individual standing in a climate mitigation case for the first time' (2024) VerfBlog. Available at: https://verfassungsblog.de/after-switzerland-comes-austria/.
[169] *Müllner v Austria*, n 164.
[170] ibid.
[171] ibid.
[172] ibid.
[173] ibid.
[174] ibid.
[175] ibid.
[176] ibid.
[177] ibid.

In his application to the ECtHR, the applicant claims that the climate crisis exposes him to a tangible and significant risk, affecting his physical, psychological, and moral well-being, as well as his personal dignity and the overall quality of his private and family life.[178] The applicant argues that the Constitutional Court's excessively formalistic approach in rejecting his complaint violated his right of access to a court, as protected under Article 6 of the Convention.[179] Under Article 8 (and subsidiarily Article 2), he contends that the Respondent State has failed to implement a sufficient legislative and administrative framework to achieve its climate targets, despite the fact that meeting these objectives would have significantly improved his well-being.[180] Additionally, under Article 13, he asserts that the domestic legal system did not provide him with an effective remedy before a national authority to challenge legislative and administrative shortcomings in this context.[181]

This case is particularly relevant in the frame of the present research for at least three key reasons. First, in this case the Strasbourg Court is called upon to rule as to what extent the *Klimaseniorinnen* case law, and the reformed criteria for granting *locus standi* to private applicants in climate cases, can now also be applied to individuals.[182] Second, this case has been brought against a Member State to the Council of Europe which is also an EU MS, that is, Austria. However, unlike in *Duarte Agostinho*, this case only concerns one EU MS, the one where the applicant is resident. The jurisdiction's requirements about the territoriality of State's protection – contested in *Duarte Agostinho* – should thus not be an issue in *Müllner v Austria*. Third, the fact that Austria is an EU MS also indirectly calls into question the adequacy of EU law *vis-à-vis* the ECHR and the application of the *Bosphorus* presumption. These aspects will be discussed in the next section.

E. EU Climate Change Law and the *Bosphorus* Presumption

Austria being an EU MS, in its defence before the ECtHR, the national government involved in *Müllner v Austria*, might have referred to its extremely narrow margin of manoeuvre set under EU law and its emission targets by 2030. This is also what the Dutch government argued in *Urgenda*, as a way to justify the Dutch emissions targets by 2020.[183] The ECtHR in its case law has already clarified that 'the member States are responsible … for all acts and omissions of their organs, whether these arise from domestic law or from the need to fulfil international legal

[178] ibid.
[179] ibid.
[180] ibid.
[181] ibid.
[182] This especially if we consider that the individual applicants in the *Klimaseniorinnen* case were denied standing.
[183] *Urgenda* (District Court of the Hague ruling), n 3, § 3.3.

obligations'.[184] Therefore, the necessity to meet obligations arising under EU law (in this case the obligation to cut down emissions in the respective MSs), does not – per se – exclude the Respondent State's responsibility under the Convention to protect citizens' human rights. Nonetheless the question of how much discretion MSs enjoy in meeting obligations arising under EU law is relevant under a different aspect of ECHR law, namely the presumption of equivalence which will be discussed below.

EU law notoriously enjoys a presumption of 'equivalence' with the standard of human rights protection guaranteed under the ECHR. This presumption – established in the *Bosphorus* case by the ECtHR[185] – could be applied if the case is ultimately deemed admissible. Under the 'Bosphorus doctrine', this presumption is justified:

> [A]s long as the relevant organisation is considered to protect fundamental rights, as regards both the substantive guarantees offered and the mechanisms controlling their observance, in a manner which can be considered at least equivalent to that for which the Convention provides … By 'equivalent' the Court means 'comparable'; any requirement that the organisation's protection be 'identical' could run counter to the interest of international cooperation pursued … However, any such finding of equivalence could not be final and would be susceptible to review in the light of any relevant change in fundamental rights protection.[186]

More specifically, this presumption only applies when (i) the State's authorities have no discretion in implementing an EU law obligation; (ii) EU law deploys the 'full potential' of its supervisory mechanism.[187] In other words, when EU law is shown to provide comparable human rights protection to that afforded under the ECHR. This implies that:

> any such presumption can be rebutted if, in the circumstances of a particular case, it is considered that the protection of Convention rights was manifestly deficient. In such cases, the interest of international cooperation would be outweighed by the Convention's role as a 'constitutional instrument of European public order' in the field of human rights.[188]

This means that, although the ECtHR has in previous cases deemed that the EU does provide a 'comparable' standard of protection, the *Bosphorus* presumption can still be rebutted if – 'in the circumstances of a particular case' – the protection of the rights granted under the ECHR is 'manifestly deficient' under the law of the Union.[189]

[184] *Bosphorus Hava Yollari Turizm Ve Ticaret Anonim Şirketi v Ireland*, n. 45036/98), ECtHR, Judgment Strasbourg 30 June 2005. Hereinafter 'Bosphorus', § 153.

[185] ibid, § 156.

[186] ibid.

[187] *Avotiņš v Latvia*, n 17502/07, ECtHR, Judgment Strasbourg 23 May 2016, § 101.

[188] ibid.

[189] To deepen the topic, see, inter alia, Nuala Mole, 'Can Bosphorus Be Maintained?' (2015) 6 *ERA Forum* 467–80; Tobias Lock, 'Beyond Bosphorus: The European Court of Human Rights' Case Law on

However, the presumption does not even apply if the EU MSs enjoy some discretion in implementing obligations stemming from EU law[190] and this is also what GLAN's lawyers have been trying to demonstrate in the *Duarte Agostinho* case.[191] In this regard, it is still worth briefly exploring whether the national authorities of the EU MSs enjoy some discretion in implementing EU climate targets and whether the *Bosphorus* presumption can find application in *Müllner v Austria*.

The point of MSs' margin of manoeuvre under EU climate law was raised in particular by Marjan Peeters, in 2016, in the aftermath of the first *Urgenda* ruling.[192] In her contribution, Peeters wondered whether a single MS could unilaterally derogate from an EU-wide climate policy, setting specific emissions targets for the whole Union. She stressed that EU climate targets are based on a 'complex mix of EU regulatory instruments …, among which the EU Emissions Trading Scheme (EU ETS) and the EU Effort Sharing [Regulation] are the most prominent'.[193]

In relation to the first policy measure, Peeters claimed that, under the EU ETS, the European Commission 'sets not only the cap but also the rules for the auctioning and free distribution of allowances, hardly leaving any discretion to the [MSs], who have to issue the allowances.'[194] However, the District Court of the Hague, in *Urgenda*, disagreed with the Dutch State on this point, namely as to whether the Netherlands truly had no possibility to deviate from the targets established under the EU ETS:[195]

> However, the court does not follow the State in this argument in so far as this means that a Member State is not allowed to reduce more than the amount adopted in EU policy. … Urgenda was right in arguing that regardless of the ceiling Member States have the option to influence (directly or indirectly) the greenhouse gas emissions of national ETS businesses by taking own, national measures.[196]

In *Urgenda*, the plaintiffs also presented concrete examples of measures adopted in other MSs, setting higher reduction targets under the EU ETS, such as: 'increasing the share of sustainable energy in the national electricity network in Denmark and the introduction of the carbon price floor … in the United Kingdom, with

the Responsibility of Member States of International Organisations under the European Convention on Human Rights' (2010) 10 (3) *Human Rights Law Review* 529–45; Cathryn Costello, 'The Bosphorus Ruling of the European Court of Human Rights: Fundamental Rights and Blurred Boundaries in Europe' (2006) 6 (1) *Human Rights Law Review* 87–130.

[190] Armelle Gouritin, *EU Environmental Law, International Environmental Law, and Human Rights Law: The Case of Environmental Responsibility* (Leiden, Brill, 2016) 22.

[191] Questionnaire filled out by Gerry Liston, n 97.

[192] Marjan Peeters, 'Urgenda Foundation and 866 Individuals v. The State of the Netherlands: The Dilemma of More Ambitious Greenhouse Gas Reduction Action by EU Member States' (2016) 25 (1) *RECIEL* 124.

[193] ibid.

[194] ibid; see also see Lorenzo Squintani, Marijn Holwerda and Kars de Graaf, 'Regulating Greenhouse Gas Emissions from EU ETS Installations: What Room is Left for the Member States' in Marjan Peeters and Marc Stallworthy (eds), *Climate Law in EU Member States: Towards National Legislation for Climate Protection* (Cheltenham, Edward Elgar, 2012) 86.

[195] *Urgenda* (District Court of the Hague), n 3, § 4.80.

[196] ibid.

which the price of CO2 emission has been increased'.[197] Such examples of good practices helped to convince the Dutch court that more could be done by the Netherlands, even under the EU ETS, to tackle climate change.

The same can probably be said in relation to the second prominent EU climate policy measure, namely the EU Effort Sharing Regulation,[198] concerning emissions not covered by the EU ETS. The Effort Sharing Regulation lays down differentiated emission reduction targets by 2030 for each MS, which have the possibility to set more ambitious targets within specific ranges,[199] in accordance with Article 193 TFEU.[200] This provision entails that 'protective measures adopted pursuant to Article 192 – being the legal basis of the Effort Sharing Regulation – shall not prevent any [MS] from maintaining or introducing more stringent protective measures'.[201] Obviously, MSs' discretion will still be subject to the general principles of EU law (eg the principle of proportionality) and the European Union Charter of Fundamental Rights (EUCFR) (eg the right to equal treatment), since national authorities will still be acting within the scope of EU law.[202]

In its written observations in *Duarte Agostinho*, the European Commission – which was granted leave to intervene – maintained that 'nothing precludes Member States from adopting even more ambitious GHG emissions reduction targets at national level'.[203] The EU executive further added that, under EU law, the MSs are required to develop their integrated national energy and climate plans (NECPs) 'covering the five dimensions of the Energy Union, ie decarbonisation (greenhouse gas reduction and renewables), energy security, energy efficiency, internal energy market and research, innovation and competitiveness'.[204] By so arguing, the Commission therefore clearly attempted to shift the responsibility for human rights violations under the ECHR from the EU to the EU MSs.

With specific regard to the *Bosphorus* presumption, the European Commission – always in the frame of the *Duarte Agostinho* dispute – curiously mentioned the *Carvalho* case,[205] holding that the CJEU

[197] ibid.

[198] Adopted in 2018, the Effort Sharing Regulation was then amended in 2023, see more specifically Regulation (EU) 2023/857 of the European Parliament and of the Council of 19 April 2023 amending Regulation (EU) 2018/842 on binding annual greenhouse gas emission reductions by Member States from 2021 to 2030 contributing to climate action to meet commitments under the Paris Agreement, and Regulation (EU) 2018/1999 (Text with EEA relevance) PE/72/2022/REV/1 OJ L 111, 26 April 2023, 1–14.

[199] See https://climate.ec.europa.eu/eu-action/effort-sharing-member-states-emission-targets/effort-sharing-2021-2030-targets-and-flexibilities_en.

[200] See also Marjan Peeters and Natassa Athanasiadou, 'The Continued Effort Sharing Approach in EU Climate Law: Binding Targets, Challenging Enforcement?' (2020) 29 *RECIEL* 205.

[201] ibid.

[202] ibid.

[203] European Commission, written observations – Case *Duarte Agostinbo and Others v Portugal and Others* (Application 39371/20), § 21. Available at: https://jusmundi.com/en/document/pdf/other/en-duarte-agostinho-others-v-portugal-and-others-third-party-intervention-of-the-european-commission-wednesday-19th-may-2021.

[204] ibid, § 23.

[205] See chapter 7.

> has not yet had the opportunity to assess in substance the claim that the implementation of the obligations under the Paris Agreement by EU law are violating [human rights], the only case brought so far to its attention, [namely *Carvalho*], having been inadmissible under [Article 263(4) TFEU].[206]

However, the Commission strongly emphasised the 'equivalent level of protection' between the ECHR and the law of the Union, arguing that (i) the values of the EU enshrined under the Treaties;[207] (ii) the EUCFR;[208] (iii) the EU membership to the Paris Agreement;[209] (iv) the 'complete system of legal remedies', which also encompasses the PRP on validity, demonstrate that the EU does guarantee for 'an equivalent level of protection of [HRs] to that of the Convention in the field of environmental protection'.[210]

In the light of this reasoning, if the ECtHR should find that the EU MSs enjoy some discretion, either under the EU ETS or under the Effort Sharing Regulation (as the Dutch judiciary found in *Urgenda*), the *Bosphorus* presumption will not find application, since the MSs will not be able to rely on the presumption of equivalence between the ECHR and the system of human rights protection established under EU law. This means that the EU MSs could be held responsible – using the words of the ECtHR – 'for all acts and omissions of their organs, whether these arise from domestic law or from the need to fulfil [EU law] obligations'.[211] Crucially, for the purpose of the argument in this chapter, a ruling of the ECtHR ascertaining that the climate targets of Austria are in breach of the Convention, even when the *Bosphorus* presumption does not find application, could mean that also the climate targets established by the EU are – indirectly – in breach of the ECHR.

Challenging EU climate standards might not be the primary intention of Mr Müllner, but public statements of leading European NGOs intervening in the case actually prove, once again, the strong will of CSOs to challenge EU climate policy *indirectly*, before the ECtHR.[212] Indeed, CAN Europe and GLAN intervened in Strasbourg in *Müllner v Austria* and released a joint statement afterwards.[213] In this statement, first, they recalled the relevance of the case for access to justice before the ECtHR in the area of climate change.[214] Second, the two NGOs declared to have brought another case to the CJEU under the new AR, where they have 'put forward similar arguments as those contained in the third party intervention just filed in the case of M. Müller'.[215] Then, the NGOs stated:

[206] European Commission, written observations, n 153, § 66.
[207] ibid, § 68.
[208] ibid, § 69.
[209] ibid, § 70.
[210] ibid, § 72.
[211] See *Bosphorus*, n 135.
[212] See https://caneurope.org/landmark-case-european-court-human-rights/.
[213] ibid.
[214] ibid.
[215] ibid.

> We are calling on the Commission to revise the greenhouse gas emissions it has authorised Member States to emit between now and 2030, as set out in their annual emissions allocations under the Effort Sharing Regulation. The current levels authorised by the Commission are contrary to environmental law because the level of climate ambition is insufficient to protect fundamental human rights.[216] It remains to be seen whether the new standards for access to justice set out in the *Klimaseniorinnen* judgement from the European Court of Human Rights could ultimately improve access to justice in climate cases before the Court of Justice of the European Union. While this ruling does not bind EU courts, it could serve as a persuasive precedent.

This statement and the strategy behind demonstrate, once again, the flexible understanding that ENGOs have of the LOS and of the opportunities available in the area of environmental and climate change litigation. CAN Europe and GLAN explicitly stated that a positive judgment in *Müllner v Austria* could be used not only as an alternative pathway to challenge the legality of EU law, but also as a 'persuasive precedent' *vis-à-vis* the CJEU, in order to push the EU judiciary to depart from the *Plaumann* formula. This also shows that the will to build TIJC does not only belong to GPI, but also to other leading European ENGOs directly involved in CCL.

Having emphasised this aspect, I would also like to stress that, if the ECtHR will find that the EU MSs do not enjoy any discretion under EU climate law – despite this being a very implausible scenario – this will trigger the application of the *Bosphorus* presumption, which can only be rebutted if, in the circumstances of the specific case, the protection of the rights granted under the ECHR is 'manifestly deficient' under EU law. To ascertain this, the ECtHR will have to review the system of human rights' protection established under EU law.

In this regard, I argue that the plaintiff in *Müllner v Austria* have a limited possibility to overturn the presumption. This is because the system of judicial protection of the EU has already been (briefly) reviewed by the ECtHR, precisely in *Bosphorus*, and deemed 'equivalent' to the system of HRs' protection granted under the ECHR.[217] There is, therefore, already a strong precedent preventing the Court of Strasbourg from changing its assessment on the adequacy of the EU system of judicial protection of human rights.

In my view, in a bid to rebound the *Bosphorus* presumption in *Müllner v Austria*, the applicant, in the frame of the domestic trial, should have also attempted to stimulate a referral to the CJEU, questioning the validity of EU law on climate change, having the form of a legislative act. Depending on the outcome of the national court's referral, only then Mr Müllner's should have tried to bring the case to Strasbourg before the ECtHR. This since the presumption can only be rebutted if, *in the circumstances of the specific case*, the protection of the rights granted under the ECHR is manifestly deficient under EU law. Therefore, in my opinion, in

[216] ibid.

[217] ibid, § 165. See Christina Eckes, 'Does the European Court of Human Rights Provide Protection from the European Community? The Case of Bosphorus Airways' (2007) 13 (1) *European Public Law* 56.

order to rebound the *Bosphorus* presumption, the applicants must show that, in the frame of the same case, they have not only exhausted the domestic remedies available at national level, but also the EU remedies laid down under the EU Treaties and, in particular, the PRP which – as mentioned already several times in this book – is the procedure identified by the European Commission as the 'gap filler' for the lack of access to justice of private applicants at EU level. The inadequacy of the PRP on validity to 'fill the gap' for the lack of access to justice at EU level – also for the reasons set out by AG Jacobs in his opinion in *UPA*[218] – has already been discussed in chapter two. Therefore, I refer the reader to that chapter for a broader evaluation of the use of the PRP in environmental litigation.

On this point, I do not know if Mr Müllner's lawyers already tried to stimulate a referral under Article 267 TFEU before bringing the case to Strasbourg. However, the scenarios discussed here below should just be considered as an intellectual legal exercise, which might be useful (or not) for future climate litigants in Strasbourg against an EU MS.

In this regard, if the *Bosphorus* presumption applies in a case triggered in Strasbourg against an EU MS, and if the ECtHR finds that the MS concerned has no room for deviating from EU climate targets, the same applicants will have to demonstrate that EU law is 'manifestly deficient' in providing adequate protection to the rights enshrined under the Convention. It is here where the 'failed'[219] referral to Luxembourg comes into play: in this way, the applicants could concretely show, to the eyes of the ECtHR, that EU law does not provide 'comparable' protection to the rights enshrined under the Convention and that individuals seeking to contest EU climate targets have no alternative other than seeking protection precisely under the ECHR. The consolidated *Plaumann* case law of the CJEU would further strengthen the applicants' argument.

Following this reasoning, the traditional 'complete system of legal remedies' argument could 'fall', as the applicant could succeed in proving the 'insufficient potential' of the EU supervisory mechanism, unlike it ruled in *Bosphorus*.[220] This would make it possible for the plaintiffs to hold the Respondent (EU) State accountable for violations of the rights protected under the European Convention, but – most importantly – could show the inadequacy of both, the EU judicial protection system and EU law on climate change, *vis-à-vis* the ECHR.

In both scenarios, the one in which *Bosphorus* does not find application and the one in which it does, there is clearly potential for legal mobilisation before the ECtHR to have an indirect impact on EU climate law. A brief summary is given below.

If the *Müllner v Austria* case is deemed admissible, this would already be a significant success for the European environmental movement, since legal standing

[218] See chapter 2.
[219] Which can either mean a denied referral at national level or a favourable referral ending with an unfavourable preliminary ruling by the CJEU.
[220] *Bosphorus*, n 135, § 164.

of individuals in climate litigation still is a barrier also before the ECtHR.[221] Furthermore, broadening access to justice in CCL in Strasbourg would send a very powerful message to the other European regional courts, including the CJEU, which – as mentioned before – would start to look even more 'obsolete' in the eyes of environmental and climate litigants across Europe. In this respect, if the plaintiff is granted standing in *Müllner v Austria* and receives a ruling on the merits of the case, this will represent a new key 'building block' for future legal mobilisation and further contribute to build TIJC in Europe.

If there is a ruling on the merits in *Müllner v Austria*, the application of the *Bosphorus* doctrine will mostly depend on the assessment, carried out by the ECtHR, of the margin of manoeuvre that the MS enjoy under EU law in relation to the emission reduction targets established by the EU. This assessment will be crucial to determine whether the Respondent (EU) State enjoys the presumption of 'equivalent' human rights protection accorded to the EU in *Bosphorus*. Moreover, it could be the first time the presumption is applied in the climate context.

If *Bosphorus* does not find application, a ruling of the ECtHR ascertaining that the climate targets of the EU MS are in breach of the Convention could still have an indirect impact on EU climate policy. This, in particular, if the Austrian emissions reduction targets do not go beyond the targets established under EU law.

Conversely, if *Bosphorus* does find application, the presumption could still be rebutted if the applicants manage to demonstrate that the EU system of protection of the human rights enshrined under the Convention is 'manifestly deficient'. In my view, this could have been proven more convincingly if the applicant in *Müllner v Austria* would have first attempted to stimulate a referral to the CJEU during the domestic trial.

Given this, it is clear that the *Müllner v Austria* case is also a test for the EU. More specifically, for its climate policy but also for its system of judicial protection of HRs.

F. The Political Impact on the EU of CCL in Strasbourg

Considering that the EU has still not adhered to the ECHR, despite an explicit mandate included in Article 6 TEU, the ECtHR's rulings cannot bind in any way the EU and its institutions.[222] The *potential* legal implications at stake in *Müllner v Austria* for the EU have already been described in the section above. Yet, the impact that CCL in Strasbourg has *already* produced on the EU political institutions also deserves considerable attention. In particular, I refer to a specific priority parliamentary question on the relevance of the *Duarte Agostinho* case, presented on 6 July 2021, before the case was dismissed in 2024, by a German MEP,

[221] Prantl, n 166.

[222] See Opinion 2/13, *Accession of the European Union to the European Convention for the Protection of Human Rights and Fundamental Freedoms* (2014) ECLI:EU:C:2014:2454, § 136.

Joachim Kuhs, to the European Commission.[223] In his request, Mr Kuhs addressed to the Commission the following questions:

> In the light of the EU's accession to the ECHR, does the Commission believe that the ECtHR's refusal to reject the clearly inadmissible application submitted by Duarte et al. could result in a judgment that conflicts with the Treaties?[224]
>
> As guardian of the Treaties, does the Commission expect that the EU's accession to the ECHR will give rise to regular conflicts between judgments of the ECtHR and the Treaties? If so, how does the Commission think these conflicts should be resolved?[225]
>
> In the Commission's view as guardian of the Treaties, and in the light of the ECtHR's quest to expand its powers, should the EU give up its claim to the supremacy of EU law and share this prerogative with the ECtHR?[226]

In his questions, Mr Kuhs has called the attention of the Commission on the impact that *Duarte Agostinho* could have had on the EU legal order and its system of human rights protection. To these questions, Ursula von der Leyen, President of the Commission, responded on 7 July 2021 as follows:

> The European Court of Human Rights (ECtHR) has not yet rendered a decision on admissibility of the application no. 39371/20 Duarte Agostinho and others v. Portugal and others, rather it has joined the question of admissibility with the merits. The Union already recognizes the rights, freedoms and principles set out in the Charter of Fundamental Rights of the European Union, which has the same legal value as the Treaties. By virtue of Article 52(3) of the Charter, rights in the Charter which correspond to rights guaranteed by the European Convention on Human Rights should be given the same meaning and scope as those laid down in the Convention.
>
> Accession of the Union to the Convention would make it possible for individuals to bring cases against the Union before the European Court of Human Rights. It would also make it possible for the Union to be held accountable under the Convention alongside its Member States in situations where an EU Member State implements Union law. However, even after accession, the Court of Justice would remain the ultimate authority with respect to the interpretation of Union law. The jurisdiction of European Court of Human Rights extends only to the interpretation and application of the Convention and its Protocols. When exercising that jurisdiction in a case involving Union law, it will have to rely on the interpretation of Union law given by the Court of Justice.[227]

[223] Priority question for written answer, P-002219/2021/rev.1 to the Commission, Rule 138, Joachim Kuhs (ID). Subject: 'Duarte Agostinho climate case pending before the European Court of Human Rights'. Available at: www.europarl.europa.eu/doceo/document/P-9-2021-002219_EN.html. In addition to this priority question, there were two more priority questions on *Duarte* asked by MEPs to the European Commission, namely the one from Michiel Hoogeveen (ECR) on 29 April 2021 and the one from Rob Rooken (ECR) on 22 April 2021. However, the one from Joachim Kuhs was the only one where the impact of the case on the EU system of access to justice emerged in Ursula von der Leyen's answer.

[224] ibid.

[225] ibid.

[226] ibid.

[227] Answer given by President von der Leyen on behalf of the European Commission (6.7.2021), EN P-002219/2021. Available at: www.europarl.europa.eu/doceo/document/P-9-2021-002219-ASW_EN.pdf.

In her reply, the President of the European Commission reminded readers that the EU has its own Charter of FRs, which lays down a clear link with the ECHR in Article 52(3).[228] However, from a legal mobilisation perspective, it is important to stress the second part of von der Leyen's answer. GLAN and the plaintiffs have succeeded in bringing the case to the attention of the European Parliament and the Commission, stimulating a political debate on the impact of the case on the EU legal order, which was even amplified after the ECtHR's climate rulings of 9 April 2024.[229]

Further, President von der Leyen confirmed what has been stated by the CJEU in opinion 2/13,[230] namely that with the adhesion of the EU to the ECHR, individuals will have the possibility to hold the EU accountable for human rights violations, which is something that would transform the EU system of judicial protection, since this is currently impeded precisely by *Plaumann*.[231] EU adhesion to the ECHR would thus certainly undermine the 'autonomy' of the EU legal order,[232] strongly protected by the EU judiciary, but also transform the way citizens and CSOs could challenge the legality of EU law.

Having the possibility to contest EU measures and hold the EU institutions accountable is precisely what most European ENGOs want. Therefore, the answer of the President of the Commission epitomises this 'clash' of different views on access to justice to the CJEU and the relevance that this has for European democracy. On the one hand, we find European ENGOs seeking to contest the legality of EU law and hold the EU accountable for the impact of environmental degradation and climate change; on the other hand, we find the EU institutions making clear that EU acts should not be subject to a judicial review which is promoted by citizens *outside* the jurisdiction of the CJEU. However, the *Plaumann* test de facto allows for the exclusion of EU acts from judicial review, namely 'direct' review promoted by citizens even *within* the jurisdiction of the CJEU.

The added 'political' value of this parliamentary request on *Duarte Agostinho* is therefore that it has forced the Commission to take a stand before the European Parliament on the way the EU executive sees and conceives the autonomy of the EU and its system of direct access to the CJEU, which – according to the Commission – should not be expanded as to enable individuals to 'circumvent *Plaumann*' and hold the EU accountable for HRs violations before the ECtHR.

In the next section, I will now draw my final conclusions on the analysis carried out throughout the whole chapter.

[228] To deepen the topic, see Stephen Brittain, 'The Relationship Between the EU Charter of Fundamental Rights and the European Convention on Human Rights: An Originalist Analysis' (2015) 11 (3) *European Constitutional Law Review* 482–511.

[229] See Eeckhout, n 134.

[230] Opinion 2/13, n 171, § 181.

[231] This in direct actions. Holding the EU accountable for HRs violations is still possible, in principle, through the PRP on validity.

[232] See chapter 3.

VIII. Conclusions

This chapter has illustrated the legal mobilisation dynamics against *Plaumann* in the 'post-Aarhus II – the CCL trend' period. Although the analysis of this timeframe will continue in the following chapter, the sections above have shed light on how CSOs are trying to 'circumvent' *Plaumann* and contest the legality of EU law by litigating before courts other than the CJEU and the national courts of the EU MSs. Despite the presence of *Plaumann*, the EU's regulatory powers in the field of climate change seems to matter for climate litigants. Indeed, ENGOs try to circumvent *Plaumann* and challenge EU emissions reduction targets by other means, as part of broader legal mobilisation campaigns.

This chapter has shown that strategic litigation can serve multiple purposes, such as winning the case in court, but also validating scientific evidence and raising public awareness. In-house lawyers working on strategic litigation for NGOs are perfectly aware of these dynamics. Depending on the goal(s) that the lawsuit intends to achieve, in-house lawyers will construct the case in order to maximise its 'impact'. This word, often mentioned in the literature on legal mobilisation, can mean different things in different cases. For instance, if a case aims at establishing a favourable legal precedent, the case will be deemed 'successful' or 'impactful' if achieves that specific goal. But the 'impact' of a case will obviously be different if the goal is empowering indigenous communities or catching media attention: winning in court in this type of lawsuits will be less crucial.

In the cases outlined in this chapter, in particular *People v Arctic Oil* and *Duarte Agostinho*, *GPI* and *GLAN*, both inspired by *Urgenda*, mainly aimed at holding national governments accountable for the negative impact of climate change on citizens' human rights. However, doctrinal and qualitative analysis has also shown that overcoming (or 'circumventing') *Plaumann* and challenging EU climate law are goals that these NGOs include in their global litigation campaigns. This has been established by the interviews carried out with in-house lawyers at *GPI* and *GLAN*, by a close reading of the application file in *Duarte Agostinho*.

More specifically, GPI seems to be adopting a more 'long-term' approach in relation to access to justice before EU Courts. This ENGO stopped litigating directly before the CJEU precisely because of *Plaumann* and is therefore trying to influence the EU judiciary by more indirect means, that is to say by building transnational judicial comfort incrementally across courts. This goal is prompted by GPI's in-house lawyers, who trigger different lawsuits in different jurisdictions. This type of strategy facilitates what Weiler and Lustig defined as a 'transplantation of constitutional ideas' from a jurisdiction to another. To make this transplantation actually happen, lawyers need to use common legal languages that all judges can 'speak', such as international law and human rights law. Human rights in particular, embedded in national constitutions and international conventions, are often framed in similar terms, making it easier for litigants to set useful precedents to be replicated in future lawsuits. A strategy which de facto shapes new legal opportunities for legal mobilisation, in a LOS that is conceived in very wide and flexible terms by NGOs undertaking CCL on a transnational scale.

Indeed, building judicial comfort aims at increasing judicial receptivity across the globe, in the attempt to push more and more judges to take bold interpretative steps in climate cases. The increasing number of favourable[233] rulings in the field of climate change shows that GPI's idea of building 'judicial comfort' is working, obviously with the support of other NGOs using litigation as a climate mitigation tool. However, so far, one specific court seems to be immune from the influence exercised by climate litigants and other judiciaries across Europe. Indeed, the spreading of 'judicial comfort' might have the effect of making the CJEU look like an 'obsolete' court in the European context, and the climate judgments of the ECtHR released on 9 April 2024 have made things worse in this regard.

The strategies and the 'impact' of the NGO GLAN must be measured in a different way, since this organisation has attempted to indirectly contest EU emission reduction targets through one crucial case, that is *Duarte Agostinho*. However, another case brought against an EU MS – *Müllner v Austria* – is currently pending before the ECtHR. Yet, this chapter has outlined what legal implications may stem from the application (or disapplication) of the *Bosphorus* presumption, under which the Strasbourg Court considers the EU system of judicial protection of the rights granted under the ECHR 'equivalent' to the one established under the human rights convention.

Besides the ultimate failure of the *Duarte Agostinho* case, the case still produced significant effects on the EU institutions, by stimulating a political debate between the European Parliament and the Commission on the relationship between the EU legal order and the ECHR. Regardless of its final outcome, the *Duarte Agostinho* case has therefore pushed the Commission to take a stand before the European co-legislator on the way the EU executive sees and conceives not only European democracy, but also the EU system of judicial protection of citizens' human rights.

The use of human rights in CCL facilitates hermeneutic harmonisation on the side of judiciaries. Harmonisation which, far from being definitive, is already happening and involves a wide range of courts, inside and outside the EU. Nevertheless, as it will be shown in the next chapter, so far, the CJEU seems to be immune from this 'constitutional cross-fertilisation' taking place in the field of climate change. After the ECtHR judgment in *Klimaseniorinnen*, where the Strasbourg Court proved its dynamic nature in reviewing the interpretation of its standing requirements for NGOs in the climate context, another 'hard blow' for the CJEU (and a key 'building block' for the CCL movement) could come precisely from *Müllner v Austria*. Indeed, as mentioned above, a positive outcome for the applicant in this case would further contribute, on the one hand, to building TIJC across the globe, and, on the other hand, also to 'isolating' the CJEU and making it feel even more 'obsolete' in the field of European CCL.

[233] For ENGOs.

In this regard, the next chapter will show that ENGOs have actually triggered lawsuits under Article 263(4) TFEU, aiming to contest the legality of EU climate policy measures, but with very poor results. As will be demonstrated, by rejecting climate actions for annulment promoted by ENGOs, the CJEU is placing itself outside of this ongoing 'judicial dialogue' occurring in the field of climate change and is therefore abstaining from giving an EU-wide interpretation of human rights in the climate context. However, the pending cases brought by ENGOs before the EU judiciary under the new AR could allow the EU judiciary to have a say on EU law on climate change *vis-à-vis* the EU Treaties.[234]

[234] On this point, see Mario Pagano, 'Climate Legal Mobilization Under the New Aarhus Regulation' (2024) 25 (6) *German Law Journal* 919–34.

7

Plaumann and Climate Change before the Court of Justice of the European Union

I. Introduction

In the previous chapters, I explored how environmental non-governmental organisations (ENGOs) have been strategically using the remedies available under EU law (ie Article 263 Treaty on the Functioning of the European Union (TFEU) and the Aarhus Regulation (AR)) and international law (ie the Aarhus Convention Compliance Committee (ACCC) and the European Court of Human Rights (ECtHR)) with the aim of acquiring standing in actions for annulment and pushing the Court of Justice of the European Union (CJEU) to abandon the *Plaumann* test. More specifically, in the previous chapter, I described how ENGOs are also using non-EU Courts to circumvent the *Plaumann* test by building TICJ across jurisdictions, on the one hand, and by *indirectly* contesting the legality of EU law *vis-à-vis* the ECHR, on the other.

In this final chapter I will continue the analysis of the last timeframe of this book, namely the 'CCL trend' period. More specifically, I will show how ENGOs and individuals have attempted to overcome *Plaumann* by continuing to contest the legality of EU climate policy measures, but this time directly before the EU judiciary.

My analysis in the present chapter will focus on the last two layers of analysis illustrated in the theoretical framework,[1] namely the one referring to 'resources' and the one referring to 'strategies' deployed by strategic litigants. Indeed, the present chapter intends to provide an original empirical and theoretical contribution to the literature analysing the micro-factors igniting legal mobilisation. As mentioned in the introduction, by the term 'resources', I refer to those dimensions or characteristics of the single agent that increase the agent's likelihood of using litigation. In the light of this, in the present chapter I will illustrate the use of coalition membership as a resource in legal mobilisation in the climate context and emphasise how this impacts the development of the legal strategy.

[1] See the introduction to the present book.

My inquiry will focus on two lawsuits, namely *Carvalho* and *Sabo*, brought by citizens and civil society organisations (CSOs). Both of these lawsuits aimed to hold the EU accountable for the negative impact of climate change on citizens' fundamental rights (FRs), this time directly before the EU judiciary. In the pages below, I will first analyse the *Carvalho* case; then the *Sabo* case. For the analysis of both cases, the same structure is followed. First, the sections below will shed light on the goals and actors involved in the 'conception' and then 'legal construction' of the cases. The people and the organisations behind the cases will be presented and their underlying reasons for mobilising the EU Courts analysed.

Second, this chapter will delve into the legal strategy adopted by the legal teams: the factors influencing the plaintiffs' selection, the eventual interlinkages with the communication strategy supporting the cases, and the arguments deployed in the application files.

Third, the chapter will engage with the actual rulings of the courts and the reasoning embedded in them. This part will show how and to what extent the EU judiciary engages with the arguments deployed by the applicants and provide a critical reading of the applicants' arguments and the courts' counterarguments. Then, I will situate the findings emerged from the analysis of resources, tactics and strategies within the existing literature on legal mobilisation and provide my own conceptualisation of such findings.

Fourth, my analysis will attempt to shed light on the aftermath of the cases and the 'impact' they actually achieved, as defined in the introduction to the present book in terms of both, 'subjective' and 'objective' impact. My conclusions stemming from the overall analysis will conclude the chapter.

II. Using Article 263(4) TFEU in CCL

Prior to 2018, CCL before EU Courts was mainly based on cases brought by Member States (MSs) and EU institutions.[2] Indeed, the narrow standing requirements laid down under Article 263(4) TFEU discouraged private applicants from seeking access to justice in actions for annulment, making this legal tool in essence an exclusive remedy for privileged applicants (namely the EU MSs, the Parliament, the Council and the Commission). Only a few climate cases[3] brought by private applicants (namely corporations) reached the CJEU through the preliminary reference procedure (PRP).[4]

However, the global developments in CCL following the Dutch *Urgenda* case have also encouraged private citizens and ENGOs to challenge the *Plaumann* test and bring direct actions against EU climate policy measures. In the next sections,

[2] Sanja Bogojevic, 'EU Climate Change Litigation, the Role of the European Courts, and the Importance of Legal Culture' (2013) 35 *Law & Policy* 199.

[3] Mainly ETS cases.

[4] C-127/07, *Arcelor Atlantique and Lorraine and Others* (2008) ECLI:EU:C:2008:728; C-366/10, *Air Transport Association of America and Others* (2011) ECLI:EU:C:2011:864.

I will shed light on two climate cases, namely *Carvalho* and *Sabo*, brought before the EU judiciary under Article 263(4) TFEU. The present analysis will focus on the objectives of the two lawsuits and on the role played by the lawyers and the other actors involved in these cases, concerning EU emission reduction targets and EU policy on renewable energy. Special attention will be devoted to unpacking the legal strategies deployed by the lawyers involved in these two lawsuits, as revealed by interviews undertaken with some of them.[5] Further attention will also be devoted to deepening our understanding of the relationship between the lawyers and the environmental organisations involved in these cases. In particular, the chapter will shed light on ENGOs' mobilisation strategies, on their dominant legal expertise and to what extent legal mobilisation fits within their broader mobilisation strategies to achieve environmental change.

III. Constructing the *Carvalho* Case

2018 was a very dry year for Europe. Likewise, the impact of climate change on indigenous communities and biodiversity across the globe was particularly severe.[6] Extreme heat and dangerous fires hit different countries in Europe in the summer,[7] helping to animate a powerful climate movement of young activists led by the Swedish teenager Greta Thunberg.[8] However, 2018 was also the year in which the EU adopted a number of climate measures, each contributing to meet the EU's obligations under the Paris Agreement.[9] It is therefore no coincidence that, on that year, a Professor of environmental law at the University of Bremen decided that time was ripe for challenging the legality of the EU climate package directly before the EU judiciary. This academic (and lawyer) is Gerd Winter, who, worried about the future for his six grandchildren[10] and inspired by *Urgenda*[11] and *Juliana v US*,[12] thought about triggering a broader 'EU-wide *Urgenda*' before the EU judiciary. Gerd Winter, who had been contemplating triggering this kind of litigation since 2016, worked on the case in its entirety, developing the legal strategy and representing the plaintiffs before the EU Courts.[13] This along with two additional lawyers, namely Roda Verheyen and Hugo Leith.[14]

[5] See methodological section in the introduction to the present book.

[6] Kelly Levin and Dennis Tirpak, World Resources Institute, '2018: A Year of Climate Extremes', 27 December 2018. Available at: www.wri.org/insights/2018-year-climate-extremes.

[7] In particular, Portugal, Sweden and Greece.

[8] See https://fridaysforfuture.org/.

[9] See below, section IV.

[10] Interview with Gerd Winter, Professor for public law, European law and Sociology of law at Department of Law, University of Bremen (13 December 2021).

[11] *Urgenda Foundation v The Netherlands* [2015] HAZA C/09/00456689 (24 June 2015).

[12] *Juliana v United States* 947 F.3d 1159 (9th Cir 2020).

[13] Interview with Gerd Winter, n 10.

[14] I want to thank the legal team involved in *Carvalho* for making their application file publicly available even before the case was decided. All the case-related documents are available here: https://peoplesclimatecase.caneurope.org/documents/. Hereinafter '*Carvalho* – AF', § 422.

Before submitting the application file, Gerd Winter had an exchange of views with the in-house lawyers of the Urgenda Foundation, who encouraged him to pursue his initiative and study in depth the science behind climate change and its impact on human rights (in particular the Intergovernmental Panel on Climate Change (IPCC) reports).[15] After a difficult initial moment of solitary work, Winter's idea started to attract more and more lawyers and environmental organisations. For instance, the initiative found the support of Roda Verheyen (mentioned above), a German lawyer specialised in environmental and international law, who also served as legal counsel in another ongoing renowned climate lawsuit, namely *Lliuya v RWE AG*.[16] Roda Verheyen joined Winter's initiative, followed by a few German ENGOs, such as *Protect the Planet* (*PP*) and *Germanwatch*.[17] *PP*, in particular, had been extremely supportive since the early phases of the lawsuit.

After having brainstormed on the case at Gerd Winter's house, PP decided to contribute concretely to the pursuit of the legal enterprise by bearing a significant part of the financial burden.[18] On this point, Gerd Winter revealed:

> Although I did and do this *pro bono* because I am paid as a professor, we did need money for the case. Roda [Verheyen] of course needed to be paid, we had a Barrister [Hugo Leith] but he also did this *pro bono*. But we had to bring scientists in. And they had to be paid as well. So, [PP] was very helpful in terms of financial background but also in terms of communication, which is core to any of this kind of [CCL] cases.[19]

PP and Germanwatch are both members of CAN Europe.[20] This stands for 'Climate Action Network Europe', a big network of 189 members across Europe (even beyond the EU MSs),[21] originally gathering mainly ENGOs working on climate-related issues and concerns. However, the network now also attracts organisations 'from the human rights and development side [which is] really helping bridge the gap between human rights and climate activism'.[22]

In relation to their involvement in the lawsuit, Harriet Mackaill-Hill, EU Climate Governance and Human Rights Policy Coordinator at CAN Europe at the time of the interview, added:

> They were looking to challenge three European texts.[23] And CAN Europe is an umbrella organisation of European NGOs and, apart from the French NGO 'Notre Affaire à tous',[24] all the other NGOs are [our] members. So, it was logical and made sense for us

[15] Interview with Gerd Winter, n 10.
[16] See www.germanwatch.org/en/15999.
[17] Interview with Gerd Winter, n 10.
[18] ibid.
[19] ibid. The interlinkages between the communication strategy and the litigation strategy will be addressed below, in section III.B.
[20] Interview with Harriet Mackaill-Hill, former EU Climate Governance and Human Rights Policy Coordinator at CAN Europe, 21 January 2022.
[21] ibid.
[22] ibid.
[23] See below section IV.
[24] Which was another partner in the case.

> to be the front-facing of that in front of the EU institutions, because there was nobody else that could do that. It just seemed like a logical formation to have us, because none of them are based in Brussels. It was kind of them, us and the institutions. And it's a job that we do for all our files, something we're used to in terms of representation and Brussels-based advocacy.[25]

The intervention of an umbrella organisation like CAN Europe provided all the ENGOs involved with better (and more uniform) representation before the EU institutions. This was crucial to ensure the achievement of the 'raising awareness' objective of the case, which aimed at mobilising not only EU citizens, but also EU policymakers.[26] In this regard, CAN Europe mainly contributed the goal-setting dimension of the lawsuit, while Gerd Winter and the other lawyers solely focused on setting the legal strategy.[27]

The interviews that I carried out revealed that the lawsuit intended to pursue a number of different objectives, ranging from holding the EU accountable for climate change to raising public awareness on the case itself as well as on the lack of access to justice at the EU level.[28] Indeed, the existence of *Plaumann* was key in the construction of the case and this is particularly visible in the process of plaintiff selection, to which the next section will be devoted.

A. Lawyers Seeking Plaintiffs

In order to effectively construct the case and overcome the *Plaumann* test, the legal team (with the support of the partner ENGOs) carefully selected the plaintiffs who formally triggered the lawsuit by relying on coalition networks and lawyers' individual relationships.[29] The selection of plaintiffs was heavily influenced by three main factors: (i) the nature of the *Plaumann* test; (ii) the scientific evidence on the impact of climate change on the environment; (iii) the geographical diversity of the plaintiffs.

In relation to the first two factors, Gerd Winter maintained that under Article 263(4) TFEU applicants seem to be required to prove a de facto differentiation 'from all other persons':

> With Plaumann we want to have claimants who are differently concerned/affected by the challenged act and it seems to mean this in 'factual' terms. Now, if you look at the 'facts' there are always differences between claimants and very much so in our case …, where we carefully selected persons who were differently concerned. Some because of the disappearance of snow, some of overflooding, some because of heatwaves, etc.

[25] Interview with Harriet Mackaill-Hill, n 20.

[26] Interview with Raul Cazan, President of 2Celsius, 24 March 2022. This aspect will be deepened below, in section V.

[27] ibid.

[28] Interview with Harriet Mackaill-Hill, n 20.

[29] Interview with Gerd Winter, n 10.

> Living in different locations of the Union and worldwide. So, the real difference is 'in fact'.[30]

Therefore, it was Gerd Winter's opinion that the 'factual' differentiation established under *Plaumann* required a selection of the plaintiffs on the basis of the 'differentiated' impact that these suffered because of climate change.[31]

> The … idea was to have plaintiffs who represented the major effects of climate change. So, in terms of water, droughts, flooding, ice and snow (the warming up of water regions), including also heatwaves.[32]

This choice produced a very strong shift from the older cases analysed in this research. Indeed, while previous environmental actions for annulment saw – almost exclusively – ENGOs acting as plaintiffs,[33] the lawsuit conceived by Gerd Winter saw a clear 'individualisation' of climate change, also justified by the presence of *Plaumann*, which led to a careful selection of natural persons across the EU.

In addition to the 'factual' differentiation of plaintiffs, the third factor also came into play. Indeed, the broad territorial reach of EU law across the MSs (and beyond) also required a certain degree of diversity relating to the geographical origin of the plaintiffs, which also had to be considered during the selection. In the light of these factors, 10 families were chosen (36 individuals in total) as well as a Swedish Association of young Sami.[34] I indicate their names[35] and their countries of origin below.

Plaintiffs from Portugal:

1. Armando Carvalho (and his family)
2. Diogo Carvalho
3. Ildebrando Conceição
4. Alfredo Sendim
5. Joaquim Caxeiro and family

Plaintiffs from France:

6. Renaud Feschet
7. Guylaine Feschet
8. Gabriel Feschet
9. Maurice Feschet
10. Genevieve Gassin

[30] ibid.
[31] Gerd Winter, 'Armando Carvalho and Others v. EU: Invoking Human Rights and the Paris Agreement for Better Climate Protection Legislation' (2020) 9 (1) *Transnational Environmental Law* 157.
[32] ibid.
[33] Apart from the initial *Greenpeace* case.
[34] *Carvalho* – AF, n 14, 38.
[35] The names of the plaintiffs are publicly available.

Plaintiffs from Romania:

11. Petru Vlad, Calene
12. Ana Tricu
13. Petru Arin Vlad
14. Maria Ioana Vlad
15. Andrei Nicolae Vlad

Plaintiffs from Italy:

16. Giorgio Davide Elter
17. Sara Burland
18. Soulail Elter
19. Alice Elter
20. Rosa Elter
21. Maria Elter

Plaintiffs from Germany:

22. Maike Recktenwald
23. Michael Recktenwald
24. Lueke Recktenwald

Plaintiffs from Kenya:

25. Roba Waku Guya
26. Fadhe Hussein Tache
27. Sado Guyo
28. Issa Guyo
29. Jibril Guyo
30. Adanoor Guyo
31. Mohammed Guyo

Plaintiffs from Fiji Island:

32. Petero Qaloibau
33. Melania Cironiceva
34. Katarina Dimoto
35. Petero Qaloibau Jnr
36. Elisabeta Tokalau

Plaintiffs from Sweden:

37. Sáminuorra, Association of Young Saami

As can be seen, the legal team added families originating from Kenya and Fiji Island to the EU-based plaintiffs. This was because the lawsuit also had a strong 'extraterritorial' component in that it claimed that:

> [The] EU's Fundamental Rights should also protect citizens who live outside the European Union if they are suffering because of EU activities. Through this case, they

> remind the EU of its international responsibilities. They underline that a higher climate target in the EU would send a strong signal to other states to increase their efforts and that the increased ambition is crucial for their survival.[36]

Indeed, the African continent and Small Island Developing States are severely affected by the negative impact of climate change.[37] The Kenyan family was chosen because the higher temperatures, lower rainfall and drought conditions that had occurred in recent years, threatening the survival of the livestock herded by the Guyo family.[38]

Similarly, the Fiji Islands family's life was essentially based on farming, fishing and eco-tourism, all dangerously compromised by higher water temperatures and rising sea levels occurring on the islands.[39] In the litigants' view, the lawsuit thus also represented a way to provide third-country nationals who were affected by the impact of EU climate policy, with access to justice before the EU judiciary.

Considering the broad geographical reach of the search, personal relationships and ENGOs' networks were crucial in the selection. Through the interviews undertaken, I only had the chance to get direct information on the selection of the plaintiffs originating from France, Italy, and Romania. In relation to the Feschet family, these were lavender growers from Provence (Southern France), who suffered a loss of 44 per cent of lavender harvest in six years.[40] On this family, Gerd Winter revealed that: 'The French farmer, Maurice Feschet, is a personal friend of mine and was the first I invited to join. We sat together with some wine under a tree in the evening discussing this and he said "ok!"'.[41]

However, the legal team also wished to ensure that some of the European mountain territories were properly represented.[42] This is why Gerd Winter first contacted various alpinist associations, but these refused to join the case.[43] Then he got in touch with a friend of his, who used to serve as Secretary General of the Alpine Convention.[44] This person proposed the name of an organic food producer from Cogne (Aosta Valley, Italy), namely Giorgio Elter, who also managed a small B&B, fully dependent on the tourism generated by the various ice climbing opportunities on the Italian Alpes.[45] Mr Elter was then formally contacted by PP, which invited him to join the lawsuit as a plaintiff, along with his family.[46] This was because the Elter's business had been heavily impacted by glacial melting and temperature changes occurring in the region.[47]

[36] See https://peoplesclimatecase.caneurope.org/plaintiff/family-guyo-from-kenya/.

[37] See https://unfccc.int/news/climate-change-is-an-increasing-threat-to-africa; see Adelle Thomas, Rosanne Martyr-Koller, Patrick Pringle and Kevon Rhiney, 'Climate Change and Small Island Developing States' (2020) 45 *Annual Review of Environment and Resources* 1–27.

[38] *Carvalho* – AF, n 14, § 66.

[39] ibid, §§ 78–81.

[40] See https://peoplesclimatecase.caneurope.org/plaintiff/family-feschet-from-france/.

[41] Interview with Gerd Winter, n 10.

[42] ibid.

[43] ibid.

[44] ibid.

[45] See https://peoplesclimatecase.caneurope.org/plaintiff/family-elter-from-italy/.

[46] Interview with Giorgio Elter, Italian plaintiff in the *Carvalho* case, 14 October 2021.

[47] See above, n 45.

Along with the Elter's family, the Romanian plaintiffs (the Vlad family) also contributed to ensuring the representation of European mountain territories in the lawsuit. Moreover, the Vlad family was also chosen to ensure the inclusion of plaintiffs coming from Eastern Europe, which was one of the areas that was still missing proper representation in the lawsuit.[48] On the selection of the Vlad family, Raul Cazan, President of 2Celsius[49] – a Romanian ENGO dealing with climate-related issues in Central-Eastern Europe – stated:

> They [the legal team] wanted Eastern Europe, Central Europe, Western Europe, probably North-South, everything to be well represented, even Kenya and Fiji. This kind of representation was on the one hand, but another sort of diversity that they wanted was about people working in agriculture and different environments, so most necessarily, they wanted someone from the mountains in Eastern Europe. As well, they wanted somebody from the lowlands, also in Eastern Europe. Most probably, that was supposed to be Poland. And people that might have been affected by the effects of climate change, one way or another, scientifically proven. I was there with this [guy] already, with Petru Vlad [the father of the Romanian family] from the Transylvanian Alps for the main reason that we were already kind of known. I was already known for all the things I did with this guy. And it just happened that we got an email from CAN [Europe], asking me: 'Listen we need somebody from the Carpathians!'. And I was like: 'Yeah sure, let's check it out and let's see how it works!'. And immediately I went to meet the guy again [Petru Vlad] and he agreed immediately.[50]

Therefore, CAN Europe asked one of its member-ENGOs (2Celsius) to help provide someone from the Carpathians whose personal conditions had been impacted by climate change. Raul Cazan – President of 2Celsius – knew the Romanian shepherd Petru Vlad (precisely from the Carpathians Alpes) from previous climate-related projects.[51] The cattle of the Vlad family had suffered greatly from water scarcity, making this family optimal plaintiffs for the case.[52] At Cazan's request, Petru Vlad accepted – along with his family – to actively engage in the lawsuit.[53]

Considering that most of the plaintiffs involved were farmers, Harriet Mackaill-Hill from CAN Europe also talked about the difficulties experienced in working with this category of persons:

> If we're talking about the [*Carvalho*] case, the plaintiffs are also farmers and they have already a very … labour-intense life. They're tired, they can't go to Paris for a conference or appear in Brussels for a Parliament interview. So, it's quite difficult to find the right people to bring the case and to challenge what you want to challenge.[54]

[48] Interview with Raul Cazan, n 26.
[49] See https://2celsius.org/.
[50] ibid.
[51] See www.youtube.com/watch?v=t2cD0jf177I.
[52] 'Year by year, the temperatures are increasing. There is no longer enough water for our cattle and sheep. I have to take my cattle from 700m altitude to 1400m for decent grass to graze, but especially for water. But I cannot go any further up with our herds, because above 2000m there is only the sky.' (Petru Vlad) from https://peoplesclimatecase.caneurope.org/plaintiff/family-vlad-from-romania/.
[53] Interview with Raul Cazan, n 26.
[54] Interview with Harriet Mackaill-Hill, n 20.

In addition to the labour-related difficulties experienced by farmers, further obstacles to their free movement were introduced by national authorities during the Covid-19 pandemic, which hit the whole world in 2020, when the appeal judgment of the CJEU was still pending. Because of the pandemic, the plaintiffs never really had the chance to meet and get to know each other in person.[55] However, they were kept up to date on the development of the case on a regular basis by the ENGOs.[56] Indeed:

> For each plaintiff there was an NGO in the consortium.[57] Apart from Fiji and Kenya, but for all the European countries, there was an NGO partner that was part of our consortium that was financed via us, so they were getting money to work on this case. I think [the case] lasted for three years in total in the end. We would organise weekly meetings with that consortium and report back to the plaintiffs, so that would mean that the plaintiffs didn't have to come to these … organisational meetings.[58]

Besides the logistical aspects of the relationship between the ENGOs and the plaintiffs, another key element of this relationship concerns the way the individual stories of the families involved were actually told to the general public. The next section will therefore attempt to deepen our understanding of the interlinkages between the litigation strategy behind the case and the communication strategy built to support it.

B. Litigation and Communication

The case was officially named 'the People's Climate case', even though it is also known as the *Carvalho* case,[59] as it is referred to in the present book. To further raise awareness of the lawsuit, a dedicated website was created by the coalition of ENGOs, gathering information on the organisations involved and the legal material gradually released – such as the application file as well as the courts' rulings – along with interviews with the actual plaintiffs.[60] Such documents demonstrate the importance of the 'awareness raising' component of the case, based on a strong storytelling of the plaintiffs' individual lives.[61] On this point, Harriet Mackaill-Hill from CAN Europe maintained that:

[55] Interview with Giorgio Elter, n 46.

[56] Interview with Harriet Mackaill-Hill, n 20.

[57] In the sense that each European family of plaintiffs had an NGO from the same country supporting it and acting as national contact point.

[58] Interview with Harriet Mackaill-Hill, n 20.

[59] The surname of the first family of plaintiffs.

[60] See https://peoplesclimatecase.caneurope.org/.

[61] See https://peoplesclimatecase.caneurope.org/who-we-are/. For instance, with regard to the French family, the official website of the lawsuit states as follows: '[the] Feschet family lives in a village in Provence in southern France. The family has been in the lavender farming business for three generations. However, due to the impacts of climate change, farming lavender is becoming increasingly difficult and is no longer fully viable'; with regard to the German family, the website states as follows: '[the]Recktenwald family lives on an island in the North Sea coast of Germany. The family has lived on that island for 4 generations and they built up a hotel and restaurant business from scratch. Their

> What I think it's really important in litigation cases is indeed to have a campaign on the side. Because in a litigation case in the end you have, in general, 3 to 4 actual 'legal moments', where they can really give you a [boost] between filing and final results. But you need to keep the case alive, otherwise it's useless. Otherwise, the result of it would just become … another piece of paper in the official journal. So, you really need to be able to use those stories and use the storytelling around it to keep it alive to really have an impact and that's really where the NGOs come in. To actually build the campaign around the actual case. Which is crucial. Without a campaign around it, a [CCL] case nowadays is not that useful.[62]

Keeping media and public attention alive – especially when the case is still 'pending' and no major legal updates are available (eg the filing of the case or the final ruling) – is therefore key, according to the members of CAN Europe. However, in order to produce interesting 'content' for viewers across the globe (especially on social media) cooperation among all the actors involved (obviously from the litigants' side) is absolutely necessary. First, cooperation was required by the legal team, which had frequent exchanges with the communication officers of CAN Europe, as revealed by Gerd Winter:

> Yes of course [we talked with the communication officers]. Then German Watch came in and CAN Europe, they also joined in and they had of course professional communication people with whom Roda [Verheyen] and I communicated very very much. And when it was to produce press statements about the state of the process and so on, the appeal … Of course, I was consulted.[63]

Second, cooperation was also relevant from the side of the plaintiffs. As aforementioned, PP bore most of the financial costs of the case, making the lawsuit completely costless for the families involved.[64] These were described as being very cooperative and 'talkative',[65] citizens who knew already a lot about climate change and the damages it causes. On this point, in our conversation Gerd Winter stated:

> I can tell you to my surprise, I was engaged in many legal actions before, concerning nuclear power and infrastructure project and so on, and very often the plaintiffs were concerned but not very talkative when they were interviewed … In this case, all of the plaintiffs came out … themselves [as people who] knew about climate change, [who] had already experienced damage of the consequences of climate change and were prepared to communicate with the press and explain them and some even became famous in their countries![66]

restaurant business is situated on top of a dune and the hotel sits just behind the dune. Now, the family's property and business are under acute risk from the continuously rising sea level, storm surges and the resulting erosion of the beach, because there is no dyke. They are also concerned about their access to drinking water. On their island, the drinking water originates from an underground lens in the Eastern part of the island. In that area, the wells are at risk of being flooded by high tides and storm waves, which means that the underground freshwater will be salinised. If this happens, the water can no longer be used.'

[62] Interview with Harriet Mackaill-Hill, n 20.

[63] Interview with Gerd Winter, n 10.

[64] Interview with Giorgio Elter, n 46.

[65] Interview with Gerd Winter, n 10.

[66] ibid.

The plaintiffs' choice (and the whole legal strategy) was thus strongly intertwined with the communication strategy set up to increase the 'impact' of the case. As mentioned before, the case was conceived not only as a 'stick' to hold the EU accountable, but also as an opportunity to raise public awareness on the lack of access to justice at EU level. As Harriet Mackaill-Hill observed:

> Not many people know about [*Plaumann*]. So, I think it was also an awareness raising litigation case. … Awareness on the lack of access to justice at the European level. How can it still be possible today (well back then in 2018) that an EU citizen, that is being drastically affected by the lack of measures taken at the Brussels level or at the national level, still not be able to challenge that? Although it is affecting their livelihood, their actual health. How is it still possible? So, I think it was also a kind of way to put pressure on the Court. Exterior pressure.[67]

Instead of discouraging the litigants from triggering litigation, *Plaumann* was actually one of the main 'drivers' of the case. As Harriet Mackaill-Hill put it, 'if it's never challenged, it will never be changed'.[68]

The 'awareness raising' component of the case was not limited to the lack of access to justice in direct actions. Indeed, the lawsuit also served as a 'megaphone' to make marginalised communities who were damaged by the consequences of climate change heard in the public arena. Video interviews were made for each family in the respective countries of origin and in their respective houses.[69] In this way, they were encouraged to tell their own stories, with a view to stimulating empathy in the public.[70] Storytelling was also part of the legal strategy, as it will be outlined in the next sections. This contributed to the creation of specific 'narratives' that will also be discussed later, in other parts of the current chapter.

Conversely, the next section will address the more 'legal' aspects of *Carvalho*, namely the claims of the plaintiffs, the reasoning deployed by the legal team to overcome *Plaumann*, and the findings on standing of the EU judiciary embedded in the two rulings.

IV. The *Carvalho* Case before the EU Judiciary

In *Carvalho*,[71] the plaintiffs challenged – under Article 263(4) TFEU – the legality of a legislative package of three EU measures,[72] by which the EU seeks to comply

[67] Interview with Harriet Mackaill-Hill, n 20.

[68] ibid.

[69] See https://peoplesclimatecase.caneurope.org/who-we-are/.

[70] 'I mean, the ABC of lobbying is storytelling and you need to hit personal and the way of hitting personal, is to talk about people in my opinion' (Interview with Harriet Mackaill-Hill, n 20).

[71] T-330/18, *Carvalho and Others v Parliament and Council* (2019) ECLI:EU:T:2019:324.

[72] Directive (EU) 2018/410 of the European Parliament and of the Council of 14 March 2018 amending Directive 2003/87/EC to enhance cost-effective emission reductions and low-carbon investments, and Decision (EU) 2015/1814 (OJ 2018 L 76, p 3); Regulation (EU) 2018/841 of the European Parliament and of the Council of 30 May 2018 on the inclusion of greenhouse gas emissions and removals from

with the 'nationally determined contributions' (NDCs), as required by Article 4(2) of the Paris Agreement. The plaintiffs also claimed compensation under Article 340 TFEU for the damages that the EU has caused to their present and future living conditions by failing to comply with higher-ranking norms of law, namely international law and EU primary law.[73]

More specifically, the applicants maintained that the climate targets laid down in the contested measures were not sufficiently ambitious to preserve their fundamental rights, protected under the EU Charter of Fundamental Rights (EUCFR). In the light of this, the EU judiciary was asked to annul the contested legislative package and order the EU co-legislators (namely the Parliament and the Council) to adopt measures requiring the EU to reduce its greenhouse gas emissions by 2030 by at least 50 per cent to 60 per cent compared to their 1990 levels, rather than by 40 per cent (as provided under the EU contested measures). This reasoning is very similar to that adopted by the applicants in *Urgenda*, to which the applicants made a direct reference in their application file.[74] This can be seen as an attempt to include the CJEU in the process of building TIJC in CCL.[75] Indeed, the lawyers involved in *Carvalho* used part of the reasoning embedded in *Urgenda* as a building block to construct their own reasoning, which was adapted to the specificities of the EU legal order. This shows once again, how the spreading of judicial comfort can open new legal opportunities, by increasing the 'perception' of a higher level of judicial receptivity in a given 'system'.

In order to overcome the *Plaumann* test and prove that they were all individually concerned by the contested measures, the applicants in *Carvalho* devoted a considerable part of their application file to the admissibility of the case. They maintained that the *Plaumann* formula is not itself based in the text of Article 263(4) TFEU, as this was originally conceived on the basis of the old text of Article 173 TEC, which referred to 'decisions' as the object of an action, not to 'acts' (as in the current wording). Given that now even legislative acts having general scope may be challenged under Treaty provisions, 'the application of the admissibility criterion must reflect the general character of legislative acts'.[76]

Moreover, the plaintiffs argued that the *Plaumann* formula has perverse results: 'the more widespread the damaging effects of a measure, the more restrictive the access to courts will be'.[77] This – according to the applicants – leads to an obvious gap in judicial protection.[78] On this point, the plaintiffs also recalled AG Jacobs'

land use, land use change and forestry in the 2030 climate and energy framework, and amending Regulation (EU) No 525/2013 and Decision No 529/2013/EU (OJ 2018 L 156, p 1); Regulation (EU) 2018/842 of the European Parliament and of the Council of 30 May 2018 on binding annual greenhouse gas emission reductions by Member States from 2021 to 2030 contributing to climate action to meet commitments under the Paris Agreement and amending Regulation (EU) No 525/2013 (OJ 2018 L 156, p 26).

[73] *Carvalho*, n 71, § 24.

[74] *Carvalho* – AF, n 14, 38.

[75] See chapter 6.

[76] *Carvalho*, n 71, § 31.

[77] ibid, § 32.

[78] ibid.

opinion in the *UPA* case,[79] where the AG proposed an alternative interpretation of the Treaty provisions allowing for access to justice of private parties before EU Courts.[80] In Jacobs' view, a natural or legal person should be regarded as

> individually concerned by [an EU measure] of general application that concerns him directly if the measure in question affects his legal position, in a manner which is both definite and immediate, by restricting his rights or by imposing obligations on him.[81]

In spite of the applicants' efforts, the Court did not engage with these arguments. It simply referred to them in its reasoning,[82] but it did not actually fully 'address' them. On the contrary, the judiciary limited itself to confirming the *Plaumann* formula without even trying to provide convincing counterarguments to dismiss those claims, proving to be just as unresponsive as it was 20 years before, in the *Greenpeace* case.[83]

Furthermore, the applicants put considerable emphasis on the interpretation of Article 263(4) TFEU *vis-à-vis* Article 47 of the EUCFR.[84] On this point the plaintiffs held that, even though, such a provision 'is not intended to change the system of judicial review laid down by the Treaties, and particularly the rules relating to the admissibility of direct actions', the conditions of admissibility must nevertheless 'be interpreted in the light of the fundamental right to effective judicial protection'.[85]

By so arguing, the plaintiffs attempted to anticipate the GC's answer on the availability of the PRP, the counterargument traditionally used by the EU judiciary in its case law to dismiss actions for annulment brought by individual plaintiffs.[86] As discussed in chapter one, the CJEU generally considers that the EU has a 'complete system of legal remedies and procedures', designed to ensure review of the legality of acts of the institutions. According to the EU judges, natural and legal persons seeking direct access to EU Courts, but who do not fulfil the conditions established under the Treaty, should plea the invalidity of EU acts before national courts, which may then refer the CJEU for a preliminary ruling under Article 267 TFEU.[87]

As it is clear from this research, the most prominent European ENGOs disagree with the Court on this point,[88] and so did the applicants in *Carvalho*. The

[79] C-50/00 P, *Unión de Pequeños Agricultores v Council* (2002) ECLI:EU:C:2002:462. Hereinafter '*UPA*'. In relation to the opinion of AG Jacobs in this case, see also chapter 1.

[80] This reinforces the argument advanced in chapter 1, according to which ENGOs used AG Jacobs' opinion in *UPA* in actions for annulment to persuade the EU judiciary that the EU system of judicial protection is 'incomplete'.

[81] *Carvalho* – AF, n 14, § 141.

[82] *Carvalho*, n 71, § 32.

[83] ibid, § 48. See also chapter 1.

[84] ibid., § 52.

[85] *Carvalho* – AF, n 14, § 144.

[86] ibid.

[87] *UPA*, n 79, § 40. On this point, see also chapter 2.

[88] Public consultation of the European Commission on EU implementation of the Aarhus Convention in the area of access to justice in environmental matters (20 December 2018–14 March 2019). Available

applicants strongly argued that the Court's 'complete system' argument is based on the premise that there is coordination of remedies before national and EU courts, including through the availability of preliminary reference'.[89] However, 'as the CJEU has held, this all depends on the availability of appropriate remedies in national law'.[90] For this reason, the applicants in *Carvalho* claimed that the case could only be fully addressed by the EU judiciary, as the action was:

> not directed against implementing measures of either MSs or EU institutions but rather against the fundamental legal basis for climate action; more precisely the allocation by the GHG Emissions Acts of an excessive and unlawful quantity of emissions. That allocation is dictated by the Emissions Acts themselves, and requires no implementing measures which could be the subject of a challenge.[91]

This argument focuses on the 'allocation' of emissions as between MSs, which may not be derogated from by EU MSs and therefore does not entail any further implementing measure at national level.[92]

However, I disagree with the applicants on this point. I argue that even such an allocation could be challenged – in principle – before national courts via PRP on validity. For instance, one of the EU measures challenged by the plaintiffs in *Carvalho* is Regulation (EU) 2018/842[93] on binding annual greenhouse gas emission reductions by MSs from 2021 to 2030. This regulation already refers to national implementing measures in recital n. 13, stating that 'the impact of Union and *national policies and measures implementing* this Regulation should be assessed in line with the monitoring and reporting obligations under Regulation (EU) n. 525/2013 of the European Parliament and of the Council' (emphasis added).

Moreover, the same contested regulation requires emissions reductions in both the ETS and non-ETS sectors amounting to 43 per cent and 30 per cent, respectively, by 2030 compared to 2005.[94] Activities falling within the ETS sectors must be specifically authorised through an administrative act issued by the competent national authority.[95] Such an act could be subject to a challenge before the competent national courts. More broadly speaking, climate policy measures usually

at: https://ec.europa.eu/info/law/better-regulation/initiatives/ares-2018-2432060_en. Many observations submitted by environmental organisations during this public consultation referred to the alleged 'incompleteness' of the EU judicial protection system. On this point, see chapter 3.

[89] *Carvalho* – AF, n 14, § 144.

[90] ibid.

[91] ibid, § 145.

[92] ibid.

[93] See above, n 72.

[94] Regulation (EU) 2018/842, recital n. 2.

[95] For instance, in Italy, AGES – Autorizzazione ad emettere Gas a Effetto Serra. See Legislative Decree n. 30, 13 March 2013, 'Attuazione della direttiva 2009/29/CE che modifica la direttiva 2003/87/CE al fine di perfezionare ed estendere il sistema comunitario per lo scambio di quote di emissione di gas a effetto serra' (13G00075) (GU General Series n.79, 4 April 2013); in France, see Article L229-6 of the French Environmental Code (Code de l'environnement) stating that 'Les installations qui entrent dans le champ d'application de la présente section sont soumises à autorisation pour l'émission de gaz à effet de serre'.

entail a number of implementing measures at national level, which could be challenged before national courts, which may then refer the question to the CJEU for a preliminary ruling.[96] On the contrary, on this point, Gerd Winter argued that the responsibility for implementing the three GHG acts lies with both the Commission and the Member States.[97] The Commission – continued the Professor – lacks the authority to permit or increase emissions beyond the reduction quotas established by these legal acts.[98] Likewise, Member States are not permitted to authorize emissions exceeding the limits set by the GHG acts.[99] However, under Article 193 TFEU and based on the classification of these acts as minimum harmonisation measures, Member States do have the right to impose stricter emission limits than those allocated to them.[100] Yet, contrary to the defendants' argument, the applicants in the case considered this point irrelevant, as it challenges the 'European Union measure' itself rather than the right to adopt stricter limits or any related national regulations.[101] The aim of the application was not to leverage national discretion but to enforce stricter emission reductions directly within the EU GHG acts.[102]

Having said that, in responding to the argument referring to the lack of national implementing measures, the GC pointed out that Article 47 EUCFR 'does not require that an individual should have an unconditional entitlement to bring an action for annulment of a legislative act of the Union directly before the [CJEU]'.[103] The Court then confirmed its traditional reasoning on the 'complete system of legal remedies' and upheld the argument proposed by the Parliament and the Council. According to the institutions, the implementation of the climate package presupposes a number of implementing measures to be adopted by national authorities. As a consequence, such measures could be challenged by private parties before national courts which may then refer the CJEU for a preliminary ruling on validity or interpretation.[104]

As already illustrated in the analysis of the 'pre-Aarhus' period, even in the 'CCL trend' period the applicants referred to a large extent to the alleged 'incompleteness' of the EU system of judicial protection in their attempt to overcome *Plaumann*. However, apart from the reference to the *Urgenda* case, most of the arguments had already been (unsuccessfully) used in previous environmental litigation.[105] This reinforces the idea of *Urgenda* as a case to be used as a source

[96] A similar solution was also proposed by Chris Hilson when he commented on the *Greenpeace* case (see analysis in chapter 1). In this regard, see Chris Hilson, 'Community Rights and Wrongs: Greenpeace before the Court of Justice' (1999) 52(1) *Environmental Law Review* 54.
[97] Winter, n 31, 157.
[98] ibid.
[99] ibid.
[100] ibid.
[101] ibid.
[102] ibid.
[103] *Carvalho*, n 71, § 52.
[104] ibid, § 53.
[105] See chapter 1.

full of convincing 'building blocks' for climate litigation, holding promise by virtue of having already reoriented the European judicial landscape in a more ENGO-friendly direction. However, at the time *Carvalho* was filed, no other key European case had been decided yet.[106] Therefore, the level of 'judicial comfort' established in CCL in Europe in 2018 was not the same as today. In light of this, the applicants in *Carvalho* probably overestimated the influence that the sole *Urgenda* ruling (perhaps just the first one, issued by the District Court of The Hague in 2015) could exert on the EU judiciary. Furthermore, the applicants did not put forward any argument on the EU system of judicial protection that the Court had not already dismissed in its previous case law. Hence, the 'bad timing' of the case might have also hampered the influence of the broader CCL trend on the EU judiciary. Below, I will now turn to analyse the plaintiffs' arguments on causation.

A. Establishing Causation in *Carvalho*

In order to meet the *Plaumann* test, the applicants were not only required to prove a causal link between the contested EU measure and the breach of their fundamental rights (a link already extremely difficult to prove in any climate case). In addition, the applicants were required to prove that the contested measure affected them in a manner that differentiates each applicant from any other person.[107] A strict requirement clearly showing that causation is not enough for plaintiffs seeking access to justice before the EU judiciary.

Therefore, in *Carvalho*, the applicants claimed that, although all persons may – in principle – each enjoy the same right, the effects of climate change, and hence the violation of fundamental rights, is distinctive and different for each individual. 'A farmer who is affected by drought is in a different position from a fisherman affected by a loss of sea ice.'[108] The plaintiffs held that, given that the EU has not adhered to the ECHR, 'the CJEU is to be the sole arbiter of the reconciliation of EU measures and [fundamental rights]'.

> It must follow – continued the plaintiffs – that an individual whose [fundamental rights] are at stake necessarily has a right of access to the EU judicature. As a consequence, it should be held that a person is 'individually concerned' where the person is 'affected in a fundamental right'.[109]

To prove the breach of their FRs, the applicants tried to rely on the *Codorniu*[110] and *FIAMM*[111] case law. Indeed, in the former the applicant established individual concern because it had an individual right (a trademark) that was adversely

[106] See chapter 6.
[107] C-25/62, *Plaumann v Commission of the EEC* (1963) ECLI:EU:C:1963:17, § 9.
[108] ibid, § 128.
[109] ibid, § 140.
[110] C-309/89, *Codorniu v Council* (1994) ECLI:EU:C:1994:197.
[111] C-120/06 P, *FIAMM and Others v Council and Commission* (2008) ECLI:EU:C:2008:476.

affected by the legislative act. This in spite of the fact that the act was of general application. In the latter, an Italian accumulator manufacturer, claimed that the EU had infringed WTO law thereby provoking US countermeasures imposing customs on accumulator imports. For this reason, FIAMM requested compensation. With regard to such cases, the plaintiffs in *Carvalho* noted that, although the application was denied in substance, 'it was found admissible without the Court … even mentioning the question of standing. This is notable because many other manufacturers of accumulators may also have been affected by the US customs duties.'[112]

The GC clarified that *Codorniu* 'concerned the loss of a specific acquired right – namely the right to use the word "crémant" in a registered graphic mark' – while, in the present case, 'the applicants have not claimed the loss of a specific acquired right'.[113] This answer of the Court is quite concerning, as it seems to subject access to justice to the loss of specific 'acquired rights'.[114] These are rights not originally owned by their holders, which are gained later and sometimes as a result of some action on the part of the right holder. Conversely, most fundamental rights are traditionally universal and – most importantly – not acquired but simply *recognised* by the Law to any human being for the simple reason of coming into existence.[115] It goes without saying that the reasoning behind *Codorniu* stays within the logic of the *Plaumann* formula, since only the applicant possessed that individual right to that specific trademark. However, the real paradox is that – by relying on this reasoning – the Court ends up granting better judicial protection to intellectual property rights than to citizens' fundamental rights.

This is why the Court's response in *Carvalho* on the reference to *Codorniu* triggers the following question: what if there is no loss of a specific 'acquired right' but rather the violation of an individual's *primary* (or *pre-existing*) fundamental right? With specific regard to climate change, the EU judges responded that this may certainly affect the enjoyment of fundamental rights.[116] However, the EU Treaties require a clear (and strict) link between the contested measure and the legal sphere of the applicant, not between climate change, on the one hand, and individuals' fundamental rights, on the other. The risk – argued the Court – would be to recognise standing for any citizen and make the requirements established under Article 263(4) TFEU completely meaningless.[117] The GC thus found that the applicants had not proved that the contested provisions of the legislative package infringed their fundamental rights and distinguished them individually from all other natural or legal persons concerned by those provisions.[118] In the light

[112] *Carvalho* – AF, n 14, § 142.
[113] *Carvalho*, n 71, § 55.
[114] Mario Pagano, 'Climate change litigation before EU Courts and the "butterfly effect"', *Blog de droit européen*, 16 October 2019. Available at: https://blogdroiteuropeen.com/2019/10/16/climate-change-litigation-before-eu-courts-and-the-butterfly-effect-by-mario-pagano/.
[115] ibid; see also https://fra.europa.eu/en/content/what-are-fundamental-rights.
[116] ibid, § 50.
[117] ibid.
[118] ibid, § 49.

of this, the case was dismissed for lack of standing of the applicants and the GC's decision was then upheld by the CJEU in 2021.[119]

The fundamental rights-based arguments advanced in *Carvalho* lead us to question the relevance of the Charter in environmental direct actions before the CJEU. Indeed, this is not the first time that the Charter is invoked before the Court by environmental litigants. Already in the *PAN* case,[120] the applicants invoked Articles 37 and 47 of the Charter – respectively enshrining the 'principle' of a high level of environmental protection, and the 'right' to an effective remedy and to a fair trial – in seeking the annulment of Commission Implementing Regulation (EU) 2015/1295 of 27 July 2015, approving the active substance sulfoxaflor.[121] With regard to Article 37, the GC maintained that such provision does not really enshrine a 'right', which can be enforced by individuals directly before the EU Courts.[122] More specifically:

> [that] article only contains a principle providing for a general obligation on the European Union in respect of the objectives to be pursued in the framework of its policies, and not a right to bring actions in environmental matters before the Courts of the European Union. The Charter of Fundamental Rights distinguishes between principles and rights, as is apparent, for example, in the second sentence of Article 51(1), and in Article 52(2) and (5) thereof. … Accordingly, those principles become significant for the courts only when such acts are interpreted or reviewed but, on the other hand, do not give rise to direct claims for positive action by the European Union's institutions or [MSs]' authorities.[123]

Conversely, with regard to Article 47 of the Charter, the GC held that:

> [it] is settled case-law that that provision is not intended to change the system of judicial review laid down by the Treaties, and particularly the rules relating to the admissibility of direct actions brought before the Courts of the European Union … Thus, the conditions of admissibility laid down in the fourth paragraph of Article 263 TFEU must be interpreted in the light of the fundamental right to effective judicial protection, but such an interpretation cannot have the effect of setting aside those conditions, which are expressly laid down in that Treaty.[124]

In the light of these answers of the Court provided in *PAN*, along with those given in *Carvalho*, the EU Charter, in the eyes of environmental and climate litigants, seems to appear like a fascinating catalogue of unavailable rights. Considering that the availability of justiciable rights constitutes one of the key elements of the legal opportunity structure (LOS), we can consider the impossibility of invoking Articles 37 and 47 in direct actions as a further 'closure' in the European LOS. This further 'closure' stems directly from two main explanations, both provided by

[119] C-565/19 P, *Carvalho and Others v Parliament and Council*, (2021) ECLI:EU:C:2021:252.
[120] T-600/15, *PAN Europe and Others v Commission* (2015) ECLI:EU:T:2016:601.
[121] ibid.
[122] ibid, § 47.
[123] ibid, § 48.
[124] ibid, §§ 50–51.

the Court. The first one is that Article 37 EUCFR does not confer any justiciable right, but it constitutes a simple 'principle' binding the EU institutions (principle perhaps already enshrined in the TFEU).[125] The second one is that Article 47 is not intended to change the system of judicial protection laid down under the EU Treaties, which is already complete as it is. This reasoning of the Court de facto makes these two (crucial) provisions completely unavailable for citizens and CSOs in environmental direct actions. In the next section, I will now turn to outline and reflect on the 'impact' of *Carvalho*.

V. The Aftermath of *Carvalho*

After the final CJEU's ruling was released,[126] the coalition of ENGOs, lawyers and plaintiffs who had been working on the case was obviously very disappointed. Harriet Mackaill-Hill from CAN Europe admitted:

> We were really disappointed, and I think it is a scandal for democracy and [fundamental rights] at the EU level. The EU goes beyond borders, talking about democracy, rule of law, etc. In the end, it's just not ok, not even under the [AR].[127]

Even Gerd Winter admitted his frustration for the 'poor' reasoning of the Court in both rulings.[128] Considering the momentum represented by the ongoing CCL trend,[129] the legal team working on the case and the people at CAN Europe saw the lawsuit also as an opportunity for the CJEU to abandon the *Plaumann* formula in transformative times for climate justice. As Harriet Mackaill-Hill from CAN Europe observed:

> We hoped [that the ongoing [CCL] trend would have affected the reasoning of the Court], but we kind of felt that now that the Court has kind of inserted themselves into a little black box, the more they give courts precedents upholding Plaumann, the more they are kind of closing themselves in. We find it very difficult to see an exit for them now. Every time they come up with this new argument of why Plaumann has to be upheld, why it's a good idea, why it's still … you know, *actio popularis*, etc., we don't see how they'll be able to exit that. I mean, if they didn't exit it, the [Carvalho] case was a wonderful opportunity to do it. Considering, as you just said, all the other litigation cases that were just coming forward, the victories … Since the [Carvalho case] ended in March last year, there have also been all of these cases that have been brought to the ECtHR. I think that could also be interesting to see how both of them will work together.[130]

[125] See Arts 11 and 191 TFEU.
[126] C-565/19 P, *Carvalho and Others v Parliament and Council*, n 120.
[127] Interview with Harriet Mackaill-Hill, n 20.
[128] Interview with Gerd Winter, n 10.
[129] See chapter 6.
[130] Interview with Harriet Mackaill-Hill, n 20.

In similar terms also Gerd Winter described the case as a 'missed opportunity' for the EU judiciary, suggesting that it is now time for the ECtHR to advance the doctrinal development of HRs in Europe in the climate context. He noted:

> They [the CJEU] lost the chance to step in. They keep themselves out of the discourse. They did it at the time when the year 2018 was not yet over. Maybe we came one year too early. And now the initiative [for] the doctrinal development of HRs in Europe would be the ECtHR and not the CJEU … We told them, 'if you don't take this case, you will lose your words to the ECtHR!' and we are now there.[131]

In their answers both Harriet Mackaill-Hill and Gerd Winter looked to the ECtHR as a source of 'hope' for supranational CCL in Europe. Considering what happened in the aftermath, with the three key climate rulings released in Strasbourg on 9 April 2024 – discussed in chapter six – I can say that their hopes were well placed.[132] Through such reading, on the opposite side, the CJEU appears more and more old-fashioned and 'obsolete' in the eyes of climate litigants, who are now redirecting their efforts toward other national and supranational fora. As mentioned above, this was already evident in the analysis set out in chapter six, especially in the words of the in-house lawyers of GPI, who do not consider the EU judiciary as a viable forum for their litigation campaigns anymore.[133] However, now even those who have directly engaged with the CJEU in the climate context seem to look at the EU judiciary in very similar terms.

Nonetheless, besides the purely *legal* outcome of the case – embedded in the final ruling – even the impact of the lawsuit on the media had its positive and negative sides.[134] As Harriet Mackaill-Hill observed:

> I think in the end of the case, the success was a bit hampered, in the sense that it was Covid, so we couldn't have all of the plaintiffs in Luxembourg, it was just COMs and me for [CAN-Europe]. … So, it was a bit of a flop at the end, when it could have been a bigger 'bang'. But just because of Covid we couldn't get everybody together in the same place. So, I think it went away too quietly in my opinion.[135]

According to Harriet Mackaill-Hill, the Covid-19 pandemic partially hampered the impact of the case. However, some relevant achievements were still acknowledged by the people working on *Carvalho*. Raul Cazan for instance revealed that the perception of the lawsuit in Brussels completely changed after climate protesters invaded the streets of Brussels in December 2018 (the 'Climate march' ahead

[131] Interview with Gerd Winter, n 10.
[132] On this point, see also Mario Pagano, 'Legal Standing in Climate Litigation before the ECtHR and the CJEU', (2024) EU Law Live. Available at: https://eulawlive.com/op-ed-legal-standing-in-climate-litigation-before-the-ecthr-and-the-cjeu-by-mario-pagano/; Jacques Hartmann and Marc Willers, Protecting Rights in Climate Change Litigation before European Courts (23 April 2021). Available at SSRN: https://ssrn.com/abstract=3832674 or http://dx.doi.org/10.2139/ssrn.3832674.
[133] See chapter 6.
[134] This in subjective terms (see introduction to the present book).
[135] Interview with Harriet Mackaill-Hill, n 20.

of COP24),[136] and occupied the entrance hall of the European Parliament in May 2019.[137] Cazan noted:

> After FFF[138] and youngsters covering the streets in Brussels, suddenly the European institutions that did not give a [s**t] about us (really), suddenly they were interested in us. [We] were very well coordinated by CAN-Europe in Brussels and we pushed it a lot at the European level. We met with MEPs in Brussels, we met with Commission officials of DG Clima and DG ENV.[139] … I think it was a little page of history. And I'm not using big words for nothing. The [Carvalho case] …, was part of a movement that started to blossom at that time (2018) especially with FFF, with the youngsters occupying Schuman[140] and Paris and Milan and Berlin, oh my God! And suddenly, this whole movement together with the [*Carvalho* case] was there, in the European public sphere.[141]

The EU policymakers thus paid attention to the lawsuit and the individual stories of the plaintiffs involved.[142] In this regard, the role of *CAN Europe* was crucial in bridging the different ENGOs working on the case (which were all spread across Europe) together with EU policymakers located in Brussels.[143] In particular, one of the Romanian plaintiffs – Vlad Petru – met with EU officials in the Belgian capital when the case was still pending, as Raul Cazan disclosed:

> I came with Vlad from the Transylvanian Alps and for the first time he came to Brussels. For the first time he flew a plane, it was so crazy! He came to Brussels, he was really impressed with everything, but his strongest impression is that he saw politicians for the very first time in his life! And those politicians were European politicians, listening to him! And he was shocked with this. 'Why … do this people listen to me? I'm so insignificant!'. 'No, you're not! Let's talk to them, tell them everything you want to say'. And he spoke freely, I was the translator. It was so mind-blowing really. And even for these Europeans [EU officials] finally, they met with people who were not picked up for them … It was like real life, coming into their office.[144]

By using such words, Raul Cazan stressed the emancipatory aspect of the lawsuit. This provided citizens who were victims of climate change with a platform to feel 'addressed' by the EU institutions, to tell their own story and try to influence the EU decision-making. In this regard, although the case did not ultimately succeed in court, it did achieve what it was mainly aiming to by other means, in particular through legislative action. Indeed, when the case was filed in 2018, the EU

[136] See www.dw.com/en/thousands-march-in-brussels-ahead-of-cop24-climate-conference/a-46545382.

[137] See https://milanoinmovimento.com/internazionale/i-ragazzi-di-fridays-for-future-occupano-il-parlamento-europeo.

[138] *Fridays for Future*, see https://fridaysforfuture.org/.

[139] Interview with Raul Cazan, n 26.

[140] 'Rond-point Robert Schuman', where the Berlaymont building of the European Commission is located in Brussels.

[141] Interview with Raul Cazan, n 26.

[142] See also the paragraph on Vlad Petru below.

[143] ibid; interview with Harriet Mackaill-Hill, n 20.

[144] ibid.

emissions reduction target by 2030 was by 40 per cent. However, in July 2021 the new EU climate law set a new reduction target aiming to cut down carbon emissions at least by 55 per cent by 2030.[145] A new objective, which was perfectly in the range requested by the plaintiffs in *Carvalho* (who were asking for a reduction of carbon emissions ranging at least between 50 per cent and 60 per cent by 2030). By putting this forward, I do not mean to imply that the new emissions reduction target was set *because* of the *Carvalho* case.[146] My intention is simply to highlight that after the case was decided, the applicants still achieved the ultimate goal of their action by other means.

In terms of 'raising awareness', the case did receive media attention, especially in the plaintiffs' respective countries of origin.[147] In particular, the case contributed to create a *David v Goliath* narrative, as national media were often framing the lawsuit with titles emphasising the individual dimension of the case, in opposition to the gigantic and complex political-administrative entity represented by the EU. Examples of such titles were 'the Romanian shepherd sues the EU'[148] or 'Portuguese families take the EU to the Court of Justice'.[149] Some of the plaintiffs were even depicted as 'climate heroes' in their respective countries.[150]

This shows, once again, how ENGOs litigating before the CJEU combine the use of legal and non-legal strategies in order to increase the effectiveness of their mobilisation campaigns. This was already observed in chapter five, when I illustrated environmental organisations' lobbying in relation to the amendment of the AR.[151] This confirms previous studies on the effectiveness of litigation in achieving change (broadly defined), stressing how litigation alone can hardly obtain what social movements strive for.[152] The analysis just concluded highlights that the same was done in relation to overcoming *Plaumann*, and raising awareness 'on' *Plaumann*, in CCL.

Having concluded my study of the *Carvalho* case, I will now turn to the other climate lawsuit here under analysis, namely the *Sabo* case.

[145] Regulation (EU) 2021/1119 of the European Parliament and of the Council of 30 June 2021 establishing the framework for achieving climate neutrality and amending Regulations (EC) No 401/2009 and (EU) 2018/1999 ('European Climate Law') PE/27/2021/REV/1 OJ L 243, 9 July 2021, 1–17.

[146] Even the people I interviewed did not know if the EU climate target was amended because of the lawsuit.

[147] See https://peoplesclimatecase.caneurope.org/press/press-coverage/.

[148] See https://business-review.eu/business/legal/video-romanian-shepard-sues-eu-alongside-dozens-of-farmers-there-is-no-longer-enough-water-for-our-cattle-and-sheep-171161.

[149] See www.dn.pt/vida-e-futuro/alteracoes-climaticas-familias-portuguesas-recorrem-ao-tribunal-de-justica-europeu-11101015.html.

[150] See www.lemonde.fr/climat/visuel/2018/12/13/en-france-maurice-feschet-le-grand-pere-inquiet-qui-lutte-contre-l-inaction-climatique_5396981_1652612.html.

[151] See chapter 5.

[152] See Emilia Korkea-Aho, '"Mr Smith Goes To Brussels": Third Country Lobbying and the Making of EU Law and Policy' (2016) 18 *Cambridge Yearbook of European Legal Studies* 45–68; Scott Cummings and Ingrid V Eagly, 'After Public Interest Law' (2006) 100 Northwestern University Law Review, UCLA School of Law Research Paper No. 05-35, 1251-1295. Available at SSRN: https://ssrn.com/abstract=834784.

VI. Contesting EU Policy on Biomass Energy

A few months before the GC released its order dismissing the Carvalho case, another climate action for annulment was brought before the same Court on 4 March 2019, namely *Sabo*[153] (also known as the 'EU Biomass legal case'). The case was prompted by the 'Partnership for policy integrity' (PFPI), a US organisation founded in 2010 by Dr Mary S Booth and Richard Wiles.[154] PFPI describes itself as a science-based organisation, using 'litigation, and strategic communications to help enact science-based policies that protect health, ecosystems, and the climate'.[155] PFPI's efforts in the last decade particularly focused on biomass energy and its impact on forests, climate and air pollution.[156]

Despite being a US-based organisation, PFPI addresses biomass energy policy on a global scale, engaging with regulators, policymakers and other ENGOs across the planet.[157] Their activities include (i) producing robust science on carbon, air pollution, and forest impacts of biomass burning; (ii) supporting community groups that oppose biomass projects; iii) training policymakers, regulators, financial institutions and the public; (iv) providing science and communications support to other NGOs working to protect forests and defeat the biomass industry; (v) bringing litigation that challenges misleading claims of the biomass industry and its advocates.[158]

PFPI's staff includes two members with a law degree, but their legal specialisation is not clearly outlined on their website.[159] As for GPI, litigation seems to be considered by PFPI as one 'tool in a toolbox', one of the diverse means available to achieve policy change. This is also clear in view of their strategy adopted in the *Sabo* case, as will be described in the next paragraphs.

The organisation claimed that 'more than a third of the EU's renewable energy comes from burning wood, which is treated as "zero carbon"'.[160] Indeed, PFPI stressed that damaging forests and burning pellets is not an effective solution to tackle carbon emissions.[161]

EU rules governing renewable energy targets (including biomass fuel) are contained in the Renewable Energy Directive (RED) which was amended in 2018 (RED II)[162] and 2023 (RED III).[163] Before triggering judicial proceedings before

[153] T-141/19, *Sabo and Others v Parliament and Council* (2020) ECLI:EU:T:2020:179.

[154] *PFPI*, 2010–2020 Ten-year report, 2. Available at: www.pfpi.net/about.

[155] ibid.

[156] ibid.

[157] ibid, 15.

[158] ibid, 3.

[159] See www.pfpi.net/about.

[160] PFPI, 2010–2020 Ten-year report, n 155, 18.

[161] ibid, 3.

[162] Directive (EU) 2018/2001 of the European Parliament and of the Council of 11 December 2018 on the promotion of the use of energy from renewable sources (Text with EEA relevance.) PE/48/2018/REV/1 OJ L 328, 21 December 2018, 82–209.

[163] Directive (EU) 2023/2413 of the European Parliament and of the Council of 18 October 2023 amending Directive (EU) 2018/2001, Regulation (EU) 2018/1999 and Directive 98/70/EC as regards

the EU judiciary, PFPI attempted to lobby EU policymakers in the course of the revision of the RED by working 'closely with US and international allies and urging EU policymakers to enact restrictions that would mitigate GHG emissions and forest damage from burning forest biomass'.[164] Despite the CSOs' efforts, the final version of the RED II did not place any substantial limitation on cutting trees for producing pellets, still counting biomass as having 'zero carbon emissions'.[165] Thus, RED II still encouraged EU countries to subsidise the biomass fuel industry, leaving PFPI and its European partners deeply dissatisfied about the concrete implications for forests across the globe. For this reason, PFPI decided to give mandate to the London law firm 'Leigh Day' to bring a suit against the EU on biomass.[166] Although Leigh Day does not have a *pro bono* policy, this is a law firm having links with many charities and NGOs and its lawyers have worked with and 'represented these bodies to challenge the behaviour of governments and public authorities'.[167] The next section will thus focus on the legal strategy deployed by PFPI and the legal team working on the case, to contest the RED II and overcome the *Plaumann* test.

A. Constructing the *Sabo* Case

Along with 'Fern',[168] PFPI coordinated the lawsuit and identified potential plaintiffs in Estonia, Ireland, France, Romania, Slovakia and the US.[169] The organisations also developed case arguments, submitted expert testimony and created a website for the case.[170] PFPI also reported that: '[the] case was funded by the Institute for Governance and Sustainable Development (IGSD) and their subsidiary, the Climate Integrity Project (CIP). We had about [ten] weeks to find the plaintiffs, write the arguments, and file the case'.[171] The plaintiffs selected were five individuals and two ENGOs:[172]

Peter Sabo and WOLF Forest Protection Movement (Slovakia)

Hasso Krull, of House of Groves Foundation (Estonia)

2Celsius (Romania)

the promotion of energy from renewable sources, and repealing Council Directive (EU) 2015/652 PE/36/2023/REV/2 OJ L, 2023/2413, 31 October 2023.

[164] PFPI, 2010–2020 Ten-year report, n 155, 18.

[165] ibid.

[166] ibid. In addition to the solicitors from Leigh Day (Rowan Smith, Anna Dews and Carol Day), also three barristers joined the legal team, namely David Wolfe (Matrix Chambers), Peter Lockley (11KBW) and Ben Mitchell (11KBW).

[167] See www.leighday.co.uk/about us/social justice and community work/#:~:text=Leigh%20Day%20does%20not%20have,legal%20rights%20or%20need%20advice.

[168] See www.fern.org/.

[169] ibid, 21.

[170] ibid; see also https://eubiomasscase.org/.

[171] PFPI, 2010–2020 Ten-year report, n 155, 21.

[172] I want to thank the legal team involved in *Sabo* for making their application file publicly available even before the case was decided. The application file is available here: http://eubiomasscase.org/the-case/. Hereinafter '*Sabo* – AF', 2.

Bernard Auric, on behalf of Association de Lutte contre les Nuisances et la Pollution (France)

Tony Lowes, of Friends of the Irish Environment (Ireland)

Kent Roberson (USA)

Most of the individuals selected were also members of ENGOs located in their respective countries of origin and, as will become clear later, they all exhibited a peculiar interest in forests. Furthermore, Raul Cazan, President of 2Celsius (an ENGO interestingly involved also in the Carvalho case) further explained the involvement of his organisation in *Sabo*:

> They [PFPI] knew about our work in Romania and Poland … on biomass issues. Previously we were fighting against [RED] and the effort sharing regulation … So, we got attention because of that and, again, they needed more people from Eastern Europe to be part of the [*Sabo*] case.
>
> … As far as I can tell you, this is not a case about being nicely represented at the geographical level. This is the mere fact that Mary [Booth] saw that the US is a market of biomass, which is hugely influenced by European policy. … So, you create this market opportunity in Europe, opened by European regulation altogether and that leads to large exploitations of biomass/forests in the US as well. This is the global/transatlantic dimension of this issue. It makes complete sense to be part of the whole effort.[173]

While in *Carvalho* the applicants contested the whole EU climate package adopted in 2018, in the *Sabo* case the applicants focused on one specific (extremely technical)[174] point, concerning the inclusion of 'forest biomass' as renewable fuel within the scope of the RED II. For this reason, the 'raising awareness' component of the *Sabo* case was much weaker than that previously shown in *Carvalho*.[175] Members of the legal team working on *Sabo* thus clarified that the fundamental rights arguments deployed in the application file were not used for 'raising awareness' purposes, but to rather try all the possible good arguments they had in order to win the case.[176]

In relation to *Plaumann*, PFPI was perfectly aware of the narrow standing requirements established under Article 263(4) TFEU,[177] but the organisation decided to bring the case anyway. As PFPI observed in its ten-year report:

> We knew it was a long shot, and we were not surprised when the case was rejected on the basis of the plaintiffs not having standing to sue, as the EU court is notoriously difficult to access. We appealed the court's rejection of the case in July 2020, but meanwhile had further developed the case argument into a major report, 'Paper Tiger', that explains why the EU's 'sustainability' criteria in the RED II do not protect forests and the climate.[178]

[173] Interview with Raul Cazan, n 26.
[174] Interview with David Wolfe, QC, Barrister, of Matrix Chambers (24 March 2021).
[175] ibid.
[176] ibid.
[177] PFPI, 2010–2020 Ten-year report, n 155, 21.
[178] ibid.

Nevertheless, the legal team thought that it was worth litigating again, not least in the light of the Aarhus 'developments' that had occurred one year earlier, relating to the adoption of the ACCC findings on EU compliance in 2017.[179] This can be seen as another 'indirect effect' produced by these findings, discussed in chapter four. As observed in that chapter, the ACCC findings on EU compliance were perceived by ENGOs as opening new legal opportunities under EU law and contributed to push more and more CSOs to trigger litigation in the attempt to overcome *Plaumann*. The *Sabo* case is another example of this type of litigation.

Having outlined the background to PFPI's decision to initiate the lawsuit, the next sections will describe the legal arguments put forward by the plaintiffs to mobilise the Court in *Sabo* and, for each argument, I will briefly engage with the answer given by the EU judiciary.

VII. The *Sabo* Case before the EU Judiciary

As mentioned above, in *Sabo* – ultimately decided in 2021[180] – the applicants contested the inclusion of 'forest biomass' – essentially trees, including, stems, stumps, branches and bark – as a renewable fuel within the RED II. The applicants provided scientific evidence that 'burning wood for energy puts more carbon in the atmosphere than burning fossil fuels, including coal; and the vast increase in industrial logging which it necessitates destroys the very forest systems that have absorbed carbon from the atmosphere'.[181] In other words, the applicants held that forest biomass fuel is ineffective as a climate mitigation tool as, on the one hand, it produces more carbon dioxide than other fossil fuels, while, on the other, it contributes to deforestation. In light of this, the applicants argued that the inclusion of 'forest biomass' in RED II breached the general principles and obligations governing EU environmental and climate change policy enshrined in Article 191 TFEU[182] as well as a number of individuals' fundamental rights protected under the EUCFR.[183] The case was ultimately dismissed by both the GC and the CJEU on appeal. Considering the scope of this research, focusing on the fight against *Plaumann* in EU environmental litigation, my analysis of this case below will be limited to the arguments deployed by the applicants in the attempt to be granted standing.

[179] Interview with David Wolfe, n 175. Wolfe added: 'That would have given the European Court an opportunity to review Plaumann and the whole jurisprudence.' On this point, see chapter 4.

[180] C-297/20 P, *Sabo and Others v Parliament and Council* (2021) ECLI:EU:C:2021:24.

[181] *Sabo* – AF, n 173, 1.

[182] Art 191(1) TFEU: 'Union policy on the environment shall contribute to pursuit of the following objectives: preserving, protecting and improving the quality of the environment, protecting human health, prudent and rational utilisation of natural resources, promoting measures at international level to deal with regional or worldwide environmental problems, and in particular combating climate change.'

[183] ibid.

A. Which Fundamental Rights?

In their submission, the applicants held that – by encouraging intensive forest harvesting – the RED II would have breached a number of fundamental rights, for example the right to health care; the right to private and family life; the right to education; the freedom to manifest religion.[184] The applicants clarified that some of these violations are not yet 'present', meaning that some of them will occur in the future. However, given that the EU Treaties allow applicants to challenge the legality of an EU measure within a period of two months from publication, they 'must look forward and anticipate the violations of their rights that the Directive itself will cause, based on the harm that has occurred as a result of the predecessor Directive' (RED).[185] As in *Carvalho*, the legal team in *Sabo* took a 'factual' approach to the 'differentiation' requirement laid down under *Plaumann*. As David Wolfe, one of the lawyers involved in the case, revealed:

> [In] that case [*Sabo*] the main problem for us was establishing standing in the court. And standing in the courts is all about the individuals. So, because that was the issue we knew we had to deal with, we probably gave more details about the individuals to give them some human characteristics than it would have otherwise been the case.[186]

To give a few examples of how the lawyers framed the 'differentiation' requirement in *Sabo*, in relation to the Slovakian plaintiff (Peter Sabo), the legal team described the choice he made to raise his family in a region:

> where he can access the forests to which he has a deep personal connection, specifically so that he can pass on this connection to his sons. … The logging threat to the forests where he lives represents an infringement on the private sphere of [his] family life, in breach of Article 7. For the same reason, his right to ensure the education and teaching of his children in conformity with his philosophical convictions has been infringed, in breach of Article 14(3) of the Charter.[187]

In relation to the applicant from the US, the lawyers described how:

> hunting in the woods he owns is an intrinsic part of his family life, and has been for over 100 years … The logging damage to surrounding woodland has had a knock-on effect on his own property, reducing the extent to which it supports the small mammals he and his family hunt, and also their ability to access it … This is an infringement of his private family life, in breach of Article 7.[188]

To support such claims, even in *Sabo* the plaintiffs tried to rely on the *Codorniu* case, but the Court confirmed the interpretation already proffered in *Carvalho*.[189]

[184] ibid, 31–32.
[185] *Sabo* – AF, n 172, 46.
[186] Interview with David Wolfe, n 175.
[187] ibid.
[188] ibid.
[189] *Sabo*, n 181, § 32. See above section III.A.

B. Establishing Causation in *Sabo*

In the Court's order in *Carvalho* the EU judges stressed the importance of establishing a clear link between the challenged measure and the alleged violation of the fundamental rights of the applicants.[190] In other words, the GC maintained that climate change may certainly affect individuals' fundamental rights. However, plaintiffs – in actions for annulment under Article 263(4) TFEU – must be directly and individually concerned by the 'challenged measure', not by climate change.[191]

Conversely, in *Sabo*, the Court stressed the necessity of challenging an 'act' which is of direct and individual concern to the applicant.[192] In this regard, given that RED II is an act of general application, 'it is not possible to identify a limited category of persons concerned by the provisions of the contested directive that are at issue'.[193] According to the EU judiciary, the applicants in *Sabo* did not 'put forward any factor recognised by case-law which would be capable of distinguishing them individually as addressees'.[194] The Court further added that:

> even assuming that the contested directive does have a negative impact as regards forests and the operation of power plants, the applicants are not in a situation that is different from that of the indeterminate and indeterminable body of Union citizens, which prevents the contested directive from being of individual concern to them.[195]

By so arguing, the GC rejected any *butterfly effect* that the relevant EU law may have on individuals' fundamental rights (even outside the EU). The expression 'butterfly effect' refers to a popular idiom saying 'when a butterfly flaps its wings in Chicago, a tornado occurs in Tokyo'. Small events compound and irreversibly alter the future of the universe.[196] With regard to the *Sabo* case, the simple inclusion of 'forest biomass' in the text of the RED II may provoke deforestation and fundamental rights violations in the EU and the US.[197]

Therefore, the Court's rejection of the 'butterfly effect' was a difficult barrier for the plaintiffs to overcome, since the chain of causal links to be connected was extremely 'long'. Indeed, the plaintiffs tried to prove that, by setting specific renewable energy targets, the EU forced its MSs to achieve such targets (with very little or no discretion on the criteria that biomass fuel must comply with).[198] For this reason, MSs are in practice pushed to continue to trade pellets with other EU and third countries.[199] Because of the increase in the pellets market, EU and third

[190] ibid.
[191] ibid, § 30.
[192] ibid, § 24.
[193] ibid, § 30.
[194] ibid.
[195] ibid, 31.
[196] Goeff Boeing, 'Visual Analysis of Nonlinear Dynamical Systems: Chaos, Fractals, Self-Similarity and the Limits of Prediction' (2016) 4(4) *Systems* 14.
[197] Pagano, n 115.
[198] *Sabo* – AF, n.173, § 70.
[199] ibid, § 36.

countries' companies are encouraged to cut down more trees and produce more pellets.[200] As a consequence, by cutting down more trees, deforestation will be increased and the fundamental rights of a number of individuals will be affected.[201]

In the light of this sequence of causal links and of the Court's narrow interpretation of the rules on standing, it is difficult to argue that it is precisely RED II that breaches the FRs of the applicants. This is why the Court found it easy to maintain that RED II does not require the cutting down of 'those' specific trees in the EU or in the US (in the areas where some of the applicants live) and that the applicants 'are not in a situation that is different from that of the indeterminate and indeterminable body of Union citizens'.[202]

Nevertheless, the 'butterfly effect' and the 'unpredictability' of all its consequences are key features of climate change.[203] Tackling climate change through judicial review will inevitably necessitate a loosening of the concept of causation. In this regard, Jacqueline Peel referred to the 'butterfly effect' as a major issue in CCL under another name (namely as the 'how many links in the chain' issue).[204] She argued that, in cases clearly showing this issue, success is deeply dependent on the extent to which courts will be willing to acknowledge that the effects or impacts of a given activity or project extend to its indirect consequences as well as its direct and immediate ecological effects.[205] This triggers the questions of how 'appropriate' the *Plaumann* test is having regard to the current challenges that the EU is facing and whether environmental protection and climate change deserve a special treatment in courts. The answer is that the laxer standard of causation required in CCL to establish standing clearly clashes with the *Plaumann* test, reinforcing once again the idea of a Court which is too 'obsolete' to rule on the adequacy of EU climate law *vis-à-vis* citizens' fundamental rights. In this regard, the applicants in *Sabo* hold that the Court:

> ought to reform the previous interpretation of 'direct and individual concern' because of the special context of environmental law cases. It is widely recognised that adequate environmental protection, more than any other area of law, relies on the involvement of the public and interest groups.[206]

As shown in previous chapters, this argument has already been used in previous environmental litigation under Article 263(4) TFEU,[207] but environmental organisations have always failed to convince the Court of the distinctiveness of the

[200] ibid, § 44.
[201] ibid, § 72.
[202] *Sabo*, n 154, § 31.
[203] eg, see V Radchuk, C Turlure and N Schtickzelle, 'Each Life Stage Matters: The Importance of Assessing the Response to Climate Change Over the Complete Life Cycle in Butterflies' (2012) 82 *Journal of Animal Ecology* 275–85. Here the authors argue that the negative effects of climate change on biodiversity (in particular on butterflies) will be even bigger than expected.
[204] Jacqueline Peel, 'Issues in Climate Change Litigation' (2011) 5(1) *Carbon & Climate Law Review* 21.
[205] ibid, 22.
[206] *Sabo* – AF, n 173, § 111.
[207] See chapter 1.

environment. Indeed, the EU judiciary has never really addressed this question, but it has usually indicated an alternative pathway for ENGOs to pursue in order to protect the environment, namely before national courts under the PRP.[208] An answer which, as reported in chapter two, is heavily, and rightly, contested by environmental associations. However, in addition to the more 'substantive' arguments used to try to overcome *Plaumann*, relating to the individual (and factual) situation of each plaintiff, the legal team in *Sabo* also referred to the 'Aarhus' development occurring in 2017. This set of arguments will be unpacked in the section below.

C. Standing and Aarhus

In the attempt to push the Court to overcome the *Plaumann* formula, the applicants in *Sabo* also referred to the 2017 ACCC findings on EU compliance with the Aarhus Convention.[209] Because of this explicit reference,[210] the GC had another opportunity to reconsider its position with regard to the recommendations put forward by the UN Committee. Indeed, as highlighted in chapter four, in *Mellifera*[211] the same Court questioned the binding character of the ACCC findings and argued that these were released only after the regulation contested by the applicants in *Mellifera* had already been adopted by the European Commission,[212] leaving open the question of how the Court would have dealt with an EU act adopted *after* the Committee's findings were released (this even without the endorsement of the MOP, achieved in 2021). The opportunity to answer this question came precisely in *Sabo*, but in this case another issue hindered the possibility of using the ACCC findings as a leverage against *Plaumann*: the 'legislative' nature of the contested EU measure.

Indeed, the RED II which was subject to direct challenge in *Sabo* is a legislative act and, in their application file, the plaintiffs did not make any reference to the explicit exclusion of 'public authorities acting in a judicial or legislative capacity' from the definition of 'public authority' provided by the Aarhus Convention.[213] This precise counterargument was thus used by the GC to dismiss the plaintiffs' request to amend the *Plaumann* formula on the basis of its alleged incompliance with Article 9 of the Aarhus Convention.[214]

On this point, in the first part of its findings released in 2011,[215] even the ACCC stressed that 'the EU institutions do not act as public authorities when they

[208] See conclusions in chapters 1 and 2.
[209] *Sabo* – AF, n 173, § 132. See also chapter 4.
[210] See chapter 4.
[211] T-12/17, *Mellifera v Commission* (2018) ECLI:EU:T:2018:616.
[212] ibid, § 86.
[213] Art 2(d) of the Aarhus Convention.
[214] *Sabo*, n 154, § 40.
[215] Findings and Recommendations of the Compliance Committee with regard to Communication ACCC/C/2008/32 (Part I) concerning compliance by the European Union (adopted on 14 April 2011).

perform in their legislative capacity, with the effect that these forms of decision-making are not covered by article 9 of the Convention'.[216] This exclusion from the scope of the Convention, actually touches upon a crucial aspect for many ENGOs, that is whether the Aarhus Convention is currently 'enough' for environmental litigants to hold States accountable for environmental protection and climate change?

In other words, should the Aarhus Convention be broadened so as to also encompass the possibility of seeking review of *legislative* acts? I asked this question to in-house lawyers working for ENGOs and external attorneys representing ENGOs and individuals before the CJEU in environmental and climate cases. In most of the answers received[217] the lawyers argued that the Aarhus Convention – in its current version – is not enough to guarantee a high level of human rights and environmental protection in the countries where it applies, including the EU MSs. As will now be reported below, according to some of the lawyers I have interviewed, the EU should also provide broader space for constitutional review of legislative acts *vis-à-vis* higher-ranking norms (such as human rights obligations and general principles of environmental law).

D. Is Aarhus Enough?

Considering the Court's rigidity on *Plaumann* and the long way ahead to revise the EU Treaties, the Aarhus Convention – if amended in a way as to also cover legislative acts – could represent an additional tool for mobilising EU primary law, allowing for broader constitutional judicial review of EU legislative acts. At the moment this may seem unlikely, but in the past ENGOs have already proven to be able to 'shape' the Aarhus Convention in a way which favours their legal mobilisation objectives.[218] Moreover, the spreading of TIJC in Europe could create more favourable conditions for pushing national governments to review the architecture of the European judicial protection system in relation to the environment, and the Aarhus Convention is an essential 'building block' in this architecture.[219] On the possibility to amend the Convention, Csaba Kiss, Executive Director of the Hungarian ENGO 'Environmental management and Law Association' (EMLA) and in-house lawyer at 'Justice&Environment' (J&E), on a pessimistic note argued that:

> It's almost HRs litigation … Going against restrictive laws, like … A bit it reminds me segregation laws in the US … So, it's more like, a fight against a whole establishment and the whole perception of the social order. I think we are a bit far from that, still. We will try at this 'technical level' that you mentioned. Like finding a new decision, a

[216] ibid, § 61.
[217] 8/10 lawyers/ENGOs members to whom the question has been asked answered that the Aarhus Convention is not sufficient for holding states accountable for HRs violations and climate change.
[218] See chapter 3.
[219] ibid.

> communication or whatever by the Commission and then go against it with a request for internal review and then go against it at the Court.[220]

In light of his words, we can infer that Csaba Kiss does not consider the re-negotiation of the Aarhus Convention to be feasible in a foreseeable future. This explains his preference for litigation under the AR, contesting EU administrative/regulatory acts via the internal review procedure and then, eventually, via Article 263(4) TFEU. On the contrary, Gerd Winter, Law Professor and lawyer in the Carvalho case, stated that:

> No, [the Aarhus Convention is] not enough. It was a bit a mistake of the recent initiative to revise the [AR] to just focus on implementing the Convention, rather than having a fresh look at the whole system of access to the Court. [A] broader approach, possibly would have also enabled better access to actions against legislative acts. So, the Aarhus Convention is in a way a good foundation for the revision of the Aarhus Regulation but it's still too narrow.[221]

Therefore, Gerd Winter saw in the revision of the AR a missed opportunity for also broadening access to the CJEU in a more expansive sense. However, he did not clarify whether he would prefer a revision of the EU Treaties or an amendment of the Aarhus Convention. On a different line of reasoning, Harriet Mackaill-Hill from CAN Europe argued that:

> That's actually something we've never really considered. We know the Convention is not enough, we know Plaumann exists, we know we'll never be able … Well, I don't want to say 'never'. We know it's very difficult – let's say – to get access to an annulment of a legislative act. So, I think that what we've been seeing a lot is also the EU trying to throw back at national courts. And right now we see that working quite well, I mean the national courts cases. There's quite a bit of success. So that can obviously challenge national targets. But in the end if the national targets are challenged, the force to increase will inherently bring up the level of ambition of the EU.[222]

Although Harriet Mackaill-Hill stressed that the Aarhus Convention is not enough to hold national authorities accountable for climate change, she still saw the potential of CCL at national level as a way to also mobilise EU climate targets. Particularly relevant were also the words of Anne Friel from ClientEarth, who advocated for a broader access to justice at EU level:

> The rights enshrined in the Aarhus Convention already provide a very good basis for environmental protection and appropriately balance the rights and obligations of the key stakeholders, ie, citizens and their organisations, parliaments, governments, competent authorities and corporations. We would like to see the Aarhus rights properly implemented and enforced in the EU and every other contracting party. Of course, legislation does enjoy more democratic legitimacy and it makes sense for the EU rules on

[220] Interview with Csaba Kiss, Executive Director at EMLA and in-house lawyer at Justice& Environment (11 January 2022).
[221] Interview with Gerd Winter, n 10.
[222] Interview with Harriet Mackaill-Hill, n 20.

> standing to recognise that. However, the ability to challenge legislation when it breaches higher-ranking environmental laws and human rights obligations would be of benefit to the environmental movement as a whole. The growing trend of [CCL] across Europe clearly demonstrates the link between human rights protection and climate change and other aspects of environmental protection. We are concerned that the avenues for judicial remedies in the EU are very limited for individuals whose human rights are violated by acts of the EU institutions, including through EU legislation. EU accession to ECHR is key here. Of course, strong procedural rights must go hand-in-hand with strong substantive environmental rights that are mainstreamed throughout policymaking. Therefore, we would also like to see stronger substantive environmental rights that are enforceable at EU level, including better use and enforcement of Article 37 of the [EUCFR] and the integration principle in Article 11 TFEU, and other environmental law principles.[223]

ClientEarth gives a much more comprehensive reading of access to justice at EU level, focusing on the shortcomings present in the EU judicial protection system, taken as a whole. By looking at Anne Friel's words from a legal mobilisation perspective, she seems to focus not only on the legal remedies provided under EU law, but also on the available legal stock, in particular on the actual rights that citizens and ENGOs could potentially invoke before the EU judiciary if standing requirements were to be relaxed. ClientEarth's reflection on the EU adhesion to the ECHR, on the possibility of invoking the rights enshrined under the EUCFR, as well as the general principles of EU environmental law, reveal that 'overcoming *Plaumann*' is just a first step for this ENGO. If broader standing were to be granted to natural and legal persons in actions for annulment, the focus would likely shift from the 'procedural' dimension of *locus standi*, to the more 'substantive' dimension of what kind of rights and principles could actually be mobilised to hold the EU accountable for environmental protection. This might bring about a crucial transformation in the nature of EU environmental litigation: from the 'administrative' litigation dimension to which European ENGOs have been relegated under the AR, to the more 'constitutional' litigation dimension hoped for by many of them.

VIII. The Aftermath of *Sabo*

Considering the very 'technical' nature of the *Sabo* case – which aimed at removing 'forest biomass' from the list of renewable energy sources within RED II – the public awareness component of the lawsuit was much weaker than in *Carvalho*. Nonetheless, the *Sabo* lawsuit received some media attention,[224] which resonated

[223] Interview with Anne Friel, Lawyer at Environmental Democracy at ClientEarth (Brussels office), 19 July 2021.

[224] See https://eubiomasscase.org/media/. Also Jemima Stratford, barrister at Brick Court Chambers, in her answer in 2022 in the questionnaire, stated as follows: 'I don't feel qualified to speak for

with the 'technical' focus of the whole case.[225] However, one of the most evident effects produced by this lawsuit – even before the EU Courts' rulings were released – was to actually push ENGOs to reorientate their strategies toward other legal mobilisation pathways. On this point, PFPI reported that:

> Recognizing that it would be difficult to get standing in the EU court, PFPI began planning how to bring and support additional legal cases internationally immediately after filing the EU case in March 2019. We found an ideal partner for this endeavour, UK-based NGO [The Lifescape Project], whose CEO Adam Eagle is an ex-litigator with an appetite for taking on big causes. Again, with backing from IGSD and CIP, in late 2020, PFPI supported a case brought by [Solutions For Our Climate], a Seoul-based NGO, against the South Korean government for its aggressive subsidizing of biomass power, South Korea being one of the biggest biomass users and importers outside of the EU. We continue to research additional cases to bring in the coming years.[226]

Hence, instead of continuing to challenge the 'policy maker' (ie the EU), PFPI decided to support litigation triggered by other organisations in one of the main 'policy taker' jurisdictions (ie South Korea), in an attempt to limit the importation of biomass fuel from the EU to the Asian country. This confirms the 'technical' focus of the *Sabo* lawsuit. Indeed, PFPI intends to counter the use of biomass fuel as a renewable energy source, but with a particular preference for the EU standards. This brought the organisation to re-organise its legal mobilisation strategy in adaptive and flexible terms, and to trigger litigation in a country trading pellets with the EU. Nevertheless, the legal dispute against the EU classification of biomass fuel as renewable energy is far from being over. This is because other ENGOs have taken over the fight on whether biomass fuel should be considered as a truly 'sustainable' source of energy, and relevant cases under the new AR are currently pending before the CJEU.[227]

IX. Conclusions

The present chapter intended to show how ENGOs have mobilised against *Plaumann* directly before the CJEU in the climate change context. Indeed, ENGOs have used Article 263(4) TFEU as a mobilisation pathway also to hold the EU accountable for climate change.

With specific regard to the two lawsuits analysed, there are analogies and differences in the mobilisation goals pursued in *Carvalho* and *Sabo*. Indeed, the

environmental NGOs in general, but it seems to me that it is desirable for them to be able to contest legislative acts'.

[225] Media reporting on *Sabo* mainly framed the case in terms of 'protecting forests', by focusing on the impact of the EU renewable energy policy on biodiversity.

[226] PFPI, 2010–2020 Ten-year report, n 155, 21.

[227] On this point, see Mario Pagano, 'Climate Legal Mobilization Under the New Aarhus Regulation' (2024) 25 (6) *German Law Journal* 919–34.

lawyers in *Carvalho* aimed at contesting the legality of three EU climate policy measures, while the ENGOs involved in *Sabo* aimed at challenging the inclusion of 'forest biomass' as a renewable energy source in the RED II. Both cases thus raised the question of whether the EU should be held accountable for the negative impact of climate change on citizens' FRs. However, *Carvalho* embedded a significant 'awareness raising' component. Indeed, the case was also conceived as a tool to raise awareness about the lack of EU ambition in tackling climate change, but also precisely on *Plaumann* and the lack of access to justice at EU level for ENGOs and citizens. Furthermore, *Carvalho* also served as a megaphone to make the voice of marginalised communities' who are victims of climate change heard. On the contrary, the *Sabo* case had a much weaker 'awareness raising' component. The lawsuit focused on a very technical point, namely the need to exclude 'forest biomass' from the EU list of renewable energy sources. As soon as the case was lost, the main actor behind the lawsuit re-organised its mobilisation tactic in order to tackle EU regulation on biomass fuel in another country, outside the EU.

This shows that European strategic litigants, despite *Plaumann*, still trust the 'radiating effect'[228] of the EU judiciary, beyond the immediate 'legal' outcome of the dispute. Furthermore, the organisations behind the two lawsuits 'perceived'[229] the opening of new legal opportunities arising respectively from the *Urgenda* ruling and the ACCC on EU compliance, which pushed them, once again despite the 'closure' of *Plaumann*, to mobilise the CJEU under Article 263(4) TFEU.

Furthermore, the two cases analysed were both conceived in 2018, a crucial year for climate mobilisation and policy in Europe. However, the cases show that contemporary CCL is not always ignited by members of environmental organisations, as it was for instance in *Sabo*. On the contrary, lawyers can also take the lead and seek the support of ENGOs at a later time, as occurred in *Carvalho*. Indeed, this lawsuit was conceived by Professor Gerd Winter, who then turned to other lawyers and ENGOs to help him build the case.

However, both cases show the importance of either using network membership or forming coalitions as a resource supporting the legal enterprise. The support of other organisations within the network having expertise in environmental advocacy is crucial for at least four main reasons, namely (i) selecting plaintiffs; (ii) securing funding; (iii) elaborating effective legal arguments; (iv) developing a communication strategy. On this last point, in-house lawyers working for prominent European climate organisations deemed campaigns built around lawsuits as 'crucial' in CCL nowadays. Lawyers and communication officers frequently interact when working on the same case, to make sure that the technical language of the law is delivered in simpler and more engaging ways to the general public.

[228] Marc Galanter, 'The Radiating Effects of Courts' in Keith O Boyum and Lynn Mather (eds), *Empirical Theories About Courts* (London, Longman Inc, 1983) 135.

[229] Sidney Tarrow, *Power in Movement: Social Movements, Collective Action, and Politics* (Cambridge, Cambridge University Press, 2012) 33.

This interaction between legal and media expertise can thus be considered as a further 'resource' to which organisations resorted to in order to maximise impact. Furthermore, this interaction stretches our understanding of legal mobilisation way beyond strategic litigation. If advocacy[230] and communication strategies deeply influence the choice of a given legal mobilisation pathway, the selection of the plaintiffs, and even the drafting of the legal arguments, then the distinction between legal mobilisation and other forms of mobilisation in practice is much more fluid and cannot be conceptualised in rigid terms.

Regarding communication campaigns, having natural persons acting as plaintiffs provided the campaign with powerful individual stories to be told to the Court and the public. The factual interpretation of *Plaumann* given by the lawyers involved in the lawsuits deeply affected the choice of the plaintiffs. These, under *Plaumann*, must be 'differentiated from all other persons'.[231] A requirement which guided the choice toward citizens living across Europe (and beyond), whose personal lives had been or would be impacted by the contested EU policy measures. In *Carvalho* the choice fell on citizens subject to the different forms climate change impact (droughts, biodiversity loss, rising sea levels, etc). In *Sabo*, considering the origin of pellets, the choice fell on citizens living in the surroundings of forests.

Moreover, the choice of having natural persons acting as plaintiffs marked a significant shift in environmental/climate litigation under Article 263(4) TFEU. Indeed, until these two lawsuits, basically all the actions for annulment brought in the environmental domain saw ENGOs acting as plaintiffs. On the contrary, thanks to CCL, individuals have appeared before the CJEU (even if 'backed up' by ENGOs), bringing their families, their individual stories and, most importantly invoking their rights.

In this regard, *Carvalho* and *Sabo* undoubtedly confirm the 'rights turn' in international CCL identified by Peel and Osofsky.[232] Indeed, even in CCL before EU Courts applicants claimed the violation of a number of fundamental rights protected under the EUCFR. This in spite of the extreme difficulties that private applicants have in proving that they are 'individually concerned' by the contested EU measure. This is because the *Plaumann* test does not only require plaintiffs to demonstrate a causal link between the contested measure and the violation of the right, but also a 'differentiation' of the legal position of the applicant from the one of any other person. Because of the hurdle of standing, CCL before EU Courts undertaken by CSOs will almost inevitably always stop at the 'admissibility' phase,[233] without even reaching the stage of 'judicial review' stage if no revision

[230] As shown in chapter 4 with regard to the strategic use of the ACCC recommendations in the reform of the AR.

[231] Part of the *Plaumann* formula.

[232] See Jacqueline Peel and Hari M Osofsky, 'A Rights Turn in Climate Change Litigation?' (2018) 7 (1) *Transnational Environmental Law* 37.

[233] Apart from the pending cases brought under the new AR.

of the TFEU occurs.[234] Unless, of course, the building of transnational judicial comfort incrementally brings about a change in the approach of the European Court. This, together with the threat of indirect review of EU law by non-EU courts discussed in the previous chapter, make this more likely than a mere reading of the case law might suggest. However, only time will tell if an EU version of *Urgenda* will be heard by the CJEU.

Moreover, the two lawsuits described also confirm the willingness of climate litigants to use rights as an 'interpretative aid' for judges, as noted in other climate cases outside the EU.[235] The applicants in *Carvalho* encouraged the GC to interpret Article 263(4) TFEU in the light of Article 47 of the EUCFR. Nevertheless, the judiciary responded by recalling that the Charter provision 'is not intended to change the system of judicial review laid down by the Treaties, and particularly the rules relating to the admissibility of direct actions'.[236] This confirms the unavailability of the rights enshrined under the EU Charter for environmental litigants seeking to challenge EU law.

Another argument deployed by the applicants to mobilise the Court against *Plaumann* referred to the ACCC findings on EU compliance. However, the EU judges recalled that legislative acts are excluded from the scope of the Aarhus Convention, easily dismissing the applicants' plea. The Court's response triggers the question of whether the Aarhus Convention is 'enough' for environmental litigants to hold States and governments accountable for environmental protection and climate change, or whether that same Convention should be amended as to also encompass legislative acts? Interviews undertaken with lawyers who have been actively involved in environmental and CCL before the EU judiciary revealed that most of them would actually prefer to be able to also challenge legislative acts, in particular when these collide with higher-ranking norms and principles of EU environmental law and fundamental rights protected under the Charter. Within the European environmental movement there is therefore a demand for a different kind of environmental and climate justice at the EU level, which at the moment is only confined into the realm of administrative law (mainly under the AR). The ENGOs' demand is to have a system of judicial protection which enables citizens and ENGOs to obtain an authentic *constitutional* judicial review of environmental and climate measures, either via revision of Aarhus or of the EU Treaties.

In terms of impact, the *Carvalho* case managed to catch the attention of EU policymakers in Brussels.[237] Some of the plaintiffs had the chance to meet with MEPs and EU officials working for the Commission, meetings which contributed to making the plaintiffs feel 'heard' by the EU institutions. In this regard,

[234] While *Carvalho* and *Sabo* stopped at the admissibility phase, on the opposite, judicial review of the Dutch State's duty of care represented the core of the Court's ruling in *Urgenda*. On this point, see Benoit Mayer, 'The State of the Netherlands v. Urgenda Foundation: Ruling of the Court of Appeal of The Hague (9 October 2018)' (2019) 8(1) *Transnational Environmental Law* 176.

[235] Peel and Osofsky, n 233, 58.

[236] *Carvalho*, n 71, § 52.

[237] See above section V.

the *Carvalho* case also served as an empowerment enterprise for the marginalised individuals involved in the lawsuit. Some of the plaintiffs involved were also depicted as 'climate heroes' by the media in their respective countries, strengthening the *David v Goliath* narrative underlying the lawsuit.[238] However, the media impact of the case was hampered by the Covid-19 pandemic which started in 2020.

In terms of policy change, the final ruling in *Carvalho* was chronologically followed by the adoption of the new EU climate law in July 2021, which increased the EU emissions reduction target from 40 per cent up to 55 per cent by 2030. A target precisely in the range requested by the applicants in *Carvalho*. However, there is lack of empirical evidence as to what extent this shift was impacted by the *Carvalho* case. With regard to the *Sabo* case, this was not followed by any relevant policy change in the RED II. The lawsuit mainly contributed to redirecting ENGOs' legal mobilisation strategies by pushing them to trigger litigation in countries outside the EU, which trade pellets with the Europe and which are indirectly impacted by EU law on renewable energy.

This chapter has demonstrated how current CCL before the EU judiciary has been affected by the global CCL trend, which is seeking to hold governments and corporations accountable for the negative effects that climate change has on citizens' fundamental rights and the environment. A major impact has been produced by the infamous *Urgenda* case, which has captured the attention of the public opinion and encouraged litigants throughout the globe to initiate climate lawsuits in a wide number of different jurisdictions, with the aim of spreading incrementally what I conceptualised in chapter six as TIJC.

Beside the successful European cases at national level,[239] the *Carvalho* and *Sabo* lawsuits show that climate litigants in the EU do not settle for actions brought before national courts, but rather continue to challenge the legality of EU climate measures directly before the EU judiciary. However, the presence of *Plaumann* makes an 'EU-wide Urgenda' de facto inconceivable for the time being. This is leading EU climate litigants to reconsider the CJEU as the sole or even primary forum for human rights-based legal mobilisation in the climate context, pushing such litigants to turn to other supranational courts to seek justice for climate related human rights violations occurring in Europe. This attitude of climate litigants toward the EU judiciary, also emerged in chapter VI, reinforces the idea of an EU judiciary looking more and more as an 'obsolete' forum for climate litigation, increasingly at odds with the European judicial landscape. It remains to be seen how the CJEU will respond to being cast in this role.

[238] For a more extensive analysis of 'transnational narratives' in climate litigation, see Phillip Paiement, 'Urgent Agenda: How Climate Litigation Builds Transnational Narratives' (2020) 11 (1–2) *Transnational Legal Theory* 121–43.

[239] See chapter 6.

Conclusions

In this final chapter, I will set out the conclusions stemming from the analysis carried out throughout the book. The conclusions will be divided into blocks, resonating with the research questions which have guided this research, namely: (i) which ENGOs have mobilised against *Plaumann* in the environmental context (ie *who*?); (ii) *why* have they done it?; (iii) *how* have ENGOs mobilised against *Plaumann* since the Greenpeace case?; (iv) *what* have they achieved so far? The main findings are set out below.

I. Who?

The names of the ENGOs mobilising to overcome *Plaumann* were clear since the introduction to the present book. But what do these names and their inner characteristics tell us about the evolution in the identity of the actors pursuing legal mobilisation to overcome *Plaumann* in environmental matters?

This book has indeed shown that the ENGOs mobilising against *Plaumann* have evolved over time. From the famous organisations, such as Greenpeace, WWF and EEB, mobilising in the 'pre-Aarhus period', the following timeframes here considered have seen the emergence of new players contributing to this legal fight. Once *Plaumann* discouraged 'old' actors, who had attempted to contest the legality of EU law in the 'pre-Aarhus period' (eg GPI), other ENGOs – with diversified legal expertise – took over the mission. In particular, since 2008 the ENGO ClientEarth contributed significantly to putting pressure on the EU institutions in relation to *Plaumann* by bringing the EU before the Compliance Committee established under the Aarhus Convention. ClientEarth was not alone in this legal enterprise but was supported by a coalition of other environmental organisations. The novelty of ClientEarth in the European ENGOs' landscape is mainly represented by its 'dominant' legal nature.[1] Indeed, this organisation has displayed a high level of legal and scientific sophistication in legal mobilisation. This is no surprise considering the hundreds of lawyers it counts amongst its employees across its eight offices. These lawyers have expertise in a broad variety of relevant domains, ranging from environmental and administrative law to finance and corporate liability law.[2] ClientEarth strongly believes in the use of the law as a tool

[1] See chapter 4.
[2] ibid.

for protecting the planet. This differentiates ClientEarth from other ENGOs which resort to the strategic use of the law as 'one tool in the toolbox', to be used along with a multitude of other instruments.[3]

What is also striking about ClientEarth is its constant presence across most of the timeframes considered in this book. Apart from the cases brought in the 'pre-Aarhus period', since its establishment in Europe, ClientEarth has mobilised against *Plaumann* at all levels in each of the timeframes identified. At the EU level (exclusively in cases brought under the 'old' and 'new' AR), at MS level (where interviews have revealed that ClientEarth also tried to stimulate validity references in Eastern Europe), as well as at the international level (before the ACCC).

On this last point, this research has shown the key role played by ClientEarth in the legal mobilisation which led to the adoption of the new AR. However, even other organisations – which lobbied the EU institutions alongside ClientEarth – contributed deeply to achieving this crucial legislative change. Indeed, umbrella organisations like the EEB and CAN Europe provided representation in Brussels to national affiliated organisations and ensured that these could speak with *one* single voice before the EU institutions when advocating for a different AR.

Precisely the adoption of the AR by the EU in 2006 favoured the emergence of other actors litigating before the CJEU in the environmental context. Considering that the initial version of the AR only applied to 'administrative acts of individual scope', this mainly included non-legislative acts having a highly technical content, targeting for instance specific substances or plans.[4] It is thus no coincidence that the procedure laid down under Article 10 AR attracted a number of highly specialised ENGOs, such as PAN (working to 'minimise the negative effects of hazardous pesticides'), Testbiotech (focusing on risks deriving from genetical engineering) or Mellifera (focusing on bees protection). While, by contrast with Client Earth, these organisations possessed a low level of internal legal expertise, they were imbued with deep and solid scientific and technical expertise.[5]

This tendency to attract highly specialised organisations with very little internal legal expertise has been confirmed (so far) even under the new AR. Indeed, the revision of the AR has further contributed to attract new players in the fight against EU administrative/regulatory acts (this time of 'general scope'). Almost half of the total number of the requests for internal review received by the European Commission since 2006 to the present comes from organisations with low[6] or no internal legal expertise whatsoever.[7] In other terms, if chapter three

[3] See for instance GPI (chapter 6) or PFPI (chapter 7).

[4] Final study on EU implementation of the Aarhus Convention in the area of access to justice in environmental matters (carried out by 'Milieu'), September 2019. Available at: https://ec.europa.eu/environment/aarhus/pdf/Final_study_EU_implemention_environmental_matters_2019.pdf.

[5] See chapters 3 and 4.

[6] Only one in-house lawyer.

[7] I calculated 45 per cent of the total amount of the requests. This data has been collected by consulting the respective official websites of the ENGOs under consideration. See https://ec.europa.eu/environment/aarhus/requests.htm.

has shown how ENGOs contributed to 'shape' the Aarhus Convention, first, and – in particular – the new AR, then, we must also notice that the internal review mechanism has 'shaped' a specific type of actors mobilising under the AR. Actors can thus shape procedures and vice versa.

Indeed, legal mobilisation under the AR sees an essential function being played by scientific expertise within ENGOs. In terms of 'resources', this seems to indicate two key aspects. The first one is that the lack of internal legal expertise does not prevent an environmental organisation from triggering legal mobilisation under the AR. This is no surprise considering the high level of technical and scientific sophistication which characterises EU regulatory acts having an impact on the environment. The second aspect is that the lack of internal legal expertise can be counterbalanced by resorting to external attorneys or networks membership.[8]

As mentioned above, the present research confirms that becoming part of networks of various kinds constitutes a key resource for ENGOs involved in legal mobilisation. Almost one-third of the requests for internal review received by the European Commission have been submitted either by established networks of ENGOs (eg EEB) or by other coalitions of ENGOs cooperating on a specific request.[9] When it comes to actions for annulment triggered by ENGOs, the rate of cases submitted by established networks or *ad hoc* coalitions is even higher (42 per cent). Qualitative analysis has shown that membership of networks in climate legal mobilisation against *Plaumann* was crucial for at least four main reasons, namely for (i) selecting plaintiffs; (ii) securing funding;[10] (iii) elaborating effective legal arguments; (iv) developing a communication strategy.[11] Moreover, membership of networks facilitates the adoption of an 'integrated' approach to advocacy, combining legal and non-legal strategies, such as political mobilisation and lobbying.[12] Indeed, as shown in chapter five, ENGOs' established networks have guaranteed a more stable representation of national organisations before the EU institutions when lobbying for an amendment to the AR.[13]

Besides the role played by organisations, this research has also shown that ENGOs are not the only ones taking the initiative to mobilise against *Plaumann*. Indeed, in most cases ENGOs, having identified the issue at stake, then search for lawyers willing to represent them before the CJEU. However, the Carvalho case constitutes an exception in this regard, since this was actually conceived by a German professor of environmental law and legal scholar, that is, Gerd Winter, who found the support of ENGOs and other lawyers only at a later stage.[14] The

[8] In this regard, this contribution has also proven that ENGOs like ClientEarth and Urgenda share their legal expertise with other lawyers and organisations in order to stimulate more legal mobilisation (see chapters 2 and 7).

[9] ibid.

[10] The analysis of the *Duarte Agostinho* case in chapter 6 has also shown the use of crowdfunding as an additional tool to secure financial resources.

[11] See chapter 7.

[12] See below, section III.

[13] ibid.

[14] See chapter 7.

qualitative analysis of *Carvalho* and *Sabo* in chapter seven has highlighted the fundamental role of individual networks in igniting litigation and coordinating the legal strategy to overcome *Plaumann*.[15]

Always in relation to CCL before the CJEU, it is worth noting that the interest to overcome the *Plaumann* test does not only come from European organisations and citizens, but also from entities located outside the EU. This underlines the extraterritoriality of the EU's regulatory power, which is contested even beyond the borders of the Union. Indeed, in Sabo the initiative to contest the legality of the RED II originated from the US organisation PFPI, which is involved in a number of lawsuits across the globe against the use of biomass fuel as a renewable energy source.[16] This point will be further deepened in the next section.

II. Why?

Beside the case-specific objectives which have been discussed for each case-study, the present research has shown an evolution in the general tendencies pushing ENGOs to mobilise against *Plaumann*. There is no doubt that each ENGO pursues its own objectives. Therefore, generalising on broader mobilisation goals can appear disconnected from the reality of many organisations. However, the analysis of the different timeframes has highlighted a major trend that is worth stressing in this concluding section. Indeed, I have argued that ENGOs' legal mobilisation efforts against *Plaumann* have displayed a clear widening of the scope of their litigation across the decades. From the project-specific lawsuits brought in the 'pre-Aarhus' period (eg Greenpeace) or the substance-specific actions brought in the 'post-Aarhus I' period under the AR (eg Stichting Natuur), legal mobilisation against the legality of EU environmental law has in more recent years shifted toward measures having broader consequences on economic operators and the environment. If the narrowness of the targeted measures in the 'post-Aarhus I' period may seem self-evident when considering the limited scope of the definition of 'administrative act' under the old version of the AR, this tendency is much less obvious in direct actions for annulment brought under Article 263(4) TFEU. Indeed, direct actions in the 'post-Aarhus – the CCL trend' period show a clear will to target EU legislative measures, which constitute the foundations of EU climate policy (eg the Effort Sharing Regulation, the RED II).[17]

[15] ibid.
[16] ibid. In this sense, the WTO can also be seen as a forum for overcoming *Plaumann*, though I have not discussed it in this contribution. This provides an alternative forum to challenge the lawfulness of EU law. In the area of biofuels see, for example, European Union and a Member State – Certain Measures Concerning the Importation of Biodiesels (DS443) which has only reached the consultations stage. Also, European Union – Certain measures concerning palm oil and oil palm crop-based biofuels (DS593) where a Panel has been composed.
[17] ibid.

Even in the chapter devoted to analysing ENGOs' litigation before non-EU courts the same tendency was observed. GPI has not simply declared as a matter of rhetoric that it aims to achieve 'systemic shifts' through its campaigns, but it has also concretely triggered litigation that is intended to realise this ambitious goal.[18] The same can plainly be said about GLAN, which in *Duarte Agostinho* sued 33 countries before the ECtHR, de facto challenging the foundation and the national implementation of the EU's entire climate policy.[19] Instead of challenging single projects or authorisations having negative consequences on human health and the environment, environmental litigants now seem to 'dream big and aim high'. This ambition was already apparent in chapter seven, in the section considering whether the Aarhus Convention is *enough* for environmental litigants today.[20] The conclusions in that chapter already highlighted a demand for a different kind of judicial review in the environmental domain and the overall analysis of the historical trajectory of environmental legal mobilisation against *Plaumann* confirms the existence of this demand. European ENGOs investing into legal mobilisation against EU law want to be able to challenge not only administrative acts (of individual or general scope), but also broader policy arrangements, including legislative acts and programmes, impacting the lives of all European citizens.

There is, in other words, a demand to challenge the EU's exercise of its overarching powers in the environmental[21] and climate change domains.[22] In more operational terms, this demand translates into a crucial shift in the nature of legal mobilisation in the EU. A shift from the more traditional *administrative* judicial review that ENGOs have been acknowledged to enjoy under the AR, to a form of more *constitutional* judicial review of broader policy measures. Here, the ENGOs have taken inspiration from the rights which they can invoke in individual Member States such as the Netherlands and Germany.[23] We can thus call this type of environmental legal mobilisation 'systemic': a type of legal mobilisation that does not settle for challenging administrative acts, but that rather aims to challenge wider policy measures – constituting the foundations of EU environmental and climate change law – *vis-à-vis* the general principles of EU environmental law and the EUCFR. The crucial point here is that the existence of *Plaumann* has not prevented this tendency from emerging. Nonetheless, the Court's rigidity on the standing of private applicants in actions for annulment is expected to postpone even further the fulfilment of this ENGOs' wish for a different kind of judicial review in environmental matters, at least as far as the CJEU is concerned.

[18] See chapter 6.

[19] ibid.

[20] ibid. On this point, see also Lorenzo Squintani, 'Is Aarhus Still a Progressive Force?' (2021) 18 *Journal for European Environmental & Planning Law* 4–7.

[21] In *Blaise*, for instance, the applicants tried to contest the validity of the PPP Regulation. See chapter 2.

[22] See chapter 6.

[23] ibid.

III. How?

This being said, how have ENGOs mobilised against *Plaumann*? This was the main research question addressed by this book, and I will set out my main findings below.

ENGOs have mobilised against *Plaumann* by shaping alternative legal mobilisation pathways and by opening new legal opportunities under national, EU and international law.[24] Indeed, the present research has clearly shown that legal mobilisation against *Plaumann* has taken the form of a 'multi-layer' approach to mobilisation, by relying on existing EU mobilisation pathways (*in primis* the action for annulment and the PRP) but also by shaping alternative ones. Both, the shaping of alternative mobilisation pathways and the opening of new legal opportunities, have been achieved essentially in two ways: (i) by turning defeats into opportunities; (ii) by combining legal and non-legal strategies of mobilisation. The next sections will deepen these two main findings.

A. Turning Defeats into Opportunities

The present research confirms that litigation can still produce significant indirect effects, even when judges' decisions themselves translate into losses in courts for environmental litigants.[25] In particular, legal mobilisation before the CJEU to overcome *Plaumann* has seen ENGOs going back and forth between the EU judiciary and supranational judicial and quasi-judicial bodies. More specifically, ENGOs have used the rejections obtained under Article 263(4) TFEU to persuade the ACCC[26] and potentially the ECtHR[27] that the EU judiciary denies access to justice in environmental matters. In this regard, this research has confirmed the value of the ACCC and the ECtHR as precious allies of ENGOs in the fight against *Plaumann*, especially after the key climate judgments released by the Strasbourg Court in April 2024.[28]

With regard to the Aarhus Committee, in 2017 this found the EU to be in breach of the access to justice provisions of the Aarhus Convention. The ACCC findings have been used by ENGOs to 'test' the judicial receptivity of the CJEU (eg in *Mellifera* and *Sabo*), but also to increase their bargaining power *vis-à-vis* the EU institutions.[29] In other words, ENGOs have been using supranational judicial

[24] For a broader overview of the theoretical framework, see the introduction to the present book.
[25] See Michael W McCann, *Rights at Work: Pay Equity Reform and the Politics of Legal Mobilization* (Chicago, University of Chicago Press, 1994). See also Gerald N Rosenberg, 'Hollow Hopes and Other Aspirations: A Reply to Feeley and McCann' (1992) 17 (4) *Law & Social Inquiry* 761–78; Douglas NeJaime, 'Winning Through Losing' (2010) 96 *Iowa Law Review*, Loyola-LA Legal Studies Paper No. 2011-03, 953.
[26] See chapter 3.
[27] See chapter 6.
[28] ibid.
[29] See chapter 4.

and quasi-judicial bodies as catalysts,[30] in a self-reinforcing cycle of litigation,[31] capable of accelerating lengthy negotiations which aim to broaden access to justice at EU level. This was evident in chapter five, where it was demonstrated how the findings of the ACCC on EU compliance gave ENGOs leverage to ask more in the decision-making process leading to the amendment of the AR.[32] Moreover, ENGOs have also relied on the ACCC as an 'external supervisor', monitoring the revision of the AR, which was amended to a large extent in the way indicated by the environmental organisations and the ACCC.[33] In light of this, I argue that the compliance mechanism established under Aarhus has been the most effective mobilisation pathway for ENGOs in the fight against *Plaumann* so far. This since it has triggered a chain of events which have led to the most tangible legal mobilisation outcome for ENGOs, that is precisely the new AR.

Besides the role of the ACCC, even non-EU judicial bodies are being used as catalysts in a bid to overcome *Plaumann* in the climate change context.[34] Indeed, through incrementalism,[35] climate litigants active before non-EU Courts are trying to increase judicial receptivity by spreading TIJC across the globe, including the EU.[36] I have theorised TIJC as a psychological mechanism that considers judges as human beings, subject – like anyone – to external and peer pressure.[37] The idea that precedents – even those coming from remote jurisdictions – have a persuasive force affects ENGOs' conception of their legal strategies. Key 'building blocks' added in previous CCL before domestic courts (eg in Urgenda) are therefore being used to push more and more judges (including those at the CJEU) to take bold interpretative steps when ruling in the climate change context.[38] To do so, climate litigants rely either on shared legal sources (eg international law) or legal texts traditionally drafted in similar terms across the jurisdictions (eg human rights). Then they warn the court that other judges in previous cases have provided a new interpretation of the law in relation to a similar argument. By doing so, climate litigants 'test' whether that judiciary is receptive to the new input or not.[39] In this regard, climate litigants active before EU Courts have 'tested' whether the spreading of TIJC has now reached Luxembourg, and therefore whether the CJEU now feels more 'comfortable' in revising its *Plaumann* formula.[40] As outlined in chapter seven, the Court has been unreceptive in both cases, *Carvalho* and *Sabo*.[41]

[30] Marc Galanter, 'The Radiating Effects of Courts', in Keith O Boyum and Lynn Mather (eds), *Empirical Theories About Courts* (New York, Longman Inc, 1983) 135.
[31] Before the CJEU, then before the ACCC and then back again before the CJEU for 'testing'.
[32] See also Michael W McCann, *Law and Social Movements* (New York, Routledge, 2006) 19.
[33] See chapter 4.
[34] See chapter 6.
[35] ibid.
[36] ibid.
[37] See chapter 6.
[38] ibid.
[39] ibid.
[40] See chapter 6.
[41] ibid.

B. Combining Legal and Non-Legal Mobilisation Strategies

The shaping of new mobilisation pathways and the opening of new legal opportunities intended to overcome *Plaumann* has also been possible thanks to the adoption of an 'integrated' approach to advocacy, based on the combination of legal and non-legal strategies of mobilisation. In the present research, three main types of non-legal strategies have emerged: (i) the use of lobbying; (ii) training judges and legal practitioners; (iii) the use of communication strategies. In the paragraphs below, I will summarise the main findings in relation to these non-legal strategies.

As mentioned above, the use of lobbying has emerged strongly in the Aarhus context. Indeed, the doctrinal analysis undertaken in chapter three has shown the essential role played by ENGOs in shaping the Aarhus Convention by lobbying national delegates in Geneva between 1996 and 1998.[42] The coalition of ENGOs who joined the Aarhus negotiation contributed significantly to the introduction of the third pillar on access to justice and, most importantly, to the conception of a compliance committee composed by independent experts.[43] Furthermore, lobbying has been crucial also in relation to the amendment of the AR, obtained in October 2021. Qualitative analysis has not provided much detail on the 'content' and the concrete operationalisation of non-legal strategies[44] in the Aarhus context. This is because such strategies were deemed not to fall within the scope of this contribution, leaving room for further research on the subject. However, the qualitative analysis undertaken does show that ENGOs have combined litigation and lobbying in order to obtain a significant number of amendments under the new AR.[45]

The use of lobbying in combination with litigation has thus been essential to establish new legal mobilisation pathways (eg the ACCC under international law; the new internal review procedure under EU law) which have expanded CSOs' opportunities for challenging the legality of EU measures. The analysis of the 'EU v Aarhus' saga, followed by the amendment of the AR, has shown that the combination of litigation and lobbying was indeed an effective strategy.[46]

Moreover, ENGOs have been training national judges and legal practitioners in the framework of the A2J EARL project. This project, funded by the European Commission and carried out by ClientEarth and Justice & Environment, aimed at increasing judges' familiarity with EU law. Indeed, judges' lack of expertise in EU law has been identified in sociolegal scholarship as one of the additional 'closures' in the EU's LOS and as capable of hindering the mobilisation of EU law before national courts.[47] In light of this, the two organisations involved approached this

[42] See chapter 3.
[43] ibid.
[44] See definition in the introduction to the present book.
[45] See chapter 4.
[46] ibid.
[47] See chapter 2.

project with the hope of increasing judicial receptivity at national level in eight MSs and with a view to obtaining, inter alia, more preliminary references to the CJEU (including those on validity). It is probably still too soon to have a clear idea about the impact of the A2J project on national courts' receptivity,[48] but in terms of 'subjective' impact, the organisations involved have both affirmed their overall satisfaction in relation to the initiative.[49]

In addition to lobbying and judicial training, ENGOs have also combined litigation with communication strategies in their fight against *Plaumann*. The use of this kind of dual strategy emerged in particular in chapter seven, in relation to climate litigation before the EU judiciary. Indeed, having an effective communication campaign beside strategic litigation has been deemed to be 'essential' in contemporary CCL.[50] An effective communication strategy can help maximise the impact of the legal case and contribute to 'keep the case alive' in the eyes of the public opinion.[51] Furthermore, an effective communication strategy can contribute to enhancing specific narratives about the lawsuit or provide marginalised individuals and communities with a platform to be heard. This is particularly relevant in cases, like *Carvalho*, aiming to raise public awareness on specific issues or empowering indigenous communities.[52] An achievement that goes beyond winning in court.

The use of an integrated approach to advocacy, combining legal and non-legal strategies, stretches our understanding of legal mobilisation, as advocacy, communication and litigation appear much more intertwined in practice than in theory. This makes it very difficult to conceptualise legal mobilisation in rigid terms and to confine it within the sole boundaries of litigation. The use of the integrated approach thus gives us a 'fluid' image of legal mobilisation, where the objectives are more important than the methods deployed. In this regard, this research has also shown the effectiveness of the integrated approach in achieving the mobilisation objectives that ENGOs were pursuing.[53]

The opportunities shaped and used by ENGOs to mobilise against *Plaumann* have shown the 'flexible' and 'wide' understanding of the concept of LOS that these environmental organisations have. As mentioned in the introduction to the present book, 'opportunities' do not only arise from the 'objective' legal stock and the available remedies.[54] These can perfectly be simply 'perceived' as being present by social actors.[55] This research confirms the value of 'perception' in legal

[48] ibid.
[49] ibid.
[50] See chapter 7.
[51] ibid.
[52] See chapters 6 and 7.
[53] The introduction of a new pillar in the Aarhus Convention; the amendment of the AR.
[54] As defined by Sidney Tarrow, *Power in Movement: Social Movements, Collective Action, and Politics* (Cambridge, Cambridge University Press, 2012) 33.
[55] ibid.

mobilisation. As a consequence, this contribution has shown that it should not be assumed that there is an exact overlap between our traditional understanding of the 'legal system' on the one hand, and the concept of LOS on the other. The latter can be much broader and more contingent than the former. Indeed, this research has shown how legal opportunities to be seized against *Plaumann* have emerged, for instance, from lost cases (eg AG Jacobs in *UPA*), from the combination of legal and non-legal strategies (eg the A2J EARL project), from non-binding findings of international compliance bodies (eg the ACCC), from successful cases at national level (eg *Urgenda*) and even from judiciaries outside the EU legal order (eg the ECtHR). The European ENGOs' understanding of the LOS is therefore not attached to the opportunities arising under a specific legal system, but it is rather based on the opportunities stemming from interactions between different legal systems that nonetheless exhibit some commonalities.

In the next section, I will turn to outline my conclusions on the 'impact' of legal mobilisation against *Plaumann*.

IV. What?

When it comes to assessing *what* ENGOs have achieved by mobilising against *Plaumann*, we can be tempted to give a simple answer: nothing! Indeed, *Plaumann* is still there, ENGOs still have no direct access to justice under Article 263(4) TFEU, and the 'closures' in the LOS are still relatively numerous. However, this contribution has provided a richer answer to this question, by looking more closely at the features, the reasons and the means deployed by ENGOs mobilising against *Plaumann* in the last 30 years.

'Impact' has been defined in the introduction in terms of both the 'political' and 'legal' consequences of legal mobilisation.[56] With regard to the 'political' impact of ENGOs' legal mobilisation against *Plaumann*, this has certainly reached the apex with the Council decision to trigger Article 241 TFEU, which has essentially unlocked the decision-making process that ultimately led to the amendment of the AR.[57] What is striking about obtaining a 'new' AR is the relationship between ENGOs and the 'old' AR. Since its entry into force in 2007 and the CJEU's ruling in *Stichting Natuur*,[58] the AR has certainly disappointed the expectations of the European environmental movement. To a large extent, this is because of the EU judiciary's unwillingness to review the AR *vis-à-vis* the Aarhus Convention. The Court's refusal, ultimately, to apply the *Fediol* and *Nakajima* exceptions,[59]

[56] See introduction to the present book.
[57] See chapter 3.
[58] ibid.
[59] ibid.

and to recognise direct effect of Article 9(3) of the Aarhus Convention,[60] has de facto represented a further 'closure' for ENGOs in the LOS.[61] Indeed, the Court's protective[62] attitude toward the autonomy of the EU legal order evidenced in *Stichting Natuur* (and in *Stichting Stop*),[63] has made it impossible for ENGOs to invoke international law provisions against EU secondary legislation hindering direct access to the CJEU. The Court's interpretation of both, the AR and the Aarhus Convention, has thus further reduced the range of justiciable rights available for CSOs, preventing the old internal review mechanism from being a satisfactory avenue for legal mobilisation.

In light of this, the new AR can be considered as the major concrete achievement of ENGOs' efforts and as a 'step forward' in the EU system of judicial protection of the environment.[64] The new AR holds a promise that will be crucial for the future of EU legal mobilisation. The new Aarhus' promise is not to increase the rate of requests being held admissible by EU administrations but – as argued in chapter five – to deliver more substantive reviews of EU administrative acts having an impact on the environment.[65] This is because, under the old AR, requests for internal review usually stopped at the admissibility stage and have rarely led to an institutional answer on the merits.[66] This is in essence because of the narrow scope of the definition of 'administrative act' under the old AR. Hence, the new definition of 'administrative act' was expected to bring more disputes on the 'science' underlying EU policy in the field of environmental protection. As a consequence, this is also supposed to bring more transparency on the technical evaluations undertaken by EU policy makers, in accordance with the spirit of 'openness' which characterises the Aarhus Convention.[67] Forcing EU administrative bodies to provide more transparency on the EU environmental decision-making process definitely represents another positive outcome of ENGOs' mobilisation efforts. Pending cases before the CJEU confirm the potential embedded in the AR reform.[68] Now it is for the CJEU to confirm whether the new AR has truly broadened access to justice for

[60] See opinion of AG Jääskinen in C-401/12 P, *Council and Others v Vereniging Milieudefensie and Stichting Stop Luchtverontreiniging Utrecht* (2015) ECLI:EU:C:2014:310. Here the AG argued that Art 9(3) of the Aarhus Convention could be read in such a way as to be recognised direct effect in the EU legal order.

[61] See Katja Rath, 'The EU Aarhus Regulation and EU Administrative Acts Based on the Aarhus Regulation: The Withdrawal of the CJEU from the Aarhus Convention', in Christina Voigt (ed), *International Judicial Practice on the Environment: Questions of Legitimacy (Studies on International Courts and Tribunals)* (Cambridge, Cambridge University Press, 2019) 52–73.

[62] ibid.

[63] See above, *Council and Others v Vereniging Milieudefensie and Stichting Stop Luchtverontreiniging Utrecht*, n 60 (ruling).

[64] ibid.

[65] See chapter 7.

[66] See chapter 2.

[67] ibid.

[68] Mario Pagano, 'Climate Legal Mobilization Under the New Aarhus Regulation' (2024) 25 (6) *German Law Journal* 919–34.

ENGOs in Luxembourg and whether this will be a viable mechanism to challenge the legality of EU environmental and climate change law.

This conclusion on the reform of the AR brings us back to the initial *why*, which motivates ENGOs to mobilise against *Plaumann*. Indeed, the question now is whether the AR will be *enough* for ENGOs considering the demand for a different type of judicial review in the field of the environment emerged above.[69] Despite the broader possibilities for legal mobilisation under the new AR, this may still be sufficiently narrow to limit the ambitions of many European organisations. Considering the emerging tendency for 'systemic legal mobilisation', which has already arisen even under the new AR,[70] it will be fascinating to discover how ENGOs will seek to bend the internal review procedure to achieve their evolving mobilisation goals.

On a different note, the ENGOs' critiques toward the exclusion from the scope of the AR of administrative acts adopted in the field of State Aid, as well as the impossibility of challenging the legality of the initial administrative act (for which internal review was sought) seem to suggest that the fight for contesting the legality of EU environmental law is far from over.

With regard to the 'legal' impact of ENGOs' legal mobilisation, this research has shown that positive outcomes in the case law of the EU judiciary have essentially arisen via PRP and in actions for annulment brought under the old version of the AR.[71] With regard to preliminary rulings, my research in chapter two has demonstrated that the CJEU has also been a trusted ally of environmental organisations in opening legal opportunities at national level.[72] The opening of legal opportunities at this level is essential to 'circumvent' *Plaumann*, since there can hardly be any preliminary ruling from the EU judiciary without a 'fair trial' before domestic courts. Legal mobilisation at national level has therefore produced positive outcomes in many MSs, which have been acknowledged by legal scholars, EU institutions and ENGOs themselves.[73] Conversely, the PRP on validity remains a tool underexploited by ENGOs, and this is mainly because of the well-known shortcomings of the PRP. However, via PRP on validity, ENGOs seeking to challenge the legality of EU legislative acts have at least succeeded in receiving rulings on the merits from the CJEU. Even though unsuccessful in the main, this is something they have never obtained in direct actions.[74]

[69] See above, section I.

[70] ibid.

[71] At present (1 March 2025), no action for annulment brough under the new AR has been decided yet by the CJEU.

[72] See chapter 2. This has also led the Court to be criticised for its 'double standard' when ruling on access to justice before national courts and when ruling on direct access before the CJEU itself. On this point, see Hendrik Schoukens, 'Access to Justice before EU Courts in Environmental Cases against the Backdrop of the Aarhus Convention: Balancing Pathological Stubbornness and Cognitive Dissonance?', in Christina Voigt (ed), *International Judicial Practice on the Environment: Questions of Legitimacy (Studies on International Courts and Tribunals)* (Cambridge, Cambridge University Press, 2019) 74–118.

[73] See chapter 2.

[74] ibid.

ClientEarth has also achieved a significant outcome in its action against the EIB, discussed in chapter three. Indeed, in this case, the GC has annulled the EIB's denial to carry out the internal review of a Resolution aiming to provide funding for a Spanish project concerning the production of renewable energy.[75] The judgment was then upheld by the CJEU. This case can thus be considered as another positive achievement for ENGOs mobilising against *Plaumann*. This is because in its judgment, the CJEU has anticipated – via judicial interpretation – some of the amendments later introduced in the Regulation.[76] In this regard, this contribution has also highlighted a difference between the GC and the CJEU, with the former usually at the vanguard and the latter pushing the GC back in appeal.[77] Future research could shed new light on this gap between the two EU Courts.

The 'legal' impact of legal mobilisation also includes the influence that legal cases exert on subsequent litigation. In this regard, this contribution has shown that ENGOs involved in transnational climate litigation are spreading what I have conceptualised in terms of 'transnational incremental judicial comfort': precedents are used as building blocks to 'incrementally' contribute to make judges feel more comfortable in taking new interpretative steps on a transnational scale.[78] As discussed in chapter six, the spreading of TIJC in CCL involves – in principle – even the CJEU. However, the persistence of *Plaumann*[79] in an increasingly progressive European judicial landscape[80] contributes to creating the impression of the CJEU as a judiciary that is more and more 'obsolete' in the eyes of environmental litigants. This argument is supported not only by the simple persistence of *Plaumann*, but also by the other numerous 'closures' in the LOS discussed throughout this book. What is clear is that transnational environmental organisations active in CCL are redirecting their efforts toward other European fora, such as domestic courts, quasi-judicial bodies and the ECtHR.[81] A real 'shock' in this regard, has come precisely from the Strasbourg Court, which – in April 2024 – delivered a crucial ruling in the *Klimaseniorinnen* case.[82] However, a new pending case before the ECtHR – *Müllner v Austria* – could also have remarkable consequences on EU climate policy and its system of judicial protection.[83]

[75] See chapter 3.

[76] ibid.

[77] See *Stichting Natuur* (chapter 3), see also C-177/19 P, *Allemagne – Ville de Paris and Others v Commission* (2022) ECLI:EU:C:2022:10.

[78] See chapter 6.

[79] Along with the impossibility of invoking before the CJEU certain rights enshrined under the EU Charter (see chapter 7) and the shortcomings of the PRP (see chapter 2).

[80] This even more after the ECtHR judgment in *Klimaseniorinnen* (see chapter 6).

[81] ibid.

[82] ibid.

[83] ibid.

In the light of the above, the overall conclusion of my analysis is that the fight against *Plaumann*, thanks to the efforts of CSOs, has delivered remarkable results, despite the superficial constant failures. In addition, this fight is – at its core – a fight for a different kind of environmental justice and it is therefore very far from being over. Considering the broader trends in environmental and climate litigation, in Europe and beyond, more legal mobilisation is expected against the legality of EU environmental and climate change law. The legal mobilisation that has already occurred – and that this research has examined – clearly shows a proactive and demanding civil society in the field of environmental protection and climate change. A wide environmental movement composed of European ENGOs which have proven to be ambitious, industrious and, some of them, technically equipped to meaningfully challenge the legality of highly complex EU measures having an impact on the environment.

V. Grounds for Future Research

I hope that this book will stimulate future scholars to carry out research in the field of legal mobilisation. In this regard, below I will outline three major suggestions for future research to be undertaken by sociolegal scholars.

My contribution has shown that ENGOs often resort to integrated advocacy by combining legal and non-legal mobilisation strategies in the pursuit of their goals. However, the way this combination works in practice and is operationalised was not included within the scope of the present research. Therefore, it could be subject to further investigation.[84] New light could be shed, for instance, on the use of litigation outcomes in lobbying, as emerged in chapter four on the 'Aarhus saga'. In other words, how are legal victories (or losses) in courts used afterwards in EU political negotiations? To what extent do ENGOs refer to legal cases when lobbying EU decision- and policy-makers? This type of research might contribute to giving a clearer picture on resources, strategies and the impact of legal mobilisation.

Another aspect which I believe would be worth exploring refers to the extent to which the use of legal opportunities, resources and strategies highlighted in the present contribution is specific to the field of EU environmental and climate change law. For instance, do strategic litigants have a broad and flexible understanding of the LOS also in other areas of EU (or non-EU) law? Do environmental litigants display more legal imagination than strategic litigants mobilising in other

[84] See, for instance, Pieter Bouwen and Margaret Mccown, 'Lobbying versus Litigation: Political and Legal Strategies of Interest Representation in the European Union' (2007) 14 (3) *Journal of European Public Policy* 422–43.

domains? The study of comparative EU legal mobilisation across the domains seems to offer unexplored potential for sociolegal research.

Legal scholars might also be interested in looking at the classical 'counter majoritarian' argument from an ethical perspective. Indeed, scholars are increasingly looking more deeply at the subject of non-State actors' legitimacy in EU and international climate governance.[85] However, it would be fascinating to explore whether the way in which, for example, lawyers' select plaintiff or academics engage in legal mobilisation, raise issues of legal ethics and legitimacy under EU or national law.[86]

[85] eg Jens Marquardt and Karin Bäckstrand, 'Democracy Beyond the State Non-state actors and the legitimacy of climate governance', in Basil Bornemann, Henrike Knappe and Patrizia Nanz (eds), *The Routledge Handbook of Democracy and Sustainability* (New York, Routledge, 2022); Karin Bäckstrand, Jonathan Kuyper and Naghmeh Nasiritousi, 'From Collaboration to Contestation? Perceptions of Legitimacy and Effectiveness in post-Paris Climate Governance' (2021) 9 *Earth System Governance* 100115; Jonathan W Kuyper, Björn-Ola Linnér and Heike Schroeder, 'Non-state Actors in Hybrid Global Climate Governance: Justice, Legitimacy, and Effectiveness in a post-Paris Era' (2018) 9 *WIREs Clim Change* e497.

[86] See Tarunabh Khaitan, 'On Scholactivism in Constitutional Studies: Skeptical Thoughts' (2022) *International Journal of Constitutional Law* moac039; (response) Adrienne Stone, 'A Defence of Scholactivism' (2022) Verfassungsblog. Available at: https://verfassungsblog.de/a-defence-of-scholactivism/.

BIBLIOGRAPHY

Case Law

EU Courts

Case 25-62, *Plaumann & Co v Commission* (1963) ECLI:EU:C:1963:17
C-26/62, *Van Gend en Loos/Administratie der Belastingen* (1963) ECLI:EU:C:1963:1
C-6/64, *Costa v ENEL* (1964) ECLI:EU:C:1964:66
Case 69/69, *SA Alcan Aluminium Raeren and others v Commission of the European Communities* (1970) ECLI:EU:C:1970:53
Joined cases 41/70 to 44/70, *NV International Fruit Company and others v Commission of the European Communities* (1971) ECLI:EU:C:1971:53
C-66/80, *International Chemical Corporation v Amministrazione delle fianze dello Stato* (1981) ECLI:EU:C:1981:102
C-283/81, *CILFIT v Ministero della Sanità* (1982) ECLI:EU:C:1982:335
Case 240/83, *Procureur de la République v Association de défense des brûleurs d'huiles usagées (ADBHU)* (1985) ECLI:EU:C:1985:59
C-314/85, *Foto-Frost v Hauptzollamt Lübeck-Ost* (1987) ECLI:EU:C:1987:452
C-302/86, *Commission v Denmark* (1988) ECLI:EU:C:1988:421
Case 79/87 *Fédération de l'industrie de l'huilerie de la CEE (Fediol) v Commission of the European Communities* (1989) ECLI:EU:C:1989:254
C-244/88, *UCDV v Commission* (1989) ECLI:EU:C:1989:588
C-106/89, *Marleasing v Comercial Internacional de Alimentación* (1990) ECLI:EU:C:1990:395
C-70/88, *European Parliament v Council* (1990) ECLI:EU:C:1990:217
C-6/90, *Francovich and Bonifaci v Italy* (1991) ECLI:EU:C:1991:428
C-69/89 *Nakajima All Precision Co Ltd v Council of the European Communities* (1991) ECLI:EU:C:1991:186
Case C-198/91, *William Cook plc v Commission* (1993) ECLI:EU:C:1993:197
C-309/89, *Codorniu v Council* (1994) ECLI:EU:C:1994:197
C-435/92, *Association pour la protection des animaux sauvages and Others v Préfet de Maine-et-Loire and Préfet de la Loire-Atlantique* (1994) ECLI:EU:C:1994:10
T-585/93, *Stichting Greenpeace Council (Greenpeace International) and others v Commission*, CFI (1995) ECLI:EU:T:1995:147
C-321/95 P, *Greenpeace and Others v Commission*, CJEU (1998) ECLI:EU:C:1998:153
C-50/00 P, *Unión de Pequeños Agricultores v Council* (2002) ECLI:EU:C:2002:462
Case C-171/00 P, *Alain Libéros v Commission* (2002) ECLI:EU:C:2002:17, § 28
C-192/01, *Commission v Denmark* (2002) ECLI:EU:C:2002:760
C-491/01, *British American Tobacco (Investments) and Imperial Tobacco* (2002) ECLI:EU:C:2002:741
C-263/02 P, *Commission v Jégo-Quéré & Cie SA* (2004) ECLI:EU:C:2004:21
C-78/03 P, *Commission v Aktionsgemeinschaft Recht und Eigentum* (2005) ECLI:EU:C:2005:761
T-142/03, *Fost Plus v Commission*, CFI (2005) ECLI:EU:T:2005:51
Joined cases T-236/04 and T-241/04, *EEB and Stichting Natuur en Milieu v Commission*, CFI (2005) ECLI:EU:T:2005:426

T-15/02, *BASF v Commission* (2006) ECLI:EU:T:2003:38
C-163/06 P, *Finland v Commission* (2007) ECLI:EU:C:2007:371
C-326/05 P, *Industrias Químicas del Vallés v Commission* (2007) ECLI:EU:C:2007:443
T-91/07, *WWF-UK v. Council*, CFI (2008) ECLI:EU:T:2008:170
C-120/06 P *FIAMM and Others v Council and Commission* (2008) ECLI:EU:C:2008:476
C-127/07, *Arcelor Atlantique and Lorraine and Others* (2008) ECLI:EU:C:2008:728
C-308/06 *Intertanko and Others* (2008) ECLI:EU:C:2008:312
C-263/08, *Djurgården-Lilla Värtans Miljöskyddsförening* (2009) ECLI:EU:C:2009:631
C-355/08 P, *WWF-UK v Council*, CJEU (2009) ECLI:EU:C:2009:286
C-115/09, *Bund für Umwelt und Naturschutz Deutschland, Landesverband Nordrhein-Westfalen* (2011) ECLI:EU:C:2011:289
C-240/09 *Lesoochranárske zoskupenie* (2011) ECLI:EU:C:2011:125
C-366/10, *Air Transport Association of America and Others* (2011) ECLI:EU:C:2011:864
T-541/10, *ADEDY and Others v Council* (2012) ECLI:EU:T:2012:626
T-338/08, *Stichting Natuur en Milieu and Pesticide Action Network Europe v Commission* (2012) ECLI:EU:T:2012:300
T-396/09, *Vereniging Milieudefensie and Stichting Stop Luchtverontreiniging Utrecht v Commission* (2012) ECLI:EU:T:2012:301
C-260/11, *Edwards and Pallikaropoulos* (2013) ECLI:EU:C:2012:645
C-287/12 P, *Ryanair v Commission* (2013) ECLI:EU:C:2013:395
C-583/11 P, *Inuit Tapiriit Kanatami and Others v European Parliament and Council of the European Union* (2013) ECLI:EU:C:2013:625
Case Opinion 2/13, accession of the EU to the ECHR – Compatibility of the draft agreement with the EU and FEU Treaties (2014) ECLI:EU:C:2014:2454
T-19/13, *Frank Bold v Commission* (2014) ECLI:EU:T:2015:520
T-168/13, *EPAW v Commission* (2014) ECLI:EU:T:2014:47
T-192/12, *PAN Europe v Commission* (2014) ECLI:EU:T:2014:152
T-685/14, *EEB v Commission* (2015) ECLI:EU:T:2015:560
Joined Cases C-401/12 P to C-403/12 P, *Council and Others v Vereniging Milieudefensie and Stichting Stop Luchtverontreiniging Utrecht* (2015) ECLI:EU:C:2015:4
Joined Cases C-404/12 P and C-405/12 P, *Council and Commission v Stichting Natuur en Milieu and Pesticide Action Network Europe* (2015) ECLI:EU:C:2015:5
T-565/14, *EEB v Commission* (2015) ECLI:EU:T:2015:559
C-78/16, *Pesce and Others* (2016) ECLI:EU:C:2016:428
T-177/13, *TestBioTech and Others v Commission* (2016) ECLI:EU:T:2016:736
C-444/15, *Associazione Italia Nostra Onlus v Comune di Venezia and Others* (2016) ECLI:EU:C:2016:978
T-600/15, *PAN Europe and Others v Commission*, (2016) ECLI:EU:T:2016:601
T-189/14, *Deza v ECHA*, (2017) ECLI:EU:T:2017:4
C-281/16, *Vereniging Hoekschewaards Landschap* (2017) ECLI:EU:C:2017:774
T-849/16, *PGNiG Supply & Trading v Commission* (2017) ECLI:EU:T:2017:924
C-622/16 P, *Scuola Elementare Maria Montessori v Commission* (2018) ECLI:EU:C:2018:873
T-12/17, *Mellifera v Commission* (2018) ECLI:EU:T:2018:616
C-57/16 P, *ClientEarth v Commission* (2018) ECLI:EU:C:2018:660
T-33/16, *TestBioTech v Commission* (2018) ECLI:EU:T:2018:135
C-416/17, *Commission v France* (2018) ECLI:EU:C:2018:811
Joined Cases T-429/13 and T-451/13, *Bayer CropScience v Commission* (2018) ECLI:EU:T:2018:280
C-441/17, *Commission v Poland (Białowieża Forest)* (2018) ECLI:EU:C:2018:255
C-528/16, *Confédération paysanne and Others* (2018) ECLI:EU:C:2018:583
C-82/17 P, *TestBioTech and Others v Commission* (2019) ECLI:EU:C:2019:719
T-108/17, *ClientEarth v Commission* (2019) ECLI:EU:T:2019:215
T-330/18, *Carvalho and Others v Parliament and Council* (2019) ECLI:EU:T:2019:324
C-616/17, *Blaise and Others* (2019) ECLI:EU:C:2019:800

C-352/19 P *Région de Bruxelles-Capitale v European Commission* (2020) ECLI:EU:C:2020:588
C-784/18 P, *Mellifera v Commission*, CJEU (2020) ECLI:EU:C:2020:630
T-9/19, *ClientEarth v EIB* (2021) ECLI:EU:T:2021:42
C-212/21 P, *EIB v ClientEarth* (2023) ECLI:EU:C:2023:546
C-458/19 P, *ClientEarth v Commission* (2021) ECLI:EU:C:2021:802
C-561/19, *Consorzio Italian Management and Catania Multiservizi* (2021) ECLI:EU:C:2021:291
C-565/19 P, *Carvalho and Others v Parliament and Council* (2021) ECLI:EU:C:2021:252
T-141/19, *Sabo and Others v Parliament and Council* (2020) ECLI:EU:T:2020:179
C-297/20 P, *Sabo and Others v. Parliament and Council* (2021) ECLI:EU:C:2021:24
C-330/22, *Friends of the Irish Environment* (2024) ECLI:EU:C:2024:19

Requests for Internal Review

European Commission, repository of requests for internal review lodged with the European Commission pursuant to Article 10 of Regulation (EC) No 1367/2006 ('Aarhus Regulation'). Available at: https://ec.europa.eu/environment/aarhus/requests.htm.

EU National Courts

Friends of the Irish Environment CLG v Minister Communications, Climate Action and the Environment, Ireland and the Attorney General (Shannon LNG Terminal) [2021] IEHC 177 (Ireland)
Neubauer and others v Germany (BvR 2656/18/1 BvR 78/20/1 BvR 96/20/1 BvR 288/20) (Germany)
Notre Affaire à Tous and Others v France, No. 1904967, 1904968, 1904972, 1904976/4-1, Paris Administrative Court (3 February 2021) (France)
Silesia (File No II OSK 3218/17, 23 January 2018) (Poland)
Sofia (ruling No 13138 on 1 November 2017) (Bulgaria)
Plovdiv (ruling No 16049 on 20 December 2018) (Bulgaria)
Urgenda Foundation v The Netherlands [2015] HAZA C/09/00456689 (24 June 2015); aff'd (9 October 2018); aff'd (20 December 2019) (District Court of the Hague, The Hague Court of Appeal, Dutch Supreme Court) (The Netherlands)

Other Courts

Avotiņš v Latvia, n. 17502/07, ECtHR, 23 May 2016
Bosphorus Hava Yollari Turizm Ve Ticaret Anonim Şirketi v Ireland, n. 45036/98), ECtHR, 30 June 2005
Carême v France, n. 7189/21, ECtHR, 9 April 2024
Duarte Agostinho and Others v Portugal and Others, n. 39371/20, ECtHR, 9 April 2024
Juliana v United States 947 F.3d 1159 (9th Cir 2020) (USA)
Massachusetts v EPA, 549 US 497 (2007) (USA)
Müllner v Austria, n. 18859/21, ECtHR (pending)
The People v Arctic Oil (Nature and Youth, Greenpeace v Norway's Ministry of Petroleum and Energy) Case Number: 18-060499ASD-BORG/03 (Norway)
The Queen on the Application of Plan B. Earth v The Secretary of State for Business and Energy and Industrial Strategy (Order of 22 January 2019) No C1/2018/1750 (EWCA Civ) (United Kingdom)
Thomson v Minister for Climate Change Issues [2017] NZHC 733 (New Zealand)
Verein Klimaseniorinnen Schweiz and others v Switzerland, n. 53600/20, ECtHR, 9 April 2024

Articles

Alberton M, 'Environmental Protection in the EU Member States: Changing Institutional Scenarios and Trends' (2012) 1 (363) *L'Europe en Formation* 287–300.

Alexander L, 'Are Procedural Rights Derivative Substantive Rights?' (1998) 17 (1) *Law and Philosophy* 19–42.

Alter KJ, 'The European Union's Legal System and Domestic Policy: Spillover or Backlash?' (2000) 54 (3) *International Organization* 489–518.

Arena A, 'From an Unpaid Electricity Bill to the Primacy of EU Law: Gian Galeazzo Stendardi and the Making of Costa v. ENEL' (2019) 30(3) *European Journal of International Law* 1017–37.

Atkinson MM, 'Lindblom's Lament: Incrementalism and the Persistent Pull of the Status Quo (2011) 30 (1) *Policy and Society* 9–18.

Bailleux A, 'Don't Judge a Case by its Cover: The Pesticides Regulation Survives Judicial Scrutiny But Is Given New Teeth: Blaise' (2020) 57 *Common Market Law Review* 861–76.

Bautista JM and others, 'An In-Depth Exploration of How Young Adults' Decision-Making Is Influenced by Peer Pressure and Conformity' (2023) A Journal Analysis presented as a final requirement For Social Psychology SOCP311.

Becker F, 'The Development of German Administrative Law' (2017) 24 *George Mason Law Review* 453–76.

Benvenisti E, 'Reclaiming Democracy: The Strategic Uses of Foreign and International Law by National Courts' (2008) 102 (2) *The American Journal of International Law* 241.

Benvenuti S, 'Access to Justice in Environmental Matters – Which Role for the European Networks of Judges?' (2014) 11 *Journal for European Environmental & Planning Law* 165–83.

Bogojevic S, 'EU Climate Change Litigation, the Role of the European Courts, and the Importance of Legal Culture' (2013) 35 *Law & Pol'y* 184–207.

Bouwer K, 'The Unsexy Future of Climate Change Litigation' (2018) 30 *Journal of Environmental Law* 483–506.

Bratspies R, 'Do We Need a Human Right to a Healthy Environment?' (2015) 13 (31) *Santa Clara Journal of International Law* 31–69.

Brittain S, 'The Relationship Between the EU Charter of Fundamental Rights and the European Convention on Human Rights: An Originalist Analysis' (2015) 11 (3) *European Constitutional Law Review* 482–511.

Burley A-M, Mattli W., 'Europe Before the Court: A Political Theory of Legal Integration' (1993) 47 (1) International Organization, 41–76.

Butler G, Sadl U, 'The Preliminaries of a Reference' (2018) *European Law Review* 120–28.

Carrubba CJ, Murrah L, 'Legal Integration and Use of the Preliminary Ruling Process in the European Union' (2005) 59 *International Organization* 399–418.

Cichowski RA, 'The European Court of Human Rights, Amicus Curiae and Violence Against Women' (2016) 50 (4) *Law and Society Review* 890–919.

Conant L, Hofmann A, Soennecken D, Vanhala L, 'Mobilizing European Law' (2018) 25 (9) *Journal of European Public Policy* 1376–89.

Costello C, 'The Bosphorus Ruling of the European Court of Human Rights: Fundamental Rights and Blurred Boundaries in Europe' (2006) 6 (1) *Human Rights Law Review* 87–130.

Cummings S, 'Law and Social Movements: Reimagining the Progressive Canon' (2018) 3 *Wisconsin Law Review* 441–501.

Cummings S, Albiston C, Abel RL, 'Making Public Interest Lawyers in a Time of Crisis: An Evidence-Based Approach' (2020) 34 (2) *Georgetown Journal of Legal Ethics* (Forthcoming), UCLA School of Law, Public Law Research Paper No. 20-30, Available at SSRN: https://ssrn.com/abstract=3712664.

Cummings S, Eagly IV, 'After Public Interest Law' (2006) 100 *Northwestern University Law Review*, UCLA School of Law Research Paper No.05-35, 1251–1295.

Cummings S, Trubek L, 'Globalizing Public Interest Law' (2008) 13 *UCLA Journal of International Law and Foreign Affairs* 1–53.

Darpö J, 'Effective Justice? Synthesis report of the study on the Implementation of Articles 9.3 and 9.4 of the Aarhus Convention in the Member States of the European Union', 2013-10-11/Final. Available at: https://ec.europa.eu/environment/aarhus/pdf/synthesis%20report%20on%20access%20to%20justice.pdf.
De Fazio G, 'Legal Opportunity Structure and Social Movement Strategy in Northern Ireland and Southern United States' (2012) 52 (1) *International Journal of Comparative Sociology* 3–22.
de Schutter O, 'Public Interest Litigation before the European Court of Justice' (2006) 13 *Maastricht Journal of European and Comparative Law* 9–34.
Delreux T, 'The EU in Environmental Negotiations in UNECE: An Analysis of its Role in the Aarhus Convention and the SEA Protocol Negotiations' (2009) 18 (3) *RECIEL* 328–37.
Donati A, 'The Glyphosate Saga, A Further but Not a Final Step: The CJEU Confirms the Validity of the Regulation on Plant Protection Products in Light of the Precautionary Principle' (2020) 11 *European Journal of Risk Regulation* 148–54.
Donati A, 'The Precautionary Principle Under European Union Law' (2021) 49 *Hitotsubashi Journal of Law and Politics* 43–60.
Donger E, 'Children and Youth in Strategic Climate Litigation: Advancing Rights through Legal Argument and Legal Mobilization' (2022) *Transnational Environmental Law* 1–27.
Early TL, 'The Scope of Preliminary Rulings on the Validity of Community Law' (1980) 15 (2) *Irish Jurist* 237–62.
Eckes C, 'Does the European Court of Human Rights Provide Protection from the European Community? The Case of Bosphorus Airways' (2007) 13 (1) *European Public Law* 47–67.
Eleftheriadis P, 'Environmental Rights in the EC Legal Order' (2007) Oxford Legal Studies Research Paper No. 24/2007, available at: http://papers.ssrn.com/sol3/papers.cfm?abstract_id=1015923.
Eliantonio M, Grashof F, 'Wir müssen reden! We Need to Have a Serious Talk! The Interaction between the Infringement Proceedings and the Preliminary Reference Procedure in Ensuring Compliance with EU Environmental Standards: A Case Study of Trianel, Altrip and Commission v Germany' (2016) 13 *Journal for European Environmental & Planning Law* 325–49.
Eliantonio M, Roer-Eide H, 'Regional Courts and Locus Standi for Private Parties: Can the CJEU Learn Something from the Others' (2014) 13 *The Law and Practice of International Courts and Tribunals* 27–53.
Epstein Y, Darpö J, 'The Wild Has No Words: Environmental NGOs Empowered to Speak for Protected Species as Swedish Courts Apply EU and International Environmental Law' (2013) 10 (3) *Journal for European Environmental & Planning Law* 250–61.
Eren O, Mocan N, 'Judge Peer Effects in the Courthouse' (2020) 13937 *IZA DP*, available at: www.iza.org/publications/dp/13937/judge-peer-effects-in-the-courthouse.
Fasoli E, McGlone A, 'The Non-Compliance Mechanism Under the Aarhus Convention as "Soft" Enforcement of International Environmental Law: Not So Soft After All!' (2018) 65 *Netherlands International Law Review* 27–53.
Fisher E, 'Is the Precautionary Principle Justiciable?' (2011) 13 (3) *Journal of Environmental Law* 315–34.
Fitzpatrick BT, 'The Ironic History of Rule 23', Vanderbilt University Law School, Legal Studies Research Paper Series – Working Paper Number, 17–41.
Galanter M, 'Why the "Haves" Come Out Ahead: Speculations on the Limits of Legal Change' (1974) 9 (1) *Law and Society Review* 95–160.
Garnett K, Parsons DJ, 'Multi-Case Review of the Application of the Precautionary Principle in European Union Law and Case Law' (2017) 37 *Risk Analysis* 502–16.
Gáspár-Szilágyi S, 'The "Primacy" and "Direct Effect" of EU International Agreements' (2015) 21 (2) *European Public Law* 343–70.
Geoff B, 'Visual Analysis of Nonlinear Dynamical Systems: Chaos, Fractals, Self-Similarity and the Limits of Prediction' (2016) 4 (37) *Systems* 1–18.
Glavina M, 'To Refer or Not to Refer, That Is the (Preliminary) Question: Exploring Factors Which Influence the Participation of National Judges in the Preliminary Ruling Procedure' (2020) 16 (1) *Croatian Yearbook of European Law & Policy* 25–59.

Glavina M, 'The Reality of National Judges as EU Law Judges: Knowledge, Experiences and Attitudes of Lower Court Judges in Slovenia and Croatia' (2021) 17 *Croatian Yearbook of European Law & Policy* 1–40.
Glazer N, 'Realizing the Public Interest: Reflections on an Elusive Goal' (2007) 136 (4) *Daedalus* 30–36.
Granger M, 'Towards a Liberalisation of Standing Conditions for Individuals Seeking Judicial Review of Community Acts: Jégo-Quéré et Cie SA v Commission and Unión de Pequeños Agricultores v Council' (2003) 66(1) *The Modern Law Review* 124–38.
Greve MS, 'The Non-Reformation of Administrative Law: Standing to Sue and Public Interest Litigation in West German Environmental Law' (1989) 22 (2) *Cornell International Law Journal* 197–244.
Hadjiyianni I, 'Judicial Protection and the Environment in the EU Legal Order: Missing Pieces For a Complete Puzzle of Legal Remedies' (2021) 58 *Common Market Law Review* 1–36.
Hartmann J, Willers M, 'Protecting Rights in Climate Change Litigation before European Courts', 12. Available at SSRN: https://ssrn.com/abstract=3832674 or http://dx.doi.org/10.2139/ssrn.3832674.
Haumont F, 'Le droit constitutionnel belge à la protection d'un environnement sain. Etat de la jurisprudence' (2005) *Revue juridique de l'Environnement, numéro spécial La charte constitutionnelle de l'environnement* 41–52.
Halpern C, Cunningham J, 'Reflections on the New Public Interest Law: Theory and Practice at the Center for Law and Social Policy' (1995) 59 *Georgetown Law Journal* 1095–116.
Harlow C, 'Towards a Theory of Access for the European Court of Justice' (1992) 12 (1) *Yearbook of European Law* 213–48.
Hilson C, 'Community Rights and Wrongs: Greenpeace before the Court of Justice' (1999) 52(1) *Environmental Law Review* 52–58.
Hilson C, 'New Social Movements: The Role of Legal Opportunity' (2002) 9 (2) *Journal of European Public Policy* 238–55.
Hofmann A, 'Left to Interest Groups? On the Prospects for Enforcing Environmental Law in the European Union' (2019) 28 (2) *Environmental Politics* 342–64.
Hunter ND, 'In Search of Equality for Women: From Suffrage to Civil Rights' (2021) 59 *Duquesne Law Review* 125–66.
Jackson V, 'Comparative Constitutional Federalism and Transnational Judicial Discourse' (2004) 2 *International Journal of Constitutional Law* 91–138.
Jans JH, Harryvan G, 'Internal Review of EU Environmental Measures. It's True: Baron Van Munchausen Doesn't Exist! Some Remarks on the Application of the So-Called Aarhus Regulation' (2010) 3 (2) *Review of European and Administrative Law* 53–65.
Jans JH, 'Who Is the Referee? Access to Justice in a Globalised Legal Order' (2011) 4 (1) *Review of European Administrative Law* 87–99.
Kangwa D and others, 'Predictors of Cheating in Online Exams Among Business Students During the Covid Pandemic: Testing the Theory of Planned Behaviour' (2022) 20 (3) *International Journal of Management Education* 100713.
Kessler M, 'Legal Mobilization for Social Reform: Power and the Politics of Agenda Setting' (1990) 24 (1) *Law & Society Review* 121–44.
Kilpatrick C, 'The EU and its Sovereign Debt Programmes: The Challenges of Liminal Legality' (2017) 70 (1) *Current Legal Problems* 337–63.
Klamert M, 'The Autonomy of the EU (and of EU Law): Through the Kaleidoscope' (2017) 42 (6) *EL Rev* 815–30.
Kokott J, Sobotta C, 'The Contribution of the Case Law of the CJEU to the Judicial Enforcement of EU Environmental Law in the UK' (2019) 16 *Journal for European Environmental & Planning Law* 109–24.
Kombos C, 'Locus Standi of Representative Groups in the Shadow of Plaumann: Limitations and Possible Solutions' (2006) 47 *Acta Juridica Hungarica* 373–404.
Korkea-Aho E, '"Mr Smith Goes To Brussels": Third Country Lobbying and the Making of EU Law and Policy' (2016) 18 *Cambridge Yearbook of European Legal Studies* 45–68.
Korkea-Aho E, Leino P, 'Interviewing Lawyers: A Critical Self-Reflection on Expert Interviews as a Method of EU Legal Research' (2019) *SI, European Journal of Legal Studies* 17–47.

Kornezov A, 'Shaping the New Architecture of the EU System of Judicial Remedies: Comment on Inuit' (2014) 39 (2) *European Law Review* 251–63.

Krämer L, 'The Open Society, Its Lawyers and Its Environment' (1989) 1 (1) *Journal of Environmental Law* 1–9.

Krämer L, 'Public Interest Litigation in Environmental Matters before European Courts' (1996) 8 (1) *Journal of Environmental Law* 1–18.

Krämer L, 'Access to Environmental Justice: The Double Standards of the ECJ' (2017) 14 *Journal for European Environmental & Planning Law* 159–85.

Krommendijk J, van der Pas K, 'To Intervene or Not to Intervene: Intervention before the Court of Justice of the European Union in Environmental and Migration Law' (2022) *The International Journal of Human Rights* 1–25.

Leachman GM, 'From Protest to Perry: How Litigation Shaped the LGBT Movement's Agenda' (2013–14) 47 *UCD Law Review* 1667–751.

Lee M, 'Access to Justice at EU Level in Environmental Law' (18 May 2012). Available at SSRN: https://ssrn.com/abstract=2062252 or http://dx.doi.org/10.2139/ssrn.2062252.

Lehoucq E, Taylor WK, 'Conceptualizing Legal Mobilization: How Should We Understand the Deployment of Legal Strategies?' (2020) 45 (1) *Law & Social Inquiry* 166–93.

Leonelli GC, 'Acknowledging the Centrality of the Precautionary Principle in Judicial Review of EU Risk Regulation: Why it Matters' (2020) 57 (6) *Common Market Law Review* 1773–818.

Leonelli GC, 'Judicial Review of Compliance with the Precautionary Principle from *Paraquat* to *Blaise*: "Quantitative Thresholds" Risk Assessment, and the Gap Between Regulation and Regulatory Implementation' (2021) 22 *German Law Journal* 184–215.

Levmore S, 'Interest Groups and the Problem with Incrementalism' (2009) 501 John M. Olin Program in Law and Economics Working Paper.

Lock T, 'Beyond Bosphorus: The European Court of Human Rights' Case Law on the Responsibility of Member States of International Organisations under the European Convention on Human Rights' (2010) 10 (3) *Human Rights Law Review* 529–45.

Lofstedt R, 'The Precautionary Principle in the EU: Why a Formal Review Is Long Overdue' (2014) 16 (3) *Risk Management* 137–63.

Marseille AT, Jans JH, 'The Role of NGOs in Environmental Litigation against Public Authorities: Some Observations on Judicial Review and Access to Court in the Netherlands' (2010) 22 (3) *Journal of Environmental Law* 373–90.

Mayer B, 'The State of the Netherlands v. Urgenda Foundation: Ruling of the Court of Appeal of The Hague (9 October 2018)' (2019) 8(1) *Transnational Environmental Law* 167–92.

Mayoral JA, Jaremba U, Nowak T, 'Creating EU Law Judges: the Role of Generational Differences, Legal Education and Judicial Career Paths in National Judges' Assessment regarding EU Law Knowledge' (2014) 21 *Journal of European Public Policy* 1120–41.

Mole N, 'Can Bosphorus be Maintained?' (2015) 16 *ERA Forum* 467–80.

Mowbray A, 'Faltering Steps on the Path to Reform of the Strasbourg Enforcement System' (2007) 7 (3) *Human Rights Law Review* 609–18.

Muir E, Kilpatrick C, Miller J, De Witte B, 'How EU Law Shapes Opportunities for Preliminary References on Fundamental Rights: Discrimination, Data Protection and Asylum' (2017) EUI Working Papers, 2017. Available at SSRN: https://ssrn.com/abstract=3782564 or http://dx.doi.org/10.2139/ssrn.3782564.

Ngaire N, 'Legal Personality and the Natural World: On the Persistence of the Human Measure of Value' (2012) 3 (68) Journal of Human Rights and the Environment 68–83.

Ozgul C, 'Beyond Legal Victory or Reform: The Legal Mobilisation of Religious Groups in the European Court of Human Rights' (2017) 45 (3–4) *Religion, State & Society* 317–33.

Pagano M, 'Climate Legal Mobilization Under the New Aarhus Regulation' (2024) 25 (6) *German Law Journal* 919–34.

Pagano M, 'Overcoming Plaumann in EU Environmental Litigation: An Analysis of ENGOs Legal Arguments in Actions for Annulment' (2019) *Diritto e Processo* 311–60.

Paiement P, 'Urgent Agenda: How Climate Litigation Builds Transnational Narratives' (2020) 11 (1) *Transnational Legal Theory* 121–43.

Panke D, 'The European Court of Human Rights Under Scrutiny: Explaining Variation in Non-Compliance Judgments' (2020) 18 *Comparative European Politics* 151–70.

Parker L, Mestre J, Jodoin S, Wewerinke-Singh M, 'When the Kids Put Climate Change on Trial: Youth-Focused Rights-Based Climate Litigation Around the World' (2022) 13 (1) *Journal of Human Rights and the Environment* 64–89.

Passalacqua V, 'Legal Mobilization via Preliminary Reference: Insights from the Case of Migrant Rights' (2021) 58 (3) *Common Market Law Review* 751–76.

Peel J, 'Giving the Public a Voice in the Protection of the Global Environment: Avenues for Participation by NGOs in Dispute Resolution at the ECJ and WTO' (2001) 12 (47) *Colorado Journal of International Environmental Law and Policy* 47.

Peel J, 'Issues in Climate Change Litigation' (2011) 5 (1) *Carbon & Climate Law Review* 15–24.

Peel J, Osofsky HM, 'A Rights Turn in Climate Change Litigation?' (2018) 7 (1) *Transnational Environmental Law* 37–67.

Peeters M, 'Urgenda Foundation and 866 Individuals v. The State of the Netherlands: The Dilemma of More Ambitious Greenhouse Gas Reduction Action by EU Member States' (2016) 25 (1) *RECIEL* 123–29.

Peeters M, Athanasiadou N, 'The Continued Effort Sharing Approach in EU Climate Law: Binding Targets, Challenging Enforcement?' (2020) 29 *RECIEL* 201–11.

Petter Graver H, 'The Holship Ruling of the ECtHR and the Protection of Fundamental Rights in Europe' (2022) 23 *ERA Forum* 19–32.

Pünder H, 'German Administrative Procedure in a Comparative Perspective: Observations on the Path to a Transnational Ius Commune Proceduralis in Administrative Law' (2013) 11 (4) *International Journal of Constitutional Law* 940–61.

Radchuk V, Turlure C, Schtickzelle N, 'Each Life Stage Matters: The Importance of Assessing the Response to Climate Change over the Complete Life Cycle in Butterflies' (2012) 82 *Journal of Animal Ecology* 275–85.

Rasmussen H, 'Why Is Article 173 Interpreted against Private Plaintiffs?' (1980) 5 *EL Rev* 112–27.

Reichel J, 'Judicial Control in a Globalised Legal Order – A One Way Track? An Analysis of the Case C-263/08 Djurgården-Lilla Värtan' (2010) 3 (2) *Review of European Administrative Law* 69–87.

Rosenberg GN, 'Hollow Hopes and Other Aspirations: A Reply to Feeley and McCann' (1992) 17 (4) *Law & Social Inquiry* 761–78.

Ryall Á, 'Djurgården-Lilla Värtans Miljöskyddsförening v. Stockholms kommun genom dess marknämnd, Judgment of the Court (Second Chamber)' (2010) 47 (5) *Common Market Law Review* 1511–21.

Ryall Á, 'The Relationship between Irish Law and International Environmental Law: A Study of the Aarhus Convention' (2018) 41 (2) *Dublin University Law Journal* 163–88.

Šadl U, Wallerman A, '"The Referring Court Asks, in Essence": Is Reformulation of Preliminary Questions by the Court of Justice a Decision Writing Fixture or a Decision-Making Approach?' (2019) 25 European Law Journal 416–33.

Samvel G., 'Non-Judicial, Advisory, Yet Impactful? The Aarhus Convention Compliance Committee as a Gateway to Environmental Justice' (2020) 9(2) *Transnational Environmental Law* 211–38.

Sanders K, 'Beyond Human Ownership'? Property, Power and Legal Personality for Nature in Aotearoa New Zealand' (2018) 30 (2) *Journal of Environmental Law* 207–34.

Sands PJ, 'Climate Change and the Rule of Law: Adjudicating the Future in International Law' (2016) 28 *Journal of Environmental Law* 19–35.

Sands PJ, 'The Environment, Community and International Law' (1989) 30 *Harvard International Law Journal* 393–420.

Schall C, 'Public Interest Litigation Concerning Environmental Matters before Human Rights Courts: A Promising Future Concept' (2008) 20 (3) *Journal of Environmental Law* 417–53.

Schoukens H, 'Access to Justice in Environmental Cases after the Rulings of the Court of Justice of 13 January 2015: Kafka Revisited?' (2015) 31 (81) *Utrecht Journal of International and European Law* 46–67.

Schoukens H, 'Articles 9(3) and 9(4) of the Aarhus Convention and Access to Justice before EU Courts in Environmental Cases: Balancing On or Over the Edge of Non-Compliance?' (2016) 25 (6) European Energy and Environmental Law Review 178–95.

Scott J, Sturm SP, 'Courts as Catalysts: Rethinking the Judicial Role in New Governance' (2007) 13 *Columbia Journal of European Law* 565.

Setzer J, Vanhala L, 'Climate Change Litigation: A Review of Research on Courts and Litigants in Climate Governance' (2019) 10 (3) *WIREs Clim Change* e580.

Shelton D, 'The Participation of Nongovernmental Organizations in International Judicial Proceedings' (1994) 88 (4) *The American Journal of International Law* 611–42.

Smith M, 'Social Movements and Judicial Empowerment: Courts, Public Policy, and Lesbian and Gay Organizing in Canada' (2005) 33 (2) *Politics & Society* 327–53.

Southworth A, 'What Is Public Interest Law? Empirical Perspectives on an Old Question' (2013) 62 *DePaul Law Review* 493–510.

Stein E, Vining GJ, 'Citizen Access to Judicial Review of Administrative Action in a Transnational and Federal Context' (1976) 70 *American Journal of International Law* 219–41.

Stewart RB, 'The Reformation of American Administrative Law' (1975) (88) *Harvard Law Review* 1667–813.

Szyszczak E, 'Article 263(4) TFEU and the Impossibility of Challenging Recovery Decisions in State Aid: Annotation on the Judgments of the General Court of 15 September 2016 in T-219/13 Pietro Ferracci v European Commission and T-220/13 Scuola Elementare Maria Montessori v European Commission' (2016) 15(4) *European State Aid Law Quarterly* 637–41.

Talesh S, 'How the "Haves" Come out Ahead in the Twenty-First Century' (2013) 62 *DePaul Law Review* 519–54.

Thomas A, Martyr-Koller R, Pringle P, Rhiney K, 'Climate Change and Small Island Developing States' (2020) 45 *Annual Review of Environment and Resources* 1–27.

Torrens DL, 'Locus Standi for Environmental Associations under EC law – Greenpeace – A Missed Opportunity for the ECJ' (1999) 8 (3) *RECIEL* 336–46.

van Loon H, 'Principles and Building Blocks for a Global Legal Framework for Transnational Civil Litigation in Environmental Matters' (2018) 23 (3) *Uniform Law Review* 298–318.

van Hoorn J and others, 'Peer Influence Effects on Risk-Taking and Prosocial Decision-Making in Adolescence: Insights from Neuroimaging Studies' (2016) 10 *Current Opinion in Behavioural Sciences* 59–64.

van Wolferen M, 'The Limits to the CJEU's Interpretation of Locus Standi, a Theoretical Framework' (2016) 12 (4) *Journal of Contemporary European Research* 914–30.

Vanhala L, 'Shaping the Structure of Legal Opportunities: Environmental NGOs Bringing International Environmental Procedural Rights Back Home' (2018) 40 (1) *Law & Policy* 110–27.

Vanhala L, 'The Diffusion of Disability Rights in Europe' (2015) 37 *Human Rights Quarterly* 831–53.

von Bogdandy A, 'Pluralism, Direct Effect, and the Ultimate Say: On the Relationship Between International and Domestic Constitutional Law' (2008) 6 (3–4) *International Journal of Constitutional Law* 397–413.

Weiler JHH, 'The Transformation of Europe' (1991) 100 (8) *The Yale Law Journal Symposium: International Law* 2403–83.

Weiler JHH, Lustig D, 'Judicial Review in the Contemporary World – Retrospective and Prospective' (2018) 16 (2) *International Journal of Constitutional Law* 315–72.

Williams GM and others, 'A Review of the Carcinogenic Potential of Glyphosate by Four Independent Expert Panels and Comparison to the IARC Assessment' (2016) 46(sup1) *Critical Reviews in Toxicology* 2–3. Erratum in: *Critical Reviews in Toxicology* (2018) Nov 30: 1–2.

Winter G, 'Armando Carvalho and Others v. EU: Invoking Human Rights and the Paris Agreement for Better Climate Protection Legislation' (2020) 9(1) *Transnational Environmental Law* 137–64.

Winter G, 'Climate Protection before the European Court of Human Rights: The KlimaSeniorinnen and Duarte Agostinho Cases in Perspective' (2024) 84 *Zeitschrift für ausländisches öffentliches Recht und Völkerrecht / Heidelberg Journal of International Law* 457–98.

Zemans FK, 'Legal Mobilization: The Neglected Role of the Law in the Political System' (1983) 77 (3) *The American Political Science Review* 690–703.

Books and Book Chapters

Abbot C, Lee M, *Environmental Groups and Legal Expertise – Shaping the Brexit Process* (London, UCLPress, 2021).

Andersen EA, *Out of the Closets and into the Courts: Legal Opportunity Structure and Gay Rights Litigation* (Ann Arbor, MI, University of Michigan Press, 2009).

Aust A, *Modern Treaty Law and Practice*, 2nd edn (Cambridge, Cambridge University Press, 2007)

Barritt E, *The Foundations of the Aarhus Convention: Environmental Democracy, Rights and Stewardship* (Oxford, Hart Publishing, 2020).

Baum L, *Judges and Their Audiences: A Perspective on Judicial Behaviour* (Princeton, NJ, Princeton University Press, 2006).

Benvenisti E, Downs G, *Between Fragmentation and Democracy: The Role of National and International Courts* (Cambridge, Cambridge University Press, 2017).

Boer B, *Environmental Law Dimensions of Human Rights* (Oxford, OUP, 2015).

Brown LN, Bell JS, *French Administrative Law*, 4th edn (Oxford, Clarendon Press, 1993).

Brunnée J, Toope SJ, *Legitimacy and Legality in International Law: An Interactional Account* (Cambridge, CUP, 2010).

Chiti MP, Greco G, *Trattato di diritto amministrativo europeo*, Tomo II, parte generale, 2nd edn (Milan, Giuffré, 2007).

Cichowski RA, *The European Court and Civil Society* (New York, Cambridge University Press, 2007).

Craig P, *EU Administrative Law* (Oxford, OUP, 2018).

Banner C (ed), *The Aarhus Convention: A Guide for UK Lawyers* (Oxford, Hart Publishing, 2015).

Dawson M, De Witte B, Muir E (eds), *Judicial Activism at the European Court of Justice* (Cheltenham, Edward Elgar, 2013).

De Laubadère A, Venezia C, Gaudemet Y, Traité de droit administratif, Tome I, 14th edn (Paris, LGDJ, 1996).

de Sadeleer N, Roller G, Dross M, Bélier S, *Access to Justice in Environmental Matters and the Role of NGOs: Empirical Findings and Legal Appraisal* (Groningen, Europa Law Publishing, 2005).

de Silva L, 'Public Participation in International Negotiation and Compliance' in Alam S, Sumudu A, Gonzalez CG, Razzaque J (eds), *International Environmental Law and the Global South* (Cambridge, Cambridge University Press, 2015).

De Witte B, 'The Impact of Van Gend en Loos on Judicial Protection at European and National Level: Three Types of Preliminary Questions' in Tizzano A and Prechal S (eds), *50th Anniversary of the Judgment in Van Gend en Loos, 1963–2013* (Luxembourg, Office des Publications de l'Union Européenne, 2013).

Donati A, *Le principe de précaution en droit de l'Union européenne* (Louvain-la-Neuve, Larcier, 2021).

Dupuy PM, Viñuales J, *International Environmental Law* (Cambridge, Cambridge University Press, 2015).

Ebbeson J, *Access to Justice in Environmental Matters in the EU* (Dordrecht, Kluwer, 2002).

Eeckhout P, *EU External Relations Law*, 2nd edn (Oxford, Oxford University Press, 2011).

Friedman LM, 'The Place of Legal Culture in the Sociology of Law' in Freeman M (ed), *Law and Sociology* (Oxford, OUP, 2006).

Galanter M, 'The Radiating Effects of Courts' in Boyum KO, Mather L (eds), *Empirical Theories About Courts* (New York, Longman Inc, 1983).

Gerbrandy A, van Kreij L, 'The Impact of the Convention of Aarhus on the Emerging European Legal Culture' in Caranta R, Gerbrandy A, Muller B (eds), *The Making of a New European Legal Culture: The Aarhus Convention* (Groningen, Europa Law Publishing, 2018) 447–48.

Gouritin A, *EU Environmental Law, International Environmental Law, and Human Rights Law – The Case of Environmental Responsibility* (Leiden, Brill, 2016).

Harlow C, Rawlings R, *Law and Administration*, 3rd edn (Cambridge, Cambridge University Press, 2009).

Hartley T, *The Foundations of EC Law* (Oxford, Oxford University Press, 2010).

Hedemann-Robinson M., *Enforcement of European Union Environmental Law – Legal Issues and Challenges*, 2nd edn (Oxford, Routledge, 2015).
Hodson L, *NGOs and the Struggle for Human Rights in Europe* (Oxford, Hart Publishing, 2011).
Hoevenaars J, *A People's Court? A Bottom-Up Approach to Litigation Before the Court of Justice of the European Union* (The Hague, Eleven International Publishing, 2018).
Huang J, Tigre MA, 'Trends in Climate Justice Litigation: The Dutch Case and Global Repercussions' in Abate Randall S (ed), *Climate Justice: Case Studies in Global and Regional Governance Challenges* (Washington, DC, Environmental Law Institute, 2016).
Jans JH, Macrory R, Moreno Molina AM, *National Courts and EU Environmental Law* (Groningen, Europa Law Publishing, 2013).
Jans JH, Vedder HHB, *European Environmental Law – After Lisbon*, 4th edn (Groningen, Europa Law Publishing, 2012).
Kilpatrick C, Scott J, *Contemporary Challenges to EU Legality* (Oxford, Oxford University Press, 2021).
Krämer L, *EU Environmental Law*, 8th edn (London, Sweet & Maxwell, 2015).
Krommendijk J, *National Courts and Preliminary References to the Court of Justice* (Cheltenham, Edward Elgar, 2021).
Kuilwijk KJ, *The European Court of Justice and the GATT Dilemma – Public Interest versus Individual Rights?* (Doctoral Thesis – European University Institute, 1995.
Lambert Abdelgawad E, 'The Enforcement of ECtHR Judgments' in Jakab A, Kochenov D (eds), *The Enforcement of EU Law and Values: Ensuring Member States' Compliance* (Oxford, Oxford University Press, 2017).
McCann MW, *Rights at Work: Pay Equity Reform and the Politics of Legal Mobilization* (Chicago, University of Chicago Press, 1994).
Naffine N, *Law's Meaning of Life, Philosophy, Religion, Darwin and the Legal Person* (Oxford, Hart Publishing, 2009).
Pallemaerts M, *The Aarhus Convention at Ten – Interactions and Tensions between Conventional International Law and EU Environmental Law* (Groningen, Europa Law Publishing, 2011.
Passalacqua V, *Legal Mobilization for Migrant Rights – Opportunities and Barriers at the European Court of Justice* (Oxford, OUP, 2025).
Pavone T, *The Ghostwriters Lawyers and the Politics behind the Judicial Construction of Europe* (Cambridge, CUP, 2022).
Rath K, 'The EU Aarhus Regulation and EU Administrative Acts Based on the Aarhus Regulation: The Withdrawal of the CJEU from the Aarhus Convention' in Voigt C (ed), *International Judicial Practice on the Environment: Questions of Legitimacy* (Cambridge: Cambridge University Press, 2019) 52–73.
Rosenberg GN, *The Hollow Hope: Can Courts Bring about Social Change?* (Chicago, University of Chicago Press, 1991).
Ryall Á, 'The Aarhus Convention: Standards for Access to Justice in Environmental Matters' in Turner SJ, Shelton DL, Razzaque J, McIntyre O, May JR (eds), *Environmental Rights: The Development of Standards* (Cambridge, Cambridge University Press, 2019).
Sands PJ, *Greening International Law* (New York, Earthscan, 1993).
Sax JL, *Defending The Environment: A Handbook for Citizen Action* (New York, Knopf, 1971).
Scott J, *Environmental Protection: European Law and Governance* (Oxford, Oxford University Press, 2009).
Schmidt SK, *The European Court of Justice and the Policy Process: The Shadow of Case Law* (Oxford, OUP, 2018).
Segal JA, 'Judicial Behavior' in Goodin R (ed), *The Oxford Handbook of Political Science* (Oxford, Oxford University Press, 2011; online edn, Oxford Academic, 5 September 2013).
Selin H, Van Deveer SD, *European Union and Environmental Governance* (Abingdon, Routledge, 2015).
Squintani L, Holwerda M, de Graaf K, 'Regulating Greenhouse Gas Emissions from EU ETS Installations: What Room is Left for the Member States' in Peeters M, Stallworthy M (eds), *Climate Law in EU Member States: Towards National Legislation for Climate Protection* (Cheltenham, Edward Elgar, 2012).

Stephens T, *International Courts and Environmental Protection* (Cambridge, Cambridge University Press, 2009).
Tarrow S, *Power in Movement: Social Movements, Collective Action, and Politics* (Cambridge, Cambridge University Press, 2012).
Thierse S, Badanjak S, *Opposition in the EU Multi-Level Polity – Legal Mobilization against the Data Retention Directive* (Basingstoke, Palgrave Macmillan, 2021).
Thornton J, Goodman M, *Client Earth* (London, Scribe, 2018).
Treves T, *Civil Society, International Courts and Compliance Bodies* (The Hague, TMC Asser Press, 2005).
Tridimas T, Poli S, 'Locus Standi of Individuals under Article 230(4): The Return of Euridice?' in Arnull A, Eeckhout P, Tridimas T (eds), *Continuity and Change in EU Law: Essays in Honour of Sir Francis Jacobs* (Oxford, Oxford Scholarship Online, 2009).
van Wolferen M, *To Justifie the Wayes of God to Men – Limits to the Court's Power of Interpretation*, Doctoral Thesis – University of Groningen, 2018. Available at: https://ssrn.com/abstract=3300703.
van Wolferen M, Eliantonio M, 'Access to Justice in Environmental Matters: The EU's Difficult Road Towards Non-Compliance With the Aarhus Convention' in Peeters M, Eliantonio M (eds), *Research Handbook on EU Environmental Law* (Cheltenham, Edward Elgar, 2019).
Vatn A, *Environmental Governance – Institutions, Policies and Actions* (Cheltenham, Edward Elgar, 2015).
Vauchez A, *Brokering Europe – Euro-Lawyers and the Making of a Transnational Polity* (Cambridge, Cambridge University Press, 2015).
Weisbrod Burton A, *Conceptual Perspective on the Public Interest: An Economic Analysis, in Public Interest Law: An Economic and Institutional Analysis* (Berkeley, University of California Press, 1978).
Worthington R, Rask M, Minna L, *Citizen Participation in Global Environmental Governance* (Abingdon, Routledge, 2011).

Guides

Fellmeth AX, Horwitz M, *Guide to Latin in International Law* (Oxford OUP, 2011 (online version). Available at: www.oxfordreference.com/view/10.1093/acref/9780195369380.001.0001/acref-9780195369380-e-1075.
UNECE, *The Aarhus Convention: An Implementation Guide*, 2nd edn, 2014. Available at: www.unece.org/env/pp/implementation_guide.html.
UNECE, *Guide to the Aarhus Convention Compliance Committee* (May 2019), 6. Available at: www.unece.org/index.php?id=54512.

Reports

Berthier A, Krämer L, The Aarhus Convention: Implementation and compliance in EU law, report of the European Union Aarhus Centre, Client Earth, June 2014. Available at: www.clientearth.org/latest/news/the-aarhus-convention-implementation-and-compliance-in-eu-law/.
Clifford Chance LLP, 'Collective Actions in Europe', July 2010. Available at: www.cliffordchance.com/content/dam/cliffordchance/PDF/collective_actions_europe_2010.pdf.
Commission Report published on EU implementation of the Aarhus Convention in the area of access to justice in environmental matters, October 2019. Available at: https://ec.europa.eu/environment/aarhus/pdf/Commission_report_2019.pdf.
Communication from the Commission to the European Parliament, the Council, the European Economic and Social Committee and the Committee of the Regions, 'Environmental Implementation

Review 2019: A Europe That Protects Its Citizens And Enhances Their Quality Of Life', Brussels, 4 April 2019 Com(2019) 149 Final.
European Commission, Science for Environment Policy, 'Wildlife law enforcement: the vital role of NGOs', July 2016, Thematic issue 56. Available at: https://ec.europa.eu/environment/integration/research/newsalert/pdf/wildlife_law_enforcement_the_vital_role_of_NGOs_56si13_en.pdf.
European Food Safety Authority, Panel on Plant Health (PLH), 'Scientific Opinion on the risk to plant health posed by *Xylella fastidiosa* in the EU territory, with the identification and evaluation of risk reduction options', EFSA Journal 2015;13(1):3989, Parma, Italy.
European Union Agency for Fundamental Rights (FRA), *Handbook on European law relating to access to justice* (2016), 176. Available at: https://fra.europa.eu/en/publication/2016/handbook-european-law-relating-access-justice.
De Sadeleer N, Roller G, Dross M, Access to Justice in Environmental Matters, Final Report, UNECE, 2002. Available at: www.unece.org/fileadmin/DAM/env/pp/compliance/C2008-23/Amicus%20brief/AnnexHSadeleerReport.pdf.
DLA Piper-PILnet, 'The Growth of Pro Bono in Europe – Using the Power of Law for the Public Interest', November 2016. Available at: www.pilnet.org/wp-content/uploads/2020/03/Pro_Bono_Final_Report_V2-1.pdf.
Greenpeace International, Annual Report, 2018. Available at: www.greenpeace.org/international/explore/about/annual-report/.
Hough A, 'Analysis of the Revised Proposal to Amend the Aarhus Regulation', EJNI Access to Justice Observatory, Final Report, 2021. Available at: https://ejni.net/resources/access-to-justice-observatory-old/.
Milieu Consulting, final study on EU implementation of the Aarhus Convention in the area of access to justice in environmental matters, September 2019. Available at: https://ec.europa.eu/environment/aarhus/pdf/Final_study_EU_implemention_environmental_matters_2019.pdf.
PFPI, 2010–2020 Ten-year report. Available at: www.pfpi.net/about.
Setzer J and Higham C (2024) Global Trends in Climate Change Litigation: 2024 Snapshot. London: Grantham Research Institute on Climate Change and the Environment, London School of Economics and Political Science. Available at www.lse.ac.uk/granthaminstitute/wp-content/uploads/2024/06/Global-trends-in-climate-change-litigation-2024-snapshot.pdf.
UNECE, Reports of the Ad Hoc Working Group for the preparation of a draft convention on access to environmental information and public participation in environmental decision-making. Available at: https://unece.org/environment-policy/public-participation/aarhus-convention/reports-negotiations-convention.
UNECE, Report of the Compliance Committee, findings and recommendations with regard to communication ACCC/C/2008/32 (Part I) concerning compliance by the European Union, 14 April 2011. Available at: https://unece.org/DAM/env/pp/compliance/CC-32/ece.mp.pp.c.1.2011.4.add.1_as_submitted.pdf.
UNECE, Report of the Compliance Committee, findings and recommendations with regard to communication ACCC/C/2010/50 concerning compliance by the Czech Republic, prepared by the Compliance Committee and adopted on 29 June 2012. Available at: https://unece.org/DAM/env/pp/compliance/C2010-50/Findings/ece_mp.pp_c.1_2012_11_eng.pdf.
UNECE, Report of the Compliance Committee, findings and recommendations with regard to communication ACCC/C/2008/32 (Part II) concerning compliance by the European Union, 17 March 2017. Available at: https://unece.org/fileadmin/DAM/env/pp/compliance/CC-57/ece.mp.pp.c.1.2017.7.e.pdf.
UNECE, Advice by the Aarhus Convention Compliance Committee to the European Union concerning the implementation of request ACCC/M/2017/3. Available at: https://unece.org/sites/default/files/2021-02/M3_EU_advice_12.02.2021.pdf.
UNECE, full Summary of the Budva Meetings – Sixth Session of the Meeting of the Parties to the Aarhus Convention. Available at: www.unece.org/environmental-policy/conventions/public-participation/aarhus-convention/tfwg/envppmop/envppmop6mopp3highlights/full-summary-of-budva-meetings.html.

Online Articles

Bäumler J, 'Sustainable Development made justiciable: The German Constitutional Court's climate ruling on intra- and inter-generational equity', EJIL:Talk!, 8 June 2021. Available at: www.ejiltalk.org/sustainable-development-made-justiciable-the-german-constitutional-courts-climate-ruling-on-intra-and-inter-generational-equity/.

Bechtel S, 'Poland and Bulgaria deny access to justice to citizens and NGOs fighting dirty air' ClientEarth, 26 April 2019. Available at: www.clientearth.org/projects/access-to-justice-for-a-greener-europe/updates/poland-and-bulgaria-deny-access-to-justice-to-citizens-and-ngos-fighting-dirty-air/.

Clark P, Liston G, Kalpouzos I, 'Climate change and the European Court of Human Rights: The Portuguese Youth Case', EJIL:Talk!, 6 October 2020. Available at: www.ejiltalk.org/climate-change-and-the-european-court-of-human-rights-the-portuguese-youth-case/.

ClientEarth, 'EU pulls down barriers for public to challenge environmental wrongdoing in court', 13 July 2021. Available at: www.clientearth.org/latest/press-office/press/eu-pulls-down-barriers-for-public-to-challenge-environmental-wrongdoing-in-court/.

Dunn G, 'The Case of the Century – The French Administrative Court Issues a Groundbreaking Ruling on State Responsibility for Climate Change', 26 February 2021. Available at: www.gibsondunn.com/the-case-of-the-century-the-french-administrative-court-issues-a-groundbreaking-ruling-on-state-responsibility-for-climate-change/.

EEB, ClientEarth and Justice & Environment, 'Letter to Environmental Ministers regarding the Commission's proposal on the Aarhus Regulation', 19 November 2020. Available at: https://eeb.org/library/letter-to-environmental-ministers-regarding-the-commissions-proposal-on-the-aarhus-convention/.

Eeckhout P, 'From Strasbourg to Luxembourg?: The KlimaSeniorinnen judgment and EU remedies' (2024) VerfBlog. Available at: https://verfassungsblog.de/from-strasbourg-to-luxembourg/.

European Eco Forum statement on the role of the European Union in relation to the finding that it is in non-compliance with the Aarhus Convention, Budva, Montenegro, Thursday 14 September 2017. Available at: www.wecf.eu/download/2017/09-September/EuropeanECOForumStatementNon-ComplianceEU.pdf.

Friel A, 'The Aarhus Regulation Amendment: Cause for cautious celebration', 6 November 2020. Available at: www.clientearth.org/projects/access-to-justice-for-a-greener-europe/updates/the-aarhus-regulation-amendment-cause-for-cautious-celebration/.

Friel A, 'People's climate case highlights lack of access to the EU courts', ClientEarth official website. Available at www.clientearth.org/peoples-climate-case-highlights-lack-of-access-to-the-eu-courts/.

GPI, 'Climate crisis hits the Supreme Court of Norway'. Available at: www.greenpeace.org/international/press-release/45579/climate-crisis-hits-the-supreme-court-of-norway/.

Hart D, 'The biter bit – EU does NOT like being criticised by Aarhus body', UK Human Rights Blog, 23 September 2017. Available at: https://ukhumanrightsblog.com/2017/09/23/the-biter-bit-eu-does-not-like-being-criticised-by-aarhus-body.

Heri C, 'The ECtHR's Pending Climate Change Case: What's Ill-Treatment Got To Do With It?', EJIL:Talk!, 22 December 2020. Available at: www.ejiltalk.org/the-ecthrs-pending-climate-change-case-whats-ill-treatment-got-to-do-with-it/.

Heri C, 'On the Duarte Agostinho Decision' (2024) VerfBlog, https://verfassungsblog.de/on-the-duarte-agostinho-decision/.

Italia Olivicola, 'Lo studio: 4 milioni di alberi morti e improduttivi, 50mila ettari desertificati, perso il 10% dell'olio italiano'. Available at: www.italiaolivicola.it/news/comunicati-stampa/xylella-lo-studio-4-milioni-di-alberi-morti-e-improduttivi-50mila-ettari-desertificati-perso-il-10-dellolio-italiano/.

Levin K, Tirpak D, World Resources Institute, '2018: A Year of Climate Extremes', 27 December 2018. Available at: www.wri.org/insights/2018-year-climate-extremes.

Murcott M, Tigre MA, Zimmermann N, 'Climate Change Litigation: What the ECtHR Could Learn from Courts in the Global South', Völkerrechtsblog, 22 March 2025. doi: 10.17176/20220322-121032-0.

Pagano M, 'Climate change litigation before EU Courts and the "butterfly effect"', *Blog de droit européen*, 16 October 2019. Available at: https://blogdroiteuropeen.com/2019/10/16/climate-change-litigation-before-eu-courts-and-the-butterfly-effect-by-mario-pagano/.

Richardson Z, Reilly P, 'Mr Justice Simons dismisses judicial review proceedings brought by Friends of the Irish Environment', Fieldfisher, 19 April 2021. Available at: www.fieldfisher.com/en-ie/locations/ireland/ireland-blog/mr-justice-simons-dismisses-judicial-review-procee.

The Irish Times, 'Government decision on Shannon LNG plant not straightforward', 24 August 2021. Available at: www.irishtimes.com/business/energy-and-resources/government-decision-on-shannon-lng-plant-not-straightforward-1.4654435.

Workman D, 'Crude Oil Exports by Country', World Top Exports. Available at www.worldstopexports.com/worlds-top-oil-exports-country/.

Conferences and Webinars

Access to justice in environmental matters: Impacts, Obstacles, Way forward, ClientEarth, Virtual Conference, 15–16 October 2020. Programme available here: www.cev6.clientearth.org/wp-content/uploads/Conference-Agenda_BAT.pdf.

Access to Justice and the Preliminary Reference Procedure, ClientEarth, Webinar, 29 October 2020.

ClientEarth Summit 2020, Online, 9–11 November 2020. Programme available at: www.bigmarker.com/series/clientearth-summit/series_summit?utm_bmcr_source=tracking_code1.

The EU Internal Review Mechanism: Access to justice for environmental NGOs under the Aarhus Regulation, ClientEarth, Webinar, 16 November 2020.

The role of cities and regions in the implementation and enforcement of environmental legislation, ClientEarth, Webinar, 14 December 2020.

Access to Justice in Environmental Matters under the ECHR, ClientEarth, Webinar, 11 January 2021.

The EU Climate Law and Access to Justice, ClientEarth, Webinar, 26 January 2021.

The preliminary reference procedure and fundamental rights, Institute for European Law, KU Leuven, 1 April 2021.

Climate Change Litigation and Human Rights: Stocktaking and a Look at the Future, Scuola Superiore Sant'Anna di Pisa, Pisa, 6–7 May 2021.

Revising the Aarhus Regulation: Securing Adequate Legal Protection for Climate Action?, Institute of International Law and Human Rights, University of Helsinki, Online, 8 June 2021. Available here: www.youtube.com/watch?v=-_65VWt51CY&t=587s.

Climate litigation before international courts and tribunals, Heinrich-Böll-Stiftung, Online, 7 October 2021. Available here: www.youtube.com/watch?v=3BdrVOfYxkI.

Climate Change Litigation in Numbers, Florence School of Regulation, 13 October 2021. Available at: www.youtube.com/watch?v=rcoU9Y4x46U&t=1036s.

Workshop 'Strategic litigation in the European Union', University of Amsterdam, 16–17 January 2023.

INDEX

Aarhus Committee 15–17, 19–20, 50–51, 95–113, 121–29, 181, 220–21, 225–27
- ACCC/C/2008/32 102–4
- composition and functions 98–99
- findings 18, 97, 103–6, 108, 111–12, 122, 127, 207, 211, 218
  - Commission study and report 113–17
  - impact 109–10
  - impact on EU decision-making 110–21
  - non-binding character 107–9
- scrutiny 99–101

Aarhus Convention 17–20, 77–79, 81–82
- Art 15 84, 98–99, 107
- EU adhesion 43, 86–87
- standing 211–12
- sufficiency 212–14

Aarhus Regulation (AR) 18–22, 87–90, 93–97, 102–6, 110–15, 117–23, 221–24
- Art 10 87–90, 92–94, 96, 105–6, 131, 135, 221
- Art 12 11, 18, 136, 140
- new Aarhus Regulation 10, 72, 124–40, 221–22, 226–27, 229–31
- reform 127, 134, 230

ACCC *see* **Aarhus Committee**

access to justice 26–27, 41–42, 53–55, 57–60, 72–73, 103–4, 115–16, 126–28, 172–75, 225–27

accountability 81, 101, 145

actions for annulment *see* **annulment, actions** 23, 105

actio popularis 126, 165, 200

active substances 66, 91, 105, 199

actors 4, 8–9, 147, 151, 158–59, 182–83, 216
- collective 2–3, 20
- social 3, 228

acts 35–36, 38–40, 49, 51–53, 92–93, 103–4, 114–20, 125, 128–30, 132–33
- administrative *see* administrative acts
- of general scope 90–91
- of individual scope 90, 92, 94–95, 105–6, 221

administrative acts 11–12, 87, 89–90, 105–6, 118–20, 127, 129–31, 133, 138–39, 224
- definition 20, 95, 114, 120, 124–25, 128–29, 133, 138–39, 223, 230
- environmental 94, 134, 139

administrative bodies 72, 79, 124, 129–31, 135, 139, 230

administrative courts 50, 67, 146

administrative law 80, 96, 144–45, 218, 220

administrative review 10, 12, 94, 103, 117, 125–26

admissibility 35, 133, 176, 193–94, 199, 217–18, 230

advocacy 10, 127, 130, 139, 216–17, 222, 227–28, 233

Advocates General (AGs) 31–33, 40, 46–47, 49, 51, 66, 74, 193–94 *see also* ***individual names***

agencies 45, 80, 87
- dispute-settlement 2, 149

agriculture 134, 139, 189

AGs *see* **Advocates General**

amendments 20, 112–14, 117–18, 121–22, 124–33, 222, 226–27, 232

annulment 30, 67, 89–90, 136–38, 180, 199, 204
- actions 7, 11–14, 23–25, 41–44, 133–36, 138–40, 149, 222–25
  - standing in 7, 23, 141, 181

appeals 12, 25, 27, 35, 53, 145, 155, 191, 207, 232
- process 17, 31, 90

applicants 31–38, 40–43, 47–48, 90–93, 105–6, 159–68, 173–75, 193–99, 206–11, 217–19
- arguments 33, 90–94, 163–64, 174, 182, 197
- privileged 7, 182

application files 16–17, 90, 162, 178, 182, 184, 190, 193, 206, 211

appraisal
- manifest error of 63, 70–71

AR *see* **Aarhus Regulation**

Arctic Oil 19, 154–56, 178

arguments 26–27, 31–33, 35–38, 44–45, 90–91, 137, 194–97, 205–7
applicants'/plaintiffs' 33, 90–94, 163–64, 174, 182, 197
defendants' 196
assessment 50, 62–64, 71, 115, 117–19, 124–25, 139, 175
manifest error of 65, 69–71
preliminary 18, 124, 128
scientific 133, 139
associations 11, 34, 36, 57, 62, 105–6, 165–66
business 113, 116
environmental 33, 64, 211
Associazione Italia Nostra 62–63, 73
attorneys, external 14–16, 21, 212, 222
Austria 19, 58, 61, 147, 167–68, 170, 172–75, 179, 232
Mineral Oil Tax Act 167
authorities 30, 63, 70–71, 163, 196, 199, 213
judicial 100, 156
autonomy of the EU legal order 86, 108, 177, 230
awareness raising 58, 117, 159, 185, 190, 192, 203, 206, 216

Barents Sea 154–55
bargaining
forums 2, 149
power 128, 139, 225
barriers 20, 45–46, 74, 116, 175, 209
hidden 60
bees protection 96, 221
Belgium 61, 146, 163
Cour de cassation 47
Benvenisti, Eyal 151–52
binding force 106, 108–9, 120–21, 125, 129, 139, 153, 211
biodiversity 141, 157, 183, 217
biomass 118, 204–7, 209, 215–16, 223
forest 205–7, 209, 214, 216
***Blaise* case** 65–69, 73
bodies 87, 89, 125, 129, 131, 138, 205
international quasi-judicial 126
judicial 2, 225
UN 127, 159
borders 163–64, 200, 223
Bosphorus 168–75, 179
boundaries of litigation 6, 10, 150, 228
Boyd, David 155–56
building blocks 153–57, 193, 197, 212, 226, 232
strategy 155–57
Bulgaria 50, 61
business associations 113, 116
butterfly effect 209–10

campaigning organisations 101, 147
campaigns 52, 148–49, 155, 191, 216–17, 224
communication 217, 228
Canary Islands 29–30
capacity 41, 84, 109, 149, 151, 164
European ENGOs 121, 138
legislative 211–12
carbon emissions 203–5
carcinogenicity 65, 67
Carpathians 189
***Carvalho* case** 12, 16–17, 19, 182–204, 206, 208–9, 213–19
case law 26–27, 31–32, 36–38, 90–91, 104–6, 108–9, 121–23, 138–39 *see also* ***individual cases/courts***
case studies 17–18, 22
catalysts 128, 139, 149, 226
categories 4, 39, 113, 116–17, 162, 189
causal links 197, 209–10, 217
causation 197, 210
in *Sabo* 209–11
Cazan, Raul 15, 189, 201–2, 206
CFI *see* **Court of First Instance**
children 6, 159–60, 208
CIFF (Children's Investment Fund Foundation) 15
CIP (Climate Integrity Project) 205, 215
citizens 77–78, 80–81, 100–102, 122, 177, 213–14, 216–18, 223–24
EU 113, 164, 185, 192
fundamental rights 182, 198, 210, 219
human rights 141, 169, 178–79
civil society 33, 80, 82, 126–27, 134, 139, 150, 233
organisations 18, 102, 141, 182
role 60, 111
CJEU *see* **Court of Justice of the EU**
claimants 53, 91, 185
ClientEarth 12–16, 50, 58–59, 118–22, 137–38, 213–14, 220–21
and ACCC/C/2008/32 102–4
ClientEarth v Commission 136–38
ClientEarth v EIB 117–21
as legal ENGO 101–2
climate 101, 158, 161, 204, 215, 219
climate action 50, 57, 145, 162, 180, 193, 195, 204
climate adjudication 10, 21, 151

climate cases 21, 143–44, 146, 168, 173, 179, 182–83, 212 *see also* ***individual cases***
climate change 7–8, 134
before non-EU courts 142–80
before the CJEU 181–219
effects/consequences/impact 141, 157, 165, 182–218
litigation (CCL) 17–19, 141–219
in Strasbourg 175–77
trend 18, 21, 140–41, 143–47, 178, 181, 196–97, 200, 219, 223
climate context 9–10, 155, 165–66, 175, 179–81, 201, 219
climate crisis 148, 159, 167–68
Climate Governance and Human Rights Policy Coordinator 16, 125, 184
Climate Integrity Project (CIP) 205, 215
climate litigants 10, 144–46, 157, 174–75, 178–79, 201, 218–19, 226 *see also* ***individual names***
climate litigation *see* **climate change**
climate policy 133, 146, 166, 170, 175, 195, 224
climate targets 143, 145–46, 168, 172, 175, 188, 193
closed category test 39
closures 9–10, 19–20, 22, 41, 88, 138, 229–30, 232
coalitions 77, 82, 84–85, 121, 128, 220, 222, 227
Codorniu 197–98, 208
collective actors 2–3, 20
common but differentiated responsibilities 155–56
communications 50, 98–99, 101–2, 121–22, 128, 204
communication strategies 182, 190, 192, 216–17, 222, 227–28
communities 26, 78, 86, 148, 228
marginalised 192, 216
Community institutions *see* **EU (European Union), institutions**
Community law *see* **EU (European Union), law**
competence 63, 83, 93, 98
exclusive 46, 84
competition 37–39
complainants 12, 25, 38, 124, 137
completeness 9, 40, 45
compliance 85, 90, 96–100, 105–10, 112–14, 121–22, 127–28, 138–39
bodies 13, 100, 104, 109–10, 121, 229
committee *see* Aarhus Committee
EU 19, 100–101, 104, 111–12, 121–22
mechanism 20, 84–85, 95, 97–98, 107, 121, 226
conferences 17, 59, 189
virtual 58
Congress 25, 80
consensus 2–3, 85, 108, 111, 121
consistency 35–37, 42, 105, 133, 137
constitutional courts 25, 146, 151, 157, 167–68
federal 146, 157
constitutional ideas 151, 178
constitutional rights 2, 28, 165
constitutions 25, 28, 145, 154–55, 167, 178
constraints 2–3, 48, 120
consultations 17, 99, 107, 114–15, 122
consumer protection 25, 79–80
contested acts/decisions/measures/ provisions 34, 89–93, 105–6, 118–20, 134–37, 193, 197–98, 217
cooperation 57, 74, 151–52, 169, 191
coordination 30, 152, 195
corporations 11, 37–38, 141–42, 144, 147–48, 157, 182, 219
costs 33, 46–47, 53–54, 126, 191
Council of Europe 109, 159, 168
counterarguments 182, 194, 211
Court of First Instance (CFI) 12, 19, 23, 27, 30, 36, 57, 108, 165
Court of Justice of the EU (CJEU) 7–14, 17–28, 31–39, 41–47, 49–56, 102–6, 171–80, 182, 230–32
contestation of EU policy on biomass energy 204–7
Court of First Instance (CFI) 12, 19, 23, 27, 30, 36, 57, 108, 165
General Court 12–13, 89–94, 105–6, 118–20, 136–37, 198–99, 211, 232
litigation and communication 190–92
Plaumann and climate change 181–219
rigidity 9, 28, 39, 116, 212, 224
courts 22–29, 31–42, 50–54, 135–38, 147–55, 161–70, 192–200, 206–11 *see also* ***individual courts***
administrative 50, 67, 146
non-EU 13–14, 18–19, 21, 140–81, 224, 226
obsolete 156–57, 179
radiating effect 2, 149, 216
referring 66–67
supreme 2, 24–25, 53, 57, 143, 145, 155–56
Covid-19 pandemic 190, 201, 219
Criminal Court of Foix 65, 67

CSOs 60, 77, 95–96, 120–21, 141–43, 165, 177–78, 205
Cumac 29–30
Czech Republic 61, 100

damages 146, 191, 193
deadlines 73, 131
decision-making process 42, 78, 119, 122, 127–28, 130, 226, 229
decisions, contested 34, 89–93, 105–6, 118–20, 134–37, 193, 197–98, 217
declarations 30, 63, 86, 95, 99
defendants 65–67, 148, 155, 196 *see also* ***individual names***
democracy 78, 81, 177, 179, 200
direct access 1, 22, 24–26, 28–29, 74, 87–88, 194, 230
  to justice 20, 22, 41, 122, 229
direct actions 38, 47–48, 50, 70, 72–73, 199–200, 223, 231
direct effect 92–94, 106, 230
Directives 53, 62–63, 83, 91, 205, 208 *see also* ***individual instruments***
direct observation 13, 16
Directors 15, 118–19
discretion 38–39, 51, 62–65, 70, 169–70, 172–73
  national 26, 169, 171, 196
discretionary acts 39
disputes 2, 10, 49, 52–53, 94, 137, 215–16, 230
District Courts 143, 155, 170, 197
diversity 62, 101, 154, 185–86, 189
domestic courts 51, 68, 158
domestic legal systems 59–60, 81, 168
domestic remedies 160, 165–66, 174
dominant legal expertise 142, 158, 183
double standards 37–39
Duarte Agostinho 13–14, 17, 19, 147, 159–66, 168, 170–71, 175–79, 224

Eastern Europe 55, 189, 206, 221
ECHA *see* **European Chemicals Agency**
ECHR *see* **European Convention on Human Rights**
ECO *see* **Environmental Citizens' Organizations**
ECSC *see* **European Coal and Steel Community**
ECtHR *see* **European Court of Human Rights**
EEB *see* **European Environmental Bureau**
effective judicial protection 31, 34–35, 40, 74, 194, 199
effectiveness 30, 81, 135, 161, 165, 203, 228
EIA *see* **environmental impact assessment**
EIB *see* **European Investment Bank**
EIPA *see* **European Institute of Public Administration**
Elter, Giorgio 16, 187–89
emission reductions 161–62, 193, 195–96
  targets 168, 170–71, 175, 179, 203
emissions 118, 143, 155, 163, 169–71, 193, 195–96, 205
  trading system 162
empirical evidence 27, 109, 219
enforcement 45, 47, 57, 60, 77, 101–2, 121, 214
ENGOs *see* **environmental NGOs**
environment *see* ***Introductory Note***
environmental associations 33, 64, 211
Environmental Citizens' Organizations (ECO) 82
environmental democracy 15, 77–78
environmental impact assessment (EIA) 29–30, 32, 34, 52–54, 57, 100
environmental information 7, 11, 78, 83, 95
environmental justice 43, 60, 81, 95–96, 109, 114, 233
environmental law 45, 89, 95, 102–4, 129–31, 183, 212, 214
  EU 45–46, 54, 60, 96, 134, 218
  principles 212, 214
environmental litigants 23, 60, 75, 155, 199, 218, 224–25, 232–33 *see also* ***individual names***
environmental litigation 46, 77, 89–90, 95–96, 207, 214
environmental NGOs (ENGOs)
  and the Aarhus negotiation 81–84
  coalition 77, 84, 102, 121, 128, 190, 200, 222, 227
  legal mobilisation 47, 69, 110, 113, 134, 223, 229, 231
  and the PRP on Validity 60–73
  specialised 96, 221
  standing 42, 54
  treating differently 33–34
environmental organisations 11–12, 46, 73, 84–85, 113–14, 126–28, 138–41, 145–46, 183–84, 231–32
environmental protection 27, 30–34, 38–39, 61, 210, 212–14, 218, 230
environmental rights 32, 40, 214
EPAW *see* **European Platform Against Windfarms**

equivalence 169, 172
ERDF (European Regional Development Fund) 29, 36
Estonia 58, 205
EU (European Union) 48–49, 86–87, 122, 169–72, 176, 186–87, 195–96, 199 *see also* ***Introductory Note***
  Aarhus Regulation *see* Aarhus Regulation
  administrative acts 19–20, 95, 105, 123, 131, 133, 230
  Charter of Fundamental Rights (EUCFR) 62–63, 171–72, 187, 193–94, 199, 207, 214, 217–18, 224
    Art 37 200
  climate law 163, 167, 170, 173–74, 178, 203, 210, 219 *see also individual instruments*
  climate policy 166, 172, 175, 188, 223, 232
  decision-making 36, 72, 97, 104
    and Aarhus Committee 110–21
  Effort Sharing Regulation 171–73, 206, 223
  environmental law, legality of 21, 44, 162, 178, 183, 219, 223, 231
  executive 64, 70–71, 115, 133, 177, 179
  institutions 7, 85–89, 94–97, 122, 127–29, 133–34, 138–39, 220–22
  judges 32, 37–38, 40–41, 53, 91–92, 105–6, 198, 218
  judicial protection system 34–35, 42, 45, 59–60, 75, 214
  judiciary 23–24, 38–39, 63–67, 88–90, 118–22, 135–37, 180–83, 192–95, 197, 218–19
  law 36–39, 49–51, 86–87, 95–96, 119–22, 141–42, 168–76, 227
    consistency 31, 35–40
    legality 11, 141, 158, 162, 173, 177–78, 181, 220
    provisions 35, 52, 121, 134
    validity 8, 13, 44, 51, 74, 166, 173
  legal mobilisation 9, 20, 124, 133, 162, 230
  legal order 111–12, 122
  measures 7, 22–23, 45–46, 50, 67–68, 194–95
  Member States 25–26, 45–48, 52–59, 61–63, 73–75, 81–83, 168–76, 195–96
  policy 30, 103, 119, 170, 183, 230
  policymakers 185, 202, 205, 218
  political institutions 72, 157, 175
  structural funds 30, 34
  system of judicial protection 167, 173, 177, 179, 196–97, 230
  Treaties 20, 32, 43, 55, 73, 174, 180, 198, 200, 208, 212–13, 218
EUCFR *see* **European Union Charter of Fundamental Rights**
euro-lawyers 5, 56–57
European Coal and Steel Community (ECSC) 26–27
European Commission 1, 29–30, 50–51, 57–59, 113, 121–22, 126, 170–71, 176–77, 221–22
European Convention on Human Rights (ECHR) 143, 152, 160–64, 167–69, 171–77, 179, 181, 197, 214
European Council 113
European Court of Human Rights (ECtHR) 10, 14, 17, 109–10, 147, 152, 157, 159–62, 164–66, 168–69, 172–77, 179, 181, 200–201, 224–25, 229, 232
European Environmental Bureau (EEB) 12–14, 42, 48, 96, 130, 220–22
European Institute of Public Administration (EIPA) 57
European Investment Bank (EIB) 13, 15, 18, 30, 117–20, 122, 232
European Parliament 41, 126–27, 138–39, 177, 179, 193
European Platform Against Windfarms (EPAW) 13–16
European Regional Development Fund (ERDF) 29, 36
evidence 69, 71–72, 131
  scientific 65, 69–70, 72, 76, 143, 148, 207
exclusions 62, 68–69, 177, 212, 231
  explicit 126, 211
  State Aid decisions 126, 138–39
expertise 56–60, 101, 158, 216, 220–22, 227
  legal *see* legal expertise
experts, independent 98, 227
external attorneys 14–16, 21, 212, 222
external supervisor 139, 226
extraterritoriality 163–64, 223

fair trial 199, 231
familiarity with EU law 56–57, 60, 227
family life 168, 208
farmers 189–90, 197
favourable precedent 153–54
federal constitutional courts 146, 157
Fediol 90, 92–94, 229
feedback 113–14, 125
Feschet family 186, 188

***FIAMM* case** 92, 197–98
Fiji 187–90
final rulings 88, 191, 201, 219
financial burden 53, 167, 184
findings 20–21, 45, 97, 103–4, 106–10, 112, 121–22, 182
  on EU compliance 20, 97, 105, 112, 121
  main 21, 142, 220, 225, 227
  non-binding 97, 104, 107, 109, 127, 229
Finland 61
fora 82, 132, 157, 201
forest biomass 205–7, 209, 214, 216
forestry 119, 193
forests 204–6, 208–9, 217
formulas 22, 141, 157, 173, 193–94, 198, 211, 226
fossil fuels 127, 148, 207
foundations 81, 213, 223–24
framework 28, 44, 122, 163, 199, 227
France 58–59, 61, 67, 73, 145–46, 162, 188, 205–6
  Criminal Court 65–67
freedoms 27, 146, 151, 176, 208
free movement 38, 190
Friel, Anne 15, 59, 127, 213–14
Friends of the Irish Environment 49, 62, 206
fundamental principles 111–12, 114, 122, 163
fundamental rights 28, 34–35, 169, 182, 193–94, 197–99, 206–10, 217–19

Galanter, M. 2, 5, 128, 149
Galicia 118–19
gap filler 44, 74, 174
general application 35, 90–91, 93, 116, 131–33, 198, 209
General Court 12–13, 89–94, 105–6, 118–20, 136–37, 198–99, 211, 232
general scope 72, 106, 139, 193, 221, 224
  acts of 90–91
genetically modified organisms (GMOs) 67, 85
geographical scope 157
Georgia 110
Germany 25, 54, 57–58, 61, 146, 187, 224
  Federal Constitutional Court 146
GHG emissions 160, 205
GHG Emissions Acts 195–96
GLAN *see* **Global Legal Action Network**
Glavina, Monika 56
Global Legal Action Network (GLAN) 14–16, 142, 147, 224
  strategic litigation 158–77
glyphosate 65–67
GMOs (genetically modified organisms) 67, 85
governments 101, 141–42, 144–45, 155, 157, 205, 218–19 *see also* ***individual countries***
  national 147, 168, 178, 212
GPEU *see* **Greenpeace EU**
GPI *see* **Greenpeace International**
GPS *see* **Greenpeace Spain**
Gran Canaria 29–30
Greece 61
greenhouse gas emissions 167, 170, 173, 193
Greenpeace 18–19, 22–23, 33–34, 36–40, 42, 148–50, 157
  and *Plaumann* test 29–31
Greenpeace EU (GPEU) 15, 67, 114, 149
Greenpeace France 145
Greenpeace International (GPI) 12, 14–15, 18, 142, 152–57, 178–79, 220
  strategic litigation 147–50
Greenpeace Spain (GPS) 30
Guyo family 187–88

Habitats Directive 54, 68
harmonization 152, 179
Harvey, Richard 15, 39
health 84, 152, 165, 167, 204, 208
  occupational 79
healthy environment 145, 156, 165
heatwaves 185–86
hermeneutic approach 41, 129, 179
higher-ranking norms 193, 212, 218
Hilson, Chris 3
houses 53, 184, 192, 205
HRs *see* **human rights**
human rights 144–45, 155–57, 159–60, 164–65, 172–73, 175, 178–80, 184
  citizens' 141, 169, 178–79
  law 110, 145, 147, 151–52, 158, 178
  obligations 145, 212, 214
  protection 169, 172–73, 175–76, 214
  violations 147, 158–59, 171, 177, 219
Hungary 55, 58
hurdles 75, 116–17, 133, 217

ice 186, 188
  sea 197
IGSD (Institute for Governance and Sustainable Development) 205, 215
illegality 34, 92, 96
  pleas of 92, 96

impairment of rights 54, 79, 84, 100, 130
implementation 20, 36, 77, 86, 93–94, 98–99, 107, 111–12
implementing measures 49, 72, 125, 129–30, 132, 134, 138–39, 195–96
national 47–49, 73, 132, 195–96
inadmissible applications 115, 176
incompatibility 86, 102–4
incrementalism 6, 153–56, 226
independent experts 98, 227
indigenous communities 149, 156, 159, 178, 183, 228
indirect effects 3, 20, 122, 149, 207, 225
individual concern 23, 102, 149, 197, 209
requirement 9, 11, 24, 39–42, 47, 116
'individually concerned' requirement 90, 132, 197, 217
individual rights 54, 197–98
individual scope 90–91, 93, 105–6
acts/measures of 89–90, 92–95, 103, 105–6, 119, 129, 221
informal meetings 84, 110
in-house lawyers 14–16, 21, 127, 147–50, 155, 178, 212
integrated advocacy 6, 233
intensity of scrutiny 69–70, 97, 100, 104
inter alia 32, 62, 66, 78, 98, 115
interest groups 9, 27, 152, 210
interests 31–32, 37, 54, 59, 70, 79–80, 169
environmental 38, 40
Intergovernmental Panel on Climate Change (IPCC) 184
interim reliefs 46–47
internal review 87–90, 115, 120, 124, 129–31, 133–40, 221–22, 230–32
mechanism 20, 72, 75, 95, 117–18, 120, 129–30
procedure 72–73, 88, 92–93, 96, 102–3, 121–22, 131, 140
requests 90, 133
international agreements 43, 92–93, 105–6, 152
international law 95–96, 108–9, 114, 121, 127–28, 145–46, 151–52, 225–27
international obligations 28, 93, 144
interpretation 8–10, 40–41, 45–46, 51–52, 74–75, 104–6, 108, 176
judicial 9, 11, 41, 232
narrow 7, 24, 27, 41–42, 102, 210
interpretative space 28, 41
interpretative steps 10, 21, 150, 153, 157, 179, 226, 232
intervention 32–33, 109, 126–27, 185
interviews 14–16, 21, 142, 178, 183–85, 188–90, 218, 221
semi-structured 13–14, 16
invalidity 35, 49, 63, 194
IPCC (Intergovernmental Panel on Climate Change) 184
Ireland 49, 51, 55, 126, 145–46, 205–6
Low Carbon Development Act 50, 145
islands 29, 188, 191
Italy 1, 62–64, 81, 133, 159, 187–88

Jackson, Vicky 151
Jacobs, Advocate-General 40, 45, 47, 194
judges 50–51, 56–57, 59–60, 74, 149–54, 156–57, 178–79, 225–26
familiarity with EU law 60, 227
judgments 1–2, 11–12, 51–52, 145, 165, 176, 232
lack of enforcement 109, 121
judicial comfort 10, 147, 149–53, 155, 157–58, 178–79, 193, 197
transnational incremental 10, 21, 157, 218, 232
judicial dialogue 52, 180
judicial interpretation 9, 11, 41, 232
judicial protection 26, 33, 151, 193, 198
effective 31, 34–35, 40, 74, 194, 199
system 173, 175, 200, 218, 232
vacuum 31
judicial receptivity 3, 60, 106, 157, 179, 193, 225–26, 228
judicial remedies 46, 160, 214
judicial review 4, 27, 70, 115, 150, 217
constitutional 10, 212
more intense 72, 136
procedural 71
judicial training 45, 55, 57, 74, 227–28
judiciaries 59, 145, 156, 179, 226, 229, 232
Dutch 156, 160, 172
jurisdiction 25, 47, 144–45, 150–57, 163–66, 176–78
jurisprudence 27, 35–37, 92, 103–5, 109, 111, 116
justice 54, 71, 106, 135, 219
gap 67, 75
pillar 84–85, 87
justiciable rights 3, 199–200, 230

Kenya 187–90
Klimaseniorinnen 162–63, 165–66, 168, 173, 179, 232
Kuhs, Joachim 176

lavender harvest 188
lawsuits 21, 144–45, 148, 160–61, 178, 182–92, 200–203, 214–19
lawyers 21–22, 131, 158, 183–85, 208, 212–13, 216–18, 220, 222
  in-house 14–16, 21, 127, 147–50, 155, 178, 212
  public interest 5, 59, 101
Leenheerenpolder 68
legal actions 147, 158–59, 191
legal acts 96, 196
legal arguments 6, 13, 23, 90, 142, 217
  effective 216, 222
legal basis 103, 119, 129, 131, 171, 195
legal culture 81, 85, 95
legal effects 7, 91, 108, 122, 125, 129, 131–33, 152
legal expertise 5, 67, 123, 220
  dominant 142, 158, 183
  internal 221–22
legal ideas, transplantation 145, 151, 156, 178
legal imagination 97, 101, 123, 233
legal impact 10, 69, 110, 122, 231–32
legality 7, 11–13, 25, 92–93, 96, 136–38, 216
  of EU climate measures 147, 163, 180–81
  of EU emission reduction targets 162
  of EU environmental law 21, 44, 223, 231
  of EU law 11, 141, 158, 173, 177–78, 181, 220
legally binding effects 107–8, 118–20
legal mobilisation 1–11, 21–22, 69–70, 122–24, 128–32, 220–25, 228–31, 233–34
  ENGOs 47, 69, 110, 113, 134, 223, 229, 231
  environmental 8, 17, 133, 224
  impact 229, 232–33
  literature 1, 7, 9, 178, 182
  pathways 4, 215, 217, 225, 227
  potential for 9, 19–20
  strategies 129, 215, 219, 227, 233
  as theoretical framework 1–7
legal opportunities, new 20, 52, 74, 95, 124, 157, 193, 225
legal opportunity structures (LOS) 3–4, 8–10, 19–20, 22, 46, 141–42, 227–30, 232–33
legal orders 28, 52, 108, 114, 152, 177, 230
legal persons 7, 23, 40–41, 54, 132, 194
legal practitioners 45, 55, 158, 227
legal reasoning 6, 13, 154
legal remedies 35, 40, 165, 214
  complete system 34, 44, 51, 74, 172, 174, 194, 196
legal scholars 1–3, 37–38, 41, 46, 106, 222, 231, 234
legal scholarship 1, 9, 22, 24, 42, 69, 108, 121
legal strategies 5–6, 8–10, 21–22, 147, 153–54, 156–57, 181–83, 192
legal systems 3–4, 9, 55, 95, 97, 109, 229
  domestic 59–60, 81, 168
legal teams 182, 185, 187–89, 191–92, 200, 205–8, 211
legislation 54–55, 77, 106, 121–22, 157, 213–14 *see also* ***individual instruments***
legislative acts/measures 10, 72, 117, 132–33, 193, 211–13, 218, 223–24
legislative proposals 17, 111
legitimacy 78, 213, 234
Lisbon Treaty 104, 131–32
Liston, Gerry 16, 159, 161
litigants *see also* ***individual names***
  climate 10, 144–46, 157, 174–75, 178–79, 201, 218–19, 226
  environmental 23, 60, 75, 155, 199, 218, 224–25, 232–33
litigation 3–5, 10, 45, 147–48, 156–58, 191, 203–4, 223–28 *see also* ***individual cases***
  boundaries of 6, 228
  campaigns 141, 154, 178, 201
  strategic 2–3, 6, 14–15, 138, 149–50, 152–55, 178, 228
  strategy 147–48, 157, 190
  triggering 55, 59, 192
loans 118, 120
lobbying 95, 203, 222, 227–28, 233
locus standi 33–34, 36–37, 39, 42, 168, 214
LOS *see* **legal opportunity structures**
Low Carbon Development Act 50, 145
Lustig, Doreen 150, 152, 178

Mackaill-Hill, Harriet 16, 184, 189–90, 192, 200–201, 213
manifest errors
  of appraisal 63, 70–71
  of assessment 65, 69–71
marginalised communities 192, 216
marginalised individuals 219, 228
maximum residue levels (MRLs) 89, 91
McCann, Michael 3
MEAs (multilateral environmental agreements) 82

Meetings of the Parties (MOPs) 84–85, 98–99, 106–8, 110–12, 121, 125, 211
Mellifera 12–14, 18, 105–6, 108, 112, 122, 211, 225
members of the public 79, 84, 98–100, 103–4, 114, 124–26, 130–31, 134
Member States (MSs) 25–26, 45–48, 52–59, 61–63, 73–75, 81–83, 168–76, 195–96
methodology 1, 11–17
migrants 6, 159
migration 6, 151, 163
Mineral Oil Tax Act 167
mobilisation 6, 8, 31, 33, 35, 89, 105, 229–30
  efforts 45, 88
  goals/objectives 6, 139, 215, 223, 228, 231
  pathways 19–20, 50, 75, 85, 95, 121, 134, 225–27
  political 20, 222
  strategies 183, 227, 233
Montenegro 110, 121
MOPs *see* **Meetings of the Parties**
MRLs (maximum residue levels) 89, 91
MSs *see* **Member States**
Müllner 147, 167–68, 170, 172–75, 179, 232
multilateral environmental agreements (MEAs) 82

Nakajima 90, 92–94, 229
narratives 51, 192, 203, 219, 228
narrow interpretation 7, 24, 27, 41–42, 102, 210
narrow scope 20, 96, 230
narrow standing requirements 46, 74, 138, 182, 206
national authorities 34, 47, 168, 170–71, 190, 195–96, 213
national courts 8, 10, 26, 35, 115, 173, 213, 228
  and AG Jacobs' opinion 47–52
  ENGOs and the PRP on Validity 60–73
  opening legal opportunities at national level 52–55
  and *Plaumann* 44–76
  training national judges and practitioners 55–60
national energy and climate plans (NECPs) 171
national governments 147, 168, 178, 212
national implementing measures 47–49, 73, 132, 195–96
national judges 25, 27, 45, 47, 49, 51, 57, 74
national judiciaries 60, 68
national law 4, 25, 35, 45–49, 51–54, 73, 92, 158
national legislation 16, 51, 79, 121
national measures/provisions 48–49, 67, 73, 100, 152, 166, 170
natural persons 32, 34, 72, 186, 217
Natural Resources Defense Council (NRDC) 101
nature protection 57, 78
NECPs (national energy and climate plans) 171
negative impact 54, 79, 127, 144, 209, 219, 221
  climate change 141, 157, 160, 178, 182, 188, 216
negotiations 3, 20, 27, 77, 81–85, 121, 226, 233
Netherlands 61, 68, 143, 146, 170–71, 224
networks 4, 170, 184, 188, 216, 222–23
  membership 10, 216, 222
new Aarhus Regulation 10, 72, 124–40, 221–22, 226–27, 229–31
  contesting EU regulatory acts 131–38
  new definition of administrative acts 128–31
  shaping 124–28
new definitions 120, 124, 128–29, 133, 139, 230
new legal opportunities 20, 52, 74, 95, 124, 157, 193, 225
NGOs 113–14, 125–26, 131, 142, 165–66, 172, 178–79, 204–5 *see also* **environmental NGOs**
non-binding findings 97, 104, 107, 109, 127, 229
non-compliance 60, 96, 99, 104, 114, 121
non-confrontational, non-judicial and consultative measures 85, 99, 107
non-EU courts 13–14, 18–19, 21, 140–81, 224, 226
non-legal strategies 6, 60, 123–24, 157, 203, 222, 225, 227–29
non-legislative acts/measures 79, 117, 129, 131, 133, 139, 221
norms 152
  higher-ranking 193, 212, 218
North Sea 42, 148
Norway 83, 110, 154–56, 160, 162
NRDC (Natural Resources Defense Council) 101

objectives 32–33, 54, 62, 77, 119, 142–43, 223
case-specific 10, 148, 223
obligations 34, 86–87, 93–95, 103–4, 118–19, 169, 172, 194–95
international 28, 93, 144
procedural 70–71
obsolete court 156–57, 179
obstacles 20, 52, 58–59, 74–75, 96, 166
hindering access to justice 52, 55, 60
oil drilling 155–56
omissions 79, 86–87, 114, 125, 129, 131, 168, 172
OPC (open public consultation) 116
openness 14, 81, 95, 230
open public consultation (OPC) 116
opportunities 3, 45, 58–59, 76, 79, 173, 225, 228–29
organisations 11, 142, 147–49, 155–56, 184–85, 204–6, 215–17, 220–23
campaigning 101, 147
non-governmental *see* NGOs
Nongovernmental 113
non-profit 147, 158
original administrative acts 127, 136, 138, 140

PAN *see* **Pesticide Action Network**
PAN Europe 12–13, 89
Paris Agreement 146, 152, 160, 162, 172, 183, 193
participation 38, 78, 81–83, 85, 95
NGOs 20, 82
spontaneous 36, 42
participatory rights 42, 78
parties 78–79, 84, 92, 97–100, 106–10, 112, 121
third 7, 80, 119–20, 122, 125, 129
Partnership for policy integrity *see* **PFPI**
pathogens 64–65
pathways 4, 11, 46, 85, 128, 138, 173, 211
peer pressure/influence 152–53, 226
Peeters, Marjan 170
pellets 204–5, 209–10, 215, 217, 219
People v Arctic Oil 19, 154–56, 178
perceptions 3–4, 104, 193, 201, 212, 228
persuasive precedents 10, 173
Pesticide Action Network (PAN) 14, 89, 114, 199, 221
pesticides 59, 89, 221
petroleum 154, 156
PFPI (Partnership for policy integrity) 204–7, 215, 223
PIL *see* **public interest litigation**
plaintiffs 14–16, 154–55, 162, 185–95, 197–98, 200–203, 205–9, 217–19
Romanian 189, 202
selection 159, 182, 185, 216, 222
Slovakian 208
plans of action 5–6
Plaumann 7–11, 17–43
and AG Jacobs 40–41
circumvention via national courts 44–76
and climate change before non-EU courts 141–80
and climate change before the CJEU 181–219
and EU law consistency 31, 35–40
and *Greenpeace* case 29–31
mobilising against in post-Aarhus period 89–90, 105–10
mobilising against in pre-Aarhus period 31–40
Rasmussen's contribution 25–27
Stein's and Vining's contribution 24–25
test 23–24
using Aarhus Convention against 97–123
van Wolferen's contribution 27–29
pleadings 47, 54, 74, 93, 154
Poland 50, 55, 58, 83, 189, 206
polders 68–69
policy arrangements 21, 133, 224
policy measures 62, 70, 133, 170, 217, 224
legality 70, 133, 147, 180–81
political impact 10, 104, 142, 229
climate change litigation in Strasbourg 175–77
political institutions 10, 150
political mobilisation 20, 222
political science 1, 152
Portugal 17, 159, 163–65, 176, 186
post-Aarhus periods 18, 20, 77, 88–89, 97, 105, 107, 109, 141, 223
powers 25, 50, 78, 80–81, 86, 137, 152
bargaining 128, 139, 225
regulatory 25, 178, 223
power stations 29–30, 32
practitioners 1, 17, 58, 60, 74
pre-Aarhus period 17–19, 21–23, 31, 35–37, 39, 42, 96, 220–21
precautionary measures 66, 70, 72, 75–76
precautionary principle 64, 66, 69–71
precedents 5, 21, 153–57, 163, 173, 178, 226, 232
favourable 153–54
persuasive 10, 173

preliminary assessments 18, 124, 128
preliminary conclusions 69, 142, 156–57
preliminary reference procedure (PRP) 9, 44–48, 51–52, 59–62, 73–76, 174, 194–95, 231
preliminary rulings 26–27, 34, 51–52, 61–62, 66–68, 115–16, 196, 231
validity 35, 51–52, 64, 69, 196
pre-litigation phase 36–38
premises 12–13, 74, 195
prerogatives 27, 70–71
pressures 20, 80, 97, 110, 127, 146, 157, 192, 220
presumptions 68, 166–75, 179
of equivalence 169, 172
primary law 31–32, 36, 52, 193, 212
principles 40–41, 62–63, 78, 146, 155–56, 164–65, 199–200
of EU environmental law 57, 70, 214, 224
proportionality 69, 114, 171
private applicants 7, 22, 24–26, 132, 168, 182
standing 38, 47, 224
private citizens 26, 61, 94, 102, 182
private parties 8, 27, 36, 194, 196
privileged applicants 7, 182
***pro bono* work** 4, 184, 205
procedural obligations 70–71
procedural rights 36, 38, 77, 214
procedures 4, 34–38, 48, 71, 96, 112, 122, 221–22
pro-climate-commitment litigation 144–45
promoters 119–20
property 65, 161, 191, 208
rights 100, 198
proportionality 64–65, 69, 114, 171
proposals 68, 84–85, 112–13, 117, 122, 125–26, 128–30, 138–39
protective measures 171
PRP *see* **preliminary reference procedure**
public authorities 59, 78, 86, 92, 101–2, 205, 211
public awareness 78, 178, 185, 192, 214, 228
public consultation 115, 117, 122, 126–28
public interest 31, 33, 42, 79, 81, 116, 126, 130
lawyers 5, 59, 101
litigation (PIL) 28, 42, 54, 79–80, 154
public opinion 219, 228
public participation 53, 81, 95, 100, 113, 115
public statements 17, 142, 172
qualitative analysis 11, 16–17, 142, 178, 222–23, 227
quasi-judicial bodies 2, 13, 107, 126, 225–26, 232

radiating effect of courts 2, 149, 216
Rasmussen, Hjalte 24–27, 42
receptivity 45, 74, 128, 228
recommendations 13, 97, 99–100, 107–11, 121, 125, 127, 211
reduction targets 162, 170, 203
reform 41, 124, 127, 138–39, 210, 231
regulations 38–39, 66, 87, 89, 91, 102–3, 138–39, 195 *see also* ***individual regulations***
regulatory acts 69, 72, 75, 125, 129–36, 139
regulatory powers 25, 178, 223
rejections 7, 89, 118, 136, 206, 209, 225
reliefs, interim 46–47
renewable energy 119, 143, 183, 204, 209, 215, 219, 232
sources 214–16, 223
Renewable Energy Directive 204
Renewable Energy Directive II 204–11, 214, 216, 219, 223
Renewable Energy Directive III 204
representation 79, 185, 189, 221–22
requirements 37–38, 53–54, 66, 98–100, 119, 168–69, 198
research 1, 7–11, 21–22, 151–53, 220–22, 227–29, 231, 233
questions 1, 7–8, 11, 13, 220, 225
resolutions 111, 118–20, 232
resources 4–5, 8–9, 142, 166, 181–82, 216–17, 222, 233
natural 32, 154
respondents 53, 113, 160–64, 168–69, 174–75
responsibilities 74, 169, 171, 196
common but differentiated 155–56
review 51, 65–66, 69–72, 92–93, 95–96, 98, 135, 212
administrative 10, 12, 94, 117, 125–26
constitutional 212
internal *see* internal review
judicial *see* judicial review
mechanisms 133, 166, 230
procedures 45, 79, 103, 125, 227
substantive 12, 45, 133, 136, 140, 230
revisions 28, 97, 111–12, 205, 213, 217–18, 221, 226

rights 54, 78–79, 164–65, 171–74, 196–200, 208, 213–14, 217–18
constitutional 2, 28, 165
environmental 32, 40, 214
fundamental 28, 34–35, 169, 182, 193–94, 197–99, 206–10, 217–19
human *see* human rights
impairment 54, 79, 84, 100, 130
individual 54, 197–98
justiciable 3, 199–200, 230
procedural 36, 38, 77, 214
turn 145, 217
risks 38, 64–65, 96, 168, 191, 198, 221
roadmap 113–14, 117, 122
Romania 55, 61, 187–89, 203, 205–6
Rosenberg, Gerald 2–3
rulings 12–13, 18–19, 37–38, 52–54, 148–50, 172–73, 175, 231–32 *see also* ***individual courts and cases***
final 88, 191, 201, 219

Sabo 12, 15–17, 19, 21, 182–83, 203–19, 223, 225–26
Samvel, Gor 109
scholarly contributions 16, 21, 24
scholars 3, 5–6, 9, 41, 71, 108–9, 121, 145
socio-legal 5, 233
scholarship 2–3, 9, 27, 109, 134, 227
science 1, 7, 10, 101, 114, 184, 204, 230
scientific assessments 133, 139
scientific error 68
scientific evidence 65, 69–70, 72, 76, 143, 148, 207
scope 14, 72, 103–4, 118, 125–26, 133–34, 138–39, 206–7
of application 86, 95
geographical 157
narrow 20, 96, 230
scrutiny 69–71, 75, 97–100, 104, 165
judicial 27, 76
SEA (Strategic Environmental Assessment) Directive 62–63
sea levels 188, 191, 217
secondary law 35, 42, 230
semi-structured interviews 13–14, 16
shops 65, 67, 83
shortcomings 45–47, 52, 55, 74–75, 114, 168, 214, 231
signals 4, 151, 188
Slovak bear 93–94, 106
Slovakia 58, 61, 93, 205
social movements 1, 4–5, 10, 41, 203
social psychology 152
societal change 2–3, 57, 147, 153, 158
socio-legal scholars 5, 233
Spain 29–30, 34, 58, 61, 118
Special Rapporteurs 155–56
special treatment 31, 33, 42, 210
stakeholders 59, 82, 114–16, 213
standards 71–72, 83, 91, 102, 151, 169, 172–73, 215
standing 22, 24, 35–40, 42, 53–54, 72–75, 165–66, 206–8, 214–15
and Aarhus Convention 211–12
in actions for annulment 7, 23, 141, 181
of private applicants 38, 47, 224
requirements 7, 24–25, 54, 79–80, 102, 139, 179, 214
narrow 46, 74, 138, 182, 206
rules 80, 157–58
state aids 37–39, 126–27, 133, 138–39, 231
Stein, Eric 24–27, 42
Stichting Natuur 12, 17–18, 20, 88–96, 103, 105–6, 223, 229–30
arguments of applicants 90–94
Stichting Stop 13–14, 230
storytelling 190–92
Strasbourg Court *see* **European Court of Human Rights**
Strategic Environmental Assessment (SEA) Directive 62–63
strategic litigants 3–4, 152, 181, 216, 233
strategic litigation 2–3, 6, 14–15, 138, 147–50, 152–55, 158–78, 228
strategies 4–6, 99, 107, 142, 156–58, 178–79, 181–82, 233
Stratford, Jemima 16, 137
structural funds 30, 34
substances 65–66, 91, 118–19, 133, 166, 198–99
active 66, 91, 105, 199
substance-specific actions 21, 223
substantive review 12, 45, 133, 136, 140, 230
sufficient interest 54, 79
supreme courts 2, 24–25, 53, 57, 143, 145, 155–56
sustainability 119, 206
sustainable development 82, 146
Sweden 53, 61, 186–87
Switzerland 110, 160, 162
systemic shifts 149, 224

tactics 139, 150, 157, 182
targets 161–62, 170–71, 175, 209, 213, 219
climate 143, 145–46, 168, 172, 175, 188, 193
emission reduction 168, 170–71, 175, 179, 203

territoriality 164, 168
Testbiotech 13–14, 96, 221
tests 18–19, 22–24, 28–32, 34–42, 102–3, 140–42, 156–58, 181–82
Teulings, Jasper 15, 150–51, 155
TFEU *see* **Treaty on the Functioning of the European Union**
theoretical framework 1, 3, 5, 7, 9, 181
third parties 7, 80, 119–20, 122, 125, 129
third-wave cases 144
Thornton, James 101–2
Thunberg, Greta 183
TIJC *see* **transnational incremental judicial comfort**
timeframes 17–19, 21–22, 72–73, 124, 131, 141, 220–21, 223
Timex 37–38
tools 51–52, 75, 101, 120, 207, 212, 216, 220–21
tort law 142–45, 155
training 45, 55, 57–59, 74, 227–28
transnational incremental judicial comfort (TIJC) 10, 21, 157, 173, 212, 218–19, 226, 232
transparency 81, 95, 134, 139, 145, 230
transplantation of legal ideas 145, 151, 156, 178
Treaty on the Functioning of the European Union (TFEU) 7–9, 70–72, 75–77, 114–16, 130–34, 136–41, 180–83, 215–18
  Art 191 32, 62–63, 103, 119, 129, 207
  Art 193 171, 196
  Art 241 112–13, 122, 229
  Art 263 28, 34, 46–47, 50, 114, 136, 199
  Art 263(4) 182–83
  Art 267 8, 20, 45–46, 48–49, 51, 56, 60, 67, 70, 72, 116, 174
trees 64, 188, 205, 207, 210
tribunals 8, 45, 64, 107 *see also* **courts**
Turkey 84, 160

Ukraine 110, 160
uncertainty
  legal 48, 114
  scientific 64, 70
UNECE region 82, 109
Unelco 29–30
unexplored potential 9, 18, 117, 234
Union *see* **European Union**
United Nations
  compliance body 100, 104, 110, 121
  Special Rapporteur on HRs 155–56
United States 2, 24–25, 80, 101, 143–44, 154, 183, 204–6, 208–10, 212
  Congress 25, 80
UPA 34, 40–41, 46–47, 55, 74, 174, 194, 229
Urgenda 141–46, 150–51, 155–56, 170, 182–84, 193, 196–97, 218–19

validity 27, 35, 45–46, 48–52, 62–64, 66–70, 73, 75
  of EU law 8, 13, 20, 44, 51, 60, 74, 166, 173
  of EU measures 44, 49, 69, 74, 132
  preliminary rulings on 35, 51–52, 64, 69, 196
  references on 13, 20, 45, 51, 61–63, 65, 69–75, 221
Vanhala, Lisa 2, 4
van Wolferen, Matthijs 24, 27–29
VCLT (Vienna Convention on the Law of Treaties) 108, 114, 121
Vereniging Hoekschewaards Landschap 68–69
Verheyen, Roda 183–84, 191
victim status 163, 165
Vienna Convention on the Law of Treaties (VCLT) 108, 114, 121
Vining, G Joseph 24–27, 42
von der Leyen, Ursula 176–77

water 63, 101, 186, 188–89, 191
  drinking 191
  management 57
webinars 17, 58–59
Weiler, Joseph 150, 152, 178
'what if' cases 49–51, 56
Winter, Gerd 183–86, 188, 191, 196, 200–201, 213, 216, 222
Wolfe, David 16, 208
World Trade Organization (WTO) 93

Xylella 63–65, 73

www.ingramcontent.com/pod-product-compliance
Ingram Content Group UK Ltd.
Pitfield, Milton Keynes, MK11 3LW, UK
UKHW020220041026
15470UKWH00012B/842

9 781509 980000